TORCH

TORCH

North Africa and the Allied Path to Victory

VINCENT P. O'HARA

NAVAL INSTITUTE PRESS
Annapolis, Maryland

Naval Institute Press
291 Wood Road
Annapolis, MD 21402

Library of Congress Cataloging-in-Publication Data
O'Hara, Vincent P., 1951–
  Torch : North Africa and the allied path to victory / by Vincent P. O'Hara.
      pages cm
  Includes bibliographical references and index.
  ISBN 978-1-61251-823-7 (alk. paper) — ISBN 978-1-61251-922-7 (ebook)
1. Operation Torch, 1942. 2. World War, 1939–1945—Campaigns—Africa,
North. I. Title.
  D766.82.O44 2015
  940.54'231—dc23

                                                    2015021195

♾ Print editions meet the requirements of ANSI/NISO z39.48-1992
(Permanence of Paper).
Printed in the United States of America.

23 22 21 20 19 18 17 16 15   9 8 7 6 5 4 3 2 1
First printing

Contents

Illustrations and Tables

Photos

Maps

Tables

Acknowledgments

I deeply appreciate the help I received writing this book. First I thank my wife, Maria, and my family—my daughter Yunuen and son Vincent. Their patient support is the foundation of my work. I thank my father, Vincent P. O'Hara Sr., for reading, commenting, and providing a moral and intellectual compass. My friend and collaborator, Enrico Cernuschi, shared photographs, material, and his fresh point of view. Michael Yakovich and Leonard Heinz reviewed the entire manuscript and made many helpful suggestions. I thank Barbara Tomblin and Robert Stern, who shared material from their own projects, and the editors of the excellent annual *Warship,* John Jordan and Stephen Dent, for illustrations and permission to adapt maps from the annual's 2012 edition. Jody Mishan generously permitted me to use photographs taken by her father, Lt. (jg) John Mishanec. Jon Parshall improved the book's maps with advice and tools. I also thank David Diaz for library access. The staff at Naval Institute Press has been, as always, a pleasure to work with, especially Tom Cutler, who has always advanced my work, and Janis Jorgensen, who searched the photographic archives. I retain responsibility for all errors and interpretations of fact.

INTRODUCTION

A particular fierceness seems to attend battles waged at the water's edge.
—JOHN LORELLI

In September 1940 a British fleet embarking Royal Marines and Fighting (or Free) French troops sailed to capture Dakar in Senegal, a colony of the neutral État Français (or French State). Great Britain's prime minister, Winston Churchill, anticipated that the very sight of the "great armada majestically steaming toward them" would precipitate Dakar's surrender. Instead the city resisted. Battleships and cruisers tried to bombard Dakar into submission, but after three days Great Britain's first major amphibious operation of World War II ended in failure when a French submarine torpedoed and nearly sank the battleship *Resolution.* Churchill called it bad luck and rightfully noted that it illustrated "the difficulties of [amphibious] operations, especially where allies are involved." The military conundrum that faced the Anglo-American alliance in early 1942 was that Germany's smashing victory over France and the United Kingdom in June 1940 had denied the Allies a continental foothold. Thus, the road to victory would begin on a beach. There was no other choice.[1]

Naturally, the United States and the United Kingdom sought to address this problem according to their own concepts of warfare. Based on experiences at the Castillo de Chapultepec and the Bloody Road to Richmond, American generals believed that victory came from hitting the enemy hard in the heart of his strength. The British, on the other hand, had a tradition of standing offshore and fighting continental powers through economic means, such as with block-ades, proxies, peripheral operations as in the Crimean War, and interventions in the enemy's hour of weakness, as at Waterloo. In terms of this tradition, the fielding of a mass land army in 1916 had been a horrible mistake. There was no military imperative to mount a risky amphibious assault across a beach in northern France as the Americans desired, especially not with a blockade in place and strategic airpower available to accelerate the enemy's economic collapse, and with the Soviet Union already heavily engaged.

In early 1942 the leaders of the Anglo-American alliance had to consider a range of political problems as well. First was the matter of the Soviet Union: At the time, Russia's survival seemed questionable. There was tremendous popu-lar demand for the Allied governments to do something, anything, to help the Soviets. Then there was Japan: After Pearl Harbor the American public cried for revenge—the more so because nearly all families receiving War Department condolences had sons fighting in the Pacific. The Anglo-American political and military leaders, however, agreed that their efforts should focus on Germany as the most dangerous foe, not Japan. Their need to shape public opinion made it essential for the Americans to start fighting Germans as quickly as possible, ideally before the U.S. elections in November. This meant that the Allies had to mount a major military operation in 1942 against the Germans. What choices were there? Not many, and each one started on a beach.

The Axis leaders knew that the seafaring "Anglo-Saxons" could attack in a meaningful way only by landing an army on the continent. Adolf Hitler and Benito Mussolini, and their military chiefs, studied amphibious operations under-taken by the British at Gallipoli, Norway, Dakar, and Dieppe and regarded the inevitable invasion as an opportunity. A disaster on the beach, particularly a defeat of the untested Americans, would, according to their calculations, force the Allies to seek terms. And who can say they were wrong? The Allies absolutely could not afford a fiasco in their first major joint amphibious offensive. A bloody repulse might have caused the United States to turn to the Pacific. A massacre might have been the final nail in the Churchill government's coffin, opening the doors of Whitehall to advocates of peace. At the very least, failure would post-pone the threat of a second front and allow Germany to settle with the Soviet Union through force, diplomacy, or perhaps a mixture of both.

Washington and London appreciated the risks just as clearly as Berlin and Rome. Nonetheless, the need to conduct a successful, mutually agreeable, large-scale land operation against the Germans, an operation that would also help the Russians, forced them to compromise vastly different strategic concepts and to undertake a risky amphibious offensive before they were ready to do so. It forced them to undertake Operation Torch, an invasion of French territory in North Africa.

Torch was, depending on the observer's perspective, brilliant or stupid, it was desperate or conservative, it was aggression or liberation. The logic of fighting Germans and helping Russia by attacking neutral territory in Africa, a thousand miles from the nearest German soldier, was so subtle that the invasion caught the Axis completely by surprise. Torch required an enormous amount of shipping at a time when German submarines were ravaging Allied traffic in the Atlantic and British imports were not sustaining the United Kingdom's economy. It forced London and Washington to learn how to fight together. It determined the future of Allied strategy—for better or worse—by precluding an invasion of northern France in 1943 as the American Joint Chiefs of Staff (JCS) so ardently desired. Torch was a rushed, half-baked experiment in the art of war, full of untested ideas and amateur touches. The politicians mandated it for political reasons over the objections of most of their military chiefs.

In the event, Torch provided no direct aid to Russia and did not bring Americans into contact with very many Germans, and it took five months longer than planned to conquer French North Africa. It did, however, force the Anglo-American allies to function as true partners on the strategic, operational, and tactical levels and to hone their system for that most difficult of military operations—the amphibious invasion. The story of how the Allies applied their systems of amphibious and coalition warfare to subsequent operations is the story of how they won World War II in Europe.

Torch is a huge subject. Many English language works on Operation Torch have been written from national and service-specific points of view. Most dismiss the French perspective, if they consider it at all. A challenge in writing this book has been keeping the material to a manageable size and picking the themes to build the narrative around. *Torch: North Africa and the Allied Path to Victory* considers the operation a study in the evolution of Allied amphibious capability and practice of coalition warfare. It examines each of the five landings—Port Lyautey, Fédala, and Safi in Morocco, and Oran and Algiers in Algeria—and discusses how the ships arrived, how the troops got ashore, and how they were supplied. It describes naval battles and air operations along with the opposition in some detail. It treats more briefly actions once the soldiers landed. To understand why events unfolded the way they did, however, requires looking at background on the war's general situation, on the planning, on the position of France, and on Torch's political aspects. The violence and duration of the Naval Battle of Casablanca, for example, makes sense in the context of French politics.[2] In fact, the matter of France is important to this work. Torch was the first major Allied offensive of the war, yet, much like Germany's early offensives, it was directed against a neutral state. The fact that Torch secured France as an ally through the actions of government members, instead of confirming it as an outright enemy, is one of the operation's seldom considered yet more important outcomes.

This book observes certain conventions. During this period France and the Axis employed the metric system of measurement while the Anglo-Americans used the imperial system. Rather than convert yards to meters or kilometers to miles, this work prefers the imperial system except when quoting or discussing French or Axis actions, when the metric system may be used. "Miles" always refers to nautical miles unless otherwise stated. Foreign ranks are translated into English; tables of conversions and equivalent ranks appear in the appendixes. French naval communications and British Ultra dispatches were expressed in Greenwich or GMT time (Z+0). This was also local time in Morocco, although during the war the French used Z+1 for Morocco, which was local for Algeria, mainland France, and Germany. Times are generally local, but if Greenwich Time is used, this is indicated. All translations are the author's.

1

SITUATION

Americans do not seem to realize, this is not a war like other wars;
it is a revolution from which a new Europe—rejuvenated,
reorganized, and prosperous—must come.
—Pierre Laval, March 1941

On 24 July 1942 on board the world's largest battleship, *Yamato*, Admiral Matome Ugaki recorded in his diary, "The Russo-German war developed in the later's [*sic*] favor and Rostov is in danger too. They are marching toward Stalingrad as scheduled." In his diary for the same day the Italian foreign minister, Galeazzo Ciano, noted, "[The Germans] have occupied Rostov. From many sources the opening of a second front in France by the Anglo-Americans is reported to be certain. At Berlin . . . the matter is not causing concern, but annoyance."[1]

Heavy fighting in southern Russia was the big news. Also on that day the Royal Air Force (RAF) conducted a fighter sweep over northern France. U.S. Army Air Force B-24s attacked near Tobruk and RAF Wellingtons bombed German bases on Crete. In the Atlantic, convoy ON 115 departed Liverpool for Boston while SC 93 left Nova Scotia for Liverpool and the lend-lease destroyer HMCS *St. Croix* sank the German submarine *U 90*. Five freighters and a tanker, survivors of the ravaged PQ 17 convoy, arrived in Archangel from Novaya Zemlya. In Australia, Japanese bombers struck Townsville and Port Darwin. The most momentous event, however, happened in London. On Friday 24 July, after three

5

days of contentious meetings, the chief of staff of the U.S. Army, Gen. George C. Marshall, and the Chief of Naval Operations, Adm. Ernest J. King, and the British Chiefs of Staff Committee (CSC), including General Alan Brooke, chief of the Imperial General Staff; Admiral and First Sea Lord Dudley Pound; Chief Air Marshal Charles Portal; and Lieutenant General Lionel Ismay, Churchill's chief staff officer, agreed that the first joint offensive operation of the Anglo-American alliance would be an invasion of French North Africa and that it would be called Operation Torch. Brooke commented in his diary, "A very trying week, but it is satisfactory to feel that we have got just what we wanted out of U.S. Chiefs."[2]

July 1942 was a difficult time for the Allies. The United Kingdom was in its thirty-fifth month of war. After two years of concentrated effort against Italy in the Mediterranean and North Africa, Britain's vital central Mediterranean outpost at Malta was isolated and the most recent relief attempt had just been roundly defeated. An Italo-German army was poised sixty miles from Alexandria. Japanese forces had closed the Indian frontier and were striking targets in Australia. Axis submarines were choking the island nation's lifelines. The Soviet Union was in its thirteenth month of conflict against Germany. The Germans had conquered that vast nation's western regions, including the Baltic States, Belorussia, and the Ukraine, and were marching toward the Volga River and the Caucasus oil fields. The United States was in its eighth month of fighting. Its troops had yet to face the Germans. In the Pacific, Japan had achieved its major war aims and was scooping up secondary objectives in the Indian Ocean and Southwest Pacific three thousand nautical miles from Tokyo. The U.S. Navy's victory at Midway was the only significant success won by American arms since Pearl Harbor.

Notwithstanding their seemingly precarious military situation and their nearly unbroken record of defeat, the Allied chiefs were eager to assume the offensive and to assist their all-important Russian ally. The question was whether they had the means to do so.

Anglo-American Strategic Objectives

The English-speaking partners established their grand strategy at the December 1941–January 1942 Arcadia Conference in Washington, DC. There they confirmed Germany as the alliance's principal foe but failed to anticipate Japan's wild success. The conference had not foreseen that British Imperial forces would become stalemated in the Mediterranean or that six months hence the Suez Canal itself would be in peril. Moreover, the entire question of how to fight Germany was a point of contention, with the Americans advocating combat in northwest Europe as soon as possible and the British seeking to delay that campaign until Germany had been all but defeated by other means, like strategic bombing, economic warfare, and (although this remained unstated) Russian blood.

The question of Russian (and German) blood was, in fact, the great consideration that drove Anglo-American strategy. Seventy percent of Germany's army was engaged in Russia. In Russia, Germany suffered more than 2.415 million deaths, or an average of 1,706 deaths every day over nearly four years of combat. During the twenty-six months of Germany's campaign in Africa, from March 1941 to May 1943, the *Reich* suffered 12,810 deaths, or an average of 16 a day. Obviously, it was imperative for the Anglo-Americans to keep the Soviet Union in the war. Rumors of peace talks between the German and Soviet foreign ministers, Joachim von Ribbentrop and Vyacheslav M. Molotov, troubled Allied deliberations throughout 1942; popular demands for a second front soon reached a crescendo that the politicians could not ignore.[3]

If the need to rely on an unreliable ally to fight its greatest foe was one cornerstone of Allied strategy, the other was shipping. The Anglo-American coalition depended on a worldwide network of sea-lanes. It needed to transport its ground forces to distant battlefields, some on the opposite side of the globe, and to supply them once they were there. It needed shipping to sustain its economy and to deliver the resources that were the ultimate key to victory. Unfortunately for the Anglo-Americans, in early 1942 shipping was a diminishing asset. As they opened or reinforced theaters of war and ramped up their economies, the need for transports increased but new construction barely offset losses, much less satisfied expanded requirements.

Shipping: Numbers and Implications

Great Britain lived off imports. In 1939 the country's merchant marine of 20 million gross registered tons (GRT) needed to supply industry, feed the population (in 1939 two-thirds of the calories consumed in the United Kingdom were imported), and meet accelerated military needs such as importing munitions and weapons, or shipping troops to France or the Middle East, among other destinations, and supplying them once there. In the war's first year this was not a problem. Through August 1940 imports totaled 44.2 million tons. With the defeat of France, however, the situation rapidly deteriorated. First, with more submarines and Atlantic ports to base them in, the Germans inflicted greater losses on the British merchant fleet. Second, the War Cabinet's September 1940 decision to make the Middle East the primary focus of the British Empire's effort shackled many tons of shipping to military requirements. Third, inefficiencies in receiving and moving goods reduced available tonnage. By April 1941 congestion at British civilian ports had subtracted from circulation 900,000 tons of shipping capacity. It was even worse at military ports. In May 1941 vessels were being unloaded at Suez at the rate of one every two days as 117 vessels waited in the roads for their turn. At the same time about 10 percent of the available dry cargo shipping was under repair. In 1941 British imports totaled 30.5 million tons, a precipitous one-year decline of 31 percent.[4]

In response to shipping shortfalls the British improved their systems for receiving and transporting imports, the government increased domestic agricultural production and imposed rationing, and it increased production of resources like iron ore. (Between 1939 and 1942 imports dropped by 3,265 million tons but domestic production increased by 5,420 million tons.) Still, efficiencies, adjustments, and compromises could accomplish only so much. By early 1941 the British were suffering a shipping crisis because there were insufficient hulls to meet the empire's multitudinous economic and military needs. In April London dispatched a mission to the United States to request accelerated production of merchantmen and to borrow shipping. It enjoyed success to the extent that by November about one-fifth of American-controlled shipping—1.6 million deadweight tons—had been assigned to British routes. Some Americans deplored this situation. One admiral warned, "If we do not watch our step, we shall find the White House en route to England with the Washington Monument as a steering oar."[5]

Then on 7 December 1941 Japan attacked the United States and on the 9th Germany and Italy declared war. London naturally hoped these events would enhance American generosity, but, in the short term, Pearl Harbor was a military, logistical, and economic disaster for the United Kingdom. For example, comparing the last quarter of 1941 to the first quarter of 1942, total imports and food imports fell by 25 and 16 percent, respectively. Not only did shipping losses accelerate, but in addition the Far East crisis required a military response and more transports to carry troops and materiel to the other side of the earth, on top of more reinforcements to the Middle East.[6]

At the Arcadia Conference the Allies approved Operation Gymnast—an invasion of French North Africa—after the shipping situation cleared up. The planners anticipated this would be in April or May 1942. In the event, however, the immediate requirement to contain the Far Eastern disaster overrode the plan to accumulate American forces in the United Kingdom. In addition, the military disregarded civilian needs in devising their plans. The price paid for this neglect was reflected by the fact that in 1942 British imports met only 90 percent of consumption with a consequent depletion of reserves.[7]

Naval Demands

In mid-1942 the U.S. and Royal navies were heavily committed. Great Britain and Canada had nearly three hundred destroyers, sloops, and corvettes escorting Arctic and Atlantic convoys, and the U.S. Navy and Coast Guard had 224 such vessels allocated to these duties. There were 397 merchant vessels at sea in the North Atlantic in twelve convoys. Two of these convoys were successfully attacked en route, with SC 94 losing ten ships, or one-third of its strength, and ON 115 losing two ships, with another damaged out of forty-one under escort.[8]

Given the horrendous casualties the Russians were suffering and their bitter complaints about a lack of help, the Anglo-Americans needed to maintain the Arctic convoys. Ten convoys totaling 137 ships sailed for Murmansk or Archangel in 1942, including the disastrous PQ 17. These convoys required the best and fastest merchantmen and first-class escorts, including fleet destroyers and cruisers, and even battleships and carriers. Moreover, returning vessels had to be convoyed back, so turnaround times for ships on this route were often months.

In the Southwest Pacific the U.S. Navy was fighting a campaign against Japan for control of the Solomon Islands. In America's first offensive amphibious operation of the war, the 1st Marine Division landed at Guadalcanal and Tulagi Islands in August 1942. This campaign absorbed much of the U.S. fleet, including all but one fleet carrier. Other campaigns were under way in the Aleutians and in the central Pacific. The losses suffered and the resources required to conduct such operations came at the expense of the Germany-first priority set by the Anglo-American political leaders and the Combined Chiefs of Staff (CCS).

The Japanese incursion into the Indian Ocean in April 1942 forced the Royal Navy to maintain a strong carrier-battleship force there. Because Italo-German forces had closed the Mediterranean to commercial traffic, the only way that the Middle Eastern theater could be maintained was via the Indian Ocean. Likewise,

India's and Australia's lifelines to the British Isles ran through the Indian Ocean. Long voyages tied up hulls: a ship traveling the North Atlantic route required a month to reach its destination and return to the port of departure, but a round trip on the Egyptian or Indian routes took six months.

By 24 July 1942 the most recent attempts to supply the beleaguered island of Malta had failed, and the Royal Navy was readying an even larger effort. The small cruiser/destroyer force remaining in the eastern Mediterranean could act as an unconvincing decoy only while the Home and Indian Ocean fleets reinforced the Gibraltar squadron to muster the required strength. In other words, at this point the Royal Navy could mount only one major operation at a time. The Arctic convoys to Murmansk and the Mediterranean convoys to Malta had to alternate and often even used the same escorts—forcing crews to go from navy whites in June to duffle coats in July.

By 24 July 1942 Allied naval resources, although tremendous, were stretched to the limit. The amphibious invasion of North Africa, which the CCS authorized on that date, would require sacrifices everywhere else. There were simply not enough escorts or shipping to meet all the demands the Allied powers faced.

Axis: Strategic Objectives

There was an Allied fear, unrealistic in light of logistic constraints but real in the minds of those facing its implications, of Panzerarmee Afrika bursting through Egypt and uniting in Iraq with German divisions spilling down through Iran and Turkey, and of Japanese forces thrusting across the broad shoulder of the Indian subcontinent and joining with their German and Italian allies somewhere on the Indo-Persian borderlands. This vision of a global strategy was not one the Axis partners themselves shared. Germany, Japan, and Italy executed a military agreement on combined warfare on 18 January 1942, but this specified only that each power would operate within broad zones, share information, and cooperate in the war against shipping. In terms of grand strategy, the Axis powers were independent agents, despite the dazzling prospects seemingly before them in the summer of 1942. The failure of Germany and Italy to cooperate with Japan was not surprising given geographic separation and cultural differences. Germany's and Italy's lack of coordination, however, was less comprehendible.

Adolf Hitler and Benito Mussolini, the German and Italian heads of state, determined joint strategy in periodic meetings. Although they had a warm personal relationship, there was tension beneath the surface: many Germans held

Architects of Operation Torch: Franklin D. Roosevelt and Winston S. Churchill enjoy the African sunrise at the Hôtel Mamounia in Marrakech during a break in the January 1943 Casablanca Conference. (National Archives and Records Administration)

their Latin allies in contempt and many Italians despised and distrusted the arrogant Teutons. There were no permanent binational committees or agencies such as the Anglo-American CCS. At times when coordination was absolutely necessary, a top figure like Hermann Göring would head for Rome or Ciano would take the train to Berlin.

In mid-1942 Germany's immediate objectives were to neutralize the Soviet Union and repulse any Anglo-American attack on the European mainland. In fact, some elements in the German high command were so confident they welcomed the idea of a 1942 Allied attack in France. Meanwhile, Germany waged the war against maritime traffic with full fury. The chief of the German navy, Grand Admiral Erich Raeder, saw this as the way to victory: "The fight against the Anglo-Saxon sea powers will decide both the length and the outcome of the war, and could bring England and America to the point of discussing peace terms." In short, Germany wanted a negotiated peace with the Western allies that recognized its European dominance.[9]

Italy entered the war as an easy way to improve its geopolitical position. However, events did not unfold as hoped, and by mid-1942 a large portion of the population and many in power would have embraced a settlement based on the situation antebellum. Although Mussolini had hitched his nation's fate to Germany's, ultimately deploying 230,000 men to Russia, the duce advocated a compromise peace with the Soviet Union and a redeployment of Axis power to the Mediterranean where he hoped victory would force the British and Americans to come to terms.

The French

On 24 July 1942 the État Français or French State, with its capital at Vichy, was technically a neutral state. This was a consequence of the trauma the nation suffered in the spring of 1940 when Germany routed the "magnificent French Army" and forced the French to request an armistice.[10]

THE ARMISTICE

The last of nearly 200,000 British troops evacuated Dunkirk on 3 June 1940. Despite its military necessity the evacuation smacked of betrayal to many French people. The French government fled Paris on 10 June and assumed a vagabond existence, camping out in scattered châteaux in the Loire Valley, some of them without telephones.

On 11 June Churchill flew across the Channel for a meeting of the joint Franco-British supreme war council and to see whether France would continue fighting. Escorted by twelve Spitfires, the prime minister and his staff arrived near Orleans at 1700. A French colonel met their plane as if he "might have been greeting poor relations at a funeral" and drove them to the Château du Muguet where the French War Cabinet waited. There they met Paul Reynaud, the bellicose and normally energetic prime minister, and a newly appointed cabinet member, Philippe Pétain, the eighty-four-year-old marshal of France and World War I hero, as well as the brand-new under-secretary of state for national defense, the "frigid, humourless and probably prickly" Brigade General Charles de Gaulle. The military chiefs, General Maxime Weygand and Admiral François Darlan, were also present.[11]

Weygand warned the British delegation that the army was at its last gasp. "Now is the decisive moment. The British ought not to keep a single fighter in England. They should all be sent to France." Churchill refused and instead recalled how, in the first war, the French were determined to fight in front of, in, and behind Paris. He suggested a street-by-street defense of the capital. Pétain stirred to life at this point and replied that in the first war there had been a reserve of sixty divisions, and that the British had sixty divisions in the line. In fact, the old marshal believed that the United Kingdom was holding back on its French partner. His perception, which he later shared with Adm. William D. Leahy, the U.S. ambassador, was that "[the British] would permit the French to fight without help until the last available drop of French blood had been shed." Churchill's refusal to commit all of Great Britain's available forces confirmed this perception. The British party returned to London the next morning but not before Churchill got at least one comfort: Darlan assured him, come what may, the Germans would never get the French fleet. "There can be no question of that. It would be contrary to [French] naval traditions and to our honour."[12]

Two days later Pétain published a manifesto that proclaimed, "The armistice is in my eyes the necessary condition of the durability of eternal France." With this manifesto the momentum within France for seeking terms accelerated, with Pétain leading the way.[13]

Worried that the French fleet and army might fight on from the empire, the Germans also desired an armistice. When the French inquired, they offered terms designed to be punishing but palatable: France would be divided into occupied and unoccupied zones. The army would be reduced to 100,000 men. French prisoners of war, nearly 1.6 million men, would remain in Germany pending the negotiation of a peace treaty. France would pay a large indemnity. The French Empire would remain intact. Warships would return to home ports and disarm, except for a small force needed for routine and overseas duties; the Germans made a solemn pledge to respect French control over the fleet. The Italians would not press for territory, especially Tunisia in North Africa. France's acceptance was predicated on the belief that the war was over. As General Weygand reportedly said, "In three weeks England will have her head twisted off like a chicken's." The armistice went into effect on 24 June 1940.[14]

HERO OF FRANCE

Marshal Pétain, the immensely popular hero of Verdun, believed he had saved his country once again, and most French people agreed. But the marshal had more in mind than just ending the war. When Pétain announced the armistice, he declared that France needed "a new order . . . [and] an intellectual and moral renewal." He and his supporters wanted to purge the nation of the perceived malaise that had led to defeat in the first place, and in this Pétain had vast support. As one historian noted of the popular climate in June 1940, "Never had so many Frenchmen been ready to accept discipline and authority." Only de Gaulle, a new and relatively minor member of the government, wanted to fight on. The British recognized him on 28 June after no one else stepped forward to don the mantle of resistance.[15]

In June 1940 Pétain was France. He was above partisan politics and beyond guilt for France's defeat, which he blamed on moral rot, politicians, and Great Britain, which had abandoned France in its hour of need. Thus, in one complete package, Pétain supplied plausible scapegoats, disguised the collective responsibility for defeat, and provided a unifying symbol of eternal France. Every military commander swore an oath of personal loyalty to the marshal. Few people outside France understood the power and perverseness of the Pétain cult and the attachment to the aura of legitimacy he embodied.

French acceptance of the armistice was predicated on the war ending shortly. When it continued, the permanency of onerous "temporary" conditions of the armistice came to drive the foreign and domestic policies of Pétain's French State, which, with Paris in the occupied zone, settled on the resort city of Vichy as its capital because of the town's abundance of hotel space. Focused on keeping the Germans and Italians out of the unoccupied zone and the rest of the empire, the government also sought to reduce the astronomical indemnity it was paying Germany for war costs, relaxation of the demarcation line that divided France into occupied and unoccupied zones, the liberation of its young men from German prisoner-of-war camps, the return of government to Paris, and postwar guarantees of its borders and empire (except, perhaps, for Alsace-Lorraine). In the longer

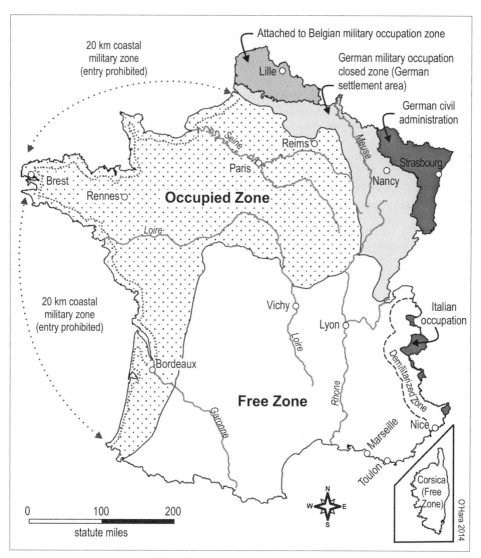

20 km coastal military zone (entry prohibited)

Attached to Belgian military occupation zone

German military occupation closed zone (German settlement area)

German civil administration

Reims

Seine

Meuse

Strasbourg

Paris

Nancy

Brest

Rennes

Occupied Zone

Loire

20 km coastal military zone (entry prohibited)

Vichy

Italian occupation

Lyon

Loire

Bordeaux

Demilitarized Zone

Rhone

Free Zone

Garonne

Marseille

Nice

Toulon

Corsica (Free Zone)

O'Hara 2014

0   100   200

statute miles

N W E S

MAP 1.1 *France under Axis Occupation, 25 June 1940–11 November 1942*

term, Pétain's government sought to secure honorable participation in a new European order commensurate with France's once and future great power status.

Despite France's sad condition, the constant message of British propaganda and thus the common perception of the Anglo-American populace was that France was an Axis puppet state—a collaborationist regime that had betrayed the Allied cause. This message was used to justify aggression against the French State beginning in July 1940 when British forces attacked French naval vessels by surprise in British and African harbors, particularly in Mers el-Kébir near Oran, Algeria. Churchill ordered this attack over the objections of many of his admirals, including Andrew Cunningham and James Somerville. He justified it as necessary to keep the French fleet out of German hands. In fact, the attack had the opposite effect, killing more than twelve hundred Frenchmen, causing the fleet to rearm, and confirming the French navy as a bitter enemy of the British. It also further rallied the French population around Pétain: most regarded it as uncontestable proof of British perfidy. The attacks of early July were followed by the assault against Dakar in September 1940, and against Gabon two months later. The British also included France in their blockade of Germany. This caused misery in France by affecting food imports. With Germany appropriating 3 million tons of food a year, the caloric consumption of the average French person dropped from 3,000 prewar to 1,327 per capita by mid-1941.[16]

The Situation by 1942

By July 1942 France was beginning its twenty-fifth month of partial occupation and 1.3 million Frenchmen remained German prisoners. Its overseas territories—Oran, Dakar, Equatorial Africa, Syria, and Madagascar—had been attacked and, in some cases, conquered by British or Allied forces. In its two years of existence, the French State collaborated with Germany, as the armistice terms required, and it made several attempts to end the armistice by normalizing relations with Germany—not for ideological reasons or to help Germany win the war, but to benefit France. What Pétain and others failed to appreciate was that Hitler intended to inflict on France a brutal peace to revenge Versailles. Joseph Goebbels, the German minister of propaganda, summarized Hitler's intentions in his diary entry for 25 April 1942: "We shall never come to a friendly agreement with them. The talk about collaboration is intended for the moment only. . . . However the war ends, France will have to pay dearly, for she caused and started it. She is now being thrown back to her borders of A.D. 1500."[17]

Thus, there was little Franco-German military collaboration beyond what the armistice terms required, in part because Hitler would not grant the concessions that French leaders demanded for such collaboration. Offsetting the collaboration that did occur was a much stronger current of French restraint. Even after Franco-German discussions about military collaboration stalled in June 1941, the British conquered the French territories of Syria in June 1941 and Madagascar in May 1942. The Royal Navy routinely stopped French shipping at sea, killing French civilians, and seized nearly sixty French vessels conducting legitimate trade. Despite these provocations, each one a casus belli under normal circumstance, the French State avoided war on its ex-ally, even though such an action would have improved its relations with Germany and convinced a skeptical Hitler, who, according to Goebbels, "wanted to see deeds first and not words," that France could be a dependable partner. In truth, the French leadership had no interest in being a dependable partner of Germany—it wanted only to restore France, and this Hitler perceived clearly.[18]

The deputy prime minister and effective leader of the French State from 27 June 1940 was Pierre Laval, a career politician who had served as prime minister in 1931–32 and 1935–36. From the first, Laval focused on Franco-German relations. In 1931 he declared, "We will always be neighbors of Germany. We face the alternative of reaching an agreement with her or of clashing every twenty years on the battlefield." Laval's policy was to ensure French sovereignty and culture in a German-dominated Europe. He dismissed British charges that he was a Fascist and pro-Nazi by asserting that he was interested in the welfare of France only and that his government would "take no step to provide military assistance to the Germans." He did, however, consider the United Kingdom a toxic influence on European peace.[19]

In December 1940 Pétain dismissed Laval, whom he personally disliked and whose policies of economic collaboration had failed to win significant concessions from Germany. In February 1941 Admiral Darlan became deputy prime minister, in addition to minister of the interior, minister of foreign affairs, navy chief of staff, and, later, minister of defense, as well as Pétain's designated successor. Darlan enjoyed power and prestige as an architect of the modern French navy, the most effective—and, after the armistice, the most powerful—of the three services. One of his ongoing priorities was to maintain French control over the fleet.[20]

As head of government Darlan sought to ease the onerous conditions of the armistice and bring home the prisoners languishing in German camps. In fact, he wanted to end the armistice altogether and negotiate a favorable peace. Like Pétain and Laval, Darlan clearly failed to appreciate the unhappy fate that awaited France in a German-dominated Europe. For example, in December 1940 he told an American diplomat, "Even if Germany wins the present war France will, given the strength and character of her people and German weaknesses, eventually be the dominating continental force." This was a view, the diplomat noted to his superiors, "curiously enough shared by a number here." In July 1940 he told the American ambassador, "If Great Britain should win the war the treatment which would be accorded to France by Great Britain would be no more generous than the treatment accorded by Germany." He believed that the Germans had no designs on French territory, other than Alsace-Lorraine, "which are lost anyway whilst the British would certainly demand much—probably Madagascar and Dakar."[21]

Early spring 1941 marked the nadir of British fortunes. Germany's rapid conquest of Yugoslavia, Greece, and Libya, and the apparent success of its air and submarine campaigns in the Atlantic, seemed to doom any prospect of British victory. When Berlin asked Vichy for help in assisting an anti-British regime in Iraq and in supplying its troops in Libya, Darlan saw a golden opportunity to realize his objectives. On 14 May he reported to the French cabinet that "Germany would win the war, and that France would receive a generous domestic and colonial settlement if she would help the Reich during the final stages." In a meeting with Hitler on 11 May, Darlan agreed in principle to Germany's requests for aircraft transit rights in Syria and the use of Bizerte in Tunisia while expressing (to Hitler's irritation) the hope that "the Führer would light up the dark road along which France was moving, so that the French nation could get a clearer picture of the future." Indeed, on 6 May France had already allowed Axis aircraft to land in Syria. Darlan expected in return major political and military concessions.[22]

On 28 May French and German negotiators concluded an accord called the Paris Protocols. These formalized the terms of French collaboration in Tunisia and Syria and provided for the future basing of German forces in Dakar. However, the concessions Germany was willing to grant fell far short of what Darlan expected, particularly because the agreement's full implementation would probably lead to war with Great Britain. Moreover, General Weygand, now the North African delegate-general, along with the governor-generals of West Africa and Tunisia, protested vigorously. In response, Darlan appended a set of political concessions that included the restoration of sovereignty over all France save Alsace-Lorraine, free transit across the demarcation line, the liberation of all prisoners, and a guarantee of the French Empire's integrity. When the German negotiator read these conditions on 6 June he called them "insane." Ribbentrop considered them a naïve attempt at blackmail. The British invasion of Syria on 8 June 1941 confirmed that London would not passively accept French military collaboration with Germany. There were additional proposals and pressure from Berlin, but in the end the Paris Protocols were never implemented. The Axis shipped only a very small quantity of goods to Libya via Tunisia, and German naval forces never used Dakar.[23]

Although Darlan continued to profess a desire to improve relations with Germany, Berlin came to believe that he was obstructing rather than advancing collaboration. After Germany's invasion of the Soviet Union he avoided military cooperation, as in the case of Dakar, or minimized it, as in the case of Bizerte. He proved recalcitrant to increased German demands for French labor and sought to improve relations with Washington, especially after Pearl Harbor. By 20 March 1942 Göring was telling Laval that "Berlin had no confidence in the Darlan government."[24]

Laval returned to power as head of government, minister of foreign affairs, and minister of the interior on 18 April 1942. Darlan continued as military chief and Pétain's heir apparent. Although Darlan had concluded that the war's outcome was now ambiguous, Laval continued to base his policies on the certainty of German victory and his personal vision of Franco-German rapport in a Europe uncontaminated by Anglo-Saxon or Bolshevik influences.

Thus, by mid-1942 the Axis powers had largely achieved their strategic aims and were fighting to convince their enemies to accept the situation and negotiate peace. The Allies, despite their weaker position, envisioned total victory. In Vichy most still thought German victory was inevitable and wanted an honorable peace.

2

THE ART OF AMPHIBIOUS WARFARE

To the world at large it seemed a glaring example of miscalculation,
confusion, timidity, and muddle.
—WINSTON S. CHURCHILL, DESCRIBING THE AMPHIBIOUS
OPERATION AGAINST DAKAR

Amphibious warfare—the delivery of troops onto an enemy-held shore and their subsequent support by naval forces—is a fundamental expression of sea power. An amphibious army could theoretically strike anywhere and at any time along an enemy coast, although in practice considerations like ports, weather, the defense, suitable landing sites, and the target's transportation network limit this flexibility. The task of getting an army ashore and keeping it supplied is enormously difficult. It is also dangerous. This was bloodily demonstrated in World War I when forces landing against Ottoman positions at Gallipoli were pinned on the beach. Thereafter, with the growth of airpower, many professionals concluded "that daylight assaults against a defended shore were suicide and folly." In the 1920s Liddell Hart, a leading British military theorist, reckoned that large-scale landings had become "almost impossible."[1]

The British Experience
In the late 1930s successful Japanese landings at Shanghai and large-scale exercises by the U.S. Marines and Army sparked renewed interest in amphibious operations among some British leaders. The military established a center in 1938 to study the tools and techniques of combined operations. This came just in time

20

for its four officers (one each from the navy, the army, the air force, and the Royal Marines) to observe Great Britain's only prewar amphibious exercise, an "opera-bouffe" affair conducted in Devonshire in 1938. The center developed a manual and submitted recommendations to the CSC, which led to the order in early 1939 for eighteen landing craft assault (LCAs), twelve landing craft mechanized (LCMs), and a pair of landing craft support (LCSs)—enough to conduct, it was envisioned, a brigade-level combat landing.[2]

The Germans invaded Norway in the war's first large-scale amphibious operation using regular troops and standard military and merchant vessels. Despite significant warship losses, it was a resounding success. The first Allied landings on hostile shores followed during the campaign to recapture Narvik in northern Norway, but did not involve British troops. Two French Foreign Legion battalions that were carried on auxiliary warships and cruisers assaulted Bjerkvik on 13 May 1940. They had carrier air support and a battleship and cruisers to soften up the beach but only seven landing craft; ship's boats carried the rest of the force. The operation was conducted in haste and in some confusion. During the landing German gunfire forced the boats to detour a mile from their intended beach, but the bombardment and three light tanks that came ashore won the day. A subsequent landing near Narvik by two French and one Norwegian battalion also succeeded despite enemy counterattacks.

In June 1940, after German victories forced Great Britain from the continent, the need to develop weapons and doctrine to facilitate a return motivated the establishment of the Combined Operations Headquarters (COHQ). A series of small amphibious operations followed. The first was an inconsequential raid near Boulogne, France, on 24 June, and the second a landing on one of the Channel Islands by an independent company and the newly raised 3rd Commando. Only one of three landing parties (carried in destroyers and then RAF rescue launches) even made it ashore. It "combed a promontory where there were supposed to be machine-guns, but found nothing" and then withdrew. Three men who could not swim were abandoned.[3]

Great Britain launched its first meaningful amphibious operation against the French African port of Dakar. The planners let politics dictate military action because they believed the French would resist half-heartedly or even rally to the Free (or Fighting) French movement—a resistance group founded by Charles de Gaulle in the United Kingdom. His organization had failed to attract significant support within France, especially after London's July attacks against the French navy, and relied on British sponsorship. For the Dakar operation the Fighting French contributed three sloops and a demi-brigade of the French Foreign Legion; the operation's only amphibious landing involved French elements.

At noon on 23 September the commander, Vice Admiral John Cunningham, sent an order from his flagship, the battleship *Barham,* to de Gaulle on board a transport to land his troops. The process of exchanging and decoding messages took two hours. Worse, there was a heavy fog and the warships assigned to support the landing could not find the transports. Cunningham finally aborted the operation at 1442, but by the time de Gaulle heard, he had already dispatched a wave of *fusiliers marins* (naval fusiliers), sixty of whom were embarked on each of his three sloops. After they established a beachhead, de Gaulle intended to land the Foreign Legion troops. First, two of the sloops tried to put their men on a jetty but withdrew behind smoke after a single 37-mm gun opened fire. Next, motor boats towed ship's boats loaded with marines toward the beach for another try, but scattered rifle fire drove them off. By that time it was growing dark, so the attempt ended there.[4]

Weather, crossed communications, and poorly trained troops defeated this landing, and when, two days later, a French submarine torpedoed the battleship *Resolution,* the British abandoned their attempt to capture Dakar. The major lesson gleaned from this fiasco was that shore batteries were difficult for warships—even battleships—to defeat, and that detailed planning and prompt and effective communications mattered. A multibrigade assault against a defended objective was not something to improvise on the fly.

More than eighteen months elapsed before the next major Allied amphibious operation. This was the British invasion of Madagascar, although there were several minor affairs in between, including an assault on Castelorizzo in the Aegean on 25 February 1941. Two hundred Commandos landed using orchard ladders to transfer from destroyers into whaleboats. They had no way to communicate with their base, and although they overcame the fifty defenders, an Italian counterlanding recaptured the island. On 19 April a Commando unit raided the Libyan port of Bardia coming ashore from the LSI (landing ship infantry) *Glengyle.* Poor intelligence and faulty navigation resulted in the Italians capturing seventy men after they hit the wrong beach. On 9 June, six weeks later, 11th Commando attacked the mouth of the Litani River in Syria, again from *Glengyle.* Most of the men disembarked on the wrong side of the river and French counterattacks foiled the operation and decimated the Commando.

Less grim were several Norwegian operations. In Operation Claymore LSI (M) *Queen Emma* and *Princess Beatrix,* escorted by five destroyers, carried 3rd and 4th Commando and fifty Norwegians to the Lofoten Islands off the country's north coast on 3 March 1941. The Commandos destroyed fish oil–processing facilities and some shipping against little resistance. Three hundred men from 12th Commando and some Norwegian personnel returned to the Lofoten Islands on 26–28 December 1941 in Operation Anklet supported by the cruiser *Arethusa* and eight destroyers. They destroyed two radio transmitters, captured two small coasters, and sank a 145-ton armed trawler. More significant was a simultaneous operation (Archer) against Vaagso and Maaloy Islands in southern Norway by 3rd Commando, elements of 2nd Commando, and some Norwegian troops, 576 men in total. They were transported in the LSIs *Prince Leopold* and *Prince Charles* and supported by light cruiser *Kenya,* flag of Vice Admiral Harold M. Burrough, who would command the Algiers naval force in Operation Torch, and four destroyers. This operation faced a company-sized German garrison. The Commandos never eliminated the resistance and suffered sixty-nine casualties with an additional thirty-one RAF personnel killed and eleven aircraft lost. Shore batteries damaged *Kenya.* The raiders destroyed two small patrol boats and five freighters (13,778 GRT).

In Operation Chariot on 28 March 1942 against the French Atlantic coast, 268 Commandos from various units carried in HMS *Campbell,* an old American lend-lease destroyer, and sixteen motor launches (MLs), supported by a motor gun boat (MGB), a motor torpedo boat (MTB), and two Hunt destroyers, attacked the dry dock at St. Nazaire. They destroyed the dock, although with such high losses—144 men killed and more than 200 captured, including navy personnel— the operation amounted to a suicide mission.

In these endeavors the stakes were small, but they allowed the British to experience the problems of ship-to-shore movements. The LSIs gained experience, marker submarines were tested, and communication protocols were refined.

The 5 May 1942 landing on Madagascar was the most significant amphibious operation of the war to date—and the first attempt since Dakar to land a force that planned to stay. It included five LSIs, four of which would later participate in Operation Torch, three personnel ships, and one tank landing ship (LST). These vessels carried three brigades and a Commando. One battleship, two modern carriers, two cruisers, eleven destroyers, six corvettes, and six minesweepers completed the support and bombardment force. There was one commander, Rear Admiral Edward N. Syfret (promoted to vice admiral [acting] by

November 1942), although his duties with Force H prevented him from participating in the planning. The CSC authorized the operation on 12 March 1942. Although preliminary planning had been under way since December 1941, the army commander received only five days' notice before sailing. He noted, "The time available for preparing this expedition was far less than previously considered necessary."[5]

Nonetheless, Madagascar incorporated lessons learned from Dakar. Because even slight opposition on the beach had proved decisive, the landings were made at night. After arriving off the disembarkation points shortly before midnight on 4 May, the first waves were away between 0227 and 0319 on the 5th. LSI *Keren's* report of proceedings noted, "The navigation of the landing craft was as good as that of their parent ships; all made accurate landings and the assault was carried out exactly as planned."[6]

By 0620 twenty-three hundred men had disembarked, fewer than planned because boats took longer than anticipated to discharge cargos and return for the next wave. Surprise air strikes attempted to neutralize French air power and sank one sloop and one of the four submarines in Diego Suarez. By day's end, 14,000 men, 339 vehicles and guns, and 615 tons of materiel were ashore.

The amphibious portion of the operation succeeded, but when the troops stalled on their advance south, Rear Admiral Syfret agreed to transfer fifty Royal Marines from the battleship *Ramillies* to the destroyer *Anthony* for a direct attack against Diego Suarez Harbor. Although some of his staff believed the operation had a less than 20 percent chance of success, the destroyer slipped past shore batteries and landed the marines directly on a quay, and they went on to secure their objective. This episode gave the dangerous impression that surprise landings against defended enemy ports, at least French ones, were a practical operation of war.

The American Experience

In January 1934 the U.S. Marine Corps published *Tentative Manual for Landing Operations*. In 1938 this document became the Navy's *Landing Operations Doctrine* and the Army's field manual on amphibious operations. From 1935 the U.S. Navy and Marine Corps held an annual event called the Fleet Landing Exercise to test and improve doctrine. This included ship-to-shore movements and gunfire support, but neglected subjects such as the landing of supplies and beach organization.[7]

By September 1941 the United States had 680 landing craft, with 410 under construction and 1,588 authorized. This was up from thirty-five in February 1940. There were thirty large attack transports (APs) and eleven attack cargo ships (AKs). The Navy Department calculated that these vessels would require 896 landing craft and could lift three divisions. However, this force, despite its impressive growth, was committed to two oceans. On 1 June 1942, when Rear Adm. H. Kent Hewitt received the job of commanding the Amphibious Force, U.S. Atlantic Fleet, he could count on only eight transports.[8]

On 7 August 1942, after rushed planning and a poorly conducted exercise, the 1st Marine Division assaulted Tulagi and Guadalcanal Islands in the Solomons. The operation's ship-to-shore aspects went well. Thirteen transports landed 11,000 Marines on Guadalcanal beginning at 0910. "All boat formations crossed the lines of departure promptly and moved in good order toward the beach. The Marine report noted proudly that the landings proceeded 'with the smoothness and precision of a well-rehearsed peace-time drill.'" Still, there were issues. The force's air and amphibious elements had different commanders. Their conflicting priorities resulted in air support being withdrawn before the amphibious commander wanted. Supplies piled up on the beach, quickly overwhelming the three-hundred-man shore party with, at one point, a hundred landing craft waiting to be unloaded while another fifty hovered offshore with no place to beach. Fire support was not a factor. Nonetheless, the experience was generally positive.[9]

The last significant Allied amphibious operations prior to Operation Torch were two large-scale raids: the 19 August 1942 landing of two Canadian brigades near the French Channel port of Dieppe (Operation Jubilee) and the assault on Tobruk on September 13 1942 by Royal Marines, Commandos, and a company of Highlanders (Operation Agreement). At Tobruk troops landed as far as two miles out of position and swells prevented disembarkation at some beaches, while craft that did land were unable to retract and load follow-up waves. When the destroyer *Sikh* ventured inshore to see why landing craft were not returning, a shore battery disabled her. The raiders lost 740 men, a cruiser, a destroyer, and six MTBs or MLs. The reasons for failure included an overly complicated plan, inexperience, poor navigation, and "a great deal of trouble . . . with the improvised landing craft."[10]

The stated purpose of the Dieppe raid was to test the port's defenses. It involved nearly five thousand Canadians, 1,075 troops of 3rd and 4th Commando, the

U.S. Rangers attached to Vice Admiral Louis Mountbatten's combined
operations train with British Commandos in the United Kingdom.
They are using live ammunition and a trench mortar to create realistic
conditions. (Library of Congress)

14th Tank Regiment, and fifty U.S. Rangers. Sea and air elements included 237
ships organized into thirteen groups, and seventy-four air squadrons, of which
sixty-six were fighters. Planning and intelligence were inadequate. "Little was
known about the strength of the positions or the whereabouts of German command posts." There were no contingencies for failure and inadequate provisions
for withdrawal and gunfire support. In the event, things went wrong from the
beginning. Surprise was lost when one landing group encountered a German
coastal convoy. Some battalions landed out of place or in the face of heavy gunfire and were unable to advance off the beach. Failure was reinforced and a fiasco
resulted with 3,367 (68 percent) of the landing force and 550 naval personnel
killed, wounded, or captured. The British also lost thirty-three landing craft, one
destroyer, and 106 aircraft.[11]

Dieppe has been explained as a necessary test of amphibious practice or a cyni-
cal British lesson to the Americans about the danger of assaulting the German-
held French coast. Both Dieppe and Tobruk affirmed the power of shore batteries

and the value of heavy gunfire support and reinforced the need for planning, intelligence, training, and surprise. Both objectives were held by supposedly second-rate troops. The danger of discounting such opposition was another lesson there for the learning.

Tools of the Trade

By late 1942 the art of amphibious warfare could be briefly described as follows: Troops were brought to beaches in vessels ranging from destroyers to large transports. Once in the objective's vicinity troops made the final voyage to the beach in specialized landing craft. These were small boats designed to run ashore and then retract to return to the transport for another load. Generally the soldiers—encumbered by up to ninety pounds of weapons, ammunition, and gear—climbed down cargo nets hung from the sides of the transports into the landing craft as they rose and fell in the swell. Even landing ships with embarked boats used this method because a fully loaded boat was generally too heavy to safely lower.

An LSI or AP attack transport with a capacity of as many as 2,500 troops could not carry enough craft to land so many men simultaneously. In British practice specialist ships called landing ship carriers (LSC), landing ship sternchute (LSS), and landing ship gantry (LSG) accompanied the LSIs. They carried few men, but between thirteen to twenty-one LCMs. In American practice APs carrying troops or supplies that were not required in the first waves would lend their landing craft to the transports bringing the assault battalions.

A central problem was navigation. Landing craft were slow and awkward to handle and faced a journey of up to eight miles toward a dark and unknown shore, using compasses that sometimes went haywire. They were often manned by sailors poorly trained for the task, yet their ability to find the right beach was critical to how troops would perform ashore in the landing's crucial first hours. Scattered units needed to establish cohesion before they could face the enemy, and that could take a long time. One solution, tested in Norway, was the use of beacon submarines. They carried pilot teams responsible for scouting the beaches beforehand. These teams would then transfer to small boats and guide the waves of landing craft to the correct beach. As an extra insurance, the submarines would move to within two miles of shore and release members of the pilot team in folding kayaks (called folbots by the British). The folbots would paddle to a position offshore and flash a light to sea for craft to home in on.

There were other specialized amphibious vessels. After Dakar, when the force commander on board a battleship lost track of the transports and did not have the communications facilities or staff to control warships and transports simultaneously, the British developed the landing ships headquarters (LSH), of which two served in Torch. These vessels were mercantile conversions and carried extensive communications gear. Next, Torch saw the second use of LSTs. These were converted shallow-draft tankers originally developed for use in Venezuela on Lake Maricumbo. They could carry twenty-one tanks and other vehicles. However, landing craft were essential for ship-to-shore movement. There were never enough. At Torch the following types were employed:

- Landing craft assault (LCA). Nine tons plus four tons cargo, speed six to seven knots, capacity thirty-five men. Crew four. Plywood construction with light armor. Troops exited via a bow ramp. This was a British Thornycroft design. The first LCA was ordered in March 1940, and the type served exclusively with British forces.
- Landing craft personnel (LCP). This was an early Higgins Eureka 36-foot type with a displacement of 6.5 tons and a capacity of thirty-six troops or four tons of cargo. Troops unloaded over the side. It was ordered by the British in 1940 and was the most prevalent type serving with British forces in Operation Torch. The U.S. designation was LCPL (landing craft personnel large) to distinguish it from a 30-foot prototype.
- Landing craft vehicle (LCV). A displacement of seven tons and a capacity of thirty-six men or four tons of cargo with a crew of four. Speed was nine knots loaded. This type served only with U.S. forces. It was considered a complement to the LCPL, to bring vehicles and cargo in follow-up waves, which unloaded via a droppable bow ramp. Operation Torch proved it more useful than its unramped cousin.
- Landing craft personnel, ramped (LCPR). Displacement 6.5 tons with a loaded speed of up to eleven knots and capacity of thirty men or three tons of cargo. A refinement of the LCP with a ramp to facilitate unloading. This type served only with U.S. forces.
- Landing craft mechanized (LCM). This was a generic name for a large type of landing craft that varied in specifications between manufacturers. The LCM(3) was the most common type used in Operation Torch. It displaced twenty-six tons empty or fifty-two tons loaded with a crew

of four men and a speed of eight knots. It could carry a light tank or up to a hundred troops.

- Landing craft support (LCS). Twenty-four and a half tons loaded with a top speed of ten knots. These were armed with a 2-pdr and a twin .50 caliber machine gun and two .303 Lewis guns. They acted as direct fire support vessels and were usually assigned one to a landing wave.[12]

In November 1942 many of the tools and techniques of amphibious warfare were in place. Practice was another matter. Most opposed landings had fared poorly. Experience indicated that failure was more likely than success. The two most successful large-scale landings—Diego Suarez and Guadalcanal—met no resistance at the crucial points and had not needed significant naval gunfire or aerial support. Moreover, questionable practices, such as sending loaded ships into defended harbors, appeared to have been validated.

In any case, the Allies were prepared to test their theories in a massive operation using thousands of ships and 100,000 men, across half the span of North Africa. The decision to take such a stupendous risk was not made lightly.

3

DECISION

When we feel what a couple of Panzer divisions and the 90th
German Light Division can do in North Africa against our greatly
superior numbers and resources, we have no excuse for underrating
German military power in 1943 and 1944.
—Winston Churchill, 21 July 1942

Genesis

Churchill considered various North Africa ventures even before the
United States entered the war. In November 1940 the prime minister
secretly approached Pétain about military aid to North Africa. He also
wrote to General Weygand in Algiers: "[The] opportunity [for military coopera-
tion] that presents itself is the most brilliant ever offered to men of courage." In
autumn 1941 the British readied four divisions in England to exploit an anticipated victory in the forthcoming Libyan offensive codenamed Crusader. One
plan—Whipcord—envisioned these divisions assaulting Sicily following the
capture of Tripoli. When the Admiralty killed Whipcord due to a lack of shipping, Churchill embraced an operation against French North Africa, dubbed
Gymnast, using the same divisions. He considered that the opportunity to inject
troops into Morocco or Algeria might "arise either through the effect of a British
victory . . . on French morale or . . . by a German demand on Pétain for the use
of this theatre in consequence of the loss of Tripoli." Such a landing would be
by invitation; it would not face immediate German opposition and the shipping

requirements would be manageable. Churchill further supported Gymnast by asserting that across the Atlantic "our friends there are much attracted by the idea of American intervention in Morocco"—so attracted, indeed, that they would land 150,000 troops there. Thus a year before Torch Churchill justified a plan to land in French North Africa in part because of American interest. How true was this?[1]

Franco-American Relations

After the Franco-Axis armistice the United States maintained full diplomatic relations with France. In July 1940 the U.S. naval attaché traveled to Morocco and Algeria and found that, contrary to rumors being broadcast from London, there was little German or Italian influence and that the army, navy, and air force officers "had not lost their traditional French fighting spirit." He concluded, "If France is going to fight anywhere in this war, I believe North Africa will be the place."[2]

In November 1940 President Franklin D. Roosevelt had the State Department summon from Vichy the chargé d'affaires, Robert Murphy, and designated him consul to North Africa. In a White House meeting Roosevelt personally instructed Murphy to report to him directly any items about North Africa of special interest. Murphy thus concluded, "The French African policy of the United States Government [was] the President's personal policy." That same month Roosevelt asked Admiral Leahy, governor of Puerto Rico and former chief of naval operations, to become ambassador to France. The president ordered Leahy to report directly to the White House and instructed him to cultivate close relations with Pétain, limit collaboration with Germany, and inform French naval officers that German use of the French fleet or bases would have dire consequences. He was also to communicate that the United States would assist France in maintaining its authority in North Africa "in any appropriate way." Roosevelt authorized limited trade and commercial traffic with North Africa to help Leahy accomplish his mission.[3]

Murphy discovered Algiers to be a political quagmire. Some authorities were willing to collaborate with the Americans and some with the Axis. There were anti-Vichy (and anti–de Gaullist) nationalists, de Gaullists, monarchists, and Arab nationalists who flourished in the atmosphere of discord and uncertainty created by the armistice. The majority, however, were loyal to Marshal Pétain and the orders of the French State.

Marshal Philippe Pétain, hero of Verdun and leader of the post-Armistice French State with its capital at Vichy. Eighty-four years old when he came to power, Pétain commanded immense loyalty from the vast majority of his compatriots. (Library of Congress)

On 26 February 1941 Murphy negotiated an agreement with Weygand for the United States to ship food and supplies to French Africa. It also authorized a Control Commission of twelve American vice-consuls in various African cities to ensure that American aid did not benefit the Axis. In practice, these vice-consuls functioned as intelligence agents, reporting on harbors, transportation infrastructure, and French attitudes toward the Germans and the Americans and encouraging military and political collaboration. Not surprisingly, their activities quickly became an open secret, especially since the diplomatic codes they used "were open to any cryptanalyst in the world who wanted to make the effort to read them." The Germans considered the American consuls amateurs and did little to interfere with their activities although Berlin did force Weygand's retirement on 18 November 1941. After the United States' entry into the war American intelligence activities intensified when the Office of Coordinating Information, precursor of the Office of Strategic Services, activated a cell in Tangiers.[4]

A theme of American diplomacy was the question of French reentry into the war on the Allied side. In January 1942 Roosevelt approached Weygand about returning to Algeria and heading a pro-Allied regime with American backing. The old general refused and reaffirmed his loyalty to Pétain. When Leahy asked Pétain whether France would accept American military aid if the Axis invaded North Africa Pétain replied, "If we ask for it." On 27 March Washington, growing frustrated, began to recognize de Gaulle's Fighting French organization in the territories that it controlled, like French Equatorial Africa, despite the antipathy to de Gaulle of Secretary of State Cordell Hull and President Roosevelt and reports emanating from France that most considered him a tool of the British. Leahy shared their distaste for the Fighting French, reporting, "The radical de Gaullists whom I have met do not seem to have the stability, intelligence, and popular standing in their communities that should be necessary to succeed in their announced purpose."[5]

Thus, Roosevelt and Churchill were independently interested in North Africa. They considered the presence of a large French army an asset because they believed this force could be enticed into Allied service. Their North African policies converged in the first Anglo-American conference, held shortly after Pearl Harbor.

The Arcadia Conference, 22 December 1941–14 January 1942

After Pearl Harbor, Churchill and his military chiefs were eager to confer with the Americans because they wanted to impress on their powerful but supposedly naïve partners the war's strategic realities and prevent them from rushing down blind alleys, especially those leading toward Tokyo. Although prominent U.S. commanders including Admiral King and Gen. Douglas MacArthur wanted to defeat Japan first, Roosevelt and General Marshall considered Germany the more dangerous foe—exactly as the Anglo-Americans had agreed at their first military staff conferences held in February 1941.

The British brought to Washington their grand wear-down strategy, developed after Churchill's rejection of Hitler's July 1940 peace offer. This consisted of blockade; attrition, via strategic bombing; subversion and sabotage (i.e., encouraging resistance movements in the conquered countries); and, finally, opportunistic military operations along the Axis fringe. These would be either butcher-and-bolt commando raids or more substantial operations like Whipcord. London envisioned a return to the continent in force only after these activities had driven Germany to the brink of collapse.

The British delegation arrived on the evening of 22 December, and Churchill immediately began describing Operation Gymnast to Roosevelt. According to Churchill's account, Roosevelt was anxious to have American troops engage the Germans "and favoured the idea of a plan to move into North Africa." The heads of state continued to discuss Gymnast the next morning. In the afternoon session, which included the American and British chiefs of staff, Churchill formally proposed a North African operation. At the time the British were poised to capture Benghazi, and the prime minister stated that 55,000 troops and the required shipping were reserved to take immediate advantage of a desert victory and a French invitation to "liberate" North Africa that he expected would follow. However, Churchill believed that it would be "essential" that some American elements, "say 25,000 men," participate. Roosevelt was intrigued and ordered a study.[6]

On 26 December a subcommittee considered the near-term implementation of Gymnast. It concluded that by mid-January there would be enough shipping in the Atlantic to lift about 25,000 American troops and that Morocco's limited infrastructure would restrict the main landing to Casablanca. From there it was fourteen hundred difficult miles to Tunisia. The committee concluded that much larger forces would be required and on 4 January reported, "It will be impracticable in the near future to capture French North Africa if important resistance is encountered." That evening the CCS, with Churchill and Roosevelt sitting in, discussed the negative impact Gymnast would have on the buildup of American forces in the United Kingdom. Churchill complained that he could not understand why, if the United States could move 2 million men to Europe in five months in 1917, they could not do the same now. "Where did all the ships go?" Despite shipping constraints, the British continued to press for a move into French North Africa.[7]

The most significant document generated during the First Washington Conference was a memorandum by the CCS, the "American-British Grand

Strategy." This affirmed that despite Japan's heavy blows, Germany was the alliance's main enemy. "It is our considered opinion . . . that only the minimum of force necessary for the safeguarding of vital interests in other theatres should be diverted from operations against Germany."[8]

The chiefs agreed that in 1942 their critical tasks were to do the following:

1. Secure areas of production in the United States, the United Kingdom, and Russia.
2. Maintain or secure both sea and air communications, with the route from the United States to the United Kingdom being the most important, followed by the Arctic route to north Russia.
3. Tighten the ring around Germany. This was defined as sustaining Russia and reinforcing the Middle East and as "gaining possession of the whole North African coast."
4. Reduce German resistance through bombardment and blockade, by encouraging revolt in German-occupied territories and by assisting Russia's offensive.
5. Develop land offensives on the continent.[9]

Although the chiefs acknowledged that a large-scale Anglo-American land offensive in 1942 did not seem feasible, they agreed to exploit any opening that may result from the wearing-down process.

At the Arcadia Conference's final session Roosevelt and Churchill decided that Gymnast would be undertaken in May when shipping was available, "if the political situation could be kept stable" until then. Churchill was less insistent on an immediate operation because the British North African offensive had stalled and was not generating the opportunities he had anticipated. Nonetheless, the British delegation left Washington believing they had won all their main points and that Gymnast was on the calendar. As one historian concluded, America's top military leaders "did not have a strategic plan of their own on hand, and they were impatient to end the conference, so they accepted the plan of the British CSC almost offhandedly."[10]

Bolero, Roundup, and Sledgehammer

Arcadia had hardly ended before Marshall and his head of planning, Brig. Gen. Dwight D. Eisenhower, rued the decisions made there. Although Arcadia had confirmed Germany as the principal foe—as both wished—there was no plan to ensure that forces would be deployed against Germany, other than the movement of three divisions to Northern Ireland and a vague agreement to land in North Africa. Meanwhile, Japanese victories were threatening even those commitments. Australia and New Zealand had recalled troops from North Africa. The British were scrambling to find shipping to dispatch nearly 300,000 reinforcements to the Far East. In mid-February Admiral King proposed that the Army increase its efforts in the Pacific and MacArthur was demanding more men.

These pressures led Marshall and Eisenhower to develop a specific program to cement the Germany-first commitment. This was Operation Bolero—the buildup of an army in Great Britain to conduct Operation Roundup, a spring 1943 invasion of the continent by forty-eight divisions supported by 5,800 aircraft, of which thirty divisions and 3,200 aircraft would be American. Marshall's plan included a provision that if the Soviet Union was in danger of collapse (or German morale appeared to be cracking), the Allies would mount an emergency invasion of northern France, Operation Sledgehammer, in 1942 with mostly British forces. Marshall's logic was simple: The direct line of communication from the new world to the old ran through the North Atlantic to the British Isles. Britain with its ports and infrastructure was the ideal place to mass an invading army. The main force of the British army was already in Britain and so did not need to be shipped elsewhere to mount an offensive. By landing in northwestern Europe near the German heartland, the Allies could meet the enemy head on and quickly win a decisive victory. By the end of January lack of shipping and the failure to secure French cooperation had put Gymnast on the back burner. Thus, on 1 April Roosevelt approved Marshall's plan and sent the general and Harry Hopkins with a small staff to London to sound out the British.

Meanwhile, in London the British CSC had, since the middle of March, been considering an emergency landing in France to help the Russians, a landing they also called Operation Sledgehammer. Because General Brooke considered it unlikely that the forces the British could devote to a mid-1942 landing (one brigade group, two armored brigades, a paratroop brigade, and a special forces brigade) would cause German withdrawals from the Eastern Front, the objective of British planning focused on making Germany "continuously employ her air forces in active operations and to cause protracted air fighting in the West in an area advantageous to ourselves in order to reduce German air support available for the Eastern Front." The landing, or a large-scale raid, would be in the Calais area because this was nearest to British airfields. Thus, when Marshall presented his

Lt. Gen. Dwight D. Eisenhower and Gen. George C. Marshall during the January 1943 Casablanca Conference. Marshall was the greatest opponent to Operation Torch, rightfully seeing it as a replacement for the 1943 invasion of France that he advocated. Eisenhower, considered inexperienced and junior, proved a genius at coalition warfare. (U.S. Army Signal Corps)

Bolero/Roundup/Sledgehammer concept on 9 April, Churchill and the British chiefs had already discussed a different Sledgehammer and even Roundup four times over the three weeks prior. At the meeting Brooke told Marshall that in the "broadest terms [the American proposal was] in line with our strategy." In a closed meeting later, however, the British chiefs correctly worried that if Allied efforts focused on Bolero "the effects of such a policy in the Middle East and Indian Ocean Theatre would be grave."[11]

Marshall presented his plan to the War Cabinet's Defence Committee on 14 April. The committee accepted with two conditions: that it not interfere with the British defense of India and that 1942 operations would be dictated by events on the Russian Front. Other than this, Churchill announced, "The British Government and people would make their full and unreserved contribution to the success of this great enterprise." "Deeply moved, Marshall cabled Secretary of War Henry L. Stimson that in an impressive statement the Prime Minister had declared his complete agreement with their plan." However, this was not the case. As one historian expressed it, "Churchill's agreement to Marshall's plans

[Sledgehammer and Roundup] had come only because of a conviction that they were impossible to implement." The prime minister remained convinced that the best actions for 1942 were Gymnast and Jupiter, an invasion of northern Norway. General Ismay wrote, "Everyone seemed to agree with the American proposals in their entirety. No doubts were expressed; no discordant note struck. [However,] perhaps it would have obviated future misunderstandings if the British had expressed their views more frankly." Thus were sown seeds of distrust that would choke future relations.[12]

Sledgehammer and Second Front Now

On 30 May Roosevelt met with the Soviet commissar of foreign affairs, Vyacheslav M. Molotov. Molotov had traveled to Washington to ask the Americans to land in Europe in enough strength to draw forty German divisions from the Russian front. He had made the same request in London, but received no assurances. Roosevelt was more forthcoming. He told Molotov that the United States expected to form a second front that year. When Churchill and his chiefs heard this, they were aghast because they assumed Roosevelt was speaking of Sledgehammer.

Marshall originally conceived of Sledgehammer as a contingency and failed to fully consider its political ramifications or that politics might trump military needs, giving Sledgehammer an unanticipated significance. The political problem, brought front and center by Roosevelt's promise to Molotov, was the need for American troops to fight Germans sometime before the November 1942 U.S. elections. In May 1942 Sledgehammer was the only operation on the books that could fulfill this need. It was no wonder that, in their evolving discussions, the British regarded it as more than a contingency and confused their plan, originally envisioned for June or July, and the larger Anglo-American operation intended for mid-September.[13]

All this time Churchill continued to champion landings in northern Norway. By 8 June things had progressed to the point where Churchill told his chiefs that there should be no substantial landing in France unless the intention was to remain, and that no substantial landing in France should be made unless the Germans were demoralized by failure against Russia. Although the reservations raised included a shortage of landing craft and difficulties in maintaining a landing force over the beaches, in fact it was the defeats in Norway, France, Greece, Crete, and Libya, as well as more recent disasters in Malaya and Burma against the Japanese, that caused Churchill and the British chiefs to lack confidence in their armies' ability to face the Germans, to say nothing of the green Americans. This was particularly true in a 1942 scenario. Thus, Churchill concluded, "Since it was extremely improbable that Sledgehammer would come off, it was all the more important that Operation Jupiter should be very carefully studied." At this meeting the CSC discussed Gymnast for the first time since March as a less risky way for the Americans to acquire some fighting experience.[14]

On 15 June Vice Admiral Louis Mountbatten, son of the former First Sea Lord and cousin to King George, met with President Roosevelt. Mountbatten, who a year before had been commanding a destroyer flotilla, had been promoted four ranks to chief of combined operations and given a seat on the British CSC. Ostensibly checking on landing craft production, he outlined to the president British objections to a cross-Channel attack in 1942. The president, who did not want to "accumulate one million American troops in Britain if all they were going to do was form a home guard," was susceptible to Mountbatten's criticisms of Marshall's plan. Marshall and King were distressed when they learned of the meeting's subject from Mountbatten's summary that their counterparts in London sent them.[15]

In the British mind Sledgehammer was effectively dead. On 16 June Churchill and his chiefs discussed a telegram from Field Marshal John Dill, the head British representative on the CCS in Washington, that suggested Marshall and Roosevelt were not in accord on the strategy to follow for 1942. Churchill regarded this as an opportunity to advance his own strategic agenda and so, accompanied by Brooke and Ismay, he rushed to Washington.[16]

Second Washington Conference

At the Second Washington Conference, held 19–25 June 1942, Secretary of War Henry L. Stimson and the American JCS dug in their heels. In a meeting between Marshall, Eisenhower, and Bedell Smith on one side and Dill, Brooke, and Ismay on the other, both parties agreed, at least according to the American record, that Operation Gymnast was a bad idea. The reasons were clear: it would cut reinforcements to the Middle East, it would reduce naval forces in all other theaters, it depended on unpredictable psychological conditions in North Africa, it would profoundly delay Operation Bolero, and, finally, it would "disperse further our available resources and weaken our efforts."[17]

On 21 June the CCS submitted a memorandum that declared the United States and Britain should continue to push Bolero "with all speed and energy,

[and] that Gymnast should not be undertaken under the existing situation." The same memorandum concluded that a 1942 attack on Western Europe should be "studied further." This seemed clear, but that same day Roosevelt and Churchill produced a document that contradicted their military leaders. It acknowledged the need for "plans and preparations for operations on the continent of Europe in 1943 on as large a scale as possible." It then asserted that operations for 1942 should likewise be "pushed forward with all possible speed, energy and ingenuity." It stated that Gymnast was the best alternative plan for 1942 and that planning for this operation should be completed as soon as possible. According to Stimson, Gymnast was Roosevelt's "great secret baby."[18]

The conference's agenda was disrupted late that day when news arrived that the British had suffered another shocking defeat. Thirty-four thousand troops had surrendered Tobruk to an Axis force half their size. After this, as General Ismay recorded, "everyone's thoughts were on the disaster in the Egyptian Desert, and the discussions centered round the steps which should be taken to restore the situation." A malady clearly infected British and Commonwealth arms, and that reinforced reluctance to assault the French Atlantic coast a few months hence.[19]

The British "Violate Their Agreement"

On 23 June Major General Eisenhower (promoted in March) and his deputy, Brig. Gen. Mark Clark (promoted to major general on 17 August 1942), left for London to head American preparations for a cross-Channel attack. In his diary Eisenhower wrote, "If the United States and the United Kingdom stay squarely behind Bolero and go after it tooth and nail, it will be the biggest American job of the war." However, he took up the task with little knowledge of the British position. The American commanders did not learn that Churchill no longer supported a cross-Channel operation in 1942 until they spent the night of 5 July at Chequers, the prime minister's residence.[20]

Although the British chiefs had informally decided on 8 June they would not undertake Sledgehammer whatever Russia's situation, they waited until 6 July before publicly stating that "Operation Sledgehammer offered no hope of success and would merely ruin all prospects of Round-up in 1943." Two days later Churchill telegraphed Roosevelt: "No responsible British general, admiral, or air marshal is prepared to recommend Sledgehammer as a practicable operation in 1942. . . . I am sure myself that French North Africa [Gymnast] is by far the best chance for effecting relief to the Russian front in 1942. . . . Here is the true Second Front of 1942." The same day Churchill ordered accelerated planning for Operation Jupiter, which he described as "a glorious opportunity to the Canadian Army."[21]

Upon receiving this notice Stimson complained to the president that the British had violated their agreements "by suddenly confronting us . . . with a Cabinet decision two months before the agreed time." He called his allies "fatigued and defeatist." Marshall was, according to Stimson, "very stirred up." In a postwar interview Marshall said that at the time he believed Churchill was reluctant to cross the Channel because of the losses suffered in the battle of the Somme in 1916 and that the British lacked confidence in American troops. There were many valid military concerns about mounting a cross-Channel attack in late 1942, including inadequate numbers of landing craft, lack of training, time, weather, potentially unfavorable force ratios, difficulty in sustaining a beach-head, and, possibly, an exaggerated fear of defeat. However, the true conflict was between military and political needs. Brooke and Marshall both agreed that militarily a 1943 operation was better than a 1942 one. However, the politicians absolutely needed action in 1942. With the British veto of Sledgehammer and the equally strong rejection of Gymnast by the U.S. chiefs, the Anglo-American partners had no prospect of meeting Roosevelt's pledge to Molotov that U.S. troops would be fighting in the European theater before the end of 1942.[22]

Bolero and Sledgehammer Again

By early July Bolero had been under way for three months but was far behind schedule. The planners had originally envisioned 100,000 troops arriving in the United Kingdom by July, 300,000 by October, and 435,000 by December. On 4 March, however, the first glitch came when Churchill requested the loan of enough American transports to move 40,000 troops from the United Kingdom to the Near East. The Axis destruction of shipping produced more delay. In the six months ending February 1942 shipping losses worldwide had averaged 382,000 tons a month with 231,000 of that coming in the Atlantic. In March these figures jumped to 834,164 and 562,336 tons, respectively, and continued at a high rate through the end of the year and beyond. Compounding this problem, the Americans had underestimated shipping requirements. When the 1st Armored Division began moving to Northern Ireland the Americans learned that a mechanized division required 200,000 tons of shipping to cross the Atlantic, far more than anticipated. The Axis advance into Egypt further disrupted

Bolero. The fall of Tobruk led to the diversion of three hundred new Sherman tanks and one hundred self-propelled guns to the Middle East from American sources while British reinforcements rushed to Suez tying up additional vessels on the long transportation cycle.

As a result, instead of 100,000 American soldiers there were 40,000 in the United Kingdom on 1 July, most of them service troops who had been given priority over combat troops so they could construct the infrastructure needed for Roundup. For Sledgehammer the Americans could contribute barely three divisions. Then there was the matter of landing craft: The original Sledgehammer plan identified a need for fifteen hundred boats to lift two infantry divisions and two tank regiments directly across the Channel. In April the U.S. War Department asked the Navy to have the required craft in Britain by 15 September. Even though Roosevelt ordered a massive expansion in the construction program, and the Navy ordered 1,100 LCMs, 600 LCPs, 1,200 LCVs, and 100 LCTs on 15 April, it could promise only 250 craft for Sledgehammer. By the end of July there were 82,000 U.S. troops in the British Isles. A month later, after stupendous efforts, there were 170,000 troops in Britain or on their way.[23]

The Politicians Choose

Marshall and King were distressed by the apparent British about-face. They sent a joint memorandum to the president on 10 July that said, "If the British attitude as to Bolero must be accepted, it is our opinion that we should turn to the Pacific [and] strike decisively against Japan." Such a reversal of American strategy was not to Roosevelt's liking. He asked to see their detailed plan for expanded action against Japan. This Marshall and King cobbled together over a weekend. After the president predictably found it inadequate, he directed Marshall, King, and Hopkins to travel to London on 15 July to resolve Anglo-American strategic issues. In a memorandum dated 16 July Roosevelt instructed them to do the following:

1. "Carefully investigate the possibility of executing Sledgehammer," and that if it were possible with "wholehearted" British support, that its execution be pushed with "upmost vigor."

2. If Sledgehammer was not possible, to continue preparing for Roundup *and* "investigate the courses of action open to us in the event of a Russian collapse." The document specified, "It is very important that

U.S. ground troops are brought into action against the enemy in 1942." Although contained in a paragraph regarding contingencies in case of a Soviet collapse, this imperative was a requirement independent of events on the Eastern Front. It was reinforced by a 16 July memorandum from the president to his chiefs: "If Sledgehammer is finally and definitely out of the picture, I want you to consider the world situation as it exists at the time, and determine upon another place for U.S. Troops to fight in 1942." Roosevelt ordered complete agreement within one week.[24]

The Americans arrived in Britain on Saturday 18 July. They declined Churchill's invitation to spend the weekend at Chequers—thereby provoking a temper tantrum that forced Hopkins to rush there on Sunday to placate the prime minister—and instead gathered with Eisenhower in London to plan strategy. Marshall learned from Brig. Gen. Lucian K. Truscott (promoted July 1942 to major general), who had been assigned to Mountbatten's COHQ, that some planners (including some British) believed an operation to seize the Cotentin Peninsula—as opposed to the original idea of provoking an aerial battle by landing in the Pas de Calais—was viable; this became the foundation of the American effort to forestall Gymnast.[25]

On Monday 20 July Marshall presented a revised Sledgehammer to the British CSC that called for a U.S. contribution of two infantry and one armored division and seven British divisions to seize the Cotentin Peninsula. He argued that it was the best action the Allies could take on behalf of Russia and that a bridgehead around Cherbourg would serve as a base for Roundup in 1943. Brooke countered that even if the bridgehead were established it would never survive the winter and would result only in the loss of the divisions committed. When the discussion turned to Gymnast the Americans stated that they would prefer to act in the Pacific. On this note the American and British chiefs broke for the day. The 21st was basically a repeat. Brooke wrote, "We went on arguing for 2 hours, during which time King remained with a face like a Sphinx, and only one idea, i.e. to transfer operations to the Pacific." On the 22nd Marshall submitted yet another memorandum presenting the case for a 1942 attack on Cherbourg, which Brooke again rejected. At this point Marshall acknowledged a deadlock and asked to speak to the prime minister.[26]

The session with Churchill took place at 1500 that day. Marshall stated there had been three meetings with the British chiefs and "a point had been reached where it was necessary for [the American chiefs] to report to the President. They had thought it right, before doing so, to have a discussion with the Prime Minister." Churchill, despite his "ardent desire . . . to engage the enemy . . . at the earliest possible moment" and his "intense dislike of 'negative attitude[s],'" agreed with his chiefs that Sledgehammer was infeasible. He stressed the need for agreement with the Americans and his "ardent" belief in Roundup, as long as the "essential prerequisites" were met: that the "operation should be on a sufficiently big scale, and . . . that there should be a certain degree of German demoraliza-tion." He would, he concluded, report to the British War Cabinet and obtain their vote on Sledgehammer so the Americans could then report to Roosevelt.[27]

The War Cabinet considered Sledgehammer that evening and predictably returned a unanimous nay. Roosevelt, accordingly, instructed his negotiators to come up with an alternative plan that would permit American troops to get into action in 1942. The choices were French North Africa, Egypt, or Norway.

On 24 July the CCS held their thirty-second meeting and, acting on the orders of their political masters, came to a consensus on military action for 1942 and strategy for 1943. This consensus was expressed in the memorandum CCS 94. It represented a partial triumph for Churchill and the British point of view and a severe setback to Marshall's roadmap for defeating Germany. However, it was not an out-and-out approval for Gymnast (now given the more inspiring name of Torch).

CCS 94 specified

- Sledgehammer is not to be undertaken, although for purposes of decep-tion and to be ready for an emergency or a favorable opportunity all preparations would continue.
- "No avoidable reduction in preparations for Round-Up should be favour-ably considered."
- "If the situation on the Russian front by September 15th indicates such a collapse or weakening of Russian resistance as to make Round-up appear impracticable of successful execution, the decision should be taken to launch a combined operation against the North and Northwest Coast of Africa at the earliest possible date before December 1942."
- Planning for the African operation would commence immediately and the supreme commander would be American.

- Should the African operation occur, Roundup would probably be "impracticable of successful execution in 1943" and the Allies would be adopting a "defensive, encircling line of action."
- It also provided for the transfer of fifteen air groups from Bolero to the Pacific and the diversion of enough shipping to send a division from the U.S. West Coast to the Southwest Pacific.[28]

The British disliked the dispatch of additional forces to the Pacific and the conditional nature of the North African venture, but Churchill and Brooke believed that they could not push the Americans any further and, after argument, secured the War Cabinet's approval.

Marshall's final attempt to save Roundup proved in vain because his commander in chief simply ignored it. On 25 July Roosevelt sent Marshall a message saying that he was delighted the decision had been made and requesting a target date of 30 October for the North African operation (before the November midterm elections). On 30 July the CCS discussed this ambiguity at their first meeting after Marshall and King's return. Leahy said that both the president and prime minister "firmly believe that the decision to undertake Torch has already been reached and that all preliminary arrangements are proceeding as rapidly as possible." Dill confirmed that this was his impression. Marshall and King, however, maintained that it was still up in the air between Roundup and Torch because Torch would mean Roundup's cancelation. They wanted a week to complete a study before advising the president that a definite decision was still pending. Roosevelt, however, with his ear to the ground, announced that evening that, as commander in chief, he had decided that Torch would be undertaken at the earliest possible date and that it "should take precedence over other operations, as for instance, Bolero." The politicians had decided. The die was cast.[29]

4

PLANNING AND PREPARATION

Material for TORCH operations had started to come in by despatch
[*sic*] and officer messenger. Soon it came in packages and rolls;
finally an armored convoy arrived to deliver 3½ tons of
papers, maps and photographs.
—REAR ADM. ERNEST MCWHORTER

French North Africa was a mosaic of peoples, geographies, and administrations. Algeria had a prewar area of 847,870 square miles and a population of 7.2 million, of whom 900,000 were Europeans. Wartime refugees greatly increased this total. The northern coastal zone consisted of three departments of the French Republic under a governor-general. The military administered southern Algeria. French Morocco had an area of 162,160 square miles and a population of 6.3 million. The sultan of Morocco, who resided at Rabat, exercised executive authority subject to the veto of a French resident-general. Tunisia had an area of 48,332 square miles and a population of 2.5 million. It was a regency under the bey of Tunisia and was subject to a resident-general's supervision.

The Anglo-American agreement to invade North Africa raised three fundamental questions: When, where, and who? Admiral King declared 7 November the earliest possible date, based on the availability of attack transports. The British chiefs wanted 7 October. This was a big range and reflected British willingness to improvise—as they had in Norway, Dakar, and Madagascar—a practice that concerned Marshall and King. As for location, the British rightfully regarded Tunisia as the crux of the matter and advocated landings as far east as possible while Washington envisioned securing the Atlantic coast of Morocco to ensure communications with the United States.

The matter of who would command was also an open question. On 26 July Marshall told Eisenhower that he, Eisenhower, would head the expedition. "My appointment was, of course, not yet official, but . . . written orders would come through at an early date." Over the next week, however, little happened. Eisenhower chaired the first planning session on the 31st—one he opened by declaring that everything was "completely tentative while awaiting the formal directive." That day Churchill telegraphed Roosevelt that it would be agreeable to him if the president appointed Marshall supreme commander and Eisenhower his deputy. The British were unanimous in thinking Eisenhower too junior for the position. Brooke said of their first meeting, "If I had been told then of the future that lay in front of him I should have refused to believe it." Ismay was "surprised that so junior an officer had been appointed to such an important command." Roosevelt, however, intended to keep Marshall in Washington and ignored Churchill's telegram. This delay fostered uncertainty, not least in Eisenhower's mind. Not until 6 August did Marshall confirm to Eisenhower that the CCS "were going to recommend him as Commander in Chief of Torch."[1]

Eisenhower distributed the first outline plan on 9 August. It envisioned landings at Casablanca, Oran, Algiers, and Bône on 7 November. The British chiefs found it unsatisfactory. They regarded the capture of Casablanca "as both unfeasible and irrelevant" and especially disliked the fact that including this objective would delay the operation's launch.[2]

While Eisenhower and his staff returned to work, the CCS finally confirmed the general as the Torch commander on 13 August. They directed him to gain complete control over North Africa from the Atlantic to the Red Sea via the establishment of lodgments in the Casablanca and Oran-Algiers-Tunis areas. This directive established that Torch would be a binational (combined) operation, and not American or British. Eisenhower reported not to the U.S. War Department, but to the CCS, a relatively new binational committee. From the start the Kansas native demonstrated that he was an excellent choice for the job. He developed his staff by including members from all services of both nations. He made it clear that his subordinates owed their first allegiance to his command, and not to their respective services or nationalities. This was new territory and threatening to many in the American and British establishments accustomed to traditional lines of authority, but it was territory the Allies needed to explore if they were to fight together effectively in the land-air-sea environment of a North African invasion.[3]

Back in Washington, Marshall and Stimson continued to drag their heels. "On no other issue of the war did the [they] differ so completely with the Commander-in-Chief. Their distrust of his military judgment, their doubts about Churchill's influence, and their deep conviction that the Torch operation was fundamentally unsound persisted throughout August." On 10 August Marshall promised Stimson that he "would not permit Gymnast to become actually effective if it seemed clearly headed to a disaster." As late as 19 August Marshall advised his Operations Division, "Apparently General Eisenhower and the British C.O.S. [chief of staff] consider that a final decision in Torch has been made. The decision to mount the operation has been made, but it is still subject to the vicissitudes of war."[4]

Questions

Eisenhower struggled to develop an acceptable plan despite many unanswered questions. Above all he needed to know how much shipping he could count on. The expedition's size depended on the answer. How many landing craft would be available? This would determine the number of assault landings. How many escort vessels would there be to screen the vulnerable transports? This would dictate the number of separate task forces. Air support was another crucial variable. What could Gibraltar's single airstrip contribute to the operation and how much of the burden could naval air shoulder? There were questions of doctrine. What could the U.S. Army borrow from the Marines? Was Madagascar the model to follow? There were many political questions: Would the French fight or bow to force majeure? Would they offer less resistance if the force were all-American? What about the attitude of Spain? The enemy's reactions and capabilities likewise needed to be considered: Would the Germans reinforce Africa? Would they invade the unoccupied zone of France? Would the Soviet Union still be in the fight? There were security and communication issues: What codes should be used and what protocols should be followed? Finally, there was a process that needed to be invented: How were decision makers in London and Washington to coordinate their supervision of the planning process? How should the Allies handle matters of joint (multiservice) command, not to mention combined (multi-national) command? Would American generals command British warships? As Eisenhower put it, "The situation was vague, the amount of resources unknown, the final object indeterminate, and the only firm factor in the whole business our instructions to attack."[5]

On 22 August 1942, only nine days after his position was confirmed (but nearly a month after the operation's approval, and only six weeks before Churchill wanted to the landings to start), Eisenhower submitted a second plan to the CCS. The essential points were a 15 October date although "every indication points to the necessity of designating a later date," and simultaneous assaults at Oran, Algiers, and Bône.[6]

A convoy direct from the United States carrying four regimental combat teams (RCTs) and one armored regiment would attack Oran. A second convoy from the United Kingdom would split once it entered the Mediterranean, and one portion would make for Algiers with a British infantry brigade and an American RCT. The other half would sail for Bône carrying the U.S. Ranger battalion and another British brigade. Follow-up convoys would reinforce the force operating against Tunisia to two armored and four infantry divisions. To move against Morocco and guard against Spanish intervention the Oran force would increase to two armored and five infantry divisions. Of these thirteen divisions four would be British and nine American. Carriers would provide air support during the landing and immediately afterward, but there were not enough carriers, and they were too vulnerable, so planes from Gibraltar would stage to captured airfields around Oran as quickly as possible and advance from there.

As this plan was completed reports about the Dieppe raid began arriving. Eisenhower considered Dieppe a fiasco and felt the need to emphasize that the forces committed to Torch were not strong enough to secure Tunis should the French vigorously resist the landings. The Spanish, should they intervene, could jeopardize communications with the landing forces and eliminate Gibraltar as an air base, which would create difficulties "of the most serious kind." The general also referred to the "inescapable costs of this expedition . . . to other allied ventures throughout the world. . . . Every other theater will have to be cut to the bone in order to provide the strength necessary to attain the prescribed object." Although he and his staff were ready to undertake the operation "determinedly and wholeheartedly," Eisenhower asked for more of everything to permit a fourth landing at Casablanca as this would greatly increase the operation's chances for success.[7]

The British CSC considered the plan on 24 August. It concluded that the initial assaults were not strong enough and did not offer a reasonable chance of seizing Tunisia before the Germans unless the French offered only token resistance. The Americans did not like it either. Marshall's representative in London, Maj. Gen. Thomas T. Handy, reported to the JCS that the plan had less than a 50 percent chance of success. He considered it "better to take a chance on the surf at Casablanca than on the closing of the Strait of Gibraltar." Marshall agreed and wired Eisenhower to prepare a new plan "commensurate with the limited military forces available." This would consist of landings in French Morocco and the Oran area. Rapid exploitation would bring Algiers and ultimately Tunisia under control.[8]

On 24 August, while the British and American chiefs were sending Eisenhower back to the drawing board for completely different reasons, Churchill and General Brooke returned from a three-week journey to Egypt and the Soviet Union. In a meeting the next morning Churchill's director of plans, Major General John Kennedy, told the prime minister that Eisenhower's plan was no good. Churchill summoned Eisenhower and Clark to dinner that evening to hear their thoughts directly. Then on the morning of the 26th the British chiefs considered Eisenhower's work. Brooke was displeased that the Casablanca landing had been scrapped because he considered it unsound to ignore the French divisions in Morocco. He also thought fighter protection insufficient for landing at Bône. Portal, Pound, and Mountbatten, however, argued that Casablanca was unnecessary, that the surf was too dangerous, and that the planning required would delay the landings past the early October date they wanted. Churchill fired off a long cable to Roosevelt that day opining that Eisenhower should "start Torch on October 14, attacking with such troops as are available and at such places you deem fit." As this message crossed the Atlantic the British chiefs learned of Marshall's instructions to Eisenhower to limit the operation to Morocco and Oran only.[9]

The British CSC responded to this "bombshell" on 26 August. It was "directly opposed to the American view" and "considered that it was essential to include landings at Algiers and Oran, and, if possible, Philippeville and Bône." Transatlantic cables followed. Churchill's began, "We are all profoundly disconcerted by the memorandum sent us by the United States Joint Chiefs of Staff." The British chiefs acknowledged that the American proposal was less risky, but identified two "overwhelming objections." First, by making Oran the easternmost point of landing, the Germans could establish themselves in Tunisia. If this happened, "All hopes of re-opening the Mediterranean would disappear and the Germans could hold or defeat us in North Africa." Second, surf conditions at Casablanca would prevent a landing four days out of five; if weather made a landing impossible, the whole enterprise would fail. They insisted on the original set of objectives—Oran, Algiers, and Bône—and recommended that Casablanca be included only if additional forces came directly from the United States. Ironically, this debate about the acceptable level of risk resembled the Sledgehammer controversy, except this time the risk takers were the British. Of course, Sledgehammer would have been a mainly British affair whereas in Torch the Americans were providing the bulk of the ground forces.[10]

On 28 August Churchill invited Eisenhower and Clark to Chequers along with Brooke, Pound, Ismay, and Anthony Eden, the foreign secretary, in an attempt to forge a compromise. In Washington it seemed the British were exerting undue influence on Eisenhower. Marshall commented to Hopkins, "You can see from this that [Eisenhower] is very much under the guns." However, Eisenhower remained sensitive to his mentor's wishes. At a meeting the next morning he pointed out that the British chiefs were focused on Tunisia whereas the American chiefs insisted on Casablanca, even if this delayed the operation. After much discussion the British chiefs agreed to drop Bône and Philippeville and to do everything possible to land at Casablanca, although this would push the operation back to early November. Brooke, who had always favored a Moroccan landing anyway, called this "a much wiser plan."[11]

On 30 August Roosevelt answered Churchill. His telegram complicated the issue by stating that the operation's success was dependent on the attitude of the French and that "there is much less probability of French resistance if the entire force making the initial landings is American." "Also it does not appear that our joint available naval resources can be extended beyond the support of two simultaneous landings." Not willing to risk a line of communications running solely through the Strait of Gibraltar, the president repeated the idea of landing at Oran and Casablanca only. He disagreed that this would certainly result in the Germans seizing Tunisia and possibly Algiers. Roosevelt ended with this: "I feel strongly that my conception of the operation as outlined herein must be accepted and that such a solution promises the greatest chance for success in this particular theatre."[12]

This was another bombshell. Brooke called the president's telegram "almost unintelligible." With Eisenhower watching on, the British chiefs drafted a reply.

They acknowledged that the operation was "primarily political in its foundation," and agreed to accede to a landing at Casablanca and for the initial assaults to be exclusively American (although "British participation in the enterprise will be perfectly obvious to the enemy owing to the presence of warships, landing craft and air forces"). After these concessions, the British telegram stated, "There is, however, one point on which we cannot give way." This was a simultaneous assault on Algiers, which they considered key to the whole position. Brooke noted in his diary that Churchill seemed "defeated, tired and depressed."[13]

London received Roosevelt's response on 3 September. The Americans proposed to reduce the Oran force by one RCT to allow a ten-thousand-man landing at Algiers. London remained unsatisfied and wanted "to cut the size of [the American] assault forces at Casablanca by another 10–12,000 men and to use the assault shipping and landing craft thus freed inside the Mediterranean. This shipping would have to come to [England] carrying trained U.S. troops."[14]

The JCS advised Roosevelt to grant this final concession. On 4 September the president agreed to reassign a transport division loaded with trained troops from Casablanca to reinforce Algiers. The next day Churchill "agreed to the military lay-out as [proposed]." Roosevelt wired back "Hurrah!" to which the prime minister replied "O.K., full blast." This settled the matter of Where. Mid-October remained the desired When, but time was flying.[15]

The Cost of Compromise

The decision to invade North Africa disrupted the U.S. Army's strategic vision. Torch's profound ramifications became apparent in the planning process and in the struggle to find the shipping and escorts, the carriers and air groups, the landing craft and specialists required. Bolero and the 1943 offensive were the first casualties. The British continued to funnel more resources than they could afford into Egypt, chasing that elusive first significant victory over a German army (that was mostly Italian). What American planners thought of this policy was expressed in a memorandum dated 21 August: "The Middle East should be held if possible, but its loss might prove to be a blessing in disguise. The British, once free of the tremendous drain upon their resources represented by Middle East requirements, might then be in a position to launch an effective offensive based on the British Isles." In the Pacific, the battle for Guadalcanal was raging: through the end of August it had already cost the U.S. Navy three heavy cruisers, one destroyer, and one assault transport sunk and two aircraft carriers,

Landing craft produced by Higgens Industries in New Orleans practice beaching techniques. In the center an LCV is about to hit shore while to the left is an LCPL, from which troops disembarked over the side. To the right sits an LCPR. All three types were used by U.S. forces in Operation Torch. (Library of Congress)

one heavy cruiser, one light cruiser, and six destroyers damaged. Despite these losses (with more to come), heavy units of the Atlantic Fleet had to be reserved for Torch.[16]

In the Atlantic, the Admiralty detached 125 escorts and 52 minesweepers from their duties and assigned them to Torch. This action degraded the protection of many convoys. For example, steam gunboats had to escort the Portsmouth-Wales routes instead of destroyers. It was also necessary to temporarily suspend convoys to the Soviet Union after convoy PQ 18 in mid-September; to and from Gibraltar (OG 89 departed Great Britain on 31 August and HG 89 sailed from Gibraltar on 17 September); the South Atlantic (SL 125 departed Freetown on 16 October); and southbound (OS 42 departed Liverpool on 29 September). Traffic from the South Atlantic to Britain continued with ships gathering at Trinidad and then joining an HX or SC convoy. Southbound ships joined ON convoys in the vicinity of the Azores and thence proceeded independently. On the other hand, traffic into Great Britain remained substantial despite the reductions in escorts. During November, 324 ships from twelve ocean convoys arrived in the United Kingdom. Thirty-three ships from three of these convoys were lost en route, including a dozen from SL 125 south of Gibraltar and fifteen from SC

107 in the North Atlantic. A total of 286 of 300 outbound vessels from twelve convoys reached their destinations. On 9 October—a week after the first Torch convoy had weighed anchor—the War Department warned Roosevelt, "The United States is waging this war on far flung fronts and demands for men and particularly materials and ship tonnage are now beyond our present capacity."[17]

More Plans

After 4 September Eisenhower was under tremendous pressure to produce a plan that reflected the Roosevelt-Churchill compromise. Much of this pressure emanated from 10 Downing Street. On 9 September Churchill minuted his chiefs, "November 8 is mentioned for 'Torch.' This is a tragedy, and every effort must be made to save at least ten days." Nonetheless, the next plan was not ready until 20 September. Eisenhower presented it to the British CSC on the 21st while Clark flew to Washington to brief the American JCS. The objective was "to secure French Morocco and Algeria with a view to the earliest possible occupation of Tunisia, and the establishment in French Morocco of a striking force which can insure [sic] control of the Straits of Gibralter [sic] by moving, if necessary, into Spanish Morocco."[18]

Three task forces would achieve this objective: a western force directly from the United States consisting of five RCTs and two armored combat teams would secure Casablanca. The U.S. Navy would provide all support and shipping. A center task force would capture Oran using American troops already in the United Kingdom: an infantry division, an armored combat team, and a Ranger battalion. The British would provide the naval and transport force. The eastern Algiers force would consist of two RCTs from U.S. forces already in the United Kingdom, two British brigade groups, and two composite U.S./British Commandos. The naval force would be British while the transports would be American and British. Reinforcements would bring the strength of the Casablanca and Oran forces up to seven divisions, all American. The Algiers group would eventually total four to six divisions of the British First Army. Thus, the troop strengths deployed remained similar to those in the 21 August plan.

Politics and Policy

The planners and politicians debated policy toward French forces. The fleet at Toulon—an important factor in the western Mediterranean's naval balance of power since June 1940—concerned Eisenhower's staff, but they also had to consider strong surface and submarine squadrons based at Dakar, Casablanca, and Oran. The CCS decided to continue existing policy and forgo preemptive strikes. French ships, even battleships, at sea or transiting the Strait of Gibraltar would not be molested unless they threatened Allied shipping. Even a French air attack against Gibraltar prior to the landings would not justify retaliatory strikes. The chiefs noted, "We consider that the present dispositions of Vichy capital ships and cruisers is the least detrimental to us. It follows, therefore, that it would be desirable to prevent any alteration."[19]

In the political arena the possibility of obtaining active collaboration from the French in North Africa excited the Americans as related, and they expended much energy in trying to achieve that collaboration. To this end American agents forged a relationship with an eclectic cabal of North African dissidents known as the Group of Five headed by Jacques Lemaigre Dubreuil, a right-wing businessman. This group's objective was to seize power in North Africa beneath the banner of anti-German patriotism. It recruited powerful supporters, most particularly Division General Charles Mast and Brigade General M. E. Antoine Béthouart, commanders of the Algiers and Casablanca divisions, respectively. Based partly on Robert Murphy's opinions and input he received from Lemaigre Dubreuil and his confederates, the Americans believed there were three prerequisites to securing French cooperation. First, exclude the British and Fighting French. Second, affirm respect for French territorial integrity. And third, produce a prestigious commander who could rally French forces and defer political complications until after victory. In September the State Department summoned Murphy to Washington, informed him about the upcoming invasion, and instructed him to redouble efforts to secure French collaboration.[20]

The U.S. JCS approved Eisenhower's plan on 29 September, followed by the British CSC on 2 October. Orders were issued on 8 October, one month before the operation's start date—and six days after the first convoy of auxiliaries and support vessels had sailed. It had taken seventy-four days from decision to orders. This left little leeway to gather needed supplies and materiel. A discussion of the logistical challenges is not possible here, but a hint of its magnitude can be suggested by the operation's needs for a single item: Most of the maps for the Algerian landings came from the British general staff's geographical section. The requirements totaled a half million items weighing approximately forty tons, not including 400,000 photomaps. The Moroccan task force sailed with sixty tons of maps. For security purposes copies issued to the troops had place names blacked out and contained a false north. Unfortunately, most maps were inadequate as they were based on outdated, large-scale sources.[21]

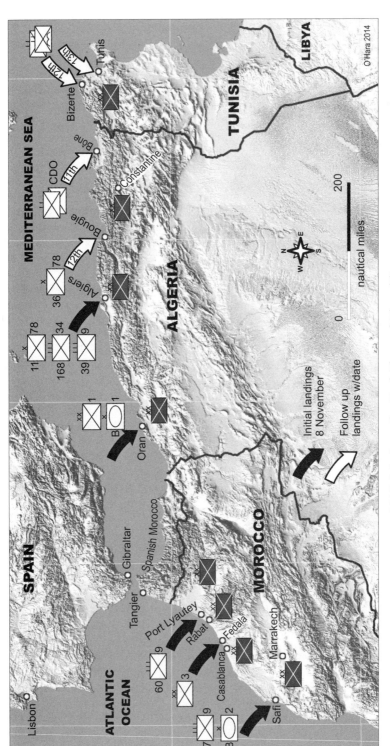

MAP 4.1 *Operation Torch Plan and Dispositions*

Joint and Combined

Torch had been difficult to decide on and plan for. Clearly, the Allies had much to learn about conducting coalition warfare at the highest levels. However, it was at the operational level as a joint and combined operation that Torch truly needed to succeed. The CCS, a binational, joint service organization, issued the orders, and from them Lieutenant General Eisenhower's authority flowed. The general seemed to truly grasp the implications, and his staff had personnel from both nations and all services with a minimum of the parochial distractions that often frustrated cooperation between parties from different services, not to mention different countries.

The general's accomplishment in this regard can be appreciated by looking at the experiences of the all-American western task force. The staffs responsible for planning and training were those of Rear Admiral Hewitt in Norfolk, Virginia, and Maj. Gen. George S. Patton Jr. in Washington, DC. Initially, they found cooperation with each more difficult than with the international team in London. "The joint planning carried out by Patton's and Hewitt's staffs was often stormy. . . . At one point the Navy considered asking the army to replace Patton with someone easier to work with." The two services eventually formed a joint committee that met as required to hash out details and resolve conflicts. Hewitt and Patton would attend committee meetings if important decisions were required while staff handled minor or routine matters.[22]

Backbone, Breastplate, and Brimstone

In conjunction with Operation Torch the Allies planned several operations to meet situations that never arose. The most significant were Backbone, Breastplate, and Brimstone. Should Spain declare war, Backbone provided for an attack on Spanish Morocco by five infantry and one armored brigade. Its big limitation was shipping. The planners hoped to use U.S. merchant shipping being held ready for the next PQ convoy and assault transports and landing craft returning from Torch. Because of the need to double up on shipping, it was envisioned that Backbone would not be possible before mid- to late December.

Breastplate was a landing from Malta onto the Tunisian port of Sousse. However, the proposed troops, one brigade of the Malta garrison, were in poor physical condition due to an inadequate diet. In addition, the requirements for air support, fuel, and escorts exceeded Malta's resources. The chiefs believed that Breastplate needed French cooperation to succeed.

Brimstone was an attack against targets of opportunity like Sardinia "if the success of Torch presented the fleeting opportunity for some further enterprise." It was contemplated only if Backbone was unnecessary as it would use the same shipping. The 1st and 4th British Infantry divisions were slotted for this force. The British chiefs cancelled Brimstone on 11 November.[23]

Training

Mountbatten's COHQ controlled amphibious operations and training in the United Kingdom. This command had experience in company- and battalion-level landings, but the Madagascar assault was COHQ's only large-scale assault. Although the planning force had been disbanded after the operation, Madagascar did provide a useful test of doctrine and several amphibious units gained valuable experience.

Admiral King established the Amphibious Force, Atlantic Fleet, in February 1942. Rear Admiral Hewitt took command on 28 April 1942. Hewitt toured the COHQ in June 1942 to familiarize himself with British equipment and practice. At the end of that month he received notice that an operation against North Africa was possible, and his command began preliminary preparations. Formal orders arrived on 25 July. As Hewitt noted in his memoirs, "An efficient and successful amphibious operation . . . involves more than the mere loading of troops on a transport, embarking them and their equipment in landing craft and setting them ashore on a selected beach. It included the proper loading of transports so that weapons, equipment, and supplies may be unloaded in the order needed (combat loading). It involved the naval gunfire and its control needed to support the landing. . . . It included a joint organization on the assault beach, where naval responsibility ends and Army responsibility takes over." As a shortcut to accomplishing these multitudinous tasks, the amphibious force adopted operating procedures propagated by the U.S. Marine Corps.[24]

Preparing the Troops

The U.S. 1st Infantry Division arrived in England on 8 August 1942 and received orders for Operation Torch on 4 September. It transferred to Glasgow and there practiced several landings. On 18–19 September it held a full-scale exercise called Oban, named after the Scottish town being attacked. This caused some concern because the name of the division's actual objective—top secret at that time—was Oran. The division moved to its embarkation ports beginning on 7 October. It sailed from the Clyde for Africa on 22 October.

The war diary of Transport Division 11, which participated in the Algiers operation, gives a flavor of the training the U.S. transports crammed into the weeks available before the operation began. The division left New York on 26 September 1942 carrying troops of the 39th RCT and units of the 9th Infantry Division. The ships included the APs *Samuel Chase, Thomas Stone, Almaack,* and *Leedstown* along with four other transports. *Chase* and *Stone* had exercised with their landing craft during August for thirteen and five days, respectively. *Almaack* and *Leedstown,* however, had just completed refit and had untrained boat crews.[25]

Five more transports joined the convoy in Halifax on the 28th and the whole force arrived off Ireland on 6 October. On the 7th the troops disembarked in Belfast and the vehicles were unloaded for waterproofing. On the 10th the reloading of vehicles and equipment began. On the 14th the troops reboarded, and the next day *Chase, Stone,* and *Leedstown* sailed to Inveraray, Scotland. They practiced boat drills for three days and on the 20th participated in Exercise Flaxman, a full-scale landing problem without vehicles. Capt. Campbell D. Edgar, USN, commander of Transport Division 11, commented, "About all the ships got out of the visit was badly needed practice in hoisting and lowering boats, and boat drills." The troops returned the next day, on the 21st, and the division conducted navigational exercises. Weather and sea conditions forced cancellation of exercises on the 22nd. On the 23rd the division sailed for the Clyde. The next two days were taken up by inspections and conferences; on the 26th, Transport Division 11 departed the Clyde as part of the Algerian-bound convoy KMF.1 (assault convoy [fast]). Thus, training was rushed and fell far short of what one officer deemed necessary for such an operation: "A minimum of ten days and nights *uninterrupted* training and preferably a month is necessary to accomplish such an undertaking against any pretense of opposition."[26]

The U.S. Atlantic Amphibious Force transports designated for Morocco had more time to practice skills including troop landing, boat tactics, gunnery, fueling at sea, deploying paravanes, and towing. For example, in August ten transports spent a collective total of fifty-eight days exercising with their landing craft, although *William P. Biddle, Chase,* and *Joseph Hewes,* with thirteen days of practice each, accounted for the bulk of this time. Older transports, such as *Joseph T. Dickman,* had relatively experienced boat crews, but this was not the case with the newer transports like *Charles Carroll.* Her captain reported, "It was noted from the time that landing boats and their crews reported for duty that instead of trained crews we had only a figurative crew. They were unskilled in handling their boats, they were unlearned in even the simplest elements of seamanship such as the rules of the road. As for items of boat smartness, such as uniforms, boat etiquette, cleanliness of boats, orderliness of equipment, stowage of gear, maintenance etc., they were in utter darkness." Maj. Gen. Ernest N. Harmon, commander of the Safi landing force, recalled his first exercise: "My troops . . . were supposed to move in orderly fashion toward specified shore points. When darkness came, a friendly lighthouse on shore provided a beacon to assist the novice navigators of the Navy's small boats. Only one boat—oddly enough, the one in which I was a passenger—arrived at its objective. The rest were scattered up and down Maryland's coast and it took until noon next day to get the erring lambs back to the fold." But even this was better than the experience of other transports in his force, *Dorothea L. Dix*'s captain noted: "This vessel was placed in commission on September 17. . . . No drill or exercise at unloading was held." *Lyon* and *Calvert* were also new vessels with unpracticed crews. Then in September training came to a halt as nearly all transports went into the yard for overhaul and the installation of additional antiaircraft guns, derricks, and communication equipment.[27]

Most transports emerged from the yard by mid-September and training intensified, leading to Operation Quick conducted 4–6 October. In this, most but not all of Transport Divisions 1, 3, and 9 practiced the loading of troops into landing craft, wave formation, and beach assault. Rear Admiral Hewitt noted in his report, "Failure of boat waves to meet schedules in exercise Quick would have been disastrous in actual operations." He ordered more training, but time was running out. On 8 October Transport Divisions 5 and 7 began loading for Torch while Divisions 1 and 3 continued practicing in Chesapeake Bay. Foul weather forced suspension of exercises scheduled for 12 and 13 October. On 16 October Transport Divisions 1 and 3 started to load and 5 and 7 rotated into the bay on the 17th. It was then back to Norfolk to meet the departure date of 24 October. As Hewitt summarized, "Except for Coast Guard–manned transports and the older naval transports, the training crews and boats left much to be desired, but the date set for the landing, November 8, 1942, was a must. We had to do the best we could with what he had."[28]

At a conference held the day before sailing, confidence ran high. "It was considered that with all the well laid plans for approaching the area by means of navigation, the submarine beacon, the use of towing spars to delineate ship's distance at night, scout boats to mark your own beach, etc., nothing could prevent a perfect performance, except insofar as enemy resistance and the treacherous surf might impose." Events would prove this assessment wildly optimistic.[29]

5

OPPOSITION

*I cannot accept that the consul general of the United States . . . would
lie on this point to the commander in chief of French forces.*
—ADMIRAL FRANÇOIS DARLAN, 6 NOVEMBER 1942

The Mediterranean Situation on the Eve of Torch

The British 8th Army launched its carefully prepared offensive at El
Alamein on 23 October 1942 and finally ruptured the Italo-German
defensive lines after twelve days of continuous attack. It failed, however, to win a decisive victory. Even the official British history complained, "The
escape of German formations that had been in contact with the British until dark
on 4th November is remarkable." A German officer who was forced to blow up
his tank after it ran out of fuel wrote, "I remember wondering why the British
advanced so cautiously." On 8 November Axis forces remained in Egypt while
Comando Supremo and Oberbefehlshaber Süd (OB Süd), the German southern command, gathered reinforcements and debated where to make a stand.[1]

In Malta the situation was growing critical. A lack of fuel and food prevented
the island from hosting surface naval forces to attack anticipated Axis movements across the Strait of Sicily to Tunisia—even if such forces could be spared
from the hundreds of warships required to escort the Torch convoys. Nor could
aircraft based there interdict shipping because aviation fuel was being hoarded
to support a desperately needed convoy scheduled to sail in conjunction with
Torch. If a convoy did not arrive in November, the population faced severe
malnutrition.[2]

Assessing the Risk

Eisenhower's planners had to assess likely reactions to Torch. The paramount question was whether the French would fight. The planners had to estimate whether the Axis powers would enter unoccupied France, if the Germans would invade Spain or pressure Franco to grant them transit rights, and if German and Italian forces would try to seize Tunisia and, if so, how fast they could act. They also had to estimate the risks the convoys faced on their passage to Africa.

The British Joint Intelligence Committee (JIC) issued rosy assessments on 7 and 19 August. It opined that French resistance would be insignificant if confronted by overwhelming force, that Spain's dependence on imports would cause it to resist German pressure, that Italy would not move into Tunisia, and that the situation in Russia and a lack of reserves would confront Germany with a strategic quandary. As for Tunisia, as long as the Allies got there first, the committee considered a combined Axis operation to recapture it unlikely. Naturally, these evaluations evolved during the planning process as the Americans challenged some of their assumptions—particularly those about the lack of danger from Spain.[3]

The final plan assumed that the French would offer only symbolic resistance and that the Germans would defer to military logic and not attempt to capture Tunisia. If they were to make that attempt, however, the JIC considered that OB Süd could transfer 14,000 light infantry by air within two weeks of the order to move, but that this force would need to be sustained by sea. They estimated that the first seaborne elements of a division could arrive in Tunisia within two weeks of an assault on Algeria, but that it would require four to seven weeks for a complete division to become operational. Axis sea and air reactions were other variables. The planners had reasonably accurate estimates of German submarine deployments, and Luftwaffe Enigma was useful for tracking German air force movements into Sicily and Sardinia, particularly in the weeks before the landings when the gathering of forces at Gibraltar was impossible to hide. For example, in early November intelligence revealed that a specialized antishipping unit of Ju 88s was moving from northern Norway to the Mediterranean. The presence of the Italian battle fleet was also a consideration, and while the JIC considered a sortie unlikely, it conceded it was possible. The problem here was that Italian naval codes were secure and the Allies could not rely on special intelligence to reveal Italian intentions. In fact, the reach of the Italian battle fleet was limited by the fuel capacity of its destroyers to five hundred miles, which put Algiers beyond range.[4]

Axis Intelligence

The Axis partners assessed Allied intentions using radio intelligence and traffic analysis, aerial reconnaissance, and reports from intelligence agents and military liaisons. The activities of the American consuls in North Africa excited the interest of Axis agents as noted. In April 1942 members of the Wiesbaden Commission toured Morocco "to investigate the possibility of an English landing [but concluded that] such an operation seemed difficult and unlikely." A contradictory assessment dated 9 June 1942, however, stated, "The Control Commission in Africa considers an Anglo-American attack to be inevitable some time during the next few months." On 24 September Italian naval intelligence (Servizio Informazioni Speciali della Regia Marina, or SIS) received a report from an agent in Great Britain that an important convoy was forming with medium and heavy tanks and corps-level army artillery. The convoy would be escorted by carriers and would enter the Mediterranean on 10 October. Supermarina, the Italian naval high command, believed that "the most probable operation would be a landing in Algeria which could even take place within the next few weeks."[5]

Valid indications of threats to French North Africa competed with many false reports. In August the Germans noted unusually heavy concentrations of shipping in British ports and monitored the situation with daily reconnaissance flights. Over the next two months rumors percolating to the German high command (Oberkommando der Wehrmacht, or OKW) from agents within the United Kingdom pointed toward Norway and northern France as targets of an impending enemy offensive. A source in Stockholm reported that on 17 October there would be simultaneous landings in France, Belgium, Holland, Denmark, and Norway, with the Americans conducting the Danish and Norwegian operations. Another report identified five towns in northern France where the Allies would disembark. The German embassy in Madrid discovered plans for a double landing in northern France and central or northern Africa. It also passed along indications of an Allied operation against northern Spain. On 5 October Hitler issued an invasion alert for northern France and ordered three more divisions transferred there.[6]

On 21 October B-Dienst, the German naval decryption bureau, reported that the number of ships in the Firth of Clyde had risen from eight to forty-three in only six days. The SIS also detected increased British shore-to-ship radio traffic starting in early October and abnormally heavy convoy traffic heading south from Britain. German and Italian agents around Gibraltar logged every arrival.

On 13 October Supermarina and Vice Admiral Eberhard Weichold, chief of the German naval command in Italy, discussed transferring the modern *Littorio*-class battleships to the western Mediterranean to forestall a landing at Bône or Bougie. Italian fuel reserves, however, were exhausted and day-by-day deliveries hardly supported routine operations. The Germans, suffering from their own oil shortages, could not promise the fuel required for such a move. On 21 October Supermarina circulated a radio decryption considered *particolarmente importante* (especially important) from the main British broadcast station at Rugby. It referred to an impending large-scale action against the enemy and was circulated to all warships. Supermarina interpreted this to mean that an important operation was commencing. The Italians shared this information with B-Dienst, which agreed the traffic was unusual but did not necessarily portend a major operation.[7]

After Brazil's August 1942 declaration of war against Germany, Dakar started generating intelligence chatter. For example, on 13 October a German agent in French intelligence reported that Dakar was preparing to defend against an overland assault from Freetown. On the 14th German military intelligence in Portugal asserted that troop convoys gathering at Gibraltar would be meeting an American task force off Freetown and thence attacking Dakar while the foreign office claimed that the Portuguese ambassador to Brazil had cabled Lisbon that the Americans were gathering assault forces at ports on the Brazilian bulge relatively close to Dakar.[8]

By late October the flow of shipping from the United Kingdom and the gathering of ships, men, and aircraft in Gibraltar made it clear to Axis leaders that the Allies were planning something. On 23 October Mussolini and Reichsmarschall Hermann Göring conferred in Rome. Göring considered the Mediterranean the area most threatened. He acknowledged an attack on French Africa was possible but considered Crete, the Peloponnese, or the "endlessly long Mediterranean coast of [Libya]" as the most threatened areas. OKW listed possible targets as Dakar, southern France, Tripoli, Benghazi, or Crete but believed another Malta convoy most likely. Corps General Alphonse Juin, commander in chief of French forces in Africa, told the Germans he did not think Algeria was threatened because the experiences of the Malta convoys showed the vulnerability of Mediterranean lines of communications. The commander of OB Süd, Field Marshal Albert Kesselring, ordered reinforcements for Fliegerkorps II and intensified reconnaissance. He wanted to transfer a German division to Sicily. OKW objected, but OB Süd kept a reinforced paratroop battalion on standby just in case.[9]

On 4 November Admiral Arturo Riccardi, Italy's naval chief of staff, observed that the long-awaited major operation had begun. The SIS had provided exact details of the force at Gibraltar, and he concluded "that beyond all doubt it would be a landing in French North Africa." The Kriegsmarine's information was not as good, and it predicted a Malta convoy because "the relatively small number of landing boats (about 50) and of only 2 transport ships does not let an immediate enemy landing operation in the Mediterranean area or on the northwest coast of Africa appear likely."[10]

French Intelligence and Preparations

The summer and fall of 1942 was a time of apprehension in Vichy. The British invasion of Madagascar in May emphasized the vulnerability of French's imperial holdings. The threat of continued British aggression provided a convenient pretext for Axis intervention in North Africa whenever Germany cared to exercise it. On 2 October Pinkney Tuck, the American chargé d'affaires in France, reported "increasing nervousness in official circles that an Anglo-American military operation against French Africa particularly Dakar is imminent." This was based on reports filtering in to French naval intelligence that the Americans were constructing many landing craft and training with them on the Atlantic coast. In French minds the introduction of American troops into Liberia (begun in July 1942 and announced on 19 October) threatened Dakar. On 22 October Rear Admiral Paul Auphan, the minster of marine, complained to Tuck about the "recent intensive British press campaign regarding Dakar," which recalled conditions preceding the invasion of Madagascar. He warned that an attack on French territory would "arouse deep-rooted animosity" against the United States. The JIC report for the third week of October noted "increasing [French] nervousness of the possibility of an attack on Dakar and preparations to meet it." On 29 October the French ambassador to the United States called on the undersecretary of state, Sumner Wells, regarding talk of "some attempted [American] invasion of North Africa." Wells assured him that it was impossible to pay attention to every rumor circulating in such troubled times.[11]

Nonetheless, indications of an Anglo-Saxon operation continued to perturb Vichy. On 2 November the French naval attaché in Lisbon reported that three important Allied convoys were off the Azores heading south. That day the prefect of the 4th Maritime Region, Vice Admiral Jacques Moreau, learned of large naval forces at Gibraltar. He concluded that this signaled another Malta convoy, especially since the week before there had been a fly-off mission to reinforce the island's fighter strength. He decided to travel to Tunisia to inspect the area's coastal defenses (he had arrived in Africa on 16 October) and then observe the "pending fight" off Cape Bon and in the Sicilian narrows.[12] On 4 November the German armistice commission advised the French admiralty that twenty-four cargo vessels and thirteen tankers were also present at Gibraltar. This report reignited fears about Dakar and the French began evacuating dependents. The first convoy, the liners *Lipari, Porthos,* and *Savoie,* carrying thirteen hundred women and children, sailed from Dakar on 4 November. Ironically, this convoy arrived in Casablanca on the morning of 8 November.

Darlan's Surprise Offer

Pierre Laval regained primacy in the French government in April 1942, but Admiral Darlan remained military chief. By this time he had concluded that German victory was unlikely and that military collaboration with the Reich was a dangerous dead end for France. In May 1942 Darlan contacted the American consul, Robert Murphy. Through an intermediary the admiral proposed that the United States "regard French Africa as a separate unit which could and would resume hostilities against the Axis at the proper time—'but only when the Americans are able to provide the material which will make such action effective.'" As the year progressed, Darlan's relations with Laval deteriorated to the point where, on 1 October 1942, the admiral attempted to resign, although Pétain refused to let him. Acting on the concern that Laval's September agreement to lease 200,000 tons of shipping to the Germans would provoke an Allied operation against Africa, Darlan considered transferring to Oran with Marshal Pétain and the fleet. On 3 October he even instructed the Oran command to prepare Mers el-Kébir to receive the Toulon squadron.[13]

On 12 October the head of Darlan's intelligence bureau, Colonel Jean Chrétien, approached Murphy the day after Murphy's return to Africa from Washington where he had been briefed about Operation Torch. Chrétien told the American diplomat that Axis sources had warned Darlan that the United States was planning to attack Dakar or Casablanca and that the French government was worried that the Germans intended to use these rumors as a pretext for occupying Africa. He dropped a bombshell by asking, "Should [Darlan] as Commander-in-Chief of French armed forces decide to come to Africa entraining with him the French Fleet," what material and economic support could the

United States provide? Chrétien also stated that should an assurance be forth-coming, there would be a "strong possibility" that Darlan would undertake such cooperation. Darlan anticipated a positive response and on 22 October he asked the sultan of Morocco to invite Marshal Pétain for a visit. Because the marshal was too old to fly, he would sail to Africa in *Strasbourg*, escorted by the fleet.[14]

Darlan's proposition gave the Allies the chance for an unanticipated politi-cal and military windfall. The trouble was that Murphy had already identified a high-level French collaborator, General Henri Giraud, whom the Group of Five regarded as possessing the prestige to lead their coup d'état and rally widespread military support. Giraud had the distinction of escaping a German prisoner-of-war camp in both world wars—most recently in April 1942 when he lowered himself down the wall of his castle prison and hopped a train for Switzerland. He was living in the unoccupied zone, having given Pétain "his word of honor as an officer" to do nothing to harm relations with the German government. The Americans considered him untainted by collaboration with the Axis and of suf-ficient stature to rally support in the Métropole. Nonetheless, when Murphy cabled the news to Roosevelt and Eisenhower, they authorized "any arrange-ments with Darlan which . . . might assist the military operations." Eisenhower immediately went to Churchill and the British chiefs to suggest a power-sharing arrangement that made Giraud the governor of North African and Darlan Eisen-hower's deputy commander. Given the propaganda war the British had been waging against Darlan ever since Mers el-Kébir, the British chiefs naturally pre-ferred Giraud, especially given Division General Mast's assurance that the Allies could enter Northwest Africa without fighting by means of Giraud's name alone. Nonetheless, they did not reject cooperation with Darlan. In fact, "the Prime Minister appeared delighted with the new developments."[15]

Darlan's offer embarrassed Murphy because it came as he was finalizing arrangements with the Group of Five. On 14 October he met with Division General Mast and learned that Giraud had agreed to join them. When Murphy asked Mast about Darlan, the general "objected vigorously" that Darlan could not be trusted. He stated that Giraud, not Darlan, commanded the army's loyalty and that the navy would "fall in line" with the army. Emphatically rebuffed, and feeling he was too deeply committed to change course, Murphy withheld the assurances Colonel Chrétien sought and in a subsequent meeting gave him the impression that Allied intervention was at least four months away. When Darlan received this news, which arrived around the same time he learned about German conclusions regarding the Allied armada gathering in Gibraltar, he discounted an operation against North Africa. Murphy stated that Darlan's "intense" dislike of the British and the fact that a firm agreement was reached with General Giraud were the reasons the Allies did not secure Darlan's cooperation before the invasion. In fact, though, Mast's refusal to work with the admiral and Murphy's commitment to Mast were the major reasons.[16]

The Meeting at Cherchell

Another reason for Eisenhower's 17 October meeting with Churchill and the British chiefs was to inform them that Division General Mast had requested a meeting with five officers from Eisenhower's staff, including a senior general. Eisenhower proposed sending Major General Clark, his deputy commander, and the chiefs agreed.

Clark and a staff of four flew to Gibraltar and thence boarded the British submarine *Seraph,* which carried them to a point offshore from an isolated farm seventy miles west of Algiers where the meeting was to be held. *Seraph* arrived in the early hours of 21 October, too late to land the Americans before dawn. Thus they had to stay on board until the following night, and their reception committee, which included Mast and Murphy, thinking something had gone wrong, drove back to Algiers. A radio message brought some of the conspirators back to the villa at midnight on the 21st and Mast returned at 0500 on the 22nd. He was likewise aided by a staff of four. In his memoirs, published twenty-five years after the event, Mast complained, "Because of its unusual nature [the Cherchell conference] has been the object of an extensive literature and certain historians, incorrectly informed, had exaggerated the number of participants and amplified the roles they held." He characterized it as a strictly military meeting to obtain details regarding the forthcoming American expedition and to share information about French preparations to help the operation.[17]

Clark confirmed that the Americans would be landing a large force in North Africa and relayed Roosevelt's assurance that the United States would assist French forces should they reenter the war on the Allied side. He told Mast that the Americans wanted to act before year's end, but he withheld the date, implying that the landings would be in five or six weeks, not sixteen days.[18]

For his part Mast recommended specific beaches, particularly Sidi-Ferruch west of Algiers, where he guaranteed a friendly reception, and he urged the Americans to rapidly occupy Tunisia. When Clark raised the subject of Darlan's participation, Mast "objected vigorously." He asserted that Darlan was responsible for the Paris Protocols that would have, but for the energetic intervention of Weygand, given Hitler bases in Bizerte and Dakar. He said that Darlan was convinced of eventual German victory and that revealing the operation to him would be "tantamount to kindling a cataclysm." Mast maintained that Giraud was the only option for commander. Clark accepted this despite the conditions Giraud placed on his participation. First, the French general wanted supreme command over all French and American forces within forty-eight hours of the landings. Second, the operation needed to include an invasion of the French Riviera. And third, the landings had to be exclusively American. Clark, of course, could agree to none of this. Instead, the American general offered a disingenuous compromise that emphasized Washington's desire to hand military command of North Africa to the French at the "earliest practicable date," but qualified that command during the landing and consolidation phases had to be retained by the United States. This compromise implied that French forces would need to reequip before command could be transferred and allowed for the possibility of a French deputy commander. Mast and his secretary, Jean Rigault, a Group of Five principal, returned to Algiers that afternoon, leaving the other French officers to continue technical exchanges with their American counterparts.[19]

The party had just sat down to dinner when the telephone rang with the warning that the police were on their way. As Clark put it, "One would have thought that fifty dead skunks had been thrown on the table at the speed with which most of our French friends disappeared." The Americans hid in a wine cellar while Murphy, his vice-consul, the house's owner, and one of the conspirators pretended they had been having a party. Once the police departed, the Americans tried to return to *Seraph*, but the surf was so high they did not reach her until 0400, after their folbots had been overturned in several earlier attempts; the general lost his money belt and another officer lost a bag with secret papers.[20]

Cherchell confirmed the American decision to collaborate with Giraud. It showed that the Group of Five had unrealistic expectations and their own political agenda, and that the Americans did not trust them, withholding crucial details like the fact that some convoys were already at sea. As Clark's compromise required Eisenhower's sign-off, he did not give Mast a copy. However, Rigault produced a paraphrase based on his notes. This version reflected what the French conspirators had wanted to hear: that supreme command of "the American army with all its resources" would come (after a very short landing phase) under French command. The conspirators rushed this language to Giraud, who interpreted it as meeting his conditions. Thus, in the end, Cherchell muddied waters it was supposed to clear.[21]

On 27 October Eisenhower forwarded a revised version of the command compromise to Murphy. This clearly spelled out that the French would take supreme command only after their forces had been reequipped (at some point in the distant future) and that their authority even then would be limited to the defense of North Africa. Murphy knew this was not what the Group of Five wanted so he requested and received permission to tell Mast that the landings would be in early November. The news stunned Mast. He told Murphy, "The Cherchell meeting took place a week ago and you hid from me that the troop transports had already sailed? Beautiful confirmation of the confidence I so firmly believed we had established between ourselves." The general considered abandoning the whole scheme but overcame his emotion, knowing that only through the American Army and the modern equipment it was bringing could the French army resume the fight. He advised Giraud, who replied that it was impossible for him to leave France before 20 November. Murphy panicked, and on 31 October he wired Eisenhower that the invasion had to be delayed two weeks. Admiral Cunningham, when he heard this request, called Murphy a "lunatic." Eisenhower told Murphy that the landings were proceeding and to do his best to secure French cooperation.[22]

The Difficulties of Working with Dissidents

In Algiers the Group of Five's plan called for the disruption of telephone and telegraph communications; isolation of naval headquarters; and occupation of the commissariat central, the police prefecture, Radio Algiers, the residences of the generals and admirals, and of the headquarters of Corps General Juin, the 19th Military Region, and the Algiers Division.[23]

Giraud received a letter from Murphy dated 2 November specifying the Allied position and the terms of his participation. From this the general learned that a landing in metropolitan France was not on the agenda. Unfortunately, because Murphy was so convinced that the Group of Five's help and Giraud's participation were critical, his letter downplayed Eisenhower's amendments to the Clark-Mast compromise. He told Giraud that he would forward the general's requirement that he take command of all forces in forty-eight hours and, finally, that he was certain that "an agreeable solution [to the question of command] can be found." In Giraud's mind it was inconceivable for an American general to command French troops fighting in French territory, and he regarded this as another endorsement of his position.[24]

With little idea of Allied intentions and severely deluded as to his intended role, the sixty-four-year-old general slipped past surveillance of his residence near Lyon and traveled to the Mediterranean coast to meet the "American" submarine HMS *Seraph* at 0140 on 6 November. His mission nearly ended when he tried to board from the deck of a tossing fishing boat. In the submarine captain's laconic description, "The embarkation was rough and the General fell between boat and submarine but was rescued by the coat collar undamaged." *Seraph* had radio problems and for hours headquarters did not know Giraud's whereabouts. The next day, however, the submarine encountered the PBY Catalina flying boat assigned to meet her—the aircraft had already concluded its search and was returning to base—and made visual contact at a distance on the barest of chance. Following another adventurous transfer in a small boat, Giraud completed his journey to Gibraltar via air on the afternoon of 7 November. The destination was Gibraltar and not Algiers because Eisenhower's political advisers, who had reviewed the communications with Giraud, realized that there were misunderstandings that needed to be resolved before the general could land in Algeria.[25]

In Gibraltar there followed what Eisenhower described as "one of my most distressing interviews of the war." The American general, commanding the greatest amphibious operation ever attempted and the largest Allied offensive of the war to date, had many things on his mind and much to do. Resolving the Giraud problem, however, devoured much of the next day. According to Clark, Eisenhower briefed Giraud and presented the text of the broadcast he wished the Frenchman to sign, whereupon Giraud stated, "Let's get it clear as to my part. As I understand it, when I land in North Africa I am to assume command of all Allied forces and become the Supreme Allied commander." Eisenhower was flabbergasted. To Clark, "It was rather like a bomb explosion." Eisenhower and Clark spent the next seven hours explaining that the French general's demands were impossible. Giraud was no less shocked. He had undertaken a dangerous journey at immense personal risk only to learn that all the assurances he believed he had received were false. Even though, as Eisenhower put it, "we offered him practically the kingship of North Africa," Giraud refused to participate because his honor and the honor of France could not be compromised by his assuming command of only the French elements. Moreover, he wished to move immediately into France and, as Eisenhower informed Washington afterward, "if he were made commander he would promptly use the entire Air Force coming into North Africa in neutralizing Sardinia and in transporting troops into Southern France." Clark recalled that the political advisers considered Giraud's participation so vital that they suggested Eisenhower give Giraud nominal command. Eisenhower, however, refused.[26]

The next day, as reports began arriving and it was clear that Torch was succeeding, Giraud agreed to command French forces only. Unfortunately, the general had missed his opportunity, if indeed it had ever existed. Although Giraud and his supporters seduced the Americans, events would show they misjudged the deep loyalty Marshal Pétain commanded.

6

MEDITERRANEAN CONVOYS

[Gibraltar] is absolutely stiff with shipping, cruisers, carriers and small fry.
How on earth the enemy are expected to take no notice beats me.
—Admiral Andrew Cunningham, 3 November 1942

The Algerian invasion fleet sailed from Great Britain in six advance convoys (numbered KX) and four assault convoys (numbered KMS [slow] or KMF [fast]). The first, consisting of colliers and minesweeping trawlers, departed the Clyde on 2 October—even before plans were finalized and orders issued—and the last on 1 November, a week before the landings. This effort upset normal convoy traffic as related; indeed, it disrupted the entire British transportation system. "Preparing for this invasion . . . 373 troop trains moved soldiers northwards from camps all over southern and midlands England to embark mainly at Liverpool and Glasgow before sailing back south. Many troops travelled almost 1,000 miles by rail and sea before clearing Land's End."[1]

Warships began heading south on 20 October when the aircraft carrier *Furious* escorted by three destroyers left the Clyde, followed three days later by the battleship *Rodney* with three destroyers and four days after that by the escort carriers *Dasher* and *Argus*, cruisers *Jamaica* and *Delhi*, and four destroyers. On the 30th the main body—Force X consisting of the battleships *Nelson* and *Duke of York*, battle cruiser *Renown*, the cruiser *Argonaut*, and eight destroyers—left Scapa Flow. Force H—the carriers *Victorious* and *Formidable* and eight destroyers—departed the Clyde the same day and joined with Force X while

TABLE 6.1

Torch Convoys from the United Kingdom to Algeria

Designation	Ships	Escorts	Speed	Depart	Arrive
KX.1	5	7	7.5	2 Oct.	14 Oct. (G)
KX.2	18	13	7	18 Oct.	31 Oct. (G)
KX.3	1	2	13	19 Oct.	27 Oct. (G)
KX.4A	20	8	7.5	21 Oct.	4 Nov. (G)
KX.4B	8	2	6.5	25 Oct.	3 Nov. (G)
KX.5	32	10	7	30 Oct.	10 Nov. (G)
KMS.1 (A&O)	47	18	8	22 Oct.	8 Nov. (A&O)
KMS.2	52	14	7	25 Oct.	10 Nov. (G)
KMF.1 (A&O)	39	12	11.5	26 Oct.	8 Nov. (A&O)
KMF.2	18	8	13	1 Nov.	10 Nov. (G)

Source: Roskill, *War at Sea* vol. 2, 316.
Note: (G) = Gibraltar; (A) = Algiers; (O) = Oran.

Force Q—the heavy cruisers *Cumberland* and *Norfolk* and five destroyers—
followed from Scapa Flow a day later. In sum, the support forces totaled six carriers, four capital ships, five cruisers, and thirty-one destroyers.[2]

Admiral Pound characterized these as the "most valuable convoys" ever to
leave Britain and fretted that Axis submarines might eviscerate the invasion
before it even began. Naval staff estimated that the Germans could concentrate
up to seventy-five submarines by 6 November should they discover what was
afoot. As a precaution the slow KX convoys were routed at around 15 degrees
west longitude to maximize air support from long-range aircraft while escort
carriers accompanied the KM convoys, which proceeded south as far west as 25
degrees.[3]

A lingering misconception in the Torch literature is that the convoys from
the United Kingdom escaped detection. Even recent assessments contain state-
ments such as, "British TORCH convoys were not observed while in the Atlantic
en route to Africa." In fact, German forces spotted *Rodney* on 26 October and on
the 31st reported "two carriers and two cruisers" heading south 280 miles west of
Portugal. These were *Argus* and *Dasher* with *Jamaica* and *Delhi*. Grand Admiral
Karl Dönitz ordered five boats, which had previously been harrowing Convoy
SL 125 to intercept, but they failed to establish contact. Two days later *U 514*

reported "seven large troop transports," probably KMS.2, in roughly the same area. Once again Dönitz dispatched five boats, but *U 514* lost contact while three of the others reported mechanical difficulties or battle damage, and engine problems prevented the one boat that did intercept, *U 440*, from maintaining contact. German forces also reported KMF.1 on 2 November and again the next day.[4]

Many accounts assert that the northbound Sierra Leon Convoy SL 125 diverted attention from the Torch convoys—some have even said it was deliberately sacrificed to draw submarines away from Torch shipping. Signals intelligence alerted the Germans to SL 125 and a group of ten submarines concentrated to intercept it. They first attacked off the Canary Islands on 26 October and in a seven-day battle sank thirteen ships, breaking off on the 1st in response to the sightings related above. While the convoy may have diverted German submarines, it was never used as a deliberate red herring.[5]

As the convoys arrived at Gibraltar, Axis observers tallied their presence. An SIS situation report dated 29 October, for example, noted the 1200 arrival of a *Nelson*-type battleship and two destroyers from the west, and that at 1800 the port held twenty-eight merchant ships, one liner, and thirteen tankers.[6]

French Dispositions

Algiers was the military and political capital of French North Africa.[7] Corps General Alphonse Juin commanded French forces in North Africa, and Corps General Louis-Marie Koeltz headed the 19th Military Region with divisions headquartered in Algiers, Constantine, Oran, and Tunis. Division General Jean Mendigal led the Armée de l'Air, which deployed ninety-nine fighters in Algeria and Tunisia, sixty-eight bombers, and fifty-one transports and reconnaissance planes. Vice Admiral Jacques Moreau of the 4th Maritime District deployed (operational units only) one *contre-torpilleur* (a large destroyer type later reclassified as light cruisers in Allied service), three destroyers, three torpedo boats, eight sloops or patrol boats, twenty-four auxiliary minesweepers or patrol craft, and five submarines. Naval air assets consisted of thirty-eight bombers.

The Run to the Landing Zone

Since 1939 many military convoys had departed Gibraltar for points east. However, nothing had ever traversed the Pillars of Hercules to compare with the mass of shipping that debouched from the Rock's crowded harbor after sunset on 5

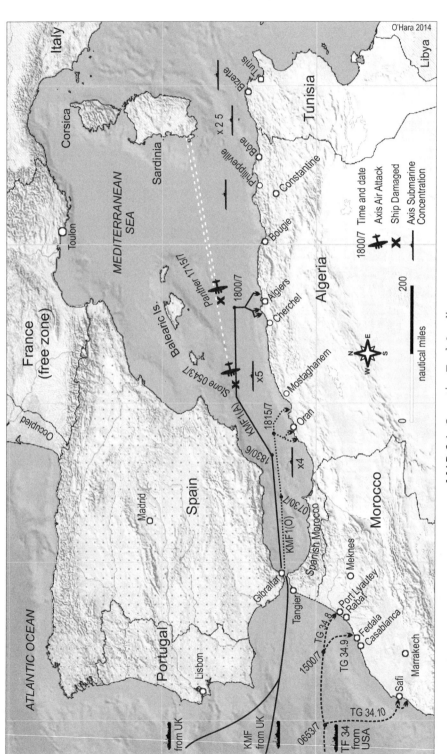

MAP 6.1 *Operation Torch Landings*

November 1942. Because of the different speeds of the forces and their various destinations and duties, it was not until dawn on 7 November that the last vessels had passed Europa Point into the Mediterranean, beyond the vision of observers in Spanish territories. These groups were the following:

- 5 November 1930: Force R. Fueling force with one corvette, two tankers, and four trawlers
- 2030: Aircraft carrier *Argus*, cruisers *Sheffield*, *Scylla*, and *Charybdis*, anti-aircraft ship *Tynwald*, and five destroyers
- 2300: Monitor *Roberts*
- 2345: Convoy KMS.1 (A) with fifteen transports, two LSGs, and eight escorts
- 6 November 0100: Convoy KMF.1 (A) with eleven LSIs, four APs, one transport, one headquarters ship, and eighteen escorts
- 0300: LSTs and four trawlers
- 0430: Force H with *Duke of York, Renown, Formidable, Victorious*, three cruisers, and sixteen destroyers
- 0445: LSIs *Ulster Monarch, Royal Scotsman, Royal Ulsterman*
- 1660: Convoy KMS.1 (O) with twenty-four transports
- 2230: Convoy KMF.1 (O) with headquarters ship and twenty transports
- 7 November 0400: carrier *Furious*, light cruiser *Delhi*, and escort

Admiral Andrew Cunningham commanded this naval conglomerate. Cunningham had led the Mediterranean Fleet from the start of the war to March 1942. By that time his star had dimmed following the Halcyon days of Taranto and Matapan due to a series of defeats and setbacks such as the bloodletting off Crete in May 1941, the December 1941 sinking of two battleships in Alexandria by Italian frogmen, and failed Malta convoys in February and March 1942. The Admiralty replaced him with Admiral (Acting) Henry Harwood and kicked Cunningham upstairs to serve on the CCS in Washington with Field Marshal John Dill. However, Harwood had not been an improvement and was responsible for the fiascos of Operation Vigorous, a Malta convoy that Italian battleships forced to abort in June 1942, and Operation Agreement, a botched attack on Tobruk in September 1942. His precipitous withdrawal of the fleet to Palestine and south of Suez when Panzerarmee Afrika neared Alexandria in June 1942 earned him no admiration in Whitehall, thus the chiefs recalled Cunningham to this important command.

The plans called for Force H to operate northeast of Algiers and, unless responding to a direct threat by the French and Italian battle fleets, keep east of longitude 4 degrees 30 minutes. KMF.1 (A) was to feint toward Malta before turning south at 1800 on 7 November to its landing zones around Algiers. KMS.1 (A) was to follow a more direct course, altering to the southeast at 1800 on the 7th for its approach to Algiers. Orders for the Oran convoys were similar. Because they had a shorter distance to cover, the fast and slow components sailed the same course. Vessels bound for the western and central beaches would turn south at 1815 while those assigned the eastern beaches turned at 1950.

As the ships passed observation points located around the strait, they were tabulated and the information quickly transmitted to Supermarina. For example, one assessment distributed at 1600 on 7 November noted that observers had seen one (probable) aircraft carrier, two (probable) cruisers, eleven destroyers, two smaller warships, eight transports, and ten merchant ships passing between 2320/6 to 0025/7 November. This was convoy KMF.1 (O). The Italians shared their intelligence with the Germans and with the French via the armistice commission.[8]

Axis naval forces in the western Mediterranean had been reinforced in response to the Gibraltar buildup. Nine German submarines waited in the relatively narrow waters east of the strait by 7 November. *U 81, 565, 593, 605* in a first line west followed by *U 77, 205,* and *660,* with *U 73* and *458* as backstops. *U 331, 431,* and *561* were steaming toward the anticipated battle zone while the other six Mediterranean boats were undergoing repair or refit. On 4 November Dönitz had ordered *U 595, 407, 596, 617, 755, 259,* and *380* into the Mediterranean to reinforce the boats already there. On 1 November Italy had thirty-nine submarines available for deployment, twenty-two under repair or refit, and fourteen serving as training boats in the Adriatic. Of these, six boats were on patrol with two stationed south of the Balearic Islands. By 5 November Supermarina had twenty-one boats at sea, most guarding the approaches to Sardinia and the Strait of Sicily. By 9 November twenty-five boats were positioned north of Bizerte, Bône, and Philippeville. This number dropped to fourteen by the 17th.[9]

Axis submarines, despite their numbers, had little impact. The convoys had strong escorts with one or more Gibraltar-based Catalinas providing direct air cover while sixteen Hudsons operated independently. On the 7th these aircraft collectively recorded six sightings, made four attacks, and incorrectly claimed one sinking. ("U-boat sank stern first after bows projecting 60° for 4 mins. Much air and oil.") *U 77* reported a contact, but the escort forced her to submerge. *U 73* stalked several transports but was depth charged and left behind. *U 81* tried to attack two aircraft carriers, but destroyers foiled her approach. *U 205* fired torpedoes at a large transport from KMF.1 (A) but missed. *U 458* discharged two torpedoes at a light cruiser and incorrectly claimed a hit. *Topazio* fired at a destroyer and was driven off in the ensuing counterattack. These events demonstrated that heavily escorted military convoys, especially those with air cover, were difficult targets even for veteran submarines with experienced commanders like *U 81* skippered by the Knight's Cross holder Friedrich Guggenberger.[10]

The only successful strike against an Algerian convoy occurred at 0543 on the 7th when a German He 111 torpedo bomber, one of six from II./KG 26 based in Sardinia, attacked KMF.1 (A) thirty miles off Cape Palos, Spain. They were the only aircraft from a group of thirty-seven to locate a target. The German aircraft claimed hits on a large warship and a steamship, but *Thomas Stone* (14,868 tons) was, in fact, their only success.[11]

The torpedo struck the transport to port and blew a hole in her bottom, breaking the propeller shaft, bending the propeller and rudder, and killing nine men. The convoy continued, leaving the corvette *Spey* with the crippled vessel. The colonel of the embarked 2nd Battalion, 39th Infantry, with the consent of the ship's captain, loaded his seven hundred men into the ship's two LCMs and twenty-two LCPs and, after dark, began a twenty-five-hour run to Algeria at a theoretical maximum speed of six knots. Not surprisingly, given that the journey was twice the designed endurance of the LCPs, there were breakdowns and other delays, as when, at night, some craft mistook another for a submarine and fired upon it. The valiant attempt to reach the battlefield was finally abandoned. *Spey* crowded the men on board and scuttled the landing craft. The battalion made Algiers at 2200 on 8 November, twenty-one hours late. *Thomas Stone* arrived in Algiers on 11 November under tow.

The Axis air forces were largely ineffective for the rest of the day. Vice Admiral Harold Burrough noted that aircraft "were in evidence at intervals during the afternoon" and that during the attack on Force H, which was north of his position, "many aircraft passed over and astern of the convoy." In fact, thirteen He 111 and forty-eight Ju 88s attacked Force H at 1715 on the 7th. This strike achieved one near miss on the destroyer *Panther*, which forced her return to Gibraltar. Warships, not transports, were the primary target of the German pilots.[12]

Destination(s)?

With the British convoys hours from their various destinations the Axis leadership scrambled to interpret what it all meant. On 6 November the German ambassador to Italy delivered to Mussolini Hitler's personal conviction that the huge Allied convoy reported departing Gibraltar was headed for Tripoli or Benghazi. Italian intelligence verified German sincerity on the 6th by wiretapping a telephone conversation between field marshals Göring and Kesselring and hearing them agree the target was a North African port, but not a French one. Surveillance of General Giraud and the French government wherein all seemed normal reinforced this conclusion.

On 7 November Giraud disappeared and Göring advised Kesselring that OKW now believed the Allies were going to attack southern France. Comando Supremo concluded that the Allied target was probably Algeria but nonetheless on the night of 7/8 November dispatched the new light cruiser *Attilio Regolo* and four destroyers to lay a barrage of 241 mines off Cape Bon while the destroyer *Corazziere* sowed a field of explosive floats, just in case the Allied convoys were headed for Libya. As the Italian force was returning, the British submarine *Unruffled* torpedoed and damaged *Attilio Regolo.* Supermarina readied the battleships *Vittorio Veneto* and *Roma* to move south from La Spezia to Naples. Following an early morning broadcast by BBC that Allied troops would be landing in North Africa, the German commander of submarines in the Mediterranean, Captain Leo Kreisch, and his superior, Vice Admiral Eberhard Weichold (promoted from rear admiral on 1 April 1942), concluded that the Allied fleets were heading for Bougie, and Kreisch ordered eight boats—*U 73, 77, 81, 205, 660, 331, 431,* and *561*—to concentrate there at top speed.[13]

The View from Algiers

Admiral Darlan and his wife had arrived in Algiers by plane on the 5th to attend their son who had been stricken with polio several weeks before and had suddenly taken a turn for the worse. As Murphy nervously telegraphed to the War Department, "Darlan's presence here on D-day might be embarrassing but it is believed he will depart before then." Vice Admiral Moreau had just left for Bizerte to observe the anticipated Allied attempt to force the Strait of Sicily. That day Italian intelligence warned Rear Admiral Auphan that the British had gathered in Gibraltar three battleships, three carriers, six cruisers, one monitor, twelve destroyers, and twenty-four smaller escorts, along with four troop transports, fifty-two merchant ships, and thirteen tankers. A convoy of such size obviously had a mission greater than just reinforcing Malta, but Auphan remained convinced that the Allies would not open a "Second Front" by invading North Africa and that they would not have sufficient landing craft for a large operation before mid-1943. Moreau was less confident. He believed that a force with so many transports would not attempt the Strait of Sicily and that more likely objectives were Sardinia or Sicily, or North Africa. One of the Italian islands seemed more logical; nonetheless, "a sudden attack on our North Africa would be in the English style." It would also be far less risky. He ordered the commanders of the Algiers and Oran naval districts to conduct aerial reconnaissance. Three aircraft scouted from Blida airfield near Algiers on 6 November but saw nothing. Another sortied from Oran and disappeared without a trace.[14]

Late on the 6th Italian intelligence advised the French admiralty that a large convoy of thirty transports and freighters had been tracked heading east between Almeria, Spain, and Melilla, Morocco, and that a second large convoy of unknown composition had left Gibraltar that day at 1100. This news alarmed Moreau, who saw in the spacing of the convoys the intent to hit multiple targets simultaneously. Meanwhile, General Jean Bergeret, an ex-Armée de l'Air minister who had maintained contacts in London, received information that there would be an Allied landing on North Africa within forty-eight hours. He had been scheduled for a trip to Bizerte but immediately diverted to Algiers on the 6th to tell Darlan. However, the admiral discounted Bergeret's information and telegraphed the admiralty on the 7th that he thought the Anglo-Saxons were acting against Axis bases in Libya to seal the El Alamein victory.[15]

On the afternoon of the 7th Moreau, who had returned to Algiers flying far inland to avoid the chance of running into British fighters, interrupted Darlan at the sick bed of his son and advised the admiral that the Allied convoys were sailing east at intervals that matched the distance between Oran and Algiers. Because the head of the first convoy was already past Algiers, he believed they would turn south to assault Bône and Algiers. According to Moreau, Darlan appeared startled by the news and responded, "This is not the report I received." Moreau wrote that Darlan had questioned Murphy about the convoy's destination and that the American had told him it was Tripolitania. Thus Darlan rejected Moreau's assessment and refused to call for aerial reinforcements from Morocco. He did agree, however, to ask the Italian armistice commission for permission to rearm as many coastal batteries as possible. Darlan also instructed Moreau to order Rear Admiral Edmond Derrien, commander of the Bizerte maritime district, to block the channel leading to Bizerte. Moreau protested that Oran and Algiers were more threatened than Bizerte, but Darlan insisted. Moreau later wrote, "He had an enigmatic and satisfied air, as if he had just played a trick on someone." The French official naval historian likewise considered this a strange order because it served little apparent purpose and similar measures were not ordered for Oran and Algiers. He believed that Darlan considered an attack against the French coast possible and wanted to ensure that Admiral Jean de Laborde, commander of the fleet at Toulon and Darlan's rival, did not take his ships to Bizerte.[16]

Thus, by the evening of 7 November when the four KM convoys began their final approaches to the landing beaches, there was still no consensus among Axis and French observers what the massive Allied movement meant. The French thought Malta or Tripoli, and OKW thought southern France or Tripoli. Comando Supremo had accepted an SIS assessment that northern Africa was the target, but Italian armistice commission staff in Algiers had not been so informed. The Allied success at preserving the strategic surprise was a remarkable accomplishment and did much to ensure the success of the subsequent landings.

7

ALGIERS

The individual equipment of our soldiers is excellent.
The only fault to be found is that there is too much of it.
—Maj. Gen. Charles W. Ryder

Plans and Objectives

Algiers, population 260,000, was the objective of the eastern task force. The broad mission was first "to occupy the port of Algiers and adjacent airfields and establish and maintain communications between Algiers and Orléansville," and then to "build up rapidly a striking force . . . to occupy Tunisia." Maj. Gen. Charles W. Ryder of the U.S. 34th Division commanded the initial landings to give the operation an American appearance, and the two landing zones nearest Algiers were assigned to U.S. troops. After the city's capture, Lieutenant General Kenneth Anderson would take over, activating the British 1st Army and spearheading the drive into Tunisia.[1]

Algiers sat on the slopes of a mountainous headland named Pointe Pescade that formed the western end of the Bay of Algiers. The planners rejected the obvious landing zone—the broad beach between the city and Cape Matifou, the bay's eastern headland, because both points had powerful shore batteries. Instead, the British contingent would land at Apples Beach twenty miles west of the city, and the Americans at Beer Beach ten miles west and at Charlie Beach, beyond Cape Matifou fifteen road miles east. After securing the beachheads American troops would advance on Algiers from both directions while the British captured

Blida airfield twenty-five miles southwest of the city. Two destroyers would bring troops into the harbor itself to secure facilities and prevent sabotage.

Forces

The British navy supported the landings with two carriers, three light cruisers, five destroyers (two assigned to the harbor assault), and ten corvettes or sloops. The assault force consisted of the 11th and 36th brigade groups of the British 78th Division (Apples), the 1st and 6th Commandos (Beer and Charlie), the 168th RCT of the U.S. 34th Infantry Division (Beer), the 39th RCT of the U.S. 9th Infantry Division (Charlie), and elements of the 3rd Battalion 135th RCT from the 9th Infantry Division (Algiers Harbor). In all the force comprised about 23,000 British and 10,000 American troops. Vice Admiral Burrough commanded the naval force from the headquarters ship *Bulolo*. Accompanying him were Ryder; Major General Vyvyan Evelegh, commander of the 78th Division; and Air Commodore George M. Lawson, the task force's air commander.[2]

French forces around Algiers came under the orders of the 4th Maritime Region and the 19th Army Corps. The Algiers Division had two regiments headquartered in Algiers, one at Blida, one at Fort National, one at Orléansville, and one at Koléa. Operational naval forces included two submarines, two patrol boats, and an auxiliary minesweeper. The Pointe Pescade and Cap Matifou coastal batteries had 194-mm guns, and there were other batteries with 120-mm, 95-mm, and 75-mm weapons. The air force deployed forty-seven D.520 fighters at Maison Blanche and twenty-eight bombers along with twenty transports at Blida. Naval air consisted of six operational bombers at Maison Blanche.[3]

At 1800 on 7 November KMF.1 (A) turned due south. The ships assigned to Charlie Sector split off at 1900 and steered southeast to their disembarkation point east of Algiers while the convoy's Apples and Beer components continued until 2130 when they likewise separated and made for their respective destinations. There was a moderate northeast breeze, a slight sea, clear sky, and good visibility. Coastal lights were burning.

Apples Sector

The British 11th Brigade Group's 2nd Battalion, Lancashire Fusiliers (2/LF) was to land at Apples Green and capture the Blida airbase twelve miles inland. The 5th Battalion Northamptonshire Regiment (5/NH) would come ashore at

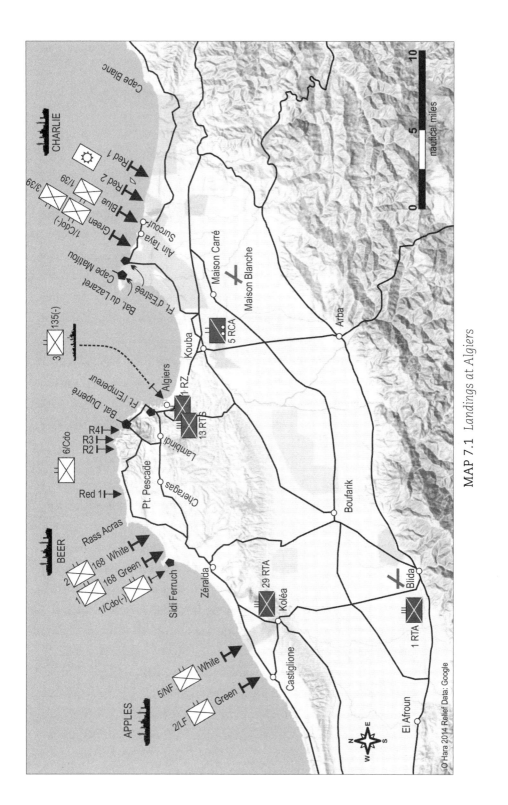

MAP 7.1 *Landings at Algiers*

Apples White and advance east toward Algiers, twenty-five miles by road. The 6th Battalion Royal West Kents (6/RWK) would stay in reserve along with the 36th Brigade Group, which would, if all went well, leapfrog to Bougie, a hundred miles east, the next day.

The LSIs came to their landing stations following the minesweeping trawlers *Rysa, Juliet,* and *Stroma* and escorted by the corvette *Rother* and the Hunt destroyers *Bicester* and *Bramham.* The convoy sighted their beacon submarine, *P 221,* at 2214. After transferring her navigation party to guide boats, *P 221* was to launch folbots two miles from shore. These would take position four hundred yards off the beach and shine a beacon to guide the landing craft in.

The LSI *Karanja* began launching boats and all were afloat by 2304. *Viceroy of India's* LCPs likewise hit the water promptly. They formed up behind the guide boat and set out for Apples Green at 2350. Coastal lights were burning and the folbot was duly flashing its light. *Karanja's* first wave landed promptly at 0100 on 8 November. *Viceroy of India's* craft beached at 0110. The boats from *Marnix* proceeded to Apples White independently because the transport's LCPs mistook a destroyer for the motor launch that was to lead them. Despite this error and the absence of a signaling folbot they hit the right beach at 0108. At the same time four transports and the LSG *Dewdale* from KMS.1 (A), rendezvoused with the Apples landing force's LSIs.

There was heavy surf at Apples White and both Apples beaches had a gradual slope. Some boats hit bottom far from shore, forcing troops to wade several hundred yards through chest-high water. Another complication was a westerly current that pushed ships as far as five miles from their release positions in just ninety minutes. Nonetheless, the commander's report asserted, "Though the beach proved very bad and dangerous, the landings were carried out safely and according to plan." The Northamptonshires captured Zéralda before sunrise. Elements of the Lancashire Fusiliers overran the defense post at Castigione at 0145 and the town of Koléa, three miles inland and headquarters of the 29 RTA (Régiment de Tirailleurs Algériens, or regiment of Algerian riflemen), before dawn. The 29 RTA's commander, Colonel Baril, was an adherent of Division General Mast, and his men remained in their barracks. This was vital because the regiment had fought in Syria and the men were strongly anti-English. After securing their immediate objectives the fusiliers moved toward Blida while the Northamptonshires started for Algiers.[4]

Beer Sector: An Orgy of Disorder

Beer Sector contained three landing zones. The 168th RCT's 1st Battalion and three hundred men of 1 Commando were assigned Beer Green, located on the southern quarter of the four-mile-wide bay between Rass Acras and Cap Sidi-Ferruch. The 2nd Battalion was to disembark at Beer White on the bay's central and northern portions, and the 3rd Battalion was to stay in reserve. The Commandos would secure the fort at Sidi-Ferruch while the 168th advanced across Pointe Pescade, occupying the high ground overlooking Algiers before sunrise and capturing the city in time to support the 135th's assault on the harbor. Meanwhile, 550 men of 6th Commando were to land at four spots designated beaches Red 1, 2, 3, and 4. Red 1 was a cove three hundred yards wide just west of the Cap Caxine lighthouse. There was a coastal defense observation post there. The other beaches were to the east. The Commandos' main task was to neutralize Batterie Duperré north of Algiers.[5]

The Beer Sector senior naval landing officer was Captain Robert J. Shaw on board *Keren*. The LSIs and transports were joined by the LSG *Ennerdale* and transports of KMS.1 (A), and then, homed by *P 48,* the amphibious force reached station seven miles offshore at 2230 and started launching boats. The first waves for Red 2, 3, and 4 were to depart at 2300 guided by a motor launch and supported by the destroyer *Wilton*. The first waves for Beer Green, White, and Red 1 were scheduled to form up behind their respective ML guides at 2330. A folbot from *P 48* was to take station two hundred yards east of Green Beach. H hour was 0100.[6]

That was the plan, but as Vice Admiral Burrough noted in his report, "The landing at B Sector was marred by avoidable mistakes." First, the planners miscalculated Beer White's position by three thousand yards. The discovery of this error "on the very eve of sailing" required last-minute adjustments, and Captain Shaw wanted to confirm that *P 48* and the guide boat understood them. Thus he ordered the MLs to wait for the beach master, Lieutenant Commander George Grandage. Meanwhile, the wind had risen to Force 3, delaying loading, and a strong current was pushing the transports west at three knots.[7]

Grandage's LCM carried the 1st Battalion's commander, Lt. Col. Edward J. Doyle, with his staff and two jeeps. Grandage wrote, "After running four miles we expected to find a submarine [*P 48*] which was stationed as a guide, and two miles farther a motor launch. To my consternation we found neither." His landfall did not resemble the carefully studied photographs and terrain models of

Beer Green, and a boat leaving shore said they were off White Beach, not Green. Grandage confessed the problem to Doyle and to his surprise found the colonel "not as unhappy as I had expected," and at Doyle's suggestion, they landed there. Grandage then shoved off and fruitlessly searched for Beer Green. When dawn revealed a landmark he realized that he had deposited Doyle at Apples White, not Beer White—that is, eight miles southwest of the correct location, not one mile northeast as thought. "I eventually landed on Beer Green Beach feeling very small at 08.30 but was much relieved to find that nearly all the other craft had had much the same experience, except those who landed in the first half hour before the current had time to have much effect."[8]

Meanwhile, *P 48* headed inshore to meet the other guide boat and launch folbots. When the guide boat did not appear the submarine put the Beer Green pilot on the first boat to come by, which happened to be an LCA from *Winchester Castle* loaded with troops from 1st Commando. The pilot transferred to an LCS and headed toward shore. After an hour's journey the wave made landfall on the wrong side of Sidi-Ferruch—but at least the pilot recognized the error and led his boats back around the point. At 0103 he ordered the first wave in, but it strayed and landed at Beer White instead of Beer Green.

The experience of other units was worse. After a detour to Apples White the regimental commander, Col. John W. O'Daniel, disembarked at Beer White at 0700. An LCM carrying most of Company H of the 2nd Battalion touched shore fifteen miles west of Sidi-Ferruch. After ascertaining the error the troops reloaded and landed at 0700 in the Apples zone only seven miles out of position. The 1st Battalion's Company C took six hours to reach shore twelve miles west of Beer Green. Companies E and F landed at Beer Green instead of Beer White. Thus, driven by the strong current and navigating without guide boats (or improperly guided boats) the 168th Regiment ended up strewn across fifteen miles of shoreline instead of arriving as a tight package in the small bay between Cap Sidi-Ferruch and Rass Acras as intended. Even the units that landed at the right place encountered difficulties: Company A made it to Beer Green only to face sandbars and heavy swells. Men disembarked in water over their heads while landing craft broached and slammed broadside onto the beach.[9]

Fortunately the Americans, like the British, encountered little resistance. The coastal defense post at Rass Acras fired on landing craft at 0045 and forced some to turn away, according to its records. Troops from the 2nd Battalion captured

Troops of the 39th Regiment landing near Sorcouf east of Cape Matifou on 8 November. Two broached craft are visible in the center of the picture. (U.S. Army Signal Corps)

this position by 0345. A company of the 29 RTA and a coastal defense detachment garrisoned the fort at Sidi-Ferruch. Division General Mast had ordered Colonel Baril to meet the Americans there because he believed it would be the main landing point and his *tirailleurs* (riflemen) prevented sailors from reporting the invasion to naval headquarters. From his vantage point Baril observed several boats capsize although the sea seemed perfectly calm.[10]

Baril greeted the Commandos as they approached the "Foreign Legion–type" fort. Mast himself arrived shortly thereafter and found his subordinate trying to talk the Commando's reluctant colonel into striking out for Blida in a collection of vehicles Mast had had assembled there the day before. Mast believed that General Giraud would be landing at the airfield that morning and that Blida's swift occupation was critical to the entire operation's success. The general spoke excellent English and finally prevailed. The Commandos began motoring toward the airfield at 0415.[11]

In fact, Giraud's welcoming committee, the commander of the Blida sector, Division General Jean Goislard de Monsabert and Jacques Lemaigre Dubreuil, the Group of Five's chief, arrived at Blida at 0300 bearing orders to permit American aircraft to land. Mast's orders also stated that a German operation against Tunisia was imminent and that the Americans were intervening in Algeria at General Giraud's request. Garrisons and coastal defense units were to facilitate their landings. Monsabert recalled that when this order was given to the colonels of the 1 and 29 RTAs, they did not seem surprised, although the mode of transmission was highly unorthodox.[12]

The air base commander, Colonel Montrelet, received Monsabert and Lemaigre Dubreuil enthusiastically. Then the colonel's superior, Division General Mendigal, telephoned from Algiers. Monsabert watched Montrelet speak on the telephone. "His face changed color. . . . The moment was sad and even slightly comical. [Upon hanging up he said], 'I have received . . . direct orders from air command to oppose the Americans with force. I do not understand this contradiction . . . but in any case I must follow air command.'" As Armée de l'Air personnel manned defensive positions, Monsabert summoned a nearby detachment from the 1 RTA to surround the base. Corps General Koeltz, meanwhile, had been freed from a short-lived imprisonment imposed by the Group of Five, and he telephoned affirming orders to resist the landings. As it became clear that Giraud was delayed and fearing he might be imprisoned, Lemaigre Dubreuil slipped away and took the coast road back to Algiers. He saw the transports offshore and later wrote, "This reassuring vision remains the most beautiful and pleasant memory that I have of 8 November 1942." Loyalists detained Monsabert, but the arrival of the caravan carrying the 1st Commando ensured that negotiations continued.[13]

Red Beach

The Commandos that landed on the Red Beaches got under way late. One account explained that this was because a swell was running and the "Merchant Navy crew of the *Awatea* were but half trained, and the landing craft were in consequence clumsily lowered." Next, on the way in some craft strayed from their guide boat. Two LCPs assigned to Red 1 landed ninety minutes late. After a short fight they captured the defense post at Caxine. Six LCPs approached the Îlot de la Marine in Algiers Harbor two miles southeast of their destination. Machine guns at l'École Indigène sank four of the boats at 0322. Shortly thereafter twenty-four Commandos climbed onto the jetty; they were captured after a short fight that cost the life of the unit's commander.[14]

Despite these mishaps, Commandos gathered to attack Duperré at 0509. The destroyer *Wilton* gave gunfire support until 0600 when a 194-mm round from the battery forced the destroyer's withdrawal "until the military situation clarified." The infantry attack likewise failed and between 1000 and 1019 *Wilton* dueled with the battery from extreme range. After noon nearly five hundred Commandos attacked again—again unsuccessfully. Five Albacores bombed the position at 1350, but Batterie Duperré resisted until the cease-fire that evening.[15]

The 168th Moves Inland

Confusion was the main foe faced by the 168th RCT's two assault battalions during their first hours ashore. The beach master closed Beer Green and directed all reinforcements and supplies to a two-hundred-yard stretch of the mile-long Beer White as the only area he judged safe to receive landing craft. Troops sat idle while their officers tried to figure out where they were or to locate missing elements. Major General Ryder complained that "all units were widely scattered and intermingled" and that there was a "lack of means of communications, either radio or vehicle." The radios either were too heavy (110 pounds for those used by regiments), had inadequate batteries, or were easily masked. The general also noted that the British beach masters gave priority to British requirements: "British staff cars were landed in place of U.S. artillery pieces which were urgently needed." The 3rd Battalion's arrival at 0730 compounded the congestion.[16]

Despite the confusion, their rough landings, and lack of experience, the Americans displayed initiative. Capt. Edward Bird of B Company scouted to the edge of Algiers. He returned to the beach at 0830 and led his unit into the hills of Pointe Pescade. Lieutenant Colonel Doyle trekked out of the British zone and joined Bird not long into his march. There was little resistance and most civilians welcomed the Americans as they climbed the lightly wooded hills. However, some French officers had unfavorable impressions: "Our valiant liberators, fatigued after three weeks at sea, were not used to the African sun, and were poorly trained for marching. . . . What disorder! What straggling! Any armed opposition would have been catastrophic." In fact, by midmorning machine guns at Lambiridi on the heights above the city caused the entire battalion to hunker down.[17]

The 2nd Battalion approached Lambiridi from the north, closing up on the 1st Battalion's left flank. The 3rd Battalion advanced on the right flank, its heavy weapons company hauling equipment and ammunition by hand. Colonel O'Daniel established the regimental command post at Cheragas and at noon he readied a three-battalion attack into Lambiridi. However, French snipers and an armored car stymied the Americans and desultory fighting continued into the afternoon. At 1500 Lieutenant Colonel Doyle infiltrated a patrol into Algiers through French lines. The group had just captured the Palais d'Été when a sniper killed Doyle. The regiment was preparing to attack Fort l'Empereur the next day when rumors of an armistice began running through the ranks.

Charlie Sector

Charlie Sector consisted of four beaches spaced along a four-mile span east of Cape Matifou. The senior naval landing officer, Capt. Campbell D. Edgar, USN, sailed on *Samuel Chase*. The torpedoing of *Thomas Stone* the day before was, as Edgar expressed it, "a severe blow, as her troops and boats were sorely needed. Moreover, she was the only one of the three transports which had actual experience in landing troops." This loss forced the 39th RCT's 3rd Battalion, formally the reserve, to land on Charlie Green—the 2nd's original destination. The 1st Battalion had Charlie Blue, the next beach east, while farthest east Charlie Red 1 and 2, with exits through the coastal bluffs, were allocated to service units and vehicles. After landing, the 39th RCT was to "defeat the enemy garrison at Maison Carré, prevent hostile reinforcements from the east and south from reaching Algiers, and advance on Algiers." In addition, five troops from 1st Commando (198 British and 114 Americans) were to land on Green Beach and neutralize Cape Matifou's Batterie du Lazaret.[18]

At 2017 Charlie Force spotted Cape Matifou's light. At 2135 the landing force established contact with *P 45,* the beacon submarine, and by 2200 the ships had reached their disembarkation position seven miles offshore. The operation was on schedule up to this point but delays accumulated as the boats loaded and formed up. Edgar identified several reasons. Except for *Almaack* the transports were "quite recently commissioned and lacked proper training." *Leedstown* blew fuses on some of her cranes, and once in the water boats had trouble finding their guide MLs. *Chase* had the first of her LCPs in the water by 2201 and completed lowering fifty-five minutes later. By 0105 all boats were loaded. *Almaack* reported her fourteen boats lowered by 2307, but her first wave did not get under way until 0145, nearly a three-hour lapse. As elsewhere, the assault transports needed extra landing craft to accommodate their assault waves. For example, half of *Almaack*'s first wave relied on six boats from *Chase, Leedstown,* and *Dempo.* The absence of *Stone* forced a whole series of last-minute adjustments that compounded delays. Fortunately, Lazaret's 194-mm guns remained quiet while landing craft circled and searched for their guide boats.[19]

The initial waves got away at 0100, but problems continued. The LCMs that were supposed to follow *ML 295* to Charlie Red instead sailed past the motor launch and followed *ML 273* to Charlie Blue. This mistake was particularly costly because it stranded vehicles and heavy weapons on a beach with no exit. The first boats grounded on Blue Beach at 0125. The 1st Battalion reported "very little resistance very little surf." Nonetheless, inexperienced crews handled their boats poorly. On some LCMs ramps splashed too quickly, or boats retracted with lowered ramps. Nearly half of *Chase*'s LCPs shipped water over the stern and six stranded. *Almaack* lost three boats in the first wave: An LCP, far astray, grounded on rocks off Cape Matifou. Surf flooded another. An LCM hit a rock and broached. Some landing craft assigned to Green ended up on Blue, including one carrying the Commandos' ammunition. Because subsequent waves were slow in forming up they lost sight of the preceding wave. "Consequently many boats landed out of position." The Commandos, occupying eleven boats from *Leedstown,* were particularly tardy because of that transport's davit problems. Then they hit a fogbank and had to proceed at half-speed to maintain contact, landing at 0250, nearly two hours behind schedule.[20]

At 0130, because the shore battery remained silent, Captain Edgar ordered the transports in to four thousand yards. *Almaack* reached her new position off Red Beach at 0321. This was only fifteen minutes after her first landing craft had returned. In fact, the battery did not sound an alert until 0150 because fog hid activity offshore even though the current temporarily pushed *Leedstown* to within five thousand yards. By 0348, however, the fog had thinned enough for Batterie du Lazaret to deploy its searchlight, and the probing beam illuminated the Hunt destroyer *Zetland* a scant five thousand meters away, by the battery's calculation. Two 194-mm guns engaged as *Zetland* turned toward shore and targeted the searchlight, which blinked out. Twenty minutes later the searchlight caught *Zetland* again. A brief gunnery exchange at nine thousand meters followed. Commandos reached the battery at 0435. The garrison of this position and the adjacent fort numbered only forty-three naval personnel and two machine-gun sections of the 13 RTS (Régiment de Tirailleurs Sénégalais, or regiment of Senegalese riflemen). Nonetheless, the defenders repulsed a predawn attack.[21]

By 0900 the transports were only fifteen hundred yards offshore. Landing operations continued except for a stoppage between 1015 and 1054 because of beach congestion. During the day *Almaack*'s fourteen landing craft managed sixty-eight ship-to-shore trips, although she lost five more boats, most of them to rough surf. *Chase* had ten boats still in service by nightfall, but three of these were lost in an air attack that followed. A contributing factor to these excessive loss rates, in addition to poorly trained coxswains and crews, was the overloading of LCMs to compensate for the loss of *Stone*'s boats.[22]

U.S. Ground Operations

At 0210 the Maison Blanche air base received orders to implement the defense plan, and two hours later Vice Admiral Marcel Leclerc, commander of Marine Alger, ordered the 4 BR (bombardment reconnaissance), a naval air squadron consisting of twin-engine Potez 63 bombers, to attack enemy transports. The squadron had, however, only six machines operational, and thick fog kept them grounded. Then reports arrived at 0530 that U.S. troops were approaching. These were the 1st Battalion's forward elements. The airbase commander organized a defense perimeter and at 0615 captured the first American patrol to arrive. Nonetheless, troops kept coming, and the airfield surrendered three hours later. Shelling delivered by the 65 RAA (Régiment d'Artillerie d'Afrique, or artillery regiment of Africa) inflicted heavy casualties and held up the 1st Battalion's further advance. The 3rd Battalion moved inland of the 1st and occupied positions a mile south of Maison Blanche.[23]

The defense of Fort d'Estrée and Batterie du Lazaret lasted most of the day. After the battery refused a surrender demand, 1st Commando's colonel asked Vice Admiral Burrough for help. The admiral reported that both positions "were bombarded by *Bermuda* and bombed by naval aircraft almost simultaneously between 1400 and 1530. Both bombing and bombardment were most successful, and having driven the defenders underground, the Commandos occupied the forts without opposition." According to a French navy report, *Bermuda* fired ten rounds and a flight of six Albacores dropped bombs "quite far from the target." After the fire had lifted, the Commandos, supported by self-propelled artillery, attacked again and overran the battery at 1630. The fort, however, did not surrender until 0920 on 9 November.[24]

Operation Terminal

To prevent sabotage of port facilities, planners devised an operation wherein two old British destroyers, *Broke* and *Malcolm,* would penetrate Algiers Harbor and land 662 men of the U.S. 3rd Battalion, 135th Regiment, along with seventy-four Royal Navy boarding personnel. This mission was a late addendum; not until 18 October did the troops receive some abbreviated training, climaxing in a nocturnal assault on Belfast Harbor. The battalion's commander, Lt. Col. Edwin T. Swenson, and his men only learned the full details of their task on 29 October, the third day of their voyage in the cruiser *Sheffield*. They were told, "Amid an atmosphere of hushed expectancy [that they would be participating in a] decisive action . . . to shorten the ultimate length of the war in Europe by at least two years." Little resistance was expected. The men were given aerial photos and charts with the name of their destination clipped out. One soldier recalled that to their untrained eyes outdoor latrines appeared "to be positive locations of coastal defense guns." Company K, half of Company I, and half of Company M (heavy weapons) transferred from *Sheffield* to *Malcolm* at 1630 on 6 November. An hour later *Broke* came alongside and embarked Company L and the remainder of Companies I and M.[25]

The port consisted of a long seawall with jetties north and south that provided two entries—both blocked by booms. Two-gun 75-mm batteries, Batterie du Musoir Nord on the north jetty and du Musoir Sud on the seawall, protected the navy-controlled northern entry. The Batterie de l'Amirauté with four 120-mm guns was located at the Îlot de la Marine where the north jetty joined land. Vice Admiral Burrough authorized the operation at 0140, and the two destroyers steered toward the city lights. *Broke* intended to discharge her troops in the southern basin at the Quai de Dieppe. Two Company K platoons would capture the port offices, the graving docks, and the Môle Amiral Mouchez. The rest would concentrate near the Grand Môle. *Malcolm* would follow fifteen minutes later and make for the Grand Môle. Company L would capture the oil depot, the power station, and the seaplane base. Planners did not expect the raiders to achieve surprise and their quick relief was crucial.[26]

The batteries came to the alert at 0310, and a searchlight illuminated landing craft approaching the north jetty carrying the Commandos who had overshot Beer Red 4 Beach. As this force was being destroyed as related, lookouts spotted the destroyers and Musoir Nord opened fire at 0320, followed at 0358 by Musoir Sud. Searchlights illuminated the British warships, and in the glare they could not locate the narrow gap between jetty and seawall. The large American flags flying at their mastheads did not diminish the fierce resistance. Just after 0400 a shell

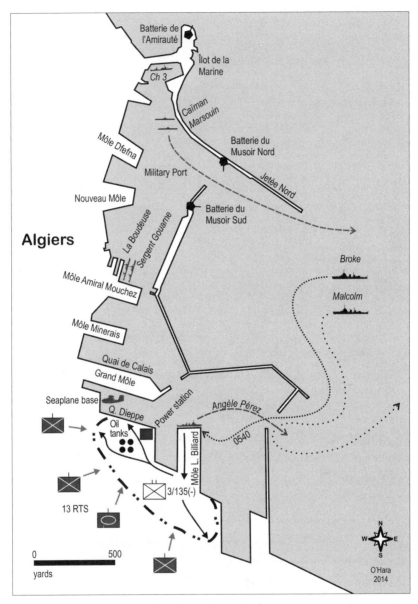

MAP 7.2 *Algiers Harbor*

struck *Malcolm* in her boiler room. The destroyer signaled, "Searchlight . . . very troublesome. Have made 3 attempts but failed to find inner channel entrance. . . . Would be easier if searchlight could be put out of action." Finally, with a fire on deck, two boilers out, and four men wounded, the destroyer withdrew. *Broke,* however, persisted and at last sliced the boom, "like a knife through butter."

After trading shots with the minesweeper *Angèle Pérez* as she passed heading out to sea, the destroyer reached the Môle Louis Billiard and at 0520 discharged her troops. At this point the city was mostly in the hands of the Group of Five, and the American soldiers secured many of their objectives, including the power station and oil depot.[27]

Shortly after 0800 Musoir Nord began to harass *Broke,* forcing her to move twice. At 0920, having been hit several times, the destroyer sounded the recall siren, but Lieutenant Colonel Swenson expected relief shortly and considered it safer for his men to hold their ground. He was probably right. The batteries heavily damaged *Broke* as she withdrew and the old destroyer eventually foundered the next day while under tow.

Swenson's men, meanwhile, hunkered down behind hay bales and wooden boxes. For several hours they stood off three companies of the 13 RTS and one company of Gardes Mobiles. After 1130 a section of Renault tanks arrived and their gunfire ignited several bales. The absence of shooting elsewhere signified to the besieged Americans that something had delayed their relief. Finally, at 1230, with ammunition running low, Swenson surrendered. Operation Terminal cost the Americans fifteen killed and thirty-three wounded. The British lost nine killed and twenty-two wounded, with one destroyer sunk and another damaged.

Air Operations

The Fleet Air Arm units flying off *Argus* and *Avenger* supported the landing. Carrier aircraft conducted major strikes against the Jetée du Nord in support of *Broke,* and against Batterie Duperré at 1350, and Batterie du Lazaret at 1400.

The senior air officer reported to Cunningham that an F4F Martlet from *Argus* had landed at Blida at 0934 "to accept surrender, and that reception appeared friendly." The U.S. Army historian George F. Howe commented, "This author has found no confirmation of this episode in contemporary records." However, a French account describing the tense standoff between Division General Monsabert and the loyalist forces at Blida noted, "This is the moment chosen by a New Zealand aircraft to land on the runway, which does not improve the atmosphere. General Mast's proclamation had stated that only Americans would land and here, suddenly a little confused and almost apologetic was a subject of His Britannic Majesty." Although elements of 1st Commando were camped outside the gate, awaiting reinforcements, French troops controlled the airfield until late that afternoon when units of the 2/LF finally arrived from Koléa. Until then the French allowed Allied aircraft to land, but not take off.[28]

The 39th Regiment's early capture of Maison Blanche permitted three fighter squadrons to fly in from Gibraltar: the 43rd (seventeen Hurricanes), the 81st (eighteen Spitfires), and the 242nd (seventeen Spitfires), which took off at 0800, 1030, and 1130, respectively, on the two-and-a-half-hour flight. Unfortunately, a lack of gasoline and ammunition prevented these aircraft from undertaking combat air patrol as anticipated. Another concern was the condition of the British carriers. *Avenger* had engine defects that limited her speed to fourteen knots. This required her to put into Algiers that night for repairs. These lasted until 12 November, after which she departed only to be sunk during her return to the United Kingdom.

French Submarines

The two operational submarines in Algiers came to combat stations at 0340, and Marine Alger ordered them to make ready for departure at 0500. *Caïman* sailed at 0620, but a fouled anchor delayed *Marsouin*. *Broke* spotted *Caïman* near the north passage and immediately raised the alarm. Thus, the submarine was barely clear of the jetty when an aircraft bombed her and forced her to crash dive. British antisubmarine forces continued to harry *Caïman*. Her report noted fourteen depth-charge attacks between 1003 and 1217 and another eight between 1647 and 1749. At 1833 she surfaced ten miles north of Pointe Pescade and headed toward France at low speed, making Toulon on 11 November at 0730.[29]

Marsouin cleared the northern exit at 0835 and attempted to patrol off Cape Matifou. Like her sister she was severely harassed counting 285 explosions in a series of attacks between 1026 and 1245, at 1510, and from 1630 to 1747. After dark she surfaced to charge her batteries and headed north. While under way she received a message from Marine Alger stating that an armistice had been signed and ordering her to return to port. Shortly thereafter Vichy ordered all submarines to Toulon. *Marsouin* arrived there at 1335 on the 11th. The French boats recorded more attacks than the British delivered. Cunningham's report specifies only two ships made depth-charge attacks off Algiers on the 8th. Beginning at 0955 *Speedwell* made "11 attacks on [*Marsouin*] 11 miles N.N.E. of Algiers harbour . . . [and] the submarine was twice blown to the surface." Only slight damage was claimed. *Hussar* dropped changes at 2325.[30]

Politics Ashore

Algiers was Algeria's political center, and there the powerbrokers, like Admiral Darlan, Corps General Juin, and Robert Murphy, were gathered. It was also the Group of Five's stronghold.

As related Division General Mast issued a general order to his division shortly before midnight. It stated, "The mission of all is simple: aid the landings of the American troops on the coast and on the airfields." He acted even though the Americans failed to satisfy several preconditions he considered essential to the coup's success. They never delivered the weapons he had requested to arm the Group of Five's volunteer militia, but more important, he lacked his figurehead. Originally Mast planned to confront Juin with General Giraud as the first troops were landing and demand the administration's cooperation. However, Giraud had seemingly vanished. On the 7th Murphy bombarded Eisenhower with "repeated radio queries asking: Where is Giraud?" Finally he learned that the general was in Gibraltar and would be arriving shortly. Mast took this to mean on the morning of the 8th and readied his reception at Blida as related rather than confront Juin directly.[31]

As Eisenhower wrestled with the misunderstanding that had delayed Giraud—a misunderstanding Murphy himself had done much to create—Murphy drove to the Villa des Oliviers, Juin's official residence near Lambiridi, to enlist the general's support. Much to Mast's horror, the American consul did this before the landings started and while Juin retained communications. Murphy told Juin that the liberation of France had started and a half million Americans were about to land all along the North African coast. Juin was, according to Murphy's account, "startled and shocked," but on reflection confessed that were it his decision, he would cooperate. However, Admiral Darlan was in town, and his orders were the ones that mattered. Murphy asked to speak to Darlan, so Juin telephoned while Murphy sent his car.[32]

The admiral arrived twenty minutes later irritated and perplexed by the late hour. When Murphy burst out with news, Darlan was furious. "After stomping for a quarter of an hour like a bear in a cage . . . he finally cried: 'Americans are definitely more stupid than their English friends; don't they see that [the Germans] are going to occupy free France? Our situation is hopeless.'" He accused Murphy of lying to him about the convoy's destination and said, "This premature action is not what we have been hoping for." Finally Darlan calmed down and asked to telegram Pétain. To this Murphy consented. The admiral sealed a message in an envelope. It read as follows: "Algiers. 8 November 0200 GMT. I was called to speak to General Juin at 0145 and I came to his residence. There Mr. Murphy told me that: Quote 'At the request of a Frenchman, General Giraud, President Roosevelt had decided to occupy North Africa this morning with a large force. The United States has only one goal: destroy Germany and save France whose integrity they wish to maintain.' End quote. I told him that France has signed an armistice agreement and that I would abide by the marshal's orders to defend our territories."[33]

At this time Juin's chief of staff attempted to leave and discovered that forty armband-wearing adherents of the Group of Five had surrounded the villa. They advised Darlan and Juin that they were prisoners. Vice-Consul Kenneth Pendar set off in Murphy's Buick purportedly to deliver Darlan's message to Vice Admiral Leclerc, who had secure communications with the admiralty in Vichy. Actually, he went to a confederate's house and steamed the message open. After reading he decided it was better undelivered. Meanwhile, there was still no sign of an invasion. Murphy wondered if he had mistaken the day. Darlan wondered if the American consul was lying again, or worse, whether the Americans were conducting only a commando raid. He eventually asked to send another telegram, in reality a duplicate of the first. However, at 0630, before this could be done, Gardes Mobiles arrived and scattered the militia. With the tables thus turned Darlan and Juin drove to Fort l'Empereur to determine the situation while Murphy and Pendar, who had returned in the meanwhile, were now the prisoners.[34]

Once free, Darlan confirmed that large-scale disembarkations were in fact under way. At 0818 he reported to Pétain that American troops carried in British ships had invaded Algiers and that in some places, such as Algiers Harbor itself, there had been an effective defense while in others the landings had achieved surprise and succeeded. At 0849 Pétain replied expressing confidence in Darlan and instructing him to react to developments as he judged best. Darlan also found waiting a message from Rear Admiral Auphan timed 0500 GMT: "OKW offers assistance from air units based on Sicily and Sardinia. In what form and where do you want this?" At 0957 Darlan telegraphed back, "On the transports off Algiers." Some historians have interpreted this reply as confirming Darlan's anti-British inclinations. However, with the Free Zone's status still pending, rejecting the German offer was not an option and the Axis was going to launch such attacks regardless. Had Darlan truly sought to harm the Allies, he would have invited the Germans into Tunisia and Algeria as they so desperately wanted.[35]

Corps General Juin, meanwhile, suppressed the uprising. Learning of Mast's role in the putsch, he put Brigade General Jean Roubertie, Mast's deputy, in command of the Algiers Division. He confirmed that landings were occurring in large numbers on both sides of the city and that the Allied columns had reached the heights overlooking Algiers and captured or neutralized the major airbases. He canceled an armored counterattack and instructed Roubertie to minimize casualties and slowly retreat toward Fort l'Empereur. Finally, at noon he advised Darlan that continued resistance was possible but pointless and recommended a cease-fire. At 1240 Darlan telegraphed Pétain that Algiers was likely to fall that day and that he was dividing the command in North Africa, putting Division General Georges Barré, commander of the Tunisia Division, in charge of the Tunisia-Constantine zone and General Auguste Charles Noguès in charge of the Oran-Morocco zone. The admiral was delaying any action that might cause the marshal to disavow him and was limiting the impact if he did come to terms with the Americans.[36]

At 1500 word arrived in the Hôtel St. Georges, where Darlan was based, that American mortars were bombarding Fort l'Empereur and enemy soldiers were descending Boulevard Gallieni in the city of Algiers itself. Staff had already begun burning secret documents. Darlan checked one last time with Auphan to see whether the Germans had entered the Free Zone (which would have allowed him freedom of action). They had not. Nonetheless, when Juin telephoned at 1530 and again requested orders, Darlan agreed to a cease-fire in Algiers. He wanted to protect French sovereignty in Africa, marginalize Giraud, and at the same time make a deal acceptable to the marshal. Juin immediately sent Pendar through French lines to locate the American commander. He did this quickly, encountering Major General Ryder outside Cheragas conferring with Division General Mast; Randolph Churchill, son of the prime minister, who was the intelligence officer of the 6th Commando; and one of Pendar's fellow vice-consuls. Ryder was ready to talk if the French agreed to an immediate cease-fire. After Pendar returned with this information, Juin dispatched Murphy in Juin's vehicle to invite the general to a parlay. They passed through French lines at Lambiridi after suffering a few bursts of machine-gun fire despite the white and French flags affixed to the car's front bumper.[37]

The interview between Ryder and Juin was "simple, short, easy and friendly." They agreed that French troops would return to their barracks with their arms. The Americans would occupy the city. The cease-fire would apply only to Algiers and its immediate suburbs and become effective at 2000. Then, in a more formal ceremony that Pendar likened to "a historical painting from a European museum," Darlan and Juin in dress uniforms stood at the head of a table covered with green baize and formally presented a sword to Ryder. An American unit, unaware of the negotiations, fired a mortar barrage at the fort just before the ceremony, killing a dozen men.[38]

Discharging

Although Ryder had been optimistic about the military situation, Burrough was not so sanguine. At 1600 the view from *Bulolo*'s flag bridge was that the city and forts were resisting, the harbor attack had failed, the 39th Regiment was reporting heavy casualties, all landings from Charlie Sector had been suspended, and the disembarkations in the other sectors were at a trickle. The admiral decided to land the West Kent Battalion, originally slotted for the advance beyond Algiers, "to give additional weight to the attack." These troops came ashore that evening in time to hear about the cease-fire and had to be ferried back to their transport the next morning. In fact, the cessation of hostilities was doubly fortunate because wind and surf were rising and landing craft losses accelerating. For example, four LCMs and five LCPs were stranded in the Apples sector as the day went on. *Almaack* had only six boats left, but by 2130 even these were gone. The seas were too rough to hoist them on board, so they were tied up astern, and all six broke loose and sank or were driven ashore. The Charlie Force transports lost forty-five boats. Ryder's frustration was obvious when he wrote, "The present landing craft are inadequate in every respect. They are too small to carry tactical units; they broach easily; they break up in moderately heavy seas; their compasses are worthless." In fact, however, operator experience rather than design flaws were more at fault as slightly modified versions of these types continued in successful use for the rest of the war.[39]

Air Attacks

Algiers was the landing zone nearest to Italian air bases. At dusk an Axis strike of fifty German Ju 88 bombers, six He 111 torpedo bombers, and fourteen Italian S.79 torpedo bombers hit the shipping clustered off Cape Matifou from several directions. *Leedstown* claimed the destruction of one aircraft, but another appeared at low altitude directly astern, "screened by the darkness and the cliffs of the beach." It dropped two torpedoes. One hit in the steering engine room compartment and carried away the transport's rudder, but pumps kept the ship afloat. *Cowdray* dodged projectiles and torpedoes until a bomb exploded in her fire room, killing five and disabling the boilers. *Algerine* eventually towed her to shallow water where she stranded. *Exceller* received minor damage from a close miss astern while *Chase* reported that a stick of bombs fell seventy-five yards off the starboard bow and another a hundred yards astern. A torpedo missed by twenty yards and another threaded the gap between her bow and anchor chain. The S.79s attacked *Bermuda* and *Sheffield* for forty-five minutes. "Attacks were well pressed home and only avoided by use of helm at high speeds." *Bermuda* claimed she evaded twenty-three torpedoes (only fourteen were dropped). The admiralty considered that "if these attacks had been made on Force O [the carriers] it is most probable that carriers would have been hit." The raid cost the Axis forces four Ju 88s, one S.79, and one Cant Z.1007 bis reconnaissance plane.[40]

Meanwhile, even before these strikes Burrough had suspended all landings and ordered the transports to the relative safety of Algiers Harbor. The admiral was delighted to find an undamaged port and fifteen deep water berths available. That evening *Spey* arrived with the 39th Regiment's 2nd Battalion. She also unloaded in Algiers.

9 November

Operation Perpetual, the landing at Bougie by the 36th Brigade Group, was scheduled for this day, but the strong northwesterly winds, which had caused such problems during the afternoon of the 8th, continued to blow, and Burrough decided to delay this crucial first step toward Tunisia.

German air forces in Sardinia, including KG.77, K.26, and K.30, mounted another large-scale effort. This consisted of fifty Ju 88s that took off before light followed by another forty Ju 88s and He 111s. The bombers slightly damaged *Leedstown* at 1255 and *Dempo* at 1302, and then at 1310 two torpedoes fired from *U 331*, which had just arrived from La Spezia and was captained by the ace Hans-Dietrich von Tiesenhausen, struck *Leedstown* on the starboard side. The ship sank to the bottom on an even keel. *Samphire* rescued 104 men and others made their way ashore, and much of the transport's cargo was eventually salvaged. At 1630 another combined bomb/torpedo attack slightly damaged *Dempo*. Fortunately for the Allies, gasoline and supplies were now flowing into Maison Blanche,

British monitor *Roberts*. She was a valuable ship specially designed for shore bombardment with two 15-inch guns. German bombers severely damaged her off Bougie on 11 November. (Stephen Dent Collection)

allowing fighters to start patrolling. Sixty-one aircraft were operational by evening. They downed nine Ju 88s and one He 111. German casualties included two group commanders.[41]

Major General Clark arrived at Maison Blanche at 1700 in the midst of an air raid. He later wrote, "Junkers were still over the harbor, and a solid wall of ack-ack fire was going up, the orange balls of fire looking like strings of Christmas tree lights across the sky. Guns around the airfield raised a tremendous clamor, and just as we drew up beside the airdrome buildings a stick of three bombs fell on the field within a hundred feet." Clark drove to Algiers and discovered there that the American investment in Giraud promised a poor return.[42]

Giraud finally arrived at Blida at 1430. The base commander, Colonel Montrelet, received the general as he stepped off his aircraft but refused to shake his hand. Giraud declared that the bloodshed needed to stop at all costs. Montrelet replied that he followed the orders of his superiors. Giraud then gave the order to cease resistance. Montrelet said, "My General, I am ready to obey you if that order comes from my superiors."[43]

This cold reception reflected the belief of the vast majority of French officers that Giraud was a dissident general who had broken his parole. A stunned Giraud retired to Lemaigre Dubreuil's house where he met with a succession of officials who confirmed that he lacked support outside the Group of Five's small circle.

As Giraud considered his options, Ryder and Darlan met at 1743 at the Hôtel St. Georges to discuss a general cease-fire for all North Africa and the maintenance of the current regime. Darlan deflected Ryder's demand for immediate action, stating only that he would transmit the terms to Vichy with a recommendation to accept. When Clark arrived he deferred further negotiations due to the hour and his desire to consult with Eisenhower and arranged to meet Darlan at 0900 on the 10th. Clark had three options: to deal with Darlan and maintain the French government; to arrest Darlan and impose Giraud, putting North Africa under American military administration; or to force an accord between Giraud and Darlan. Eisenhower had already announced that Giraud "has assumed the leadership of the French movement to prevent Axis aggression in North Africa and will organize the French North African Army." This made it difficult for the Americans to completely abandon Giraud.[44]

In preparation for their showdown the French leaders spent the night conferring. Giraud asked to see Juin, who was originally reluctant but finally received him at the Villa des Oliviers at 0300 on the 10th, on the condition he keep the meeting secret. Mast joined them from Sidi-Ferruch where he had spent the day under American protection. Juin wanted to prevent French leadership from fracturing, but when Giraud asked to meet Darlan, the admiral refused. Darlan spent an anxious night in conferences and studying radio reports. He received a telegram from Auphan that Pétain agreed with his recommendation to come to terms, but no official response could be forthcoming until Laval returned from his meeting with Hitler.[45]

10 November

On this day the Allies further organized Algiers Harbor. Vice Admiral Burrough reported "port authorities, shipping agents and local labour most co-operative." The weather moderated early and *Chase* resumed unloading over the beach. Operation Perpetual finally got under way. This and fighters based at Maison Blanche gave relief from Axis air attacks.[46]

At 0900 the Americans and French reconvened at the Hôtel St. Georges. Clark and Darlan chaired their respective delegations, which included, for the Allies, three staff officers (the French refused to shake the hand of the British attendee,

Cunningham's chief of staff, Commander Royer Dick) and Robert Murphy, who interpreted. In addition to Darlan the French had generals Juin, Koeltz, and Mendigal and admirals Moreau and Raymond Fenard, secretary-general of North Africa. Clark was under intense pressure to secure French cooperation. The situation at Port Lyautey remained in doubt. Fighting continued at Casablanca and Oran, and, worst of all, the advance east had not begun despite reports that German aircraft and troops were already in Tunisia. Clark stationed an infantry platoon around the hotel "mostly for psychological effect" and to show "that we meant business."[47]

Clark opened by asking if the French were ready to sign a cease-fire for all of Africa. Darlan replied that he had communicated American terms to Vichy and expected a reply following that evening's cabinet meeting. Clark, who Juin characterized as a "big American who does nothing but shout and pound the table," demanded a decision within a half hour stating that Darlan had the marshal's confidence and the authority to deal. Darlan repeated that he needed authorization and did not want to take an action that would lead to the Free Zone's occupation. Clark countered that in that case he would be under the "painful obligation" to put Darlan under the protection of American troops and have Giraud order the cease-fire. Juin observed that such an order would only be obeyed in areas the Americans already controlled.[48]

With negotiations degenerating, Juin requested a recess. After the Americans left the room he told Darlan that the mission to defend North Africa had been accomplished. Koeltz agreed, saying, "We can hold out four or five more days but in the meanwhile the Germans will install themselves in Tunisia." Juin added that prolonging the situation would sacrifice French lives and lead to Giraud's unilateral elevation and perhaps civil war. Confronted with this possibility Darlan relented as long as the Americans recognized him as Pétain's (and France's) representative. When Clark returned he accepted Darlan's conditions, so at 1105, in the name of the marshal, Darlan ordered all land, air, and naval commands in French North Africa to immediately stop hostilities against the Americans. "Our battles are over and further bloodshed is useless." He added that all military and civilian authorities would retain their positions.[49]

Summary

Algiers was the riskiest landing because it was closest to Axis bases. It suffered the greatest shipping losses in the operation's first three days and was the only landing wherein the Axis prevented a portion of the assault force from reaching the beach as scheduled. While the Apples operation went broadly according to plan and the Charlie landings were a partial success, the Beer operation was a fiasco. Raising surf caused nearly all unloading to be suspended by the afternoon of the first day. A French historian wrote, "If the defenders had had a common viewpoint about repelling the Americans they would have been thrown back into the sea."[50]

In fact, Algiers surrendered two days before the other objectives. The presence of Admiral Darlan and the actions of the Group of Five contributed to this rapid success. During the critical first hours French troops remained in their barracks, and there was considerable command confusion thereafter. Corps General Juin ordered light resistance once he had suppressed the Group of Five's rising. After they confirmed that they faced a major operation, Darlan and Juin aligned themselves with the Allies (as they would have done in the beginning, had their feelers about collaboration been acted upon). The critical harbor facilities were not sabotaged, and, in fact, French authorities cooperated fully with the Allies in returning the port to full use. That Spitfires greeted German bombers over the harbor on 9 November was a direct consequence of French collaboration.

8

ORAN

Cease fire. Don't shoot. We are your friends. We are Americans.
—Lieutenant Paul Duncan, RN

Plans and Objectives

With a population of 165,000 Oran was western Algeria's largest city and major port. It was the objective of Maj. Gen. Lloyd R. Fredendall's central landing force that included the U.S. 1st Infantry Division and Combat Command B of the U.S. 1st Armored Division. Commodore Thomas Troubridge commanded the all-British naval contingent. The operation's objectives also included two important airbases south of the city, the small harbor and naval airbase at Arzew to the east and the military port of Mers el-Kébir three miles west. The central force was also to establish communications between Oran and Casablanca and to "prepare to seize Spanish Morocco, if necessary."[1]

The assault plan specified landings at Mersa bou Zedjar, a village thirty-four miles west of Oran (Beach X); at Andalouses Bay fourteen miles west (Beach Y); and at Arzew and along the Gulf of Arzew twenty-five miles east (Beach Z). There were also two special attack missions: two ex–U.S. Coast Guard cutters in Royal Navy service would land U.S. infantry directly in Oran Harbor and five hundred American paratroops would fly from Cornwall and drop on Latigue and La Sénia airfields to destroy aircraft and hold Latigue until relieved.[2]

The Group of Five contingent in Oran was led by Roger Carcassonne, an industrialist, and Colonel Pierre Tostain, chief of staff to Division General

Robert Boisseau, commander of the Oran Division. They planned to seize strategic locations in the city in support of the landings, but as the date approached Tostain got cold feet. On 6 November he told Boisseau of the impending operation and asked for his help. The general did not take Tostain seriously because he believed the United States incapable of mounting a major operation before 1943 and did not forward the information to his superior, Corps General Koeltz. In a meeting that night with Carcassonne; Ridgeway Knight, American vice-consul at Oran; and other conspirators, Tostain confessed what he had done. Under these conditions they canceled the uprising and Knight radioed that the landings may have been compromised, although it was far too late to act on this warning.[3]

The Eastern Landings

The 1st Infantry Division's 18th RCT was to land on Beach Z Green, with two battalions abreast, seize Arzew, and then advance toward Oran. The 16th RCT was to land two battalions on Beach Z White and cover the disembarkment of the 1st Armored Division's Combat Command B, which would then drive inland through the unit. The 1st Ranger Battalion would come ashore directly in Arzew Harbor and at a cove north of town. Its mission was to seize the port intact and to neutralize the four 105-mm guns at the Batterie du Nord and a pair of 75-mm weapons at Fort de la Pointe.

The transports arrived at the disembarkation point five miles offshore at 2300 on 7 November and located the beacon submarine, *Ursula,* without difficulty. Conditions were calm, dark, and hazy, and the light at Arzew was burning.

THE RANGERS

The 1st Ranger Battalion consisted of 478 men in seven companies. Companies A and B disembarked from *Royal Scotsman* into four LCAs, escorted by one LCS. They were to motor directly into the harbor. Companies C, D, E, and F, and the Headquarters Company, led by the battalion's commander, Lt. Col. William Darby, disembarked from *Royal Ulsterman* and *Ulster Monarch* in eight LCAs escorted by two LCSs. Their objective was a cove three miles north of town. In contrast to the standard practice of descending on cargo nets, the men boarded first and the landing craft were then lowered into the water. The reason why preloading was not a standard practice was demonstrated when a davit jammed on *Royal Ulsterman,* dumping forty Rangers into the water. The men were rescued, but important radio and signaling gear sank to the bottom. The little fleet of

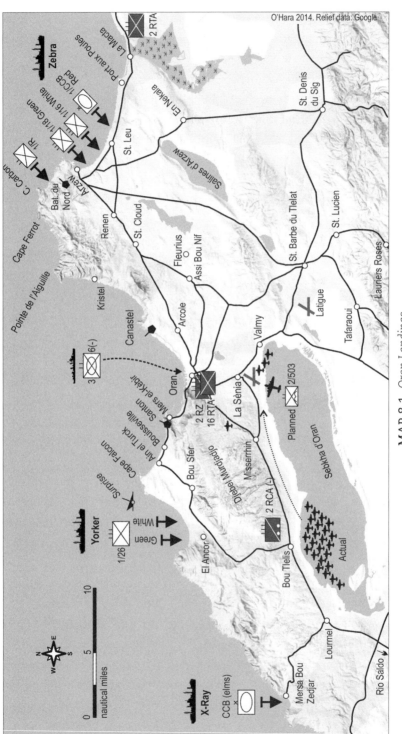

MAP 8.1 *Oran Landings*

O'Hara 2014. Relief data: Google

landing craft then set out in the wrong direction, compounding the delay caused by this misadventure and forcing *Royal Ulsterman* to head them off and point them toward land.

A and B Company arrived off Arzew at 0100 and found the harbor lights burning and the boom open. Somehow the entry of 130 men in five large motor boats and the clamor of their climb up a slippery seawall passed unnoticed. Not until 0200 did a siren sound the alarm. As B Company masked the naval air base, A Company captured Fort de la Pointe, taking forty-two prisoners, including the commander, who was wearing pajamas under his coat.[4]

The main force landed north of town as planned, and the troops traversed shrubby, gullied terrain toward Batterie du Nord. Arriving shortly before 0200 D Company set up 81-mm mortars in a ravine five hundred yards away while the other companies closed the position. At 0300 sentries detected American scouts cutting the perimeter wire and machine guns rattled into action. The scouts retreated as the mortars opened up. Darby wrote that the eighty-round barrage "[turned] the French machine guns off as if someone had pulled a switch." The Rangers then stormed the battery at the cost of two dead and eight wounded, taking sixty prisoners. It was just after 0400. This was the only occasion in the Algerian landings when a special operations force completed its mission as planned.[5]

Because Arzew seemed quiet, an Anglo-American antisabotage detachment, which included a dozen U.S. Marines, entered the port at 0200. At 0400, after seeing the green flare that signaled Darby's success, the men boarded the steamers docked there, *Meonia* (5,218 GRT), *Richebourg,* (1,074 GRT), the aviation repair ship *Petrel* at Môle Number 3, and *Parme* at Le Grand Quai. The crews surrendered peacefully.

French resistance was centered at the naval air station and Fort du Nord, a strong point above the harbor. At 0400 heavy machine guns from the air station engaged landing craft, both in the harbor and those carrying 18th Regiment troops south of the harbor. The French incorrectly claimed they sank six boats. The fusillade delayed troops advancing from the south who answered with 60-mm mortars and machine guns of their own. At 0647 Fort du Nord's defenders surrendered, having exhausted their ammunition, but the airbase continued to resist. The .50 caliber guns on the LCSs proved useful as the troops advanced and finally overran the base at 0830. The French suffered twelve dead and twelve wounded. The Americans took sixty-two prisoners and captured the thirteen naval bombers, which were fueled and loaded with torpedoes.[6]

Z BEACH 1ST INFANTRY DIVISION

The 7,092 men of the 18th RCT, under the command of Col. Frank U. Greer, came ashore on Zebra Beach Green from the transports *Tegelberg, Reina del Pacifico,* and *Ettrick.* On board *Reina del Pacifico* one officer remembered that, as engines came to a stop, the lights ashore shown brilliantly off the port bow and that a lighthouse was winking reassuringly. "The troops who had been waiting by their landing craft in perfect silence, and chewing gum so that one could smell the mint up on the bridge, quietly manned their craft. There was what seemed an appalling roar in the stillness as the landing-craft engines were started up and they were lowered into the water."[7]

The first wave of 1,120 men landed between 0120 and 0130. On the right the 3rd Battalion advanced north toward Arzew, hitting resistance at 0400 as related. At 0600 a 75-mm gun from the 68 RAA firing from the hills west of Arzew struck *Reina del Pacifico* three times before landing craft wrapped the transport in smoke and she withdrew out of range. The gun then tried its luck against the LSTs disembarking the vehicles of the 1st Armored Division, but they were beyond range. When the destroyer *Vansittart* approached to return fire, the gun fell silent.

The 1st Battalion landed on the left and advanced inland. West of Renan it broke up an attack by five armored cars of the 2 RCA (Régiment de Chasseurs d'Afrique, or chasseurs regiment of Africa). Then, just before noon, it encountered elements of the I/16 RTA outside St. Cloud, a town of 3,500 a third of the way to Oran. Machine guns drove the American troops to cover, "and officers had difficulty in getting [the men] to move forward." The battalion finally attacked with two companies abreast, but the *tirailleurs* had been reinforced by two batteries of the 66 RAA and a battery of the 68 RAA occupied a ridge north of the village. Their barrage repulsed the American assault with heavy losses that included two company commanders killed and one wounded.[8]

The 18th RCT's 2nd Battalion and elements of the 32nd Field Artillery Battalion landed on Green Beach between 0730 and 0840. Colonel Greer ordered the battalion to circle around and attack St. Cloud from the southwest. However, its maneuver was not broad enough and the result was a frontal assault by two battalions abreast. Once again French artillery broke up the attack. Late that afternoon the bulk of the 3rd Battalion advanced from Arzew and concentrated north of St. Cloud in preparation for a massed regimental attack the next day.

The 16th Regiment, 5,608 men under Col. Henry B. Cheadle, landed at Beach Z White. The 1st Battalion came ashore on the left at 0055 and wheeled

U.S. troops landing in calm conditions near St. Leu east of Oran. Seven transports stand close offshore including the LSI (L) *Ettrick* and, to her left, the Dutch transport *Tegelberg*. (U.S. Naval Institute Photo Archive)

east to clear Red Beach for the armored troops, capturing the small town of St. Leu by surprise. The Americans rousted the garrison, a company of the I/16 RTA and one battery of the 68 RAA, from their barracks in the town's racetrack. Continuing east American troops pushed through light resistance to Port-aux-Poules. One company then turned south and advanced six miles, reaching En Nekala. However, as Company B entered La Macta it was ambushed by a platoon from the 2 RTA. The battalion deployed and at 1230 two companies counterattacked, supported by the destroyer *Farndale*'s 4-inch guns. They had captured La Macta by 1330. The battalion then organized a defensive line to meet an anticipated French counterattack.

The 3rd Battalion on the right beached without major incidents and advanced against light opposition all the way to Fleurus, five miles south of St. Cloud, where it stopped and organized a defensive position. The 2nd Battalion landed at 1000 and followed the 3rd Battalion toward Fleurus.

Z SECTOR COMBAT COMMAND B

The elements of Combat Command B assigned to Z Sector (Task Force [TF] Red under the command of Brig. Gen. Lunsford E. Oliver) consisted of 4,772 men and included two armored battalions, an armored infantry battalion, self-propelled artillery, tank destroyer, reconnaissance, and armored engineer companies. Elements of these units were to form a task group called the Red Flying Column to secure the Latigue (called Tafaraoui in many English language sources) and La Sénia airfields (with the assistance of paratroopers, should they have made it there) and then swing north to attack Oran.[9]

The first troops of Combat Command B landed from *Derbyshire* and *Durban Castle* at 0057. The LSTs beached just before dawn and had completely unloaded by 0800. After the 16th Regiment cleared St. Leu, Brigadier General Oliver established his headquarters there. At 0820 the 13th Armored Regiment's reconnaissance company began advancing toward St. Barbe du Tlelat and St. Denis du Sig. The Flying Column followed fifteen minutes later. The first tanks arrived near Latigue airfield twenty-five miles southwest of the beachhead at 1050 to find six French bombers and five fighters about to take off. A single 75-mm and a few machine guns could not withstand the American armor, and the column had secured the field by 1215, taking three hundred prisoners, although skirmishing continued in the general area until 1430. The flying column remained near Tafaraoui the rest of the day fending off French incursions from the south. This included a brush near Lauiers Roses with a column from the 9 RCA that included ten tanks. To the north elements of the 2 RCA and the 32 DCA (*défense contre avions*, or antiaircraft) established a defensive position several miles northwest at Valmy. During the night portions of the main body reinforced the Flying Column in preparation for thrust toward La Sénia the next day.

Landing at Mersa Bou Zedjar (X-Ray)

The westernmost of the three landing zones consisted of two beaches separated by a rocky headland. White Beach was a fifty-yard-wide strip of sand adjacent to the village of Mersa Bou Zedjar. Green Beach to the southwest was wider with a gentle slope, soft sand, but only one exit. The landing force contained 2,257 men of the 1st Armored Division's Combat Command B, including armored infantry and armored battalions and companies of armored field artillery, tank destroyers, engineers, and other supporting troops. Their orders were to advance along a road that cut through the coastal range to the town of Lourmel on the western end of the Sebkra d'Oran and capture a landing strip there. Then they were to follow the salt lake's north shore to La Sénia, or the south shore to Tafaraoui, as the situation required.

The assault ships were nearing the disembarkation point when a fully lit convoy appeared to port. This was K 39, which had just departed Oran bound for Casablanca. It consisted of five vessels—*Agen* (4,186 GRT), *Carthage, Montaigne* (2,770 GRT), the trawler *Capitaine Armand* (585 GRT), and the liner *Eridan* (9,928 GRT)—escorted by the armed trawler *La Sétoise*. At 0045 the destroyer *Wivern* ordered *La Sétoise* to bear off. The patrol boat complied and turned the convoy around. Nonetheless, the confusion caused delay and the LSIs lowered landing craft a mile farther offshore than planned. Vice Admiral Burrough reported, "The wind was nil, the sea smooth, and even the stars obscured by cloud. Conditions were perfect." Perfect, that is, except for a strong and unexpected westerly current.[10]

The boats swung out beginning at 2347 for the long journey toward shore. The first wave, one company of the 1/6 Armored Infantry, navigated the tricky passage to White Beach and landed at 0125. Things were not so ordered at Green. The guide boat was late. The first wave from *Queen Emma* could not locate the beach and fell behind the second wave from *Batory*. One landing craft caught fire during the run in and had to be scuttled. The British beach party, which was to mark the landing zone, arrived ninety minutes late. Many boats beached outside the zone, resulting in damage and vehicles mired in soft sand.

Fortunately, there was no resistance. The few troops in the village "promptly welcomed the Americans to Africa and set to work helping unload landing craft." By 0345 the invaders had occupied the headland and high ground around the beaches, and the LST *Bachaquero* nosed into Green Beach at 0405. She grounded on a sandbar 360 feet from shore, but engineers improvised a platoon bridge and she had finished unloading by 0815. However, steep exits through soft sand and rising surf forced Green Beach's abandonment before noon and unloading continued only at White Beach despite congestion and shallow water. Bulldozers had to help LCMs retract, and ten of the thirteen LCMs available suffered damaged rudders or propellers. Narrow exits meant that supplies were beached faster than they could be transferred inland, and by 0700 "1,500 barracks bags and other supplies had been dumped on the sands." Troops used sleds to move material, but not until 1800 did engineers, employing troops and Arab labor as stevedores, finally clear the beach and lay tracking.[11]

The reconnaissance platoon headed for Lourmel before dawn. It encountered slight opposition and occupied the town by 0903. The Green Flying Column consisting of half the 1/13 Armored followed, arriving at Lourmel at 1125. Shortly after noon this group received orders to advance toward La Sénia north of the Sebkra d'Oran. They left an armored infantry platoon to garrison Lourmel while the reconnaissance platoon drove southwest toward Rio Salado.

At 1408 the Green Flying Column hit a roadblock manned by a unit of the 2 RCA a mile west of Bou Tlelis and lost two tanks in a sharp, thirty-five-minute engagement. At 1517 the column broke through another roadblock at the cost of a halftrack. The next town was Misserrhin, eight miles southwest of Oran, but here resistance from a squadron of the 2 RCA was so strong the column bypassed the town and bivouacked for the night in Sebkra. Meanwhile, the Green Force Headquarters moved into Lourmel, Lourmel's garrison advanced to Rio Salado, and the reconnaissance platoon leapfrogged southwest toward Ain Temouchant.

Convoy K 39 continued to disrupt Allied naval activities. At 0330 Vice Admiral André Georges Rioult, commander of Marine Oran, ordered the convoy to Nemours, a small port near the Moroccan border. Two hours later, as the French ships again crossed the landing zone, the destroyer *Antelope* sent a party to board *Eridan*. The liner increased speed and accidently collided with *Montaigne*. *La Sétoise* then ordered the ships to scuttle. *Montaigne, Carthage,* and *Agen* rounded Cape Fegalo west of the X beaches and ran aground. *Eridan's* crew sabotaged their ship's engine and pumps. The two trawlers continued west and at 0830 arrived at Beni Saf. To finish this episode, at 1130 a British corvette ordered *Eridan* to follow her. The master, described as "most obstructive," responded that his ship had been crippled, so *Antelope* embarked an armed party and towed her to an anchorage off Cape Fegalo. On the 12th she was taken to Arzew. *Agen* was refloated and both eventually entered British service.[12]

Landings at Y Beach

Yorker Beach was located in Andalouses Bay twelve miles west of Oran, separated from the city by the rugged Djebel Murdjadjo, a coastal ridge that reared to an elevation of nineteen hundred feet. It was the destination of the 26th RCT (Brig. Gen. Theodore Roosevelt Jr., son of President Theodore Roosevelt) which was to land two battalions abreast: the 2nd at Green Beach and the 3rd at White Beach to the east while the 1st Battalion stayed in reserve. The regiment was to occupy the heights of Djebel Murdjadjo and then "seize all coast defense installations and docking facilities in Oran and Mers-el-Kebir."[13]

The transports began lowering boats at 2320 on 7 November. Loading troops laden with ninety pounds of weapons and gear onto bobbing boats in the dark proved time consuming—especially from *Monarch of Bermuda,* whose boarding ladders had rungs two feet apart. Nonetheless, the first landing craft guided by *ML 1128* began the six-mile run to shore at 2345. Navigation was not a problem because the beacon submarine, *P 54,* had unloaded pilots and the folbot teams were duly flashing signals. *Monarch of Bermuda's* craft carrying units of the 2nd Battalion landed on Green Beach at 0100 while the 3rd Battalion's first wave from *Glengyle* reached White Beach at 0116. There was no opposition, but the boats hit an unexpected sandbar that ran parallel to the shore and was in some places just inches below the surface. Most LCAs churned over the obstruction, but some damaged their propellers and rudders doing so. The second wave, eight LCPs from *Llangibby Castle,* arrived at Green Beach at 0138. The third, consisting of LCMs from *Glengyle* carrying vehicles and guns, reached the bar at 0145 and could not cross. The first jeeps to roll off disappeared into deep pools between the obstruction and shore.

After dispatching the initial waves the transports moved inshore and by 0340 had anchored a mile off the beach. Even from so close the trip to shore was hardly routine. One platoon leader, who set out at 0400, remembered that "silence combined with the utter blackness of the night brought up the doubt as to whether the boat was hitting the right beach and whether the other troops had landed. It was a weird, uneasy feeling." Nevertheless, by 0500 the beachhead held 2,670 men and thirty-three vehicles. Before dawn 2nd Battalion's G Company and the antitank platoon established a roadblock a mile beyond the village of El Ancor south of Green Beach while other units moved east. At 0900 three armored cars and a pair of motorcycles from the 2 RCA approached the position, but American 37-mm antitank guns destroyed all three vehicles. Elements of the 3rd Battalion occupied Bou Sfer and began advancing east.[14]

At dawn Fort du Santon started shelling the landing area. At 0845 *Aurora* approached to return fire but Santon beat her to the punch, closely straddling with its first salvo. *Aurora* made smoke and fled out of range as 194-mm shells dropped to either side, "some shots falling very close." At 0917 Santon hit *Llangibby Castle* several times, forcing the transport to withdraw. This bombardment provoked the battleship *Rodney's* intervention. Her 16-inch rounds temporarily silenced the battery, but at 1050, after the battleship had withdrawn, Santon landed a shell on *Monarch of Bermuda.* An observer described the fire as "quite rapid" and observed a direct hit on a landing craft. In response, *Monarch of Bermuda* dropped smoke pots and moved away.[15]

Soldiers of the U.S. 26th Regiment/1st Infantry Division descending a boarding ladder from *Monarch of Bermuda* in Andalouses Bay west of Oran. The rungs were two feet apart, and troops from the initial waves found it slow going descending in the dark. (U.S. Army Signal Corps)

Two companies of the 2 RTA stationed at Ain el-Turck counterattacked 3rd Battalion troops on the road to Bou Sfer but were stopped by "very intense fire." The Americans captured a platoon and the rest of the unit retreated. The 75-mm antiaircraft guns of the 124 and 160 DCA at Bouisseville proved more effective: they halted Brigadier General Roosevelt's troops and even forced a withdrawal, but the Americans encircled the 125 DCA just northwest of Ain el Turck, and that night the French unit destroyed its guns.[16]

Attack on Oran Harbor

The Allied planners wanted to capture the major ports intact and were willing to risk much to do so. In Oran two ex–U.S. Coast Guard cutters in British service, *Walney* and *Hartland,* were loaded with 393 men from Companies G and H of the 3rd Battalion, 6th Armored Infantry/1st Armored Division. These troops received a week of training in "commando-type tactics." Their mission was to sail directly into Oran Harbor, seize the docks, and hold out for as long as two days before being relieved. There was also a detachment of twenty-six naval specialists, six Marines, and a dozen British Special Boat Service Commandos with six folbots. They were to drop explosive mines from the folbots to trap the French squadron in port. The U.S. Navy commander who supplied the antisabotage specialists considered the plan "suicidal and absolutely unsound." He protested to Eisenhower, Cunningham, and Troubridge, but to no avail.[17]

The cutters made landfall at 0200 on 8 November and stood offshore while two smoke-making motor launches, *HMML 480* and *483,* approached the harbor. Sounds of gunfire and sirens drifting across the water put the lie to a reassuring message *Walney* received at 0250 from Commander Troubridge, "No shooting thus far; landings unopposed. . . . Don't start a fight unless you have to." Five minutes later a searchlight briefly illuminated the cutter and a machine gun fired a burst in her direction. As other guns engaged, the ships sheered away and the motor launches started generating smoke. Then, accelerating to fifteen knots, *Walney* headed toward the boom as a British officer broadcast in heavily accented French, "Cease fire. Don't shoot. We are your friends. We are Americans." In response, a rocket arced overhead and searchlights probed the channel. *HMML 480* ran into the boom and *483,* in the process of avoiding her, rammed *Walney* abeam. Nonetheless, *Walney* sliced the boom at 0305 with barely a tremor; she then slowed to launch the folbots before heading down channel. Thanks to the intense smoke, French gunfire was largely inaccurate, although it did sink a folbot.[18]

At 0320 *Walney* encountered the sloop *La Surprise* sailing toward her and tried to ram. *La Surprise,* mistaking the cutter for a friendly trawler returning to port, steered to miss. The two ships passed within yards and neither opened fire. *Walney* next approached the end of the port where she encountered the *contre-torpilleur Epervier* docked at the Quai d'Alger, the destroyer *Tramontane* and

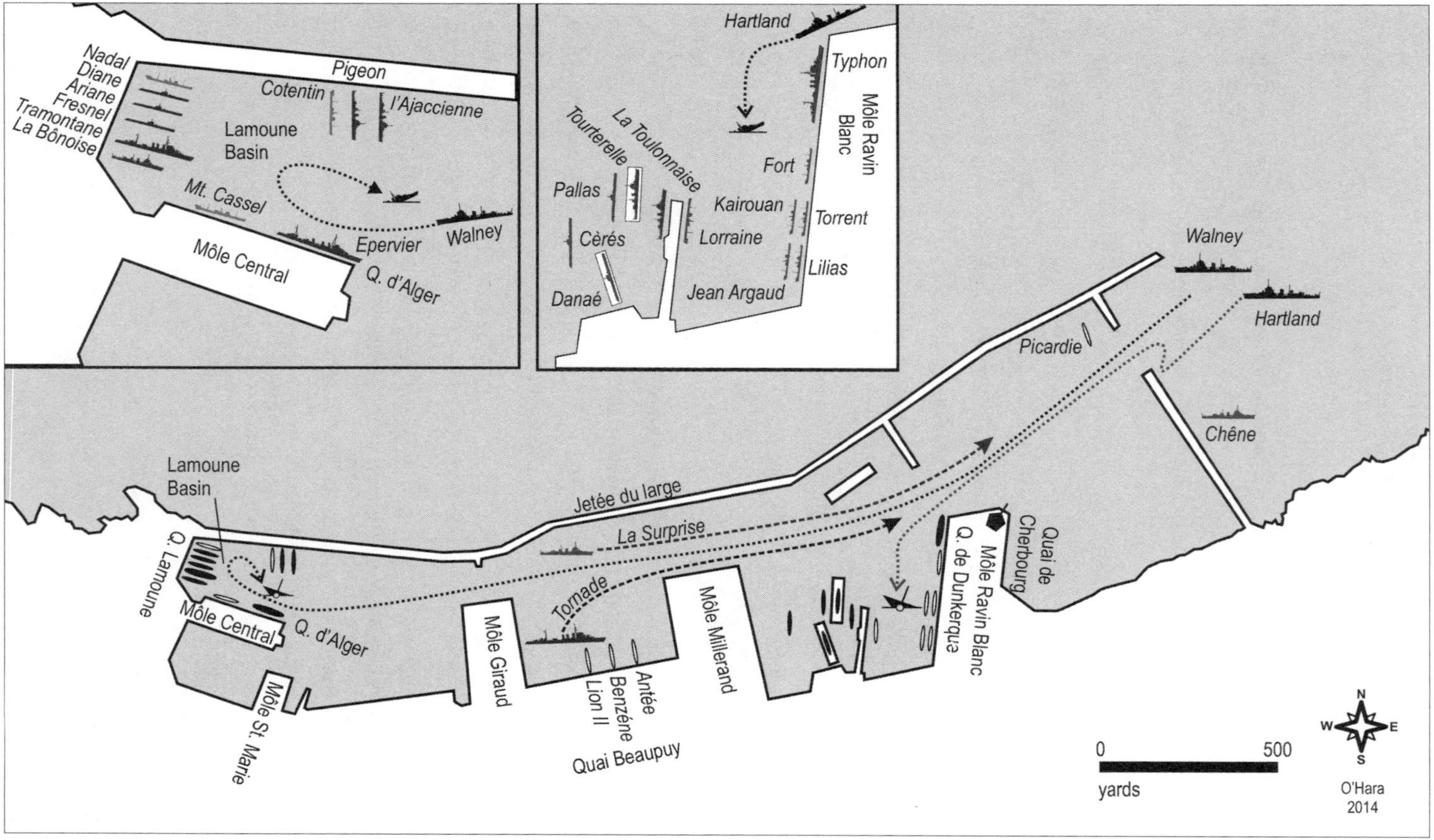

MAP 8.2 Attack on Oran Harbor

patrol boat *La Bônoise* at the Quai Lamoune, and along the jetty the minesweepers *Pigeon* and *L'Ajaccienne.* The plan was to grapple *Epervier* and winch alongside, clear the French warship's decks with hand grenades, and drop boarding parties from boats swung out on davits. These boats were out, each loaded with fourteen men while another sixteen soldiers crouched behind a sandbag parapet erected on the cutter's bow ready to fling grenades.

Epervier's watch saw a vessel approaching and assumed it intended to dock behind her. Then a searchlight revealed that the ship was flying a large American flag. This revelation was followed by a burst of bullets that swept the *contre-torpilleur*'s deck, killing four men. The gangplank machine gun responded while the navigation officer rushed to a 37-mm weapon and the gunnery officer manned the aft 138-mm mount. As *Epervier* returned fire more ships joined the action. *La Bônoise* discharged a dozen 100-mm shells and riddled the cutter's bridge with a thousand 7.7-mm rounds. *L'Ajaccienne* laced *Walney*'s superstructure with two thousand machine-gun bullets and a pair of 102-mm shells. *Tramontane* fired ten shells from her forward 130-mm mounts and many 25-mm and machine-gun rounds. On *Epervier* the other 138-mm mounts took aim. In total the *contre-torpilleur* expended seventeen main battery shells and hundreds of 37-mm rounds.

At first *Walney* fought back. Her gunners set *Tramontane*'s starboard aft 130-mm ammunition locker ablaze and wounded six men. Automatic fire punctured *Epervier*'s bridge and fire control director and damaged her searchlight platform (extinguishing the light in the process). But the cutter's resistance was short lived. The intense barrage slaughtered her huddled men. A shell ripped through one of the boarding party lifeboats, tumbling the occupants into the sea. *Tramontane*'s 77-pound 130-mm shells smashed the bridge, wardroom, steering compartment, and captain's cabin. A 90-pound 138-mm projectile exploded in the boiler room, decimating the engine room crew. Another shell scythed through infantrymen huddled in the mess deck waiting to disembark. Splinters cut down the grenadiers on the bow, including the battalion commander, Lt. Col. George F. Marshall, who had stood to hurl a grenade.

The last survivor on the cutter's bridge was a war correspondent, Harold Disher. He described his experience a year later: "[The man] behind me was dead. So were the lookouts and the helmsman. Peters had been knocked into the water by a shell and had been hit in the shoulder by a bullet. I dropped to my knees again and began crawling behind the bridge toward the port ladders. I reached them. They were swept by flame but I went down. . . . Pushing my helmet from my head, I toppled through a shell-torn gap in the rail to the water. . . . I began swimming away from the ship while bullets and bits of metal rained down on the water."[19]

With three-quarters of her nearly 250 crew members and passengers dead or wounded, abandoned by the survivors, and heavily on fire, *Walney* drifted toward the northwest corner of the Lamoune Basin, compelling *Tramontane, L'Ajaccienne,* and *Pigeon* to get under way by 0400. The wreck then drifted back toward *Epervier.* The *contre-torpilleur's* crew fended it off by hand as firefighters vainly attempted to quell the blaze. At 0730 after a large explosion *Walney* capsized and sank. She absorbed, according to a French count, seventeen 138-mm, twenty 130-mm, and twenty-two 100-mm shells in addition to thousands of small caliber rounds.[20]

Hartland's experience was equally horrific. Her captain, Lieutenant Commander G. P. Billot, waited five minutes before following *Walney,* and in the interval the protective smokescreen dissipated. The cutter's first entry attempt failed after a piece of shrapnel struck Billot in the eye, causing him to steer his ship into the breakwater. *Hartland* backed off and navigated the gap on the second try. She rounded the Môle du Ravin Blanc to the Quai de Dunkerque and found *Typhon* occupying the berth she was heading for. The French destroyer's searchlight revealed a strange vessel flying a large American flag, whereupon her stern mounts rapidly fired thirty 130-mm rounds from ranges that one American soldier guessed were only a hundred feet. "Shots from these guns set fire to the bridge, scored directly in the forward messing compartments, after living spaces, fireroom, and the wardroom, which was being used as an emergency dressing station." Ravin Blanc's two 37-mm antiaircraft weapons contributed a hundred rounds. The destroyer *Tornade* passed on her way toward the open sea, and her guns added to the cutter's agony, hitting the bridge, wardroom, aft living spaces, and fire room. *Hartland* lost control and drifted alongside *Typhon,* tearing off a davit and crushing the destroyer's guardrail. The survivors abandoned the burning cutter. According to the senior American naval officer, "Many men were machine gunned in the water." *Hartland* burned in the narrow basin until 0925. Then, after a massive blast that damaged buildings around Ravin Blanc, the unfortunate ship finally disappeared beneath the harbor's oily waters.[21]

The two hundred prisoners taken in this episode were marched through Oran at 1100 on the 8th. One participant recalled, "This was unpleasant as many men were oil-soaked; some had no shoes, and all were wet." A jeering crowd gathered and even threatened the prisoners. However, once the French army took custody of them that afternoon and they were concentrated with other prisoners, "all hands were treated in a friendly and courteous manner."[22]

Battles in the Bay

After *La Surprise* passed *Walney,* she emerged into the roads, where Ravin Blanc and *Chêne* briefly fired on her by mistake, wounding three men. The sloop then headed west to investigate landings reported at Andalouses Bay. She arrived at 0620 but saw nothing until a gap in the fog exposed four transports and several ships she believed were destroyers. She signaled this information to Vice Admiral Rioult. At 0630 the British destroyer *Brilliant* challenged. The sloop's captain and his replacement, who was on board observing and who was scheduled to take over in two days, conferred and decided they needed to do more than just report, so at 0640 *La Surprise* engaged *Brilliant* with her single 100-mm gun from a distance of 3,500 meters. After seeing her second round hit (in fact it missed) she dropped a pair of smoke floats, hoping to confuse the larger warship's reply, but the range was too close and *Brilliant,* which closed to two thousand yards, shredded the sloop's hull and superstructure with several rapid 4.7-inch salvos. *La Surprise* started listing to starboard and sank by the stern at 0703. Fifty-five French sailors, including both captains, died. *Brilliant's* boats rescued the rest of the crew, of whom twenty-one were wounded.[23]

At 0220 Rioult ordered the 7th DT (Division de Torpilleurs, or torpedo division), *Tramontane* (Commander Adrian de Féraudy, division head), *Tornade,* and *Typhon* to raise steam and investigate enemy forces reported in Arzew Bay. *Epervier* was completing a five-month refit and was not yet combat ready. *Tramontane* could man only three guns after several of No. 4 Mount's crew had been lost in the action with *Walney.* At 0435 she cast off, signaling *Typhon* and *Tornade* to follow as soon as possible. *Tramontane* cleared port shortly before 0500 and headed north, cutting through a light fog. *Typhon* exited at 0515, but *Tornade,* blinded by thick smoke roiling up from *Hartland,* smashed into the môle and crumpled her bow.[24]

Tramontane was eight miles north of Oran making twelve knots when at 0542, in the predawn twilight, lookouts reported a ship off her port bow. This was *Aurora,* skippered by Captain William G. Agnew. The veteran light cruiser had been steering southwest ready for shore bombardment duties when, five minutes earlier, she turned to investigate a radar contact fine off her port bow. Both ships

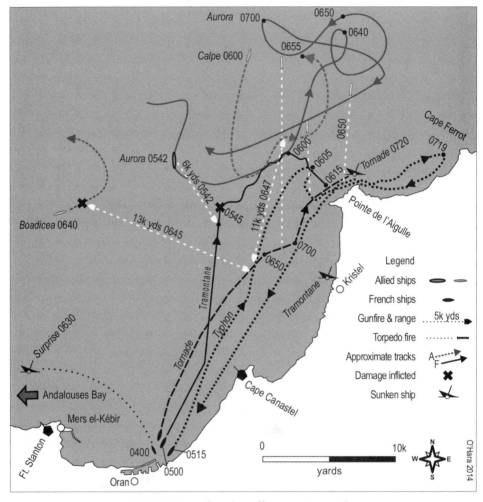

MAP 8.3 *Naval Action off Oran, 8 November*

reported making recognition signals, but Agnew fired first, from six thousand yards. The British warship had the advantage of light, and at 0543 a shell from her fourth salvo wounded several men of *Tramontane*'s No. 3 Mount, then a 6-inch shell from the following broadside exploded beside No. 1 Mount. The French destroyer's No. 2 Mount continued in action until a third blow sent splinters slicing through its crew and rained metal fragments on *Tramontane*'s bridge, killing de Féraudy. The navigation officer, although seriously wounded, swung *Tramontane* northeast at 0545 and started zigzagging to confuse *Aurora*'s deadly aim. No. 3 Mount briefly returned to action, but access to the aft shell room hoist was blocked and it fell silent after it had expended its ready ammunition. As *Aurora* closed, her starboard 4-inch guns fired six broadsides, but all rounds missed.[25]

The cruiser turned to unmask all her guns, and at around 0550 crewmen spotted a man in an oil slick crying for help. Agnew directed the destroyer *Calpe,* which was approaching from the north, to search the area. Then, as return fire tapered off, *Aurora* continued to close. Her port-side 40-mm pom-poms discharged sixty rounds but without effect, as "an error was made and shell self-destructed some two hundred yards short of the target." However, with the range down to three thousand yards, "a hit forward with at least four shells of the 15th broadside set the enemy heavily on fire." At 0600, burning from deckhouse to bridge, *Tramontane* turned southeast toward Pointe de l'Aiguille. The ship was down by the head and listing to starboard. Speed was falling and there was no communications with the engine room. Consequently, the executive officer ordered the crew to abandon ship.[26]

Typhon, following farther inshore, witnessed her flotilla leader's plight and at 0605 spotted *Aurora* five miles to the northwest. *Aurora* had observed her as well and stood off, assuming her intent was rescue. At 0610, however, *Typhon* launched two torpedoes at the British warship. She then looped back to succor *Tramontane's* crew. *Aurora* spotted the oncoming torpedoes and turned to outrun them. Meanwhile, *Calpe* searched the oil slick and rescued a badly wounded Lieutenant Fresse from *Tramontane.* Then, still following *Aurora's* orders, the Hunt-type destroyer headed northeast to intercept two French merchant vessels reported off Pointe de l'Aiguille. She reported conditions as calm and clear.

After colliding with the jetty, *Tornade* shored up her bow and headed into the bay at ten knots. Enemy ships were visible to the north and northwest from 0615, with the destroyer *Boadicea* closest. *Boadicea's* signalman wrote, *Tornade* was "almost invisible against the cliffs. . . . Challenge it with unknown call sign—no reply. Challenge it with secret call sign—still no reply! Skipper gives order to open fire." It was 0645. *Tornade* was seven thousand yards north of Pointe du Canastel and *Boadicea* 13,000 yards west-northwest of the French ship. *Tornade's* report described the British fire as "in salvoes of three or four, dispersed and taking a long time to find range." Her reply hit the British destroyer to starboard with a 130-mm round that burst in the forward 4.7-inch shell room and ignited several ammunition boxes. *Boadicea* turned away, making smoke and taking water. She rigged a collision mat over the hole to slow the flooding and eventually required a month in dock.[27]

Calpe, sailing to investigate the reported convoy, was surprised at 0646 by a geyser spouting a hundred yards off her starboard bow. She turned to starboard and returned *Tornade*'s fire from 11,000 yards, claiming a hit with her second broadside. In fact, a shell fell close and splinters shattered one of *Tornade*'s searchlights, forcing the French ship to risk a burst of speed to confuse *Calpe*'s aim. Then at 0650 *Tornade* turned to starboard, aligned her tubes on *Aurora,* and five minutes later sent six torpedoes on a long run north.

As *Tornade* approached Pointe de l'Aiguille, *Typhon* suspended rescue efforts and, shooting at *Calpe,* circled to follow *Tornade.* The British destroyer recorded that *Typhon*'s first salvo fell only fifty yards ahead. *Aurora* joined the action at 0650 from 13,600 yards but discharged only three salvos before maneuvering to avoid *Tornade*'s torpedoes. She reengaged at 0655, ordering *Calpe* to follow.

A running fight at an average range of 12,000 yards developed as the French destroyers headed east hugging the shoreline. *Aurora*'s report noted that "rate keeping was made difficult by the enemy snaking the line and altering speed and was greatly handicapped by him merging with the coastline over which was a considerable haze." The French ships straddled *Aurora* several times, but it was the British cruiser's gunnery that proved deadly. Just before 0710 three shells hammered *Tornade,* the most damaging exploding in the engine room. A minute later *Typhon* launched a torpedo at *Aurora* from 12,000 yards. At 0715 another cluster of 6-inch shells crashed into *Tornade:* one hit the engine room causing flooding and killing five men; another burst beside No. 4 Mount, cutting down the gun's crew; and a third penetrated below the waterline, flooding the aft magazine. The battered destroyer lost way and began to list to starboard. At 0720 she drifted onto the rocks just north of Pointe de l'Aiguille, and the crew abandoned ship. *Tornade* expended several hundred rounds in her half hour of action.[28]

As *Tornade* foundered, *Typhon* continued past Pointe de l'Aiguille. She was nearing Cape Ferrot when, at 0719, short of torpedoes, with half her ammunition expended, her decks crowded with *Tramontane*'s survivors, and *Aurora* to the north, her captain decided to return to Oran. Zigzagging at high speed she was hit once off the semaphore station by a 6-inch shell that exploded near her forward funnel, killing three men. She suffered considerable splinter damage as well. *Aurora* ceased fire at 0727 to conserve ammunition: she had expended 213 rounds against *Tramontane* and another 301 against *Tornade* and *Typhon.*

Typhon made port at 0755 and tied up at the Millerand Quay. There she loaded 220 130-mm shells and three torpedoes. *Aurora* returned to her bombardment duties. A 130-mm round had exploded underwater six feet from the cruiser's portside outer propeller. This indented thirty-two square feet of side plating, distorted two frames, and resulted in a rate of flooding of sixteen tons per hour, controllable by the ship's pumps. *Tornade* capsized and sank at 0825. She lost twelve men. *Tramontane* continued to burn, and after the last of her men had been taken off, she drifted down the coast and finally grounded near the village of Kristel. Twenty-eight of the ship's crew died.

L'Ajaccienne exited Oran at 0640 intending to patrol between the harbor and Canastel, but at 0710 Marine Oran ordered her to evacuate the wounded sailors gathered at the semaphore station. The 738-ton trawler engaged *Boadicea* at 0745 with her 102-mm gun. The Canastel battery also targeted *Boadicea*. As one British crewmember recalled, "Skipper increases speed to thirty knots and zigzags. He ordered smoke floats to be dropped and the engine room to make smoke. . . . He stood up on the bridge watching the splashes and judging where the next shell was going to drop and altered course immediately. Not one shell hit us and after a hectic quarter of an hour, we were out of range." *L'Ajaccienne* was back in Oran at 1235 with four dead and twenty-four wounded. She then returned to the semaphore station and embarked 120 survivors. In other rescue activity the tug *Cotentin* attempted to salvage *Tramontane* but the task proved impossible. She returned to Oran on the 9th, bringing eighty survivors.[29]

The Submarines

At 0250 Vice Admiral Rioult ordered his three operational submarines, *Argonaute, Actaéon,* and *Fresnel,* to sail as soon as possible. *Actaéon* and *Fresnel* had been in Oran only sixteen hours, having arrived from Casablanca escorted by *Tramontane.* He directed them to operate off Cape Falcon and assigned *Argonaute* the eastern zone.

Argonaute exited the harbor at 0334 coming under fire from Ravin Blanc's eager gunners as she passed. The other two got under way ten minutes later as the battle between *Epervier* and *Walney* was at its height. A shell fragment from *Epervier* punctured one of *Fresnel*'s stern torpedo tubes, and telltale fluids bubbled up in her wake.

Argonaute submerged once clear of the harbor and presumably headed toward Pointe de l'Aiguille. At 0740 *Aurora,* having returned to her bombardment sector in Oran Bay after her naval battle, reported avoiding three submarine-fired torpedoes. This was in *Argonaute*'s patrol sector. At 1517 the destroyer *Achates,* escorting the carrier *Furious,* developed a sonar contact eighteen miles north of Cape Ferrot. She dropped depth charges at 1519 and 1531. After the second attack a large quantity of debris surfaced. *Argonaute* disappeared and *Achates* is regarded as the agent of her loss.

Actaéon likewise submerged once clear of the jetty and crossed the first line of enemy vessels without incident. After fourteen hours underwater she surfaced sixty-five miles north-northwest of Oran to recharge her batteries. Unfortunately for her, the destroyer *Wescott* was just a few hundred yards away. *Wescott* turned toward *Actaéon* at full speed. The submarine submerged as the destroyer launched six depth charges ahead. Shortly after she crossed the submarine's position, a compact mass of bubbles rose two hundred feet long, marking the French boat's demise.[30]

Fresnel cleared harbor at 0355 and headed west by northwest. British warships dropped more than a hundred depth charges against her in attacks delivered at 0610, 0630, 0640, 0835, and 0855. At 1045 *Fresnel* spotted a *Southampton*-type cruiser. While setting up her attack a torpedo discharged prematurely, causing another destroyer to harass her with twenty depth charges. An hour later an aircraft spotted her trail of oil (the damage was unknown to the captain) and planes bombed *Fresnel* five times between 1225 and 1537. She was shaken but not damaged, and at 1753 she surfaced to recharge her batteries.

On the 9th *Fresnel* patrolled northwest of Haibas Island. During the day aircraft attacked four times and destroyers twice, but she sustained light damage only. The routine on 10 and 11 November was similar, with repeated air attacks. Finally, on the evening of the 11th, the captain decided to abandon his seemingly jinxed patrol. *Fresnel* docked at Toulon on the 13th.

Air Actions

The Royal Navy aircraft carriers *Furious, Biter,* and *Dasher,* with twenty-four Seafires, twenty-four Sea Hurricane IIs, and eight Albacores, supported the landings. In an effort to obtain air superiority from the start the Albacores attacked La Sénia airfield, dropping six 250-pound bombs. D.520 fighters rose to contest the raid, but escorting Hurricanes counterattacked and claimed five kills. Next, Seafires piled in and strafed the field. The British lost three aircraft over La Sénia and others were forced down elsewhere or ran out of fuel. Moreover, the attack was hardly as effective as claimed. ("8 Albacores and 22 Naval fighters attacked the aerodrome at dawn today and destroyed 47 aircraft which were bombed up, alerted and ready to fly.") At 1345 three Albacores and five fighters bombed Latigue field (and the Americans occupying it).[31]

At Gibraltar, Maj. Gen. James Doolittle, commander of the U.S. Twelfth Air Force, sent the 31st Fighter Group to Oran at 1520 on the 8th. The twenty-four planes of the 308th and 309th Squadrons flying Spitfire Vs arrived at 1700. Almost simultaneously, thirteen D.520s took off from La Sénia to hit Latigue. The 308th began landing at Latigue as four aircraft believed to be Hurricanes orbited the airfield. They turned out to be the D.520s. The French fighters shot down one Spitfire. Three Spitfires waiting to land counterattacked. The French acknowledged three losses but claimed four kills.[32]

Paratroop Task Force

The planners assigned the 2nd Battalion, 503rd Parachute Regiment, and the 60th Troop Carrier Group the audacious task of flying from England to conduct a night drop. Originally one company was to jump over La Sénia field at 0100 on 8 November and destroy aircraft there before joining the other three companies, which would drop over Latigue, eight miles southeast. The united battalion would then defend Latigue until relieved by the 1st Armored Division. However, at Cherchell on 22 October Division General Mast had assured Major General Clark that the C-47s could land unopposed, so an alternative plan was devised that called for a daylight landing at La Sénia, permitting the 2/503 to be used in a subsequent move into Tunisia. At 1625 on 7 November the paratroopers received orders to conduct this alternative plan. This delayed takeoff by six hours and required signaling their new arrival time to Gibraltar and the antiaircraft ship *Alynbank,* which was to broadcast a homing beacon.

At 2200 on 7 November four companies of the 2/503, in total 531 men, took off from two Cornish airfields in thirty-nine C-47s. Col. William C. Bentley Jr.'s guide plane was to lead the formation to Oran twelve hundred miles away. Poor weather, radio difficulties, and the "burning out of formation lights" caused the planes to scatter by the time the 60th had ascended to ten thousand feet to transit Spain. Once over the Mediterranean, solid cloud cover complicated navigation. *Alynbank* was transmitting on the wrong frequency and a back-up beacon had shut down because the operative had not been informed the aircraft would be arriving after sunrise instead of 0100 as originally planned. As a result, six C-47s wandered off course. One landed at Gibraltar, two in French Morocco, and three in Spanish Morocco.[33]

The largest group of aircraft followed Colonel Bentley's plane. It erroneously homed in on a lighthouse in Spanish Morocco and arrived over Oran behind schedule. There Bentley's aircraft found a dozen C-47s already landed on the western end of the Sebkra d'Oran. They had been attacked approaching La Sénia and had used the lake bed as an alternative landing site. Dewoitines had forced down four C-47s and strafed the paratroopers. Bentley's group jumped to reinforce the men at Sebkra d'Oran while Bentley himself continued to La Sénia. However, engine problems forced the plane down on the dry lake near the airfield, and French troops captured Bentley and the crew of two other transports (one still loaded with troops) that had landed nearby. Meanwhile, the Sebkra contingent began marching toward La Sénia. The aircraft tried to taxi in that direction, but mud quickly forced the paratroopers to slog ahead on foot. After they had disappeared orders arrived to fly the aircraft to Latigue and these planes safely landed there.

Of the thirty-nine C-47s involved in the operation, six were lost as related, twenty-eight landed on Sebkra, and one landed between Misserrhin and Oran; the French shot down four. Later French artillery shelled Latigue and only fourteen C-47s remained serviceable by nightfall on the 8th. The operation demonstrated a breathless readiness to accept risk, but it contributed nothing to the battle's outcome—it seemed that the planners wanted to use every resource at their disposal, regardless of need. In any event, only three hundred paratroopers were available on 15 November for the advance into Tunisia.[34]

By the end of the day, Sunday 8 November, the Allies had landed 10,472 men of the 1st Infantry Division, 1,026 men of the TF Red/1st Armored Division, 2,522 corps troops, but only 340 vehicles. Rising surf had forced the suspension of landings on all beaches except X White. Scores of landing craft had been damaged. Arzew Harbor was being utilized to the utmost, but unloading was seriously behind schedule.[35]

9 November

The 1st Infantry Division faced several difficulties on this day. The 16th Regiment's 2nd Battalion, having advanced to within nine miles of Oran on the 8th, found the going much harder, advancing just three miles along the Oran road to Assi Bou Nif. The 3rd Battalion followed through Fleurus and turned north, hitting the St. Cloud–Oran highway five miles west of St. Cloud and advancing along that road toward Arcole, four miles short of Oran. Meanwhile, units of the 2 RTA crossed the Macta River on the eastern side of the beachhead and infiltrated south of La Macta during the night. At dawn they reached the coast near Port-aux-Poules, cutting off units of the 1st Battalion, 16th Regiment in La Macta. The Americans called for help, describing the situation as horrible. Brigadier General Oliver diverted elements of the Armored Task Force to assist while the 1/19 Engineers and a Ranger company rushed up. By noon they had forced the French *tirailleurs* to retreat; the armored troops, which were never needed, turned back.

All three battalions of the 18th Regiment attacked the units of the 16 RTA and 2 RCA defending St. Cloud on the morning of the 9th. Forward elements penetrated into the village, but snipers drove them back. The regimental commander ordered a heavy artillery bombardment to be followed by an all-out assault, but the divisional commander, Maj. Gen. Terry Allen, arriving on the scene decided this would inflict too many civilian casualties. He ordered the 1st Battalion to mask the village while the 2nd and 3rd continued toward Oran. These units were halfway to Arcole by dark.

West of the city the 26th Regiment faced two companies of the 2 RTA. During the day the 2nd Battalion captured Ain El Turk and advanced to Bouisseville. The battalion had been given the recognition password "Hi Ho Silver," to which the response was "Away." One officer noted "during the day when the Arab children approached to ask for candy, they would greet us with 'HI HO SILVER.' They apparently thought that our password was a greeting of some kind and was the proper way to begin a conversation with the American troops." The 3rd Battalion's attack against Ferme Ste. Marie in the hills north of Mers el-Kébir stalled. That afternoon the 1st Battalion reinforced the 3rd for a combined attack the next day.[36]

1st Armored

At 0750 TF Red advanced north from Tafaraoui toward La Sénia, but 75-mm batteries located in the intervening town of Valmy halted its advance. Near St. Lucien, Spitfires flying reconnaissance strafed a French armored column from the 2 RSA that was advancing from Tlemcen. After dispatching an armored company and an infantry platoon to reinforce the Green Column, TF Red turned south and battled the French tanks north of St. Lucien, claiming the destruction of fourteen R35 Renaults at the cost of one tank and one half-track. That night the 2/6th Armored Infantry moved up from St. Leu and relieved the Latigue garrison, permitting them to move toward Oran for the next day's assault.

The Green Flying Column attacked east toward La Sénia airfield at 0745 and captured the base an hour later, taking 160 prisoners. However, the American troops stalled there under fire from the Batterie du Santon and the guns at Valmy. At 1700 two platoons attacked Valmy and destroyed the 32 DCA, which had been troubling the American advance.

The main body of Task Group (TG) Green moved out from Bredea to join the Flying Column, but the 2 RCA at Misserrhin repulsed three American assaults. Finally, at 1800 two companies along with trucks carrying gasoline and ammunition bypassed Misserrhin and joined the Flying Column at 0100 on the 10th.

U.S. Army Spitfires flew forty-five sorties from Latigue on the 9th, mostly against the French mechanized column to the south and to support the attack against Valmy. Major General Doolittle landed at 1605 in a B-17 escorted by twelve Spitfires of the 52nd Fighter Group. During the operation five Spitfires were lost in action, including two to friendly ground fire. Accidents cost two more aircraft, and six planes of the 52nd Group ran out of gas en route to Latigue. Twenty C-47s were operational by the end of day.

The Second Naval Battle of Oran

Workers hastily readied *Epervier* for sea as thirty-three replacements, mostly submariners, supplemented her crew. At 0822 Vice Admiral Rioult ordered her and *Typhon* to break out to Toulon. The *contre-torpilleur's* captain, Commander Joseph Laurin, sallied his ship at 0900 and headed up the coast at twenty-three knots with *Typhon* trailing. One of *Typhon's* officers recalled, "The sea was beautiful, and a slight mist gave us the hope of passing undetected." This hope, however, quickly proved vain. At 0930, as they drew level with Pointe du Canastel, a reconnaissance plane passed overhead followed by three fighters. As they came abeam Pointe de l'Aiguille fifteen minutes later, lookouts could see four enemy warships ten miles off *Epervier's* port bow heading southeast, a force including cruisers to port, a convoy to the west, and the aircraft carrier *Furious* and her escort on the northern horizon.[37]

Laurin steered northeast at 0955 to slip into a fog bank. However, at 0959 *Aurora,* which was 25,000 yards north of Cape Falcon waiting for a bombardment call, spotted the French squadron to the east-southeast. Followed by *Calpe* she rang up twenty-eight knots and turned to close. The cruiser lost sight of the enemy formation at 1012 in the fog but picked it up again eight minutes later.

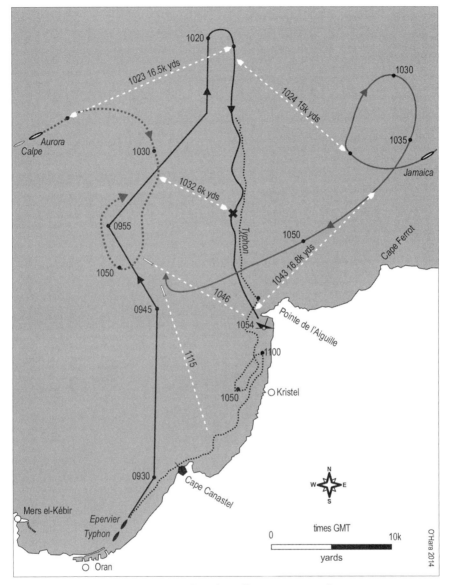

MAP 8.4 *Naval Action off Oran, 9 November*

At 1020 when *Epervier* emerged from the fog at a point fourteen miles north of Pointe de l'Aiguille she sighted light cruiser *Jamaica* nine miles off her starboard beam approaching at high speed in response to *Aurora*'s sighting report, and *Aurora* herself closing from the west. Laurin concluded his mission was impossible and came about for Oran.

Aurora engaged at 1023 from 16,500 yards and straddled *Epervier* with her third salvo. The French warships replied and, according to an *Aurora* account, "much too accurately for comfort. . . . A prolonged action followed in which we were lucky not to be hit." At 1024 *Jamaica*, now 15,000 yards to the east, fired a few salvos from her forward turrets before making a broad loop to the north to bring her broadside to bear. *Aurora*, veteran of four surface actions against the Italians, had the sun behind her targets and held a steady course. She continued to close and maintained a heavy fire, claiming her first hit at 1026, although French reports do not substantiate this. *Calpe*, steaming at her best speed of twenty-four knots, engaged at 1027 from 13,900 yards. Her 4-inch guns maintained a rapid fire during the nineteen minutes she was in action, discharging 318 rounds and claiming many straddles and some hits.[38]

At 1030 *Jamaica* returned to action. *Epervier* turned her guns against *Jamaica* while *Typhon* concentrated on *Aurora*. In response *Jamaica* made a large alteration to starboard. At the same time an *Aurora* broadside struck *Epervier*'s forward boiler room. (*Aurora* timed this blow at 1032 on her 31st broadside when she observed *Epervier* stop and disappear "in a dense cloud of smoke." French records put it at 1035.) At 1035 *Jamaica* ceased fire and started steering west. She reported, "Difficulty was experienced in finding line owing to the swinging of the ship and frequent alterations of course by the enemy, and considerable delays occurred between broadsides as the director trainer lost the target on firing."[39]

Aurora and *Calpe* were now on a parallel course off the French column's starboard quarter. At 1034 *Aurora* switched targets and engaged *Typhon* after a round disabled *Epervier*'s forward engine. Meanwhile, *Jamaica*'s guns fell silent at 1035. She unleashed a few salvos at 1043 from 16,800 yards just before the enemy disappeared behind Pointe de l'Aiguille. At 1045, according to *Epervier*'s record, a round completely destroyed the *contre-torpilleur*'s bridge and another exploded aft, igniting a shell room fire. The French attributed this blow to the eastern cruiser. However, *Calpe* is also a possibility. With the rudder frozen and a large fire astern, Laurin decided to beach his ship. As he turned toward Pointe de l'Aiguille, *Typhon* sailed past laying a thick curtain of black smoke. She launched one of her three torpedoes while firing rapidly at *Calpe*. Salvos bracketed the British destroyer and splinters punched through her forecastle deck. As *Epervier* limped toward shore a shell hit near the sickbay, inflicting many casualties, and another hit in the after engine room, forcing its evacuation. With that, however, the *contre-torpilleur*'s agony ended as *Calpe* ceased fire at 1046 and *Aurora* at 1050.[40]

At 1054 *Epervier* stranded on the rocks below the point. *Typhon* turned back to assist, but at 1100 *Jamaica* rounded Pointe de l'Aiguille and opened fire at 1103. *Typhon* reported, "The English cruiser reappeared and again began shooting with astonishing precision so that *Typhon* could avoid her shells only with difficulty despite zigzagging at a speed of thirty knots." One of *Jamaica's* first salvos achieved a near miss that slightly damaged *Typhon*. Otherwise her fire was ineffective, particularly because the destroyer was "almost impossible to see against the dark background of the land." At 1115 as *Typhon* ran south she launched a second torpedo. Then at 1117 the Batterie du Canastel's 240-mm guns opened fire and straddled *Jamaica*. This caused the cruiser to immediately sheer away ending the surface action.[41]

Typhon returned to Oran at 1135 largely undamaged. *Epervier* lost twelve men killed, nine missing, and thirty-one wounded. She shot 240 rounds while *Typhon* expended 200. *Jamaica* used 501. *Jean Argaud* and *Chêne* sailed up to Pointe de l'Aiguille and brought *Epervier's* men back to Oran.

At 1630 after the rescue operations were completed Vice Admiral Rioult ordered all shipping in Oran Harbor scuttled. At 1730 the first bottleneck at the Môle du Ravin Blanc was thoroughly blocked by the wrecks of seven merchant ships, the submarine *Diane,* the sloop *La Bônoise,* and the minesweeper *Pigeon.* *Typhon* was moored precisely in the center of the narrow entrance to the port and scuttled there at 2030. Other vessels sunk at their moorings included, in the Bassin Poincaré, three floating docks, three commercial vessels, and the submarines *Cérès* and *Pallas.* Farther up harbor three merchant ships were demolished while at the harbor's extreme end around the Quai d'Alger a merchantman, the minesweepers *Chêne, Tourterelle, Nadal,* and *Jean Argaud,* the sloops *L'Ajaccienne* and *La Toulonnaise,* and the submarine *Ariane* all joined *Walney* as wrecks and hazards to navigation.[42] In other naval activity on this day the British corvette *Gardenia* collided with the auxiliary minesweeper *Fluellen* in the fog while patrolling off X Beach. *Gardenia* sank with the loss of three men.

10 November

Early on this day the 18th Regiment's 2nd and 3rd battalions advanced toward Oran while the 1st masked St. Cloud. The 3rd bore to the right and captured the Batterie du Canastel while the 2nd entered the outskirts of Oran at 1000 and the town itself at noon, shortly before the cease-fire. The 18th, which reportedly lacked élan, had faced the hardest fighting and suffered higher casualties than any other unit. The 26th Regiment captured Ferme Ste. Marie and occupied the heights of Djebel Murdjadjo, its first-day objective.

At 0730 the 1st Armored Division's Green and Red TGs attacked up parallel roads toward Oran. A roadblock north of La Sénia and persistent artillery fire from guns near Valmy delayed the Red Column for two hours, but both forces penetrated Oran before noon. The French agreed to a cease-fire at 1215.

The amphibious landings went better than in Algiers, but the 1st Infantry Division was slow in achieving its objectives and resistance was stiff compared to Algiers. The occupation of Oran cost the French navy 243 killed or missing and 146 wounded, the army 94 killed or missing and 194 wounded, and the air force 10 killed and 13 wounded. Losses totaled 347 killed or missing and 353 wounded. Total Allied losses through 10 November were 593 killed and 569 wounded, mainly in the ill-advised attempt to capture the port. The mass scuttlings subtracted from the port's usefulness for the balance of the year, but the incomplete military port at Mers el-Kébir suffered little damage and accommodated commercial vessels and the capital ships of Force H, which, ironically, berthed beside the wrecks of the French battleships it had sunk in July 1940.[43]

9

ATLANTIC CONVOY

On 25 October the Air Group sailed. . . . The course followed
resembled the track of a reeling drunk.

—Rear Adm. Ernest McWhorter

TF 34, commanded by Rear Adm. H. Kent Hewitt, carried the Morocco
invasion force. It consisted of five amphibious task groups: TG 34.8 (Rear
Adm. Monroe Kelly) was bringing the reinforced 60th Regiment/9th
Division to Port Lyautey in the north, TG 34.9 (Capt. Robert M. Emmet) held
the 3rd Infantry Division destined for Fédala just north of Casablanca, and 34.10
(Rear Adm. Lyal A. Davidson) had the 47th Regiment/9th Division and Combat
Command B of the 2nd Armored Division bound for Safi, 120 miles south of
Casablanca. A heavy surface support group, TG 34.1 (Rear Adm. Robert C. Giffen)
and a carrier group, TG 34.2 (Rear Adm. Ernest McWhorter) were in support.

This mighty undertaking started in humble fashion when the first of five
scout submarines cast off from New London on 19 October. TGs 34.8 and
34.10 departed Hampton Roads, Virginia, on 23 October and headed southeast. Rumors were circulated to suggest they were bound to Haiti for maneuvers.
The next day TG 34.9 left Hampton Roads as if headed for Great Britain while
Giffen's TG 34.1 with battleship *Massachusetts,* two heavy cruisers, and four
destroyers left Casco Bay, Maine, the same day. McWhorter's carrier group with
Ranger, three escort carriers, a light cruiser, and nine destroyers had been exercising in isolated waters off Bermuda since 3 October. They sailed on 25 October.

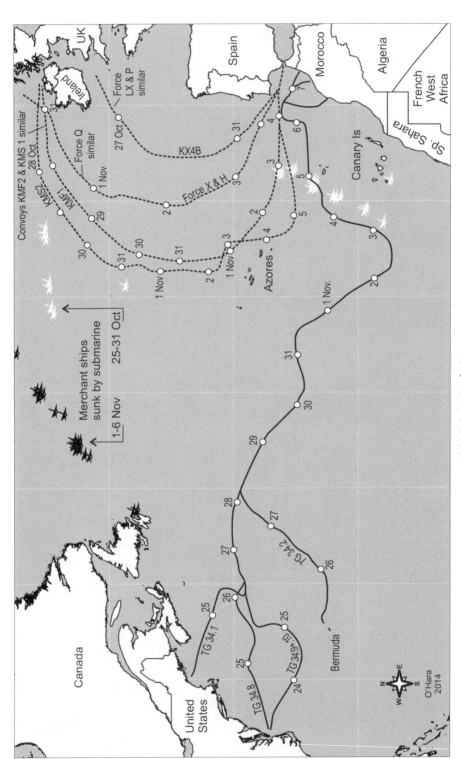

MAP 9.1 *Torch Convoys*

Once land dropped from sight the groups converged toward a rendezvous in the western Atlantic, and by midafternoon on the 26th Hewitt's central group and Giffen's force had united. Before sundown they sighted the northern and southern groups, and all joined Hewitt after dawn on the 27th. Finally, at 1000 on the 28th, the carrier force approached from the southeast and took station astern body so the flattops could conduct aerial operations without interference from the transports, which were sailing in nine five-ship columns. The sight of the combined fleet stirred even a lubber's soul. The newly promoted Maj. Gen. Lucian Truscott, commander of the northern landing force, remembered it like this: "A great convoy at sea is a magnificent sight. . . . Forward of us was the battleship *Texas,* broad of beam, bristling with guns. . . . We followed at a distance of perhaps half a mile. Behind us spaced at similar distances followed other transports. Off to our right, or starboard, there was a similar column; beyond it another, another and still another."[1]

Harvard history professor Lt. Cdr. Samuel E. Morison was on board *Brooklyn* to record events for the semi-official naval history he had asked President Roosevelt to commission him to write. He noted that the weather was magnificent and that there were no breakdowns, no straggling, and no submarine attacks.[2] However, while he was correct on the last point, the first breakdown occurred even before the task force had cast off when the transport *Harry Lee*—known as *Leaning Lena* for her tendency to list—had to be replaced by *Calvert.* The need to transfer all of *Lee's* combat-loaded cargo (first needed first off) to *Calvert* meant that *Calvert* sailed two days after the main body escorted by the destroyers *Eberle* and *Boyle. Calvert* and her escort joined TF 34 on the morning of the 29th. Other than that, there were minor breakdowns on the 25th and 26th and periodically throughout the voyage, but nothing so serious the ships involved could not resume station by nightfall. Destroyers darted back and forth between the columns to minimize straggling.

On October 30 through 31—about two thousand miles into the journey— the fleet steamed in a straight line at eight knots to refuel smaller vessels that lacked the range to cross nonstop. Hewitt believed the mid-Atlantic location was free of enemy submarines, but he doubled the air patrols nonetheless. He was nervous when, during this period, Truscott asked to take a motor whaleboat to inspect the transports in his group and was relieved when the general finally returned to his own ship.[3]

The crew of the light cruiser *Philadelphia* enjoys a concert while in transit to Africa. (Jody Mishan collection)

As refueling was being completed the fleet picked up a distress call from *Alaska,* a Norwegian freighter with Convoy SL 125. She had been torpedoed, but her position was a thousand miles east. A review of Axis submarine attacks shows that from 25 October to 6 November TF 34 was well outside threatened areas. From the 26th to the 31st a German wolf pack harried SL 125. Their attacks lay across TF 34's future track but were long finished when the American fleet reached the area five days later. The British convoys converging on Gibraltar had been sighted by that time and German submarines were making for the strait, vacating the area the Americans were moving into. German submarines were also active in the North Atlantic traffic lanes thirteen hundred miles northeast of the convoy's route and in the central Atlantic and Caribbean, three thousand miles southeast and two thousand miles southwest, respectively. By early November a convoy battle was occurring to the northeast of Newfoundland, and in the first six days of November TF 34 was two thousand miles from the nearest submarine sinking.[4]

After the fleet refueled, the voyage continued. An aircraft was sighted on 1 November; on the 2nd one of the destroyers suffered a minor act of sabotage;

on the 3rd one of *Ranger*'s aircraft crashed close alongside the destroyer *Wilkes,* which rescued the pilot. The delivery of a massive amphibious attack across the entire breath of an ocean had never before been attempted, and naturally the commanders worried. Hewitt fretted about things like how many destroyers he should leave behind should a transport be torpedoed, but weather was his main concern. On the night of the 3rd the fleet entered a storm front. On the 4th excessive roll forced the converted minelayer *Miantonomah* to drop out. The minesweeper *Raven* stayed with her until she rejoined on the 7th while the escort carrier *Suwannee* had an "engineering casualty" that forced her to leave formation briefly.[5]

The weather raised the possibility that high surf might prevent a landing on the Atlantic coast, as the British chiefs had repeatedly warned. In this case the task force would enter the Mediterranean and disembark troops east of Spanish Morocco. The army formations would then march hundreds of miles west to attack Casablanca and their other objectives. Rough seas made refueling impossible, and bunkers on some of the small vessels were getting so empty that Hewitt considered the possibility of towing. In addition, as it neared Africa the fleet began to encounter coastal steamers and fishing vessels. Those that sighted the Americans were boarded and prevented from communicating until after the landings commenced.

On 6 November the weather started to moderate. The fleet refueled and then Hewitt faced a decision that had to be made on the morning of 7 November—whether to proceed to the landing beaches, now to his southeast, or continue into the Strait of Gibraltar, several hundred miles east. Weather forecasts emanating out of Washington were pessimistic. The fleet meteorologist, however, a lieutenant commander who had been studying the relationship between North Atlantic weather and African surf for several months, bravely predicted that Atlantic landings would be possible and that conditions on the 9th would be less favorable. Hewitt also had the British Admiralty forecast of 6 November that predicted decreasing winds, moderate seas, and mostly fair conditions. The admiral considered these and decided to make for Morocco. At 0700 on 7 November the flag signal "proceed on service assigned" broke out on *Augusta*'s mast, and Rear Admiral Davidson separated TG 34.10 from the fleet to head south toward Safi. At 1100 the covering and air groups split off, followed by the Northern Group, TG 34.8, at 1500. Finally, the Central Group turned toward Casablanca.[6]

Task Force 34 sailed in nine columns. Here the ships are making a simultaneous turn to port. Taken from one of USS *Philadelphia*'s SOC Seagull float planes. (Jody Mishan Collection)

The U.S. Navy in late 1942

The Atlantic Fleet, which provided the ships and men of TF 34, had been the poor sister of its Pacific counterpart. It had failed to adequately protect Allied shipping against Axis submarines off the American coastline for several critical months after Pearl Harbor. There had been no great carrier battles like Coral Sea, Midway, Eastern Solomons, and Santa Cruz, and no surface actions like Balikpapan, Java Sea, Savo Island, and Cape Esperance. This fleet was a polyglot of old ships, like the World War I–era dreadnoughts *Texas* and *New York* and new, unbloodied vessels, like the battleship *Massachusetts* or light cruiser *Cleveland*. Its "fleet" aircraft carrier, *Ranger,* was considered unfit for the Pacific's more demanding environment. The personnel were a mix of veterans, reserve, and draftees. Light cruiser *Brooklyn,* for example, although five years in commission, had a crew of 1,050 men; for more than half of them, this was their first voyage. Few men had experienced a naval engagement. On board *Massachusetts* the crew stood at general quarters for an hour each day and spent the rest of the day, from before sunrise to 2200, drilling and exercising.[7]

En route the soldiers were trained at the whim of their commanders, which varied from vessel to vessel. On one transport, "Signal Personnel spent periods of 'general quarters' handling drill traffic, routing, encoding and decoding. . . . Troops studied plans, contour maps, and models. The non-specialists practiced more mundane tasks." Maj. Gen. Ernest N. Harmon, the ground commander of the southern landing force, later recalled, "Rope ladders were rigged forward

USS *Ranger* with a pair of *Gleaves*-class destroyers screening astern at dusk of the first day's operations. On deck eight F4F Wildcat fighters and one Douglas SBD-3 Dauntless dive bomber are visible. (Library of Congress)

and aft on the ship and soldiers scrambled up and down like monkeys during certain hours of the day." On a third transport, an officer recalled, "'very little' training was done en route and on the others 'apparently less.'" On a fourth, "All boat crews and soldiers familiarized themselves with the plan, harbor and facilities. Everyone rehearsed their detailed duties."[8]

French Dispositions

General Augustin Noguès was resident-superior and chief of French forces in Morocco.[9] Under him Corps General Georges Lascroux commanded army forces that consisted of 55,000 troops organized into four divisions headquartered at Casablanca, Fez, Marrakech, and Meknès. The Armée de l'Air was under Division General Auguste Lahoulle. The Armée de l'Air and Aéronautique Navale deployed more than two hundred aircraft, about two-thirds of which were serviceable. Vice Admiral François Michelier headed Marine au Maroc. His forces included an immobile battleship, *Jean Bart,* with improvised fire control, a light cruiser, three *contre-torpilleurs* (one in dock), seven destroyers (two under repair), three sloops, four patrol boats (two inactive), and eleven submarines. Coastal defenses included the powerful Batterie d'El Hank with four 194-mm and four 138.6-mm guns defending Casablanca and other batteries up and down the coast.

Some American accounts criticize French preparations. "No other enemy would have failed to lay mines and prepare beaches at least in the vicinity of strategic points. No other enemy equipped with air and submarines would have failed to detect the approaching force by or before dark the day before their appearance off shore." This assessment seems harsh. The invasion convoy did catch the French by surprise, but this was hardly remarkable. By late 1942 the French navy rationed its scant stocks of fuel oil and gave priority to convoy escorts. Air units could not routinely train, much less patrol into the Atlantic on the scale required to detect unexpected enemy forces undertaking a transoceanic invasion—something never before attempted—at a sufficient range to make a difference. Instead, the French command had to frame its response based on piecemeal scraps of information. While such information indicated a major Allied operation, there was nothing to suggest that a huge fleet had departed the United States bound directly for Morocco.[10]

As it happened, French authorities in Morocco received several hours' warning of the impending invasion through the efforts of the Group of Five's Brigade General M. E. Antoine Béthouart, the Casablanca Division's commander. He ordered his division to permit American landings and proceeded to army headquarters in Rabat where—accompanied by the colonel of the RICM (Régiment d'Infanterie Coloniale du Maroc, or colonial infantry regiment of Morocco) and protected by elements of that regiment—he arrested Corps General Lascroux and sent him to Meknès. Béthouart's men occupied the telephone exchange and at 0030 on the 8th the general dispatched a representative to General Noguès. He advised Noguès that American troops were landing and presented a package of documents that included the text of General Giraud's planned radio address, information from Robert Murphy regarding American intentions for North Africa, and an assertion that Axis forces were invading Tunisia. He asked Noguès for cooperation, or at least his neutrality.

At the same moment in Casablanca Béthouart's chief of staff was handing Vice Admiral Michelier an identical set of documents. The admiral already suspected that some type of plot was impending. At 0100 he telephoned Noguès. Béthouart did not know that the resident-superior had a secure telephone line independent of the exchange. Michelier told Noguès that the convoys observed at Gibraltar or approaching the strait had all passed into the Mediterranean and that there was no evidence of American landings in Morocco and, moreover, that the weather seemed too rough for such landings to even be possible. They finally concluded they were facing some type of dissident putsch, possibly combined with an American commando raid. Noguès then summoned loyal troops who freed him and arrested Béthouart. Michelier, meanwhile, countermanded Béthouart's orders and sounded the alert. The time was 0200.[11]

Events at Port Lyautey demonstrated the impact of Béthouart's action. At 0130 on the 11th a staff officer appeared at the quarters of Colonel Jean Petit, commander of the 1 RTM (Régiment de Tirailleurs Marocains, or regiment of Moroccan riflemen) in Port Lyautey, and handed him orders to cooperate with the Americans. Petit wrote, "My surprise, I admit, was total. My emotion considerable." He summoned the area's military and civil authorities and described their reaction as "an explosion of general joy." Then the port's naval commander, Commander Cadoret, pulled him aside and stated he had just spoken with Marine au Maroc. Vice Admiral Michelier had instructed him to implement the defense plan. Brigade General Béthouart was in a state of rebellion. Petit wrote, "I was stunned. . . . The clock was ticking. The landing was near. Who to believe?" Finally at 0430 he reached Noguès. The resident-superior confirmed Michelier's orders. Petit hung up the telephone. "My hopes collapsed under this new, hard perspective." But "I was a soldier with a formal mission and orders that I would execute without hesitation, regardless of how hard and cruel it was."[12]

"By 0300, the Americans in the consulate [in Casablanca] observed truckloads of soldiers, a stream of little 'Citroëns,' and many motorcycles and bicycles hastening trough the city toward the port and coastal batteries." Thus, an hour before the first landing, the French authorities were aroused and ready for a fight, one they believed they could win.[13]

10

PORT LYAUTEY

Unloading a transport on an open sea beach under threat from air,
surface, and sub-surface, with only flimsy surf boats and inexperienced
personnel is a prodigious, dangerous, and nerve wracking undertaking.
—CAPTAIN PAUL A. STEVENS, *HENRY T. ALLEN*, 24 NOVEMBER 1942

Plans and Objectives

TG 34.8 carried 9,079 men from the 60th Regiment (9th Division), the 1st Battalion, 66 Armored Regiment, elements of the XII Air Support Command, and other attached units. Under the overall command of Major General Truscott they were to land around the village of Mehdia, eighty miles northeast of Casablanca. Their objective was the only all-weather airfield in Morocco located near Port Lyautey six miles up the twisting Wadi Sebou (Sebou River). Seventy-seven P-40s of the 33rd Fighter Group embarked on the escort carrier *Chenango* along with fighters from Gibraltar were supposed to occupy the field the evening of the first day so they could support a subsequent attack on Casablanca.

Truscott, who had served with Mountbatten's COHQ, was assigned to Torch in July and led Eisenhower's planning team. He considered two options for taking the airfield: a landing on a narrow front and a concentrated drive to the objective, or a broad-front attack where a failure on one beach would not necessarily doom the whole affair. Geography limited Truscott's choices. The airfield was tucked into a horseshoe bend of the river and was separated from the coast by steep ridges. Beaches were plentiful, but they were open to the Atlantic surf and, backed by lagoons, dunes, and ridges, had few vehicle exits. Truscott had observed firsthand the slaughter at Dieppe. His plan, completed on 10 October, assigned five beaches along a nine-mile front to his three battalion landing teams (BLTs).

In the center the 2nd Battalion under Maj. John H. Dilley would land at Green Beach around the resort of Mehdia Plage, funnel through a marshy bottleneck between the coastal ridge, a lagoon, and the river and then climb a second two-hundred-foot-high ridge. After this, the battalion would storm the Kasba, a large sixteenth-century Portuguese fort that dominated the river passage, in a surprise predawn bayonet attack. After capturing the fort and a nearby shore battery, Dilley's men would advance four miles and be ready to attack the airfield by 1100.

In the north the 3rd Battalion commanded by Lt. Col. John J. Toffey would land above the Wadi Sebou. A third of the force would use Red 1 Beach four miles north of the river mouth, traverse a belt of sand dunes, ascend the coastal ridge, and trek to a position across the river from the airfield by 1100. From there they would cross the river in rubber boats and attack the airfield. The bulk of the battalion was to land at Red Beach a thousand yards north of the river mouth, push up the Wadi Sebou's north bank, and support with mortars and artillery the 2nd Battalion's attack on the Kasba. It would then cross the river in rubber boats and secure Brown Beach on the river below the Kasba within two and a half hours of landing. Finally, the troops would march three miles and join the rest of the battalion at the airfield.

South of Mehdia Plage the three-mile-long Sidi Bou Rhaba lagoon paralleled the beach creviced between a wooded, seventy-foot-high ridge to the west and a two-hundred-foot escarpment to the east. Maj. Percy McCarley's 1st Battalion was to come ashore at the lagoon's southern end on either Blue Beach, three miles below the river mouth, or on Yellow Beach, five miles south. One company was to land on each beach and report to Truscott, who would then decide where to disembark the rest of the battalion and the armored landing team, a battalion of Stuart light tanks. The southern prong's missions were to block reinforcements from Rabat and threaten Port Lyautey from the south.

The plan included one special attack operation. Sixteen men were to boat up the river and cut a boom anchored on the bank below the Kasba. Then *Dallas,* an adapted four-stack destroyer, was to bring seventy-five specially trained troops six miles up the Wadi Sebou to help secure the airfield.

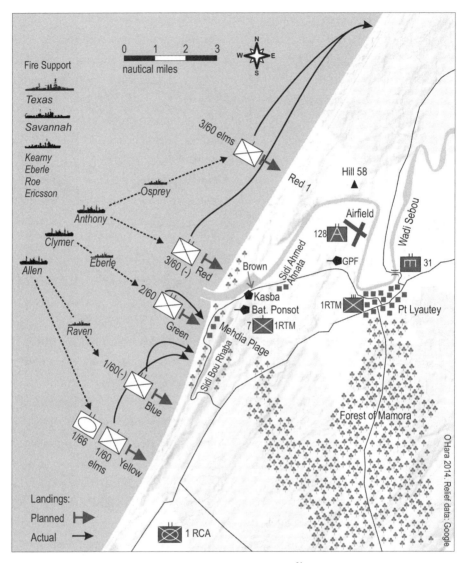

MAP 10.1 *Port Lyautey Landings*

French Dispositions

French forces included the navy-manned Batterie Ponsot with two 138-mm guns, situated on the ridge three hundred yards southeast of the Kasba, and the Défense des Passes—two 75-mm weapons on railroad flatcars parked beside the river directly below the Kasba.[1] The 1 RTM under Colonel Petit had three battalions barracked in Port Lyautey with the 7th Company forward. The 7th had one platoon on the Wadi Sebou below the Kasba, a reinforced platoon in the Kasba itself, and another reinforced platoon protecting the lighthouse and Batterie Ponsot. Units in the immediate area included three Renault FT-17 tanks, the 1st Battery of the 2 REI (Régiment Étranger d'Infanterie, or foreign infantry regiment) with four 75-mm guns, the 5th Battery of the II/64 RAA with four 75-mm guns, the 1st Battery GPF (*grande puissance de feu,* or heavy firepower) with four 155-mm guns, and the 31 Génie (Engineer) Battalion. The 128 DCA defended the Port Lyautey naval air station. At the airbase itself the 1st Fighter Flotilla had twenty-seven D.520 fighters (twenty-two operational) and the 3rd Bombardment Flotilla with eleven Glenn Martin bombers (nine operational). Strong ground and air units were based at Meknès sixty miles east and Rabat twenty miles south. The French naval commander in the area, Commander Cadoret, fielded an ad hoc company of naval infantry to supplement the base's ground defense.

The Final Approach

TG 34.8 separated from TF 34 at 1500 on 7 November. Rear Adm. Monroe Kelly in *Texas* headed one of the group's columns while *Savannah* led the other. The minesweepers *Raven* and *Osprey* swept ahead while the carriers trailed well behind. The transports were to take station eight miles off the mouth of the Wadi Sebou by 2300 on 7 November, and the first waves were to hit the beach by 0400 on 8 November.

Things went wrong from the beginning. The submarine *Shad* had been scouting the landing zone for four days. At 1900 the destroyer *Roe* steamed ahead to find *Shad* at one of three designated rendezvous points. After this *Roe* was "by means of SG Radar and navigational fixes" to direct the transports to the disembarkation point. *Shad,* however, had submerged to avoid detection by a "possible patrol craft." Accordingly, *Roe* missed the submarine and hastened to obtain her own fix on the river mouth. She then steamed back toward the fleet, broadcasting bearings to Kelly beginning at 2246. After that she took station a mile off the jetty.[2]

The convoy, meanwhile, sighted the lights of Rabat at 2228. Truscott recalled, "We were sliding along silently in darkness at reduced speed under a star-studded sky. Off to starboard glittered the lights of a good-sized town only a few miles distant. . . . But what town? Neither Commodore [*sic*] Gray nor any Navy officer on the quarterdeck would hazard a guess, but some thought that it was Rabat some twenty miles south of our objective area." In fact, Capt. Augustine Gray, who was commander of Transport Division 5 and who stood on *Henry T. Allen's* quarter-deck next to Truscott, believed they were still a "considerable distance from [their] destination" because he had been briefed to expect a southerly current (in fact it was running north). After *Roe* began transmitting, Rear Admiral Kelly ordered a series of large course changes. According to Gray, "During this wheel the formation was slowed and brought to a stop, the transports getting considerably out of position." At 2336 Kelly (correctly) advised Gray that the transport area "was about two miles to the westward" and gave him command of the landing force. Gray, however, still considered the transports were too far south. Although *Shad* had surfaced at 2300 and trained an infrared light on radar and visual contacts, this did no good. As Gray remarked, "We were unable on the *Allen* to pick up the marker submarine at any time."[3]

Gray spent a frustrating half hour trying to correct a nonexistent problem. He signaled the transports to head west, but this order was not executed "due to disorder of formation." At 2350 he instructed *Susan B. Anthony,* which had a pilot embarked, to proceed to the landing zone, but due to a signaling ambiguity *Anthony* misunderstood. Next Kelly ordered *Roe* to help Gray locate the proper area, but *Roe* and *Allen* could not establish visual contact. Finally, at 0036, ninety-six minutes behind schedule, Kelly radioed to Gray that he was close enough and ordered him to start loading boats. There was an overcast sky, a smooth sea, and a five-knot breeze.[4]

The Landing

Susan B. Anthony carried the 3rd BLT bound for the Red Beaches; *George Clymer* the 2nd BLT assigned to Green Beach; and *Henry T. Allen* the 1st BLT bound for Blue and Yellow Beaches. *John Penn* transported the personnel of the armored battalion while *Electra* carried the unit's thirty-seven tanks. *Florence Nightingale, Anne Arundel,* and *Algorab* held the personnel of the XII Air Support Command, engineers, and other support units.

Allen began lowering boats at 0040, followed minutes later by *Anthony* and *Clymer.* Seven waves were to be loaded before departing on the ninety-minute run to shore—the first three using the transport's organic landing craft while the ships loaded with support troops lent their boats for the next four. *Anne Arundel's* twenty-two boats, for example, reported to the *Susan B. Anthony,* the last one not leaving her mother ship until 0425. Sixteen of *Algorab's* eighteen boats reported to *Clymer* while two LCMs went to *Anthony*. Vehicles were boomed on board the small craft while the burdened troops clambered down nets. Although the sea was calm, a heavy swell caused the nets to swing away from the ships on the down roll. The transports maintained headway swinging from port to starboard to create lees as the craft were loaded first down one side and then the other. It was a slow and tricky process.[5]

The plan called for the waves to form around their mother transport and then rendezvous with a control vessel: *Osprey* for *Susan B. Anthony*/Red Beach; *Eberle* for *George Clymer*/Green Beach; and *Raven* for *Henry T. Allen*/Blue and Yellow Beaches. The three control vessels were to guide the assault waves to departure lines five thousand yards from shore. Succeeding waves would follow at ten-minute intervals, "each keeping the preceding wave in sight and exercising care not to 'pile up.'"[6] There were several exceptions: *Clymer*'s first two boats carried the special net-cutting party detailed to open the Wadi Sebou for the raiders who had to be transferred from *Anthony* to *Dallas*. Each of the attack transports also dispatched a boat to mark the beach. *Allen*'s scout boat, unfortunately, fixed on a point two miles north of the correct position.

The first seven waves were to land between 0400 and 0500, but uncertainty in locating the disembarkation point was the first in a chain of delays. Truscott, who had planned to remain on board *Allen* during the initial landings, became nervous. He later wrote, "I wondered what the troops on the other ships were doing. In the confusion, would commanders wait for orders? Would they proceed with the plans? . . . Radios were still silent. I had to find out." The general clambered down a net, commandeered a scout boat, and searched for *Clymer* and *Anthony* so he could "verify plans with troop commanders and ship's officers." He boarded *Clymer* at 0200 to find she had three waves ready to go. *Anthony*'s log, on the other hand, records that Truscott arrived at 0231 and left at 0310; perhaps there was more there to discuss. Gray implicated Truscott himself for some of the delay: "Loading of boats proceeded slowly on all assault vessels. Major General Truscott made the rounds of the assault ships and as a result the Hypo (0400) hour was delayed."[7]

As the laden soldiers inched down the swinging nets and landing craft swarmed about to find their guides, another disruption occurred, one beyond the control of planners or commanders. Lookouts reported lighted ships to the north and Kelly sent *Parker* to investigate. This was Convoy R 42, which had departed

Oran on 5 November bound for Casablanca. It included the steamships *Stras-bourgeois* (2,895 GRT) and *Dahomey* (5,851 GRT), the trawlers *Foudroyant, Simon Duhamel,* and *Loup de Mer,* and their escort, the patrol boat *Estafette*. A French history asserts that "between 0400 and 0600 on 8 November the convoy traversed, unmolested, the American naval force operating off Mehdia." In fact, at 0335 *Parker* signaled the leading vessel to change course and head out to sea. When the French ignored this order Lt. Cdr. Bay, *Parker's* captain, asked Kelly for permission to open fire, but the admiral told him to play shepherd instead. The "bewildered French merchant ships" proceeded to thread their way through the convoy formation, further delaying the process. Bay reported them clear by 0430.[8]

1ST BATTALION/BLUE AND YELLOW

At 0408 *Raven* began leading the 1st Battalion's first three waves toward the Blue Beach departure line at seven knots, although not without some confusion because two waves mistook *Osprey* for their control vessel and initially followed her. *Raven* had orders to steer 130 degrees true, but her captain calculated this would take the boats north of their destination, so he adjusted to the south. A searchlight was visible "signaling five French fishing boats which have been mill-ing thru area all night." Even after the course correction, the first two waves landed between 0500 and 0525 directly athwart the lagoon, two miles north of the proper location. *Raven* directed the third wave, assigned to Yellow Beach, farther south, but it landed at Blue Beach, three miles north of its intended destination. Fortunately, according to Captain Stevens of *Henry T. Allen,* "the surf conditions were extremely favorable. Landing parties had few if any casualties and boats got on and all but two got off without difficulty."[9]

2ND BATTALION/GREEN

Green Beach was the destination of *Clymer's* landing craft led by *Eberle*. The destroyer headed for the departure line at 0414 and released the first wave at 0454. Like other vessels, *Clymer* commented on "a number of French . . . ships passing close aboard as we commenced unloading."[10] The boats hit the correct beach, helped by the scout boat's flashing light; although an hour behind the revised schedule, they were still among the first ashore. By 0540 twenty-four boats and 860 men in three waves had landed. Although the surf was running five to six feet and the tide ebbing, the boats discharged rapidly and began retracting at

0545. *Clymer's* captain commented, "About dawn boats from our first three waves started returning which was a great source of satisfaction and relief to me." French aircraft strafed the landing craft and men at Green Beach in the first two hours of daylight.[11]

3RD BATTALION/RED

The 3rd Battalion came ashore late and far out of position. Dispatching the raiders to *Dallas* delayed the loading of the assault waves. Then the first boats had trouble locating *Osprey* and were not in formation for their long run to shore until 0500. *Osprey* led the landing craft north, except for the first wave, which "had no idea where they were" and strayed between the jetties at the mouth of the river forcing *Clymer's* scout boat to redirect them. After motoring north for an hour the craft turned toward shore at 0600. The battalion commander, Lieutenant Colonel Toffey, decided, because it was so late and the force was clearly past Red Beach, to land his entire unit together at Red 1. Two French D.520s confirmed the wisdom of this decision. According to *Osprey,* they "approached close ahead and began strafing attack on our troops in landing boats close by. The two planes were taken under fire by our 20-mm battery and were quickly driven away." Two boats foundered but fortunately no troops were lost. Unfortunately, *Osprey* had led the landing craft five miles past Red 1.[12]

The French Reaction 0545 to 0730

At 0400 the Batterie Ponsot came to the alert and at 0440 observed light flashes out to sea and one near the jetty's north end, probably a scout boat. A searchlight probed the river approaches and illuminated a small craft offshore, but the river itself was clear and so the defenders held fire.[13]

Between 0545 and 0549 *Texas, Eberle, Roe,* and *Clymer* all recorded seeing a red flare arching from the south jetty. A sentry had spotted the net-cutting party sneaking upstream. Fifteen minutes later a searchlight at Ponsot illuminated the landing craft while the 75-mm guns of the Défense des Passes and machine guns from both banks opened fire. *Eberle* responded at 0603, flinging in two minutes fifty-eight 5-inch rounds on the old, unmanned battery just south of the Kasba. The searchlight switched off, and the firing died away when the net-cutting party retreated. Their orders permitted the American ships to return fire but not to otherwise engage unless the army requested, and so for the most part they circled as the landing craft beached and started to retract. *Savannah* launched four aircraft beginning at 0607 and *Texas* one at 0622 to spot for the gunners when the call came.[14]

At 0629 Batterie Ponsot took a pot shot at *Roe* and the destroyer briefly fired back. By 0635 it was light enough for Ponsot to observe *Clymer*'s landing craft swarming off Mehdia Plage and the two guns targeted them. French records state that *Savannah* and the destroyers immediately replied, but this is not indicated in the American reports. At 0645 the GPF 155-mm battery, which was positioned southwest of the airbase, began shelling Mehdia Plage. At the field itself crews rushed to ready aircraft for action.[15]

At 0600, anticipating a dawn attack, five D.520s lifted off to patrol over the field while another pair reconnoitered south. As individual fighters made it aloft they sped west to attack enemy shipping. One fighter buzzed *Savannah* at 0646 and another *Roe* six minutes later. The destroyer reported, "Fighters made only one attack then returned into the clouds. Ship unable to return fire due to rapidity with which attack developed." At 0704 *Savannah* recorded shell splashes within 150 yards and two of her spotters sparred with D.520s. At 0708 Batterie Ponsot again targeted *Roe*. The squadron commander reported that the "second salvo landed just astern of *Roe* where *Roe*'s stern had just been. . . . Third salvo landed immediately astern and about 50 yards on the starboard quarter." The concussion knocked men off their feet as *Roe* made smoke and twisted away at thirty knots. The air attacks also continued. At 0717 a D.520 stitched *Kearny*'s topsides with .30 caliber bullets. The destroyer chased the aircraft with 5-inch and 20-mm gunfire, but it escaped.[16]

At 0715 Ponsot targeted *Clymer*. The transport cleared boats and got under way at full speed to open range. Her captain recorded that "at 0717 we were straddled, two shells falling about 25 yards short of the port quarter, one close under the starboard bow, cutting the main radio antenna and one dead astern about 50 yards." *John Penn* and *Algorab* also noted shellfire in their vicinity and withdrew, terminating ship-to-shore movement at a critical time.[17]

The Battle Aloft

French naval aircraft were first over the battle zone to the discomfort of American warships and landing craft. They encountered, however, fierce antiaircraft fire that damaged five fighters. *Kearny* fired on a Glenn Martin bomber at 0801 and observed the aircraft crashing in the water about a mile from the ship. She had less luck at 0817 against another Glenn Martin even though she expended twenty-two 5-inch rounds.[18]

The Kasba, a sixteenth-century fortification on a bluff above the Wadi Sebou near Port Lyautey. Scheduled to be taken at dawn on 8 November, the Kasba held out until the afternoon of the 10th. (U.S. Army Signal Corps)

Sangamon embarked nine TBF 1 Avenger torpedo bombers, nine SBD 3 Dauntless dive bombers, and twelve F4F Wildcat fighters. Light winds delayed the launch of the first Avenger until 0610. The third TBF stalled into the water, and after the fifth launch the remainder of the air group catapulted off with the last plane airborne at 0720. Once all aircraft were aloft a strike group of seven TBFs, eight SBDs, and ten F4Fs proceeded to the naval air station. Two fighters scouted while the rest circled to the south. At 0755 the Wildcats observed the last of the Glenn Martins taking off while nine Dewoitines waited on the tarmac, propellers spinning. American bombers immediately dove into action. "[They] emerged from the cloud layer, about 500 meters altitude and attacked simultaneously the ground installations, fighters on the runway, and the bombers that had just taken off." F4Fs downed three Glenn Martins and heavily damaged two others. They also destroyed three D.520s on the ground and another in a dog fight. The French claimed the destruction of two American aircraft in the air and two more with flak. In fact, throughout the day fifteen U.S. aircraft were damaged but none shot down. The American pilots characterized their enemy as half-hearted. "Two or three French fighters attacked our bombers and fighters but these attacks were rather listless and were not pressed to close range." Surviving French aircraft headed for Meknès seventy miles inland as they completed their missions and by 1000 French air activity had largely ended.[19]

The Battle Ashore

At 0630 the 3rd Battalion landed on an isolated mile-long strip of sand five miles beyond its designated destination. D.520s strafed the scrambling men as they moved inland and scaled the 165-foot-high ridge behind the beach. On this height they quickly emplaced machine guns that claimed the destruction of two fighters. Then the battalion began lugging weapons, ammunition, and supplies over ridges and through thick brush five miles to their first objective, Hill 58. Patrols reached it only an hour behind schedule. Unfortunately, they arrived without heavy weapons and rubber boats needed to attack the airfield, but this signified little since the other battalions had even bigger problems.

Between 0535 and 0730 most of the 1st Battalion landed two miles north of Blue Beach. This forced the troops to march three miles south to round the lagoon and it was 1000 before the battalion arrived at its intended starting point. Company A continued south to block the road to Rabat while B, C, and D companies ascended the plateau and headed toward Port Lyautey. Two hours later, directly opposite their original landing point, the battalion encountered the III/1 RTM, which was advancing south. As the two battalions skirmished, French tanks and truck-borne infantry of the 1 RCA attacked from the south and overran two Company A outposts, capturing the company commander but losing three tanks.[20]

While the 1st and 3rd battalions undertook the long marches required by Truscott's plan—marches extended because both battalions landed miles out of position—the 2nd Battalion, which arrived where it was supposed to, never delivered its scheduled surprise assault on the Kasba. The troops had to thread the gap between the northern end of the lagoon and the river and then scale an escarpment before they could reach the Kasba atop a bluff commanding the river. On the same plateau running south by southwest from the Kasba were situated the inactive battery of four old 138-mm/81 guns, the command post, the Batterie Ponsot, and a lighthouse.

The first troops were past the lagoon when at 0755 sixteen 5-inch rounds from *Savannah* smashed into the ridge above them. Seventy-two 6-inch shells aimed at Batterie Ponsot followed between 0759 and 0807. "The troops, inexperienced in the actual effects of such fire and not trusting its control, melted back into cover in considerable disorder and waited for it to stop."[21]

The question of naval gunfire vexed the operation. The navy considered it essential to suppress shore batteries that threatened transports. Useful support of troops, however, required careful coordination. Each battalion had a naval Shore Fire Control Party (SFCP) attached that was supposed to call down naval fire as needed, but this was a little-tested practice and the army naturally trusted its own artillery more. In fact, the 2nd Battalion left its SFCP on the beach. An extract from *Texas's* report further illustrates the problem: "The planned operations called for the Army to attempt to take the Kasbah and adjacent battery at Mehdia with cold steel early the morning [sic] of 8 November. If this attack failed our troops were to withdraw from the vicinity and bombardment of the two positions by the *Texas* would be called for. . . . No call came for the *Texas* to fire on these targets. It was therefore assumed that the Army had reached their objectives."[22]

After *Savannah* ceased fire the 2nd Battalion overran the lighthouse at 0830. It was preparing to advance toward the batteries when, at 0840, the bombardment began again. Over the next fifteen minutes 268 6-inch shells hit the area. The U.S. Army history asserts that "naval gunfire held up the infantry attack at a time when the Kasbah's defenders were fewest, and thus inadvertently helped prolong the whole operation." In fact, the first French reinforcements, one company of the I/1 RTM and two guns of the 2 REI, arrived at 0715. The "very violent" naval bombardment caused heavy casualties to the I/1 and forced the legionnaires of the 2nd to pull back. The real problem was American inexperience. "Many troops 'froze' when hearing friendly naval gunfire and friendly artillery for the first time." The Marines on Guadalcanal could have testified to the terrifying effects of a bombardment from 14-inch rifles. How the Kasba's defenders would have reacted had *Texas* subjected them to such violence can only be imagined.[23]

From 0918 to 0926 *Savannah* flung another 120 rounds against the battery while *Roe* and *Ericsson* (349 rounds) chipped in. The shelling disabled one of Batterie Ponsot's two 138-mm guns and American infantry finally overran the position. At this point, the commander of the 60th Regiment, Col. Frederick J.

de Rohan, appeared at the lighthouse and ordered the attack to continue. Major Dilley understood this as an order to bypass the Kasba. He left one company to occupy trenches near the fort and, "in spite of much straggling and confusion," pushed the balance of his unit forward.[24]

The French, meanwhile, were massing to counterattack. A company of the I/1 RTM accompanied by a battery of the 64 RAA had trucked to Mehdia before the American attack. The rest of the formation covered the five miles on foot. Two companies of the II/1 RTM protected I Battalion's southern flank while III/1 RTM advanced southwest on the Rabat road, running into the 1st BLT as related. By 1030 the 1 RTM's first and second battalions had united and faced Dilley's troops who were occupying the village of Sidi Ahmed Ahnata. This "formed, with its reed huts and cactus hedges, a favorable cover to their advance." Supported by 75-mm artillery the I/1 RTM attacked along the highway and the II/1 from the south. By 1130, after an intense fight and despite heavy casualties, Moroccan riflemen had recaptured the village.[25]

At 1140, as French counterattacked, Rear Admiral Kelly ordered *Dallas* to head upriver. Twice, however, after only several hundred yards, the 75-mm battery forced her to make smoke and withdraw, the last time at 1215.[26]

At 1230 three Renault light tanks rumbled forward to add their weight to a renewed advance by I/1 RTM. With the situation becoming dangerous, both ground and air spotters directed the fire of *Savannah, Ericsson,* and *Roe* against French troops. Between 1355 and 1557 *Ericsson* fired 250 rounds in four short bombardments; *Savannah* added 130 6-inch and 60 5-inch in three bombardments; and *Roe* added an unspecified number of rounds in five installments. The main target was the 64 RAA. At 1341 *Texas* finally deployed her powerful artillery against an ammunition dump on a reverse slope near the airport. Major General Truscott selected this target because it was safely behind the front. *Texas* fired fifty-nine 14-inch bombardment rounds from four thousand yards offshore and 16,500 yards from target while cruising at five knots. Initial estimates that she had destroyed 10 percent of the dump proved exaggerated.[27]

At 1635 Moroccan infantry recaptured Batterie Ponsot in a bayonet attack, pushing most of the 2nd BLT off the plateau. The battalion's Company E lost five of its six officers: one was killed by naval gunfire near the Kasba, French artillery killed another on the beach, a third died near the lighthouse, and a fourth died at Sidi Ahmed Ahnata. The French captured two hundred Americans but lost a quarter of the 1 RTM's officers. In the only bright spot for the invaders, the 60th Regiment's antitank unit successfully held the lighthouse. After this the center stabilized and the French relieved the 1 RTM during the night.[28]

At 1253 Commander Cadoret ordered the freighters *St. Emile, Nyhorn,* and *Ste. Madeleine* to scuttle at the narrows where the river made a hairpin turn to the south. *St. Emile* sailed at 1445 and scuttled at 1640 but settled parallel to the bank. *Ste. Madeleine* got under way at 1900 but missed her location in heavy mist and sank below the turn, leaving the channel open. Engine problems prevented *Nyhorn* from sailing.[29]

For the rest of the day the 3rd Battalion brought up heavy weapons, cut exits off the beach, and bulldozed a jeep trail to its position. The SFCP established communications and directed naval gunfire against the French 155-mm battery. The III/1 RTM stalled the 1st Battalion's advance five and a half miles south of Port Lyautey until late afternoon. Elements of the armored battalion relieved the shaken Company A after dark. It had seven tanks to meet French reinforcements expected from Rabat the next day.

Savannah and *Kearny* sparred with French batteries until dark (sunset was at 1735). At 1558 eight shells from the 155-mm battery fell within fifty yards of the cruiser and a dozen small fragments peppered the ship, wounding one man. The cruiser replied with a rapid-fire burst of 293 6-inch rounds that cut the battery's contact with its observation post and killed one man.[30]

Truscott had intended to direct the first day's battle from afloat, but found communications inadequate and so at 1545 the restless general landed at Blue Beach through "pounding surf." Immediately his jeep became "embedded in heavy sand a few yards from the water's edge." He wrote, "There was much confusion on the beach for craft destined for Green Beach were also landing on Blue. The soft, powdery sand, much worse than we had anticipated, was causing trouble. . . . Some landing craft had broached to in the surf and had been abandoned by their crews. Some weapons and equipment had been dumped into the surf, but everywhere men were working."[31]

9 November

The first day's combat had shaken the 60th Regiment. When Truscott returned to Blue Beach after visiting the 1st Battalion, he found "men wandered about aimlessly, hopelessly lost." And to compound the general's problems, the surf was up that morning running fifteen to twenty feet and making ship-to-shore movement perilous. *Penn* described unloading as "very slow on account of lack of boats and the increasingly heavy surf at Beach." *Algorab* commenced unloading at daybreak and had five boats swamped by the time operations were suspended. *Arundel* lost six boats that day, including two that swamped and two that broke up in the surf. *Clymer's* report states, "Boating was discontinued most of the day." At 0645 the destroyer *Hambleton,* part of *Sangamon's* screen, came upon an LCM that had been lost for twelve hours and gave her directions to the transport area.[32]

Meanwhile, French reinforcement had arrived from Meknès. The I/7 RTM relieved the I/1 RTM, which had suffered heavily in the prior day's fighting, and the 8 Tabor (the 79 and 80 Goums) was sent forward to capture the lighthouse. The 79 Goum moved out at 0545 and overran several American outposts, but defensive fire from the lighthouse threw the Moroccans back and killed their commander. At 0730, however, the 80 Goum swept past the lighthouse, and by 0900 Moroccans had reached Green Beach while others infiltrated along the coastal ridge.[33]

In one of the day's truly bizarre episodes American troops cornered a French lieutenant from the 80 Goum near the U.S. headquarters at the Mehdia Plage casino. The English-speaking officer convinced Colonel de Rohan that—despite the attack—the French were seeking a cease-fire. De Rohan allowed the officer to return to his lines to arrange this event and sent the good tidings to Truscott. The general considered this "thrilling news" and immediately headed for de Rohan's headquarters. He borrowed a razor and shook the worst of the dust and grime from his clothing and discussed with de Rohan the terms they would grant the French. However, the firing continued and no white flags appeared from the French lines. Truscott later wrote, "The whole incident was invented. . . . We had allowed our wishes to father our thoughts, a dangerous practice in war."[34]

The incident of the false surrender illustrated the American mindset. The French military had a strong tradition of professionalism, but Truscott, among others, did not think they would act professionally because he considered their cause unworthy. In this regard he concocted a scheme whereby two officers of "good appearance and persuasive personality" would present the French commander a letter "in fine Old English lettering on a scroll which we bound with ribbons and seals." In essence, this called on the French commander to surrender. The messengers were Col. Demas Craw, the operation's air commander, and Maj. Pierpoint Hamilton, both fluent French speakers. Shortly after the landing these officers and a driver set out in a jeep festooned with American, French, and white flags. They enjoyed free passage past the Kasba and along the road south of the airfield.[35]

By chance, Colonel Petit, preceded by his intelligence officer in another car, was driving toward the Kasba to review the situation. He related that he was heading along a road lined with tall eucalyptus trees when the first car suddenly returned, driving rapidly, the officer waving his arm through the window to follow him. "Behind him coming at the same speed was a greenish-gray vehicle, perhaps some enemy mechanized device harbinger of an armored column." Petit made a quick U-turn and headed back toward the town with the strange vehicle following. Then there was gunfire. Petit stopped and he walked back to see the American vehicle halted and surrounded by a small group of soldiers. "This was a 'jeep,' the first example to land on the Moroccan coast of this small all-terrain vehicle that would later become so popular here but still at that moment a strange and curious object." A machine gunner had fired a burst that killed Craw instantly. Hamilton related that he berated Petit for not respecting a flag of truce. The colonel apologized but noted that the car's speed gave a warlike impression and the flags could not be seen from ahead in any case. Petit took Hamilton to his headquarters. After reading Truscott's missive, he checked with Rabat but wrote, "It was clear to me once again that my mission had not changed."[36]

To the south seven Stuarts took position along the Rabat road and in the predawn darkness scattered a company of French infantry. At 0630 elements of the 1 RCA renewed their advance, a movement Truscott considered the most dangerous threat to his command. The Stuarts withdrew behind a small rise as a column of fourteen Renault FT-17s with a short-barrel 37-mm gun approached. The SFCP radioed for gunfire support and *Savannah* responded, launching two Seagulls for spotting at 0656. The tanks traded rounds from ranges down to a hundred yards, but neither side inflicted damage because the French shells could not penetrate the frontal armor of the Stuarts while the Americans shot wild, not having had time to adjust their sights. At 0750 the cruiser's 6-inch battery ended the stalemate with 121 rounds in twelve minutes. This barrage disabled two French tanks and drove the others off. Both sides claimed honors. Truscott who arrived as the skirmish ended remembered, "The dust had barely settled, smoke trailed upward from four French tanks in the foreground, and a number of bodies were sprawled about in the various postures of sudden death." A French author wrote of the same engagement, "We clearly had the upper hand since we destroyed four enemy tanks and lost only two of our own."[37]

Truscott reinforced Col. Harry H. Semmes, the armored battalion's commander, with ten Stuarts from Company C, 70th Tank Battalion, just in time to face a renewed assault by the Chasseurs. The French tankers had learned from the first battle and bushwhacked the Americans, knocking out two Stuarts with side hits. Semmes, however, had an ace in the hole. At 0825 *Savannah* and *Kearny* renewed their bombardment and up through 0913 the cruiser fired thirty-two 5-inch and 114 6-inch rounds. At 0922 her SOC Seagulls bombed the retreating armor with depth charges. A French historian complained they "inaugurated that day a new way of attacking tanks: with depth charges equipped with contact fuzes. The technique was good and caused us heavy losses."[38]

At 0900 the 1st Battalion renewed its advance. The troops slowly pushed three miles past positions held by III/1 RTM in the Forest of Mamora. That afternoon, however, they bogged down outside Port Lyautey in the face of heavy resistance from the III/7 RTM. At 1430 Truscott transferred the tanks of Company C/70 north to maintain momentum. The Stuarts arrived two hours later, but, contrary to the general's intentions, the 1st Battalion stayed put. Still, the French considered the situation threatening. Colonel Petit tried to infiltrate newly arrived units of the 3 REI supported by two squadrons of the 1 REC (Régiment Étranger de Cavalerie, or foreign cavalry regiment) and the 64 RAA through the forest to flank the enemy, but the Stuarts foiled this attempt. In response, Petit moved artillery from the central front to provide antitank support.[39]

On the central front, engineers and air group personnel reinforced the 2nd Battalion, which was reeling from 8 Tabor's morning attack. American troops then cleared the beach and the first ridge and clung to positions on the western slope of the higher ridge despite harassing fire from the 155-mm guns near the airport. "The rest of the day passed in a sort of deadlock with the 2nd BLT unable to arrange a successful coordinated attack despite the availability of artillery, naval gunfire, and air support." Part of the problem was that companies were down to forty or fifty men. Truscott wrote, "A casual inspection of beach and village showed an unduly large number of soldiers wandering about," and ordered de Rohan to "search every house in the village from ground to roof and comb the wooded areas between the village and the lagoon." This netted more than two hundred stragglers to restore unit strengths.[40]

The 3rd BLT remained north of the river bringing up weapons and rubber boats. At 1630 Companies K and M advanced down the narrow peninsula formed by a 180-degree bend in the river toward the highway bridge north of Port Lyautey. Company I was tasked with paddling across the river after dark.

At 1400 the French scuttled the merchantmen *St. Benoît* and *St. Hughes* in the river just above the town. Once again poor placement squeezed the channel but did not block it.

During the afternoon Major General Truscott appealed to Captain Gray for supplies and armor. This "led to pushing boats in although the loss of boats was very heavy. . . . Landings were discontinued when none of the last group to land was able to return." Fifteen of *Allen's* thirty-five landing craft were stranded on the beach and some soldiers and crews drowned. *Clymer* recorded that by the end of the day she had only "one tank lighter, four personnel boats and one ramp" still in service. Of two salvage craft sent to recover boats, one swamped and the other recorded no success after "five or six" hours of operation.[41]

The 3rd Battalion attacked the highway bridge just before dark. The 31 Génie and the 100-mm guns of the sloop *Ailette,* anchored nearby, laid down a vigorous fire and repulsed the Americans. The troops retreated to Hill 58, leaving a heavy weapons detachment to mask the bridge. Company I successfully crossed the river but after becoming disoriented in the dark dug in on the field's outskirts to await dawn. Lashed by Truscott, the 1st Battalion's Companies B, C, and D moved out at 2300 in three columns. They were to slide north before the town and block reinforcements from reaching the airfield.

10 November

After dark a boat from *Clymer* carrying sixteen men set out to meet an army unit on the river's southern bank. They were to cut the boom blocking the Wadi Sebou so *Dallas* could undertake her long-delayed mission. "It was an exceptionally dark night and raining, with the surf rolling high over the jetties." The boat negotiated the channel at 0100, but the ground elements failed to appear. Crossing to the north bank and harassed by machine guns, *Clymer's* men nonetheless severed the main cable at 0230. They returned to their ship with half the party wounded. When news of this success reached Rear Admiral Kelly he ordered *Dallas* up river.[42]

The 1st BLT's advancing columns encountered a machine-gun nest outside Port Lyautey at 0100. The troops flowed around this obstacle, but in the darkness and rain, the columns lost touch and drifted east and south of their intended line of advance. At 0300 an American squad encountered Colonel Petit who was out inspecting positions. According to the U.S. Army history, he was captured and paroled to the custody of Major Hamilton, who had been languishing at

French headquarters since his failed mission; from there Petit ordered his men to cease fire. According to a French historian, "he escaped with great difficulty." According to Petit himself, American troops stopped his car, but he slipped unseen out the door on the far side and, "taking a path next to a house and wading in a veritable stream," he returned to the city on foot.[43]

At 0400, as troops sparred outside Port Lyautey, *Dallas* steered toward the jetties. Due to "extremely low" visibility, the destroyer could not locate the river mouth until 0600 when *Roe* and *Livermore* took station off the breakwaters to guide her in. These two destroyers would also provide fire support should *Dallas* require. A French pilot with Gaullist sympathies took the helm; he had worked on the Wadi Sebou and had been smuggled out of Morocco for this specific mission. The seas were breaking astern and the ship yawed violently, but the pilot navigated the perilous passage only to ground on a bar just inside the channel. "A very heavy vibration was felt as the propellers dug into the mud. . . . The engine room called and proudly announced we were making twenty-five knots. A glance over the side, though, showed we were making less than five." As the destroyer plowed forward the barrier chain came into view. Although cut, anchored buoys held most of it in place. Accelerating to eighteen knots the destroyer kept to the deepest channel and at 0629 severed the hawser with scarcely a tremor. She rushed past the Kasba troubled by only a few small-caliber rounds.[44]

As *Dallas* neared the hairpin turn, periodically touching bottom in the ebbing tide, two *Savannah* Seagulls appeared overhead. French 75-mm rounds slashed the water two hundred yards short of target. The ship's 3-inch battery replied and silenced the enemy fire. Arriving at the bend, the pilot neatly slipped between the block ships even though one had capsized and was three-quarters submerged. *Dallas* scraped bottom again, but churned ahead at ten knots while making revolutions for twenty. At 0737 she reached the concrete ramp on the airfield's east side and the troops deployed rubber rafts. A 75-mm battery near the bridge two miles southeast opened rapid fire and shells splashed within ten yards of the ship. Buildings masked *Dallas's* guns so *Kearny* replied, discharging seventy-six rounds in ten minutes. Then a Seagull dived on the position and released two 325-pound depth charges that silenced the 75s. Although the captain assessed enemy gunfire as extremely accurate, no one on board *Dallas* was injured. The ship's only damage was five shell fragments found embedded in the shielding around the fire control platform.[45]

USS *Dallas*, an adapted *Clemson*-class destroyer, in the Wadi Sebou off the French naval air station. *Dallas* was two days late delivering her raiders to their objective but was still in time to help capture the airfield. (U.S. Army Signal Corps)

The troops from *Dallas* and I Company secured the airbase by 0800. The Americans were anxious to use the field and the first P-40 touched down at 1030. However, after seventeen aircraft were damaged on the cratered runway, *Chenango* discontinued launchings. The fighters landed over the next two days with some going to Cazès airfield near Casablanca.

Dallas anchored opposite the airfield as elements of the 1st Battalion's Company B occupied the southwestern corner of Port Lyautey surrounding the II/7 RTM, which was defending the city's western outskirts. With dawn, Companies C and D drove toward the airbase, surrounding the I/1 RTM in the process, two companies of which surrendered to men of B Company on the encirclement's eastern side. These troops had reached the racetrack southeast of Port Lyautey. However, realizing their position was exposed they began withdrawing with their prisoners and were, in turn, trapped by elements of the 7 RTM. The French took forty prisoners of their own, including Major McCarley, the battalion commander. The Americans were marched east, but at 1600 that afternoon during a meal break McCarley escaped into the woods and returned to friendly lines the next morning.[46]

In fact, the defense was beginning to crumble. Division General Maurice Mathenet, who had arrived from Petitjean to take command, ordered the Sebou highway bridge blasted, and Commander Cadoret directed the remaining ships in the port to scuttle. Companies C and D supported by Stuarts drove north through diminishing resistance, "accounting for four French antitank guns and twenty-eight machine guns." The column arrived at the airfield's western edge by 1045, in time to see P-40s landing.[47]

The Kasba was the other critical objective. The 2nd Battalion had been reinforced by a pair of assault guns and a provisional assault company of engineers, but elements of 7 RTM attacked first. The *tirailleurs* recaptured Batterie Ponsot and reached the lighthouse, but this was the resistance's last gasp. The assault guns led a counterattack and overran the battery, taking many prisoners. However, heavy fire kept them away from the Kasba itself. A flight of three TBFs armed with a dozen 100-pound bombs and four F4Fs that had been searching for artillery to attack were called in to hit the fort instead. At 1010 they conducted a glide attack from the north. Two TBFs released all their bombs, and the third just one. One of the fighters also dropped a pair of 100-pound bombs. When the dust and smoke cleared the Americans rushed the fort through the broken gate and gaps in the walls, and the 250 defenders surrendered after a short fight. Following this long-sought success the 2nd Battalion drove to the high ground southwest of the airfield, their H+6 objective.[48]

Amid the positive reports flowing into Truscott's command post were several troubling ones, including news that more French troops were approaching Port Lyautey from the east. Reconnaissance aircraft flew to investigate. One pilot from *Texas* later reported, "I found instead of tanks coming westward into Port Lyautey, motor trucks and vehicles were moving eastward leaving Port Lyautey." *Texas* bombarded the road between 0848 and 0951, expending 150 14-inch rounds, and from 1057 to 1131 shooting another sixty-four heavy shells. Afterward aircraft radioed that the road was "littered with wreckage and stalled vehicles."[49]

Reports about the supply situation also troubled Truscott. Food, fuel, and ammunition were running short and replenishments were not arriving ashore in the quantities required. *Clymer,* for example, had only eight boats available after strenuous salvage efforts. A crew recovered her second LCM "although broached broadside to the water and 30′ above high water line by proper use of a bulldozer and shovels." The fall of the Kasba meant that craft could finally use Brown Beach up the river, but this proved a mixed blessing because the small strip of sand was quickly congested and the high swell meant a wild passage between the jetties. *Penn's* LCM (17), loaded with a tank, capsized in the channel at 1045; fortunately the personnel made it to the jetty or were rescued by other boats.[50]

Submarine scares further impeded unloading. At 1041 *Roe* obtained a sound contact. All transports got under way while the destroyer crisscrossed the area and dropped depth charges at 1051, 1159, and again at 1258. At 1306 *Roe* and *Livermore,* which joined her, finally concluded that the contacts were reverberations from the bottom. This mistake cost hours of unloading time. *Algorab,* for example, had just anchored off the jetties at 1015. The alert forced her to get under way at 1033 and she did not return to the anchorage until 1452. *John Penn* started maneuvering at 1058 and did not anchor again until 1412. For *Clymer* the times were 1100 to 1424. Once unloading resumed the Navy employed captured shipping including a small tug and "Dutch and Belgian ships sabotaged by the Germans" to offset the landing craft shortage. *Contessa,* loaded with aviation fuel and munitions for Patrol Squadron 73, Navy Catalinas to be based at Port Lyautey, sailed upstream during the afternoon floodtide. She hit bottom above the port, so lighters transferred her cargo ashore.[51]

The fall of Port Lyautey and the airbase did not end the fighting. To the south reinforcements brought the armored battalion to a strength of seventeen Stuarts and two assault guns. This front was quiet until 1100 when twenty FT-17s appeared. After a short battle between six Stuarts supported by the assault guns and a section of six Renaults, naval gunfire and aircraft forced a French retreat. The pilot of a *Texas* Seagull reported, "I was ordered to strafe tanks which were attacking our troops about two miles south of the lagoon. TBF's and F4F's were already strafing and dive bombing. Occasionally a tank, official car, or truck would make a run for Rabat but few if any were successful."[52]

By 1730 Port Lyautey was considered secure. Organized resistance ceased at 0400 after Division General Mathenet received authorization to terminate hostilities, and at 0800 on 11 November a formal ceremony was held in the Kasba to mark this fact.

The End of the Operation

TG 34.8 remained in the area unloading supplies. On 11 November the seaplane tender *Barnegat* headed up river under the French pilot's guidance and at 1745 moored off the airport. On the 12th she began unloading her cargo of depth charges, aviation gasoline, and supplies and equipment. She also began salvaging the scuttled ships.

Surf remained a problem and several boats swamped trying to navigate the river mouth. At 2000 on the 11th unloading had to be suspended until the next day. Submarine alarms continued to disrupt. For example, on 12 November there were alarms at 1123 when *Livermore* attacked a contact. *Livermore, Parker,* and *Kearny* made additional attacks at 1133, 1226, 1320, 1340, and 1750. The surviving landing craft were being worked hard, and while several were salvaged, losses continued to accrue.[53]

The crews proved resourceful in using expedients to unload ships. On the 12th one of *Arundel's* men noticed a dredge lighter that had formed part of the net barrier. They towed it to the ship and, securing an LCP on each quarter, loaded it with 8,500 gallons of fuel. On the 13th poor visibility and heavy surf at the bar once again halted unloading from midnight until the next morning. On the 14th *Raven* and *Osprey* along with a small ex-Dutch steamer, *Export,* pitched in. Still, the swells and congested beaches continued to impede progress.[54]

Early on the 15th the transports proceeded to Casablanca. By this time *Allen* was only 60 percent discharged and only thirteen of her landing craft survived. At 0640 *U 173* torpedoed *Electra,* which was sailing independently. The explosion sparked a secondary blast from her cargo of ammunition and opened a hole nineteen by forty-three feet that filled two holds with water. *Electra* turned toward the beach, but the engines flooded at 0703. The destroyer *Cole* removed all hands except a salvage party at 0720. The tug *Cherokee,* along with the minesweepers *Raven* and *Stansbury,* stood by towing and pumping. Finally at 0400 on the 16th they successfully brought *Electra* to Casablanca. The ships were unloaded in Casablanca after two nights and one day of nonstop effort by stevedores and crew. *Clymer* landed about two thousand of the 3,400 tons of cargo she carried along with 130 vehicles and 1,400 troops.[55]

Two aspects of the operation stand out: the heavy loss of landing craft and the role of naval gunfire support. Heavy surf after the first day was a factor, but even on the 8th, despite relatively favorable conditions, losses were excessive, mainly due to boats being swamped and colliding. *Allen,* for example, lost twenty boats: nine were swamped, six suffered mechanical breakdowns, and collisions sank four. *Penn* recorded the loss of nine boats, all as the result of swamping. Only one of *Clymer's* thirteen LCVs survived. Boats were overloaded, risks were taken to bring supplies ashore, but the major problem was lack of operator experience. Overall, losses totaled 70 boats of 161 used.[56]

Naval shore fire successfully disrupted the movement of French reinforcements from the south. In the counterbattery role it reduced the effectiveness of French batteries. However, naval guns were underutilized, as reflected by the remarkably light expenditures of ammunition in this role. The failure to use *Texas* effectively on the first day was particularly unfortunate.

American forces prevailed in an unexpectedly hard fight, but they hardly distinguished themselves. Truscott had to prod his regimental and battalion commanders, although this also may have been his personal style. The U.S. Navy turned in a mixed performance, committing errors of navigation and failing to see all the boats to the right beaches. *Osprey* leading the 3rd Battalion so far astray was a particularly puzzling error. Nonetheless, in this, the most difficult of the nine major landings, the American forces persisted and prevailed over a stronger foe, a faulty plan, difficult geography, and unfavorable weather.

11

CASABLANCA

I'm just glad of just one thing—that I learned how to swim.
—S2C FRED BULLOCK, USS *LEONARD WOOD*

Plans and Objectives

Casablanca, the main American objective in Morocco, had a population of 260,000 and the most important harbor between Dakar and Oran. Forces assigned to capture the city were under the overall command of Maj. Gen. George S. Patton Jr. and included the 3rd Infantry Division (Maj. Gen. Jonathan Anderson) and its three regiments, the 7th (Col. Robert Macon), 30th (Col. Arthur H. Rogers), and 15th (Col. Thomas Monroe). The 7th and 30th were assault regiments and reinforced with fourteen hundred more men than the 15th. The 1st Battalion of the 67th Armored Regiment, units of the XII Air Support Command, an engineer, and a coastal artillery battalion completed the invasion force of 19,870 men and 1,701 vehicles.[1]

The plan called for four BLTs from the 7th and 30th regiments to land around Fédala, a fishing port fifteen miles northeast of Casablanca. Each regiment's third battalion would serve as floating reserve while the 15th Regiment would come ashore once the beachhead was secure.

The 1st BLT of the 7th Infantry under Lt. Col. Roy Moore was embarked on *Leonard Wood*. It was to land on Red 2 Beach, a twelve-hundred-yard strip of sand in the Bay of Fédala, and capture Fédala and the shore batteries located there. Lt. Col. Rafael Salzmann's 2nd BLT on board *Thomas Jefferson* was to

170

land at Red 3 Beach, separated from Red 2 by a rocky outcropping. This unit was to advance a mile inland and then swing west and secure the highway and railroad bridges over the Wadi Mellah (Mellah River). The regiment's reconnaissance troop, outfitted in black uniforms, was to paddle stealthily ashore to a small beach west of the Wadi Mellah called Yellow and help seize the Batterie de Fédala. The 3rd BLT's L Company was to follow over the same beach an hour later. The rest of the 3rd BLT was to arrive at Red 2 seventy minutes after the 1st BLT had landed.[2]

The 1st BLT of the 30th Regiment under Lt. Col. Fred Sladen was embarked on *Charles Carroll.* Their destination was Blue 1 Beach, immediately east of Red 3. This battalion would push inland five miles and seize a ridge south of the Casablanca-Rabat highway. Continuing east Lt. Col. Lyle W. Bernard's 2nd BLT was to land from *Joseph T. Dickman* on Blue 2 Beach, a cove just west of the Wadi Nefifik (Nefifik River). Their objective was the Batterie de Pont Blondin. After capturing these guns they were to block French reinforcements from Rabat. Company L of the 3rd Battalion was to land at Blue 3 Beach, three and a half miles east of Blue 2 Beach, and assault Pont Blondin from the other side. The 30th's 3rd BLT less Company L was to land on Red 3 ninety minutes after H hour. The 15th Infantry, the armor, and the engineers would deploy at Major General Patton's discretion.[3]

The Final Approach

After TGs 34.8 and 34.10 steered away for Safi and Mehdia, the rest of TF 34 continued toward the disembarkation area off Fédala. Rear Admiral Giffen's covering group (TG 34.1, with the battleship *Massachusetts* and the heavy cruisers *Wichita* and *Tuscaloosa*) was tasked with containing the French warships in Casablanca, neutralizing the immobile battleship *Jean Bart,* and guarding against a sortie by the other modern French battleship, *Richelieu.* That battleship, along with three light cruisers and three *contre-torpilleurs*, was based at Dakar, 1,350 miles south. Giffen had previously commanded Cruiser Division 7 in the Atlantic neutrality patrol. In April 1942, six months after attaining flag rank, he assumed command of TF 99, consisting of the battleship *Washington,* the cruisers *Wichita* and *Tuscaloosa,* and four destroyers, when his predecessor, Rear Adm. John W. Wilcox, fell overboard in the mid-Atlantic. The Air Group, TG 34.2 commanded by Rear Adm. Ernest McWhorter, had 110 aircraft embarked on the carriers *Ranger*

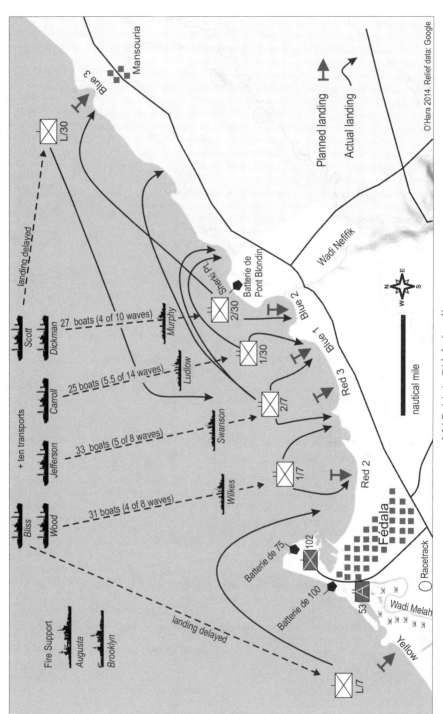

MAP 11.1 *Fédala Landings*

and *Suwannee*. McWhorter had previously commanded the Atlantic Fleet's air patrol wing and became Commander Carriers, Atlantic Fleet, in April.

Capt. Robert Emmet in *Leonard Wood* assumed command of the Central Attack Group, TG 34.9, consisting of the transports and the fire support group, at 1500 on 7 November. He needed to guide his sixteen transports to the designated anchorage six miles off Fédala in time for them to start launching landing craft at midnight. The landings were to commence at 0400 so the troops could secure their initial objectives before dawn.

As the transports approached the coast, Emmet sent the destroyer *Boyle* ahead to locate the picket submarine, *Gunnel*. The captain of *Charles Carroll* wrote, "The sea was smooth as glass, except for swells. The stars were out and the night seemed to be made 'to order.' Great cheerfulness and enthusiasm prevailed among crew and troops. . . . We were marking in to the 'kill.'" At 2137 radar revealed shoreline twenty-five miles away and the loom of the El Hank lighthouse emerged through the dark and the intermittent rain squalls. An unexpected northeasterly current, however, caused confusion. "To rectify navigational position" the formation made a series of course adjustments, generally in 45-degree increments from due south to due east and then back again to south by southeast. On *Carroll* "this atmosphere [of cheerfulness] did not prevail very long, because showers of rain made station keeping difficult, especially as changes in speed were being made. . . . At one time this vessel could not see any other ship in the convoy. . . . At 2327 an emergency turn of 45 degrees to starboard was executed. Was this a submarine contact? At 2343 another emergency turn of 45 degrees was executed." Not all transports had TBS (talk between ships VHF radio), and instructions had stressed that turns would be made in increments of not more than 5 degrees, at five-minute intervals. Not surprisingly, when the screened lights of the column leaders disappeared, the rear vessels became disoriented, and the four columns of transports "straggled badly."[4]

Leonard Wood stopped at 2353. Radar alerted Emmet to the disorder and he dispatched destroyers to collect the lost transports. However, this proved a lengthy process, and some ships took four hours to reach position. These delays played havoc with the complicated landing plan that required the lost vessels to lend landing craft to the assault transports for the initial waves.

Emmet had expected to rely on *Gunnel's* signals to pinpoint his position, but the submarine was invisible and static drowned the designated radio channel. In fact, *Boyle* found *Gunnel* at 2312 and both the destroyer and submarine were in position by 2330. Her captain noted that El Hank light switched off at 2347. At 0012 on the 8th the destroyer ceased signaling and proceeded to screen the transport area to the west as per orders. Although the marker vessels remained invisible, *Leonard Wood* lowered the first boats at 0012. Four destroyers—*Wilkes, Swanson, Ludlow,* and *Murphy*—were to lead the assault waves and then provide gunfire support. Scout boats would sail well ahead of the landing waves to ensure proper navigation.[5]

French Dispositions

French defenses around Fédala consisted of the 102 Coastal Defense Company of the 6 RTS, a section of tanks, and the 53 DCA with four old 105-mm weapons.[6] More worrisome to the Americans were Batterie de Fédala and Batterie de Pont Blondin. In a pre-operation conference Emmet had gone so far as to assert, "It would be worth two destroyers to knock those guns out." The Batterie de Fédala included three 100-mm and two 75-mm weapons. Fifty-four troops under a naval officer, Lieutenant Salmon, manned the positions. The Batterie de Pont Blondin had four 138-mm guns, one of which was inoperable, and fifty-four men under a chief petty officer. The auxiliary minesweeper *Abbé Desgranges* was docked in Fédala's little harbor.[7]

The Landings

At 0145 the scout boats from *Wood, Dickman,* and *Carroll* set out to mark their beaches. *Jefferson*'s boat had engine problems and followed fifteen minutes later. At 0306 Captain Emmet postponed the landing by a half hour because, as Capt. R. G. Coman, commander of Transport Division 3, complained, "None of the [assigned] landing craft arrived as scheduled." *Dickman*'s report noted, "Only one boat out of twenty allocated from other units reported." *Carroll* wrote, "A careful lookout was maintained for the boats [but] none were seen anywhere. . . . No little confusion resulted." Overall, six boats from *Procyon* failed to report to *Wood* on time because *Procyon* did not finish launching her boats until 0545. It was worse elsewhere. Thirty boats were supposed to join *Carroll* from *Oberon* (fourteen), *Hugh L. Scott* (four), *Stanton* (one), *Thurston* (one), and *Arcturus* (ten). *Dickman* needed twenty from *Hugh L. Scott* (nine), *Stanton* (one), and *Arcturus* (ten). These stragglers did not begin lowering their boats until much later than the assault transports. For example, *Edward Rutledge* and *Ancon* did not even reach the disembarkation area until 0330.[8]

The Batterie d'El Hank west of Casablanca. The four 138.6-mm guns are visible in the lower right of the photograph while the main 194-mm guns were emplaced in the structure facing the ocean above the pier at the top center. The battery was intensely bombarded by *Massachusetts*, heavy cruisers, and navy bombers but remained largely undamaged until the 11 November armistice. (U.S. Naval Institute Photo Archive)

These delays forced *Carroll* and *Dickman* to shift personnel and equipment and dispatch their assault waves using organic boats only. There were other problems. On board *Jefferson* someone sliced the lashings on a debarkation net, and when laden soldiers began descending, the ropes snapped, dumping several men into the ocean. All nets had to be checked before unloading could continue. The landings were postponed another fifteen minutes to 0445, but the scout boats never received word and duly began flashing blinkers at 0350. Not until 0402 did the abbreviated landing waves start, following the control destroyers on the hour-long run to the release point.[9]

Wilkes led thirty-one boats comprising four of *Wood*'s eight scheduled waves for Red 2. The reconnaissance platoon from *Tasker H. Bliss* assigned to Yellow Beach as part of this wave never arrived. *Swanson* led thirty-three boats comprising five of the eight scheduled waves from *Jefferson* for Red 3. *Ludlow* led twenty-five boats comprising five and a half of *Carroll*'s fourteen scheduled waves for Blue 1 (fewer boats per wave because of the constricted approaches). *Murphy* led twenty-seven boats comprising four of ten scheduled waves from *Dickman* for Blue 2. *Scott*'s boats carrying Company L/30 for Blue 3 did not appear until 0645.[10]

Wood's boat group commander commented, "On a dark night with no land-marks it is extremely difficult not to get lost." He lost track of *Wilkes* while assisting a disabled landing craft, which forced him to navigate alone, "guiding by occasional glimpses on Polaris astern." Nonetheless, most boats followed their destroyers without problem and by 0500 all the scout craft were in view and "observed to be blinking violently." The control destroyers accordingly released their waves for the final run to shore. So far, all had been quiet and the men hunkered down in their small boats had reason to be optimistic.[11]

In fact, the French had several forewarnings. At 0210 Pont Blondin reported unidentified speedboats. Then Vice Admiral Michelier ordered an alert after Brigade General Béthouart's failed coup. At 0338 Cape Fédala reported engine noises offshore but saw nothing suspicious. At 0400 lookouts spotted a light flashing out to sea. At first Lieutenant Salmon, who had just arrived from Casablanca, presumed these were fishing vessels. Shortly after 0500 he ordered the Pont Blondin searchlight to search the water, but this revealed nothing. Then the control arm malfunctioned and the light unintentionally swept the beach. It momentarily illuminated a landing craft that, incidentally, the operators did not notice.[12]

American accounts time this event at 0515 (*Ludlow*), 0516 (*Murphy*), 0523 (*Brooklyn*), or 0530 (*Wilkes*), and all relate that a light on Cape Fédala briefly flashed vertical. The support boats swung their machine guns on the light and sprayed the area with bullets, "ineffectively as far as could be ascertained from the *Wilkes*." Pont Blondin returned fire briefly. *Wood*'s boat group commander wrote that the shooting started at 0523 and lasted ten to fifteen minutes. He said that machine guns from Cape Fédala also fired but were ineffective. These were the Naval Battle of Casablanca's first shots.[13]

Going from west to east the initial waves had the following experiences:

- Red 2. The 7th Regiment's 1st BLT from *Wood* landed at 0515. *Wood* was a Coast Guard–manned transport, so the boat crews and coxswains had more small-craft experience than most of the Navy-manned boats. However, the scout boat had drifted east and was off the rocky outcrop between beaches Red 2 and 3. The coxswains were instructed to keep the scout boat to port, which they did, so the error in position resulted in many boats running full gun onto the rocks. The boat group commander reported that "some of the boats . . . backed off and found the correct beach and landed there. The majority of coxswains held their boats on the rocks while troops disembarked. Those boats that were not then too badly damaged backed off. . . . A great many of them, however, were in a sinking condition and were abandoned." Overall, twenty-one of thirty-one boats in the first four waves were wrecked. The troops lost or soaked much equipment coming ashore. The unit's commander, Lieutenant Colonel Moore, landed at 0530. By 0600, after swimming and struggling over rocks, he joined Companies A and C concentrating behind Red 2.[14]

- Red 3. BLT 2/7 from *Jefferson* was jinxed from the beginning. Engine problems forced her scout boat to proceed independently without receiving the corrected compass bearing. She strayed miles east of the assigned position and started flashing off a rocky cove on the wrong side of Sherki Point. Relying on this signal, the control vessel, *Swanson,* took the wrong position as well. The Wave 1 leader deployed his boats for landing. Then, he reported, "At this point I could see the surf breaking on huge rocks and that there wasn't a beach to land on." He backed off just in time except for one boat that tore its bottom on the rocks. Wave 1 returned and informed the scout boat of the problem. The boats then headed west searching for the proper beach. "On looking back," the wave leader continued, "I saw a group of boats which I took for the 2nd wave. We tried to stop them from landing on the rocks by shouting but to no avail." After finding what seemed to be a sandy beach, Wave 1 came ashore. Nonetheless, four boats hit submerged rocks. In Boat 1 a crewman swam to shore with a line and the boat was unloaded by having the soldiers grasp the rope until they could "get to the rocks where they could walk onto the beach." The wave's other two boats beached successfully, but only one could retract.[15]

The second and third waves landed between Blue 2 and Blue 3, two to three miles too far east. The Wave 2 leader followed the scout boat's lights until they suddenly vanished (when the scout boat discovered it was in the wrong location), so he proceeded by compass, "scraped over rocks beneath the water and then crashed into a rock ahead." The other five boats backed off and landed a mile even farther east. Wave 3 also saw the lights disappear and proceeded "by compass, which was totally unreliable, and by instinct." The leader tried to pick out landmarks, but "the whole coastline looked much the same and each beach seemed to answer the description . . . we were given of Red 3." Wave 3 finally went in realizing too late they had the wrong beach. The boats scraped onto rocks four hundred yards east of Sherki Point where the ebbing tide stranded them. Some men were reluctant to get wet and had to be "coaxed." The battery was under fire by this time and splinters from American shells damaged two landing craft. The wave leader noted, "My wave suffered most from the barrage of our own guns for this barrage killed eight men. We lost no men in the landing itself." Wave 4 hit Bluc 2, close to its correct location. One LCV ground up on a rock twenty-five feet offshore, and when the coxswain lowered the ramp, it filled with water. Wave 5 landed on Blue 1 at 0605, losing one boat "hopelessly beached on rock and leaking badly." There was heavy artillery fire and shrapnel caused several casualties. Sixteen of *Jefferson's* boats were lost and six damaged. The thirty-three boats in the first five waves landed along a five-mile span.[16]

- Blue 1. This narrow cove framed by rocky outcroppings was the destination of the 30th Regiment's 1st BLT from *Carroll*. Heavy stress placed on beach recognition during the voyage paid off as the majority of craft deposited their men on target, except for part of Company C and the Headquarters section, which landed east of Sherki. However, eighteen of *Carroll's* boats were wrecked in the first landing and five more in the second: three due to flooded engines, four by collision, four on the rocks, ten by broaching, and two to other causes. This included Lieutenant Colonel Sladen's craft that foundered, forcing the battalion commander to swim ashore. Lack of experience was a major cause. "Boats that had been broached were abandoned at the critical time when a little judgment might have saved them. And having been abandoned to the mercy of the surf, soon were hopelessly battered to pieces." A correspondent, Harold Boyle, who was in the third wave, dramatically recalled his experience: "There came a grinding crash as our landing boat smashed full speed into a coral reef. . . . We plunged from the sides of the settling craft up to our armpits in the surf and struggled to the reef. Waves washed over our heads, doubling the weight of our 60-pound packs with water, but sweeping us nearer safety." Machine guns on Pont Blondin harassed all but the first wave.[17]

American soldiers landing near Fédala on 8 November 1942. There is very little surf and the beach has a slight gradient, but there are clearly underwater troughs. In places the water is ankle deep fifty yards from shore and knee deep ten yards out. (U.S. Naval Institute Photo Archive)

- Blue 2. The sandy outlet of the Wadi Nefifik was the 30th's 2nd BLT's destination. Technically, this was the most difficult beach, but *Dickman's* Coast Guard–manned craft met the challenge. All twenty-seven boats but two threaded their way into the cove and landed as planned, unloaded, and successfully extracted before dawn. The two delayed boats, one of which carried Lieutenant Colonel Bernard, strayed east. When the bombardment against the Batterie de Pont Blondin began, Bernard decided to land east of the battery. Both boats were wrecked coming ashore.[18]

- Blue 3. *Hugh L. Scott,* the next-to-last transport in the eastern column, was late arriving at the disembarkation point. Her boats assigned to land Company L, 30th Regiment L/30 on Blue 3 Beach missed the rendez-vous with *Murphy* and did not arrive until 0645. At that time Captain Emmet ordered them to head for Blue 1 instead.

French Convoys

The U.S. sailors remarked how, when they approached the coast, navigation lights were burning at El Hank and Fédala. This was because several convoys were at sea. One had just arrived at Casablanca from Dakar and two were due in from Oran. All ran afoul of the invasion fleet.

Convoy R 41 had left Oran for Casablanca on 5 November and included *Lorrain* (3,819 GRT), *Capitaine Paul Lemerle* (4,945 GRT), the trawlers *Porrou* and *Joseph-Elise*, and their escort, the auxiliary corvette *Victoria.* At 0505 *Tillman,* screening the oiler *Miantonomah* east of the anchorage, beheld *Lorrain* steering straight for the transports at twelve knots, burning her running lights and displaying an illuminated French flag on either side. The destroyer signaled her to reverse course, punctuating the order with a 20-mm burst. *Lorrain* attempted to contact *Victoria,* which was following some distance astern, but the minesweeper *Hogan* had already accosted the French corvette.

Hogan had left station at 0515 "to investigate two vessels with running lights on approaching Fédala on a course which would take them through the transport anchorage." The minesweeper placed herself across *Victoria's* bow and broadcast bilingual orders to come about. Instead *Victoria* steered to ram. *Hogan* backed and sent a burst of .30 caliber across the corvette's bow. *Victoria* fired back to hit, so *Hogan* blasted her with 150 rounds from her three 20-mm guns, "obtaining a great many hits in hull and superstructure" and wounding six of the crew. According to *Hogan's* report, *Victoria* hove to and at 0545 the minesweeper returned to her duties. *Victoria's* captain reported that he masked his running lights and turned toward the coast. However, a destroyer blocked his way and he saw by her flag she was American. This was the minesweeper *Auk.* The French captain stopped, "thinking to be able to escape later." However, as the light grew he saw that he was in the midst of "a large naval force." *Auk* dispatched a boat at 0600 and *Victoria's* captain acceded to force majeure. The minesweepers put prize crews on board the rest of the convoy's ships.[19]

Meanwhile, *Lorrain* had turned toward shore. *Tillman* sent more 20-mm rounds across the steamer's bow, and when that had no effect the destroyer aimed a single 5-inch round that burst on *Lorrain's* funnel and peppered the ship with splinters. This was at 0605, according to *Tillman's* report. The ship halted a half mile from the coast. *Tillman,* thinking her target had grounded, returned to screening duties.[20]

The other convoy approached Fédala six hours later. This was Convoy R 42, which had already run through the American task group off Mehdia. At 1100 *Tillman* spotted vessels approaching down the coast and at 1135 left station to investigate. She approached *Estafette* and signaled the escort to follow her to Fédala. *Estafette's* commander, Lieutenant Perrin, instead ordered the convoy to head for shore and scuttle. He ignored *Tillman's* increasingly strident signals until he finally replied that honor forbade him from following the destroyer's orders. At 1235 *Tillman* laid a 5-inch round across the escort's bow. *Estafette* rapidly fired five 75-mm rounds in reply. This provoked several full 5-inch salvos from *Tillman.* The second obliterated the escort's bridge and killed Perrin. On fire and severely damaged *Estafette* eventually ran aground. The larger ships evacuated passengers and crews and scuttled. The three trawlers survived and on the 10th an American warship conducted them into Fédala.[21]

The Bombardment of Fédala

The four control destroyers were supposed to vacate their exposed positions near the beach before morning twilight lest they be sitting ducks for the shore batteries. However, because the landings had been so delayed and there had been no resistance, Cdr. Edward R. Durgin of Destroyer Division 26 on board *Wilkes,* decided to linger on the departure line. Shortly after 0604 *Wilkes's* executive officer saw a light flare up at the northern tip of Cape Fédala. He remarked to the captain that it looked like a gun flash. An instant later a geyser erupted four hundred yards to port. The next salvo straddled. *Wilkes's* weapons barked in reply as she rushed to get under way. Batterie de Fédala's 75-mm guns in fact loosed the first shots, but they were quickly followed by 100-mm shells. The French recorded the time as 0607.[22]

Meanwhile, six miles offshore *Brooklyn* had closely observed the searchlight-instigated exchange of fire. The light cruiser radioed Captain Emmet that she was "moving into position to take care of eventualities." At 0614 Emmet picked up the TBS and ordered, "Play Ball," the code term authorizing his forces to open fire. At 0618 *Brooklyn* launched a spotter aircraft and a minute later lofted star-shells over Pont Blondin, although these failed to penetrate the haze. Meanwhile, *Ludlow* and *Murphy* targeted Pont Blondin at 0614 and 0616, respectively. *Swanson* joined *Wilkes* against Fédala at 0625.[23]

At 0620 a round from *Wilkes* struck an oil storage tank on Cape Fédala (purportedly the only one actually containing oil), igniting a fire and sending black smoke roiling out to sea. Another hit the battery's range finder. After a quarter hour "the smoke of bursting shells, of burning buildings, and of oil tanks ablaze, combined with the early morning low-lying haze or ground fog, completely obliterated the shore line of the Fédala area."[24]

At 0621 *Murphy* reported she was dodging straddles and requested *Brooklyn's* support. The light cruiser probed with three-gun salvos fine-tuned with aerial corrections. When she believed she was on, fifteen-gun rapid-fire salvos followed. From 0622 to 0649 *Brooklyn* blasted the battery with 363 HC 6-inch rounds, pausing periodically to let smoke and dust clear. Her report later noted that with several ships firing on the same target, "some erroneous spotting, with attendant misses resulted." The men of the 7th Regiment's 2nd Battalion who had landed next to the battery by mistake could attest to this.[25]

At 0643 a 138-mm round struck *Murphy,* penetrated the after engine space on the port side, and exploded in the crew's quarters. The ship lost power aft but could still steam on her starboard engine. Her captain, Lt. Cdr. Leonard W. Bailey, noted that because the other destroyers had withdrawn to their shore bombardment positions, *Murphy* was "presenting a solitary target to the one remaining gun firing from [Sherki]. This gun peppered splashes at us all the way out to 9000 yards." He also proudly noted that 60 percent of *Murphy's* crew had less than a year's service, but that "this ship whose inexperienced loading crews had never yet fired a practice without various foolish personnel errors and loading casualties, expended some 486 rounds, generally in full 4-gun salvoes, without casualty interruptions."[26]

Having driven off *Murphy*, Batterie de Pont Blondin targeted the transports at 0656 with ten rounds. Then *Brooklyn's* 6-inch shells started raining in once again. The cruiser's second salvo killed three men and disabled the battery's rangefinder. Within minutes Pont Blondin was completely obscured by smoke and the guns ceased fire. *Brooklyn* remained in action until 0728, expending another 569 6-inch rounds.[27]

As the larger French guns targeted warships and transports, the lighter weapons focused on landing craft. At 0645 *Jefferson's* scout boat reported that "shrapnel was whipping the water into foam" off the beaches just east of Blondin; when the boat headed toward Cape Fédala it drew fire from the 75-mm battery. Eight shells splashed within twenty-five yards before, at 0740, one struck the craft's bow and sank her. At 0820 *Jefferson's* boat group commander was a thousand yards offshore leading a wave of thirty boats when the 75-mm guns engaged his flotilla. His report also complained that "the beaches were strafed and bombed by enemy planes unopposed by friendly aircraft." The beach master for Red 2 related, "When about five miles away from Beach Red-2, the coastal battery at [Sherki] opened fire on us and the shells started dropping all around the boats, and after getting in a little closer the batteries at Fedala and one battery on Cape Fedala also opened fire on us. . . . As we got closer to Fedala, the shelling became heavier, and although some were close enough to splash water into the boat, there were no direct hits until we stopped on the beach." After landing, a shell smashed his boat. He also noted, "All boats that landed on Beach Red-2 on the morning of D-day, that could not get off the beach right away were destroyed by gun fire from the batteries at Cape Fedala."[28]

During this time *Augusta* was circling 14,000 yards offshore. She had launched four aircraft but could not establish radio contact with them. This, along with the smoke and haze, made accurate gunnery impossible. Nonetheless, between 0710 and 0717 she discharged five nine-gun salvos at Cape Fédala. The battery fired back. "No direct hits were made on the ship, although several came very close." Between 0723 and 0726 the heavy cruiser loosed another eighteen rounds from ranges under ten thousand yards. One damaged Fédala's fire control station and wounded Lieutenant Salmon.[29]

At 0738 Pont Blondin's guns flung another ten rounds at the transports. *Brooklyn* responded, with her last salvo discharged at 0749. Pont Blondin was in any case finished as troops were assaulting the perimeter. During ninety minutes of action the battery had fired 150 138-mm rounds and had lost eleven men killed and six wounded. Otherwise the results achieved by the storm of American shellfire were, according to a French account, "mediocre."[30]

The Fall of Fédala

Despite losing so many boats the 3rd Division landed nearly thirty-five hundred men—most relatively near their objectives—with forty-five minutes of dark and twilight remaining. Given the twelve-to-one superiority in troops and the powerful naval support they enjoyed, the landings would have succeeded even had they been more confused and dispersed than they already were, but casualties were reduced because the commander of the Senegalese 102nd Coastal Defense Company had received Brigade General Béthouart's orders to welcome the Americans. At 0600—with telephone connections out and the naval batteries clearly following a different policy—he traveled to Lieutenant Salmon's command post to confirm these instructions. Salmon informed him the orders were to fight the invaders. They fired a red flare to signal this, but it was misinterpreted or disregarded by nearly all troops.[31]

Elements of the 1st BLT, 7th Regiment, entered Fédala before dawn, "passing along the way small groups of Senegalese who gave no trouble." At 0630 Company A's 1st Platoon captured the Hôtel Miramar, headquarters of the Axis Armistice Commission. The commission head escaped, but American troops nabbed nine other members and a treasure trove of documents.[32]

Company C entered the town to attack the 100-mm battery from the rear, but U.S. naval gunfire stopped it 150 yards from its objective. After shelling wounded several men the company withdrew three hundred yards and then, at 0945, retreated farther south to the racetrack to wait out the bombardment. However, this put the troops into 53 DCA's line of fire. Pinned by Hotchkiss guns, the Americans replied with their heaviest weapon, a bazooka, and at 1100 secured the unit's surrender.

Four Stuarts of the 765th Tank Battalion reinforced Company A at 0900, but hindered by the naval bombardment, the attack against the 100-mm battery developed at a snail's pace. The battery finally surrendered at 1230 after suffering nineteen casualties. It had expended six hundred 100-mm rounds. After taking twenty-two prisoners Company A pushed on and captured the 75-mm battery at 1500. This position had been particularly pesky, sinking boats and constantly driving shore parties to cover.

Within the port the minesweeper *Abbé Desgranges* fired her machine gun on landing craft as opportunity presented. Naval gunfire damaged her slightly at 0620 and then more seriously at 0730 when two shells fell close alongside, staving in the hull and sinking the trawler *Jeanne d'Arc* moored alongside. *Abbé Desgranges* machine gunned troops from Company B as they entered the port at 1330 and was subjected to heavy automatic weapons fire in return. Finally, after running out of ammunition, the minesweeper scuttled at 1430.

The 7th/2nd BLT's Companies E and F, which had landed far out of place beyond Sherki Point, reached their initial objectives, the road and rail crossings over the Wadi Mellah, at 1700 after a long march punctuated by occasional strafing attacks. Company G was scattered from Red 3 Beach to locations east of Sherki. Lieutenant Colonel Salzmann of the 2nd, who also landed east of Sherki, mustered most of Company G and a section of mortars from Company H and led an attack against Pont Blondin from the east.

After organizing themselves most of the 30th Regiment's 1st BLT Companies B, C, and D moved south from Blue Beach. At 0700 they intercepted a train and captured seventy-five French soldiers. They reached their objective line by 1600. The 30th/2nd Battalion's Company F spearheaded the attack on Pont Blondin from the west. It crossed the Wadi Nefifik, but *Brooklyn's* 0656 bombardment killed six men and halted its advance. After the cruiser ceased fire at 0728 Company F moved out again. Pressured from both sides, Batterie de Pont Blondin surrendered at 0800.

Radio communications were established between the 7th Regiment and *Wood* at 1123. *Carroll* and the 30th Regiment had a connection by 1225. Tactical networks for beach-to-beach, shore party–to–advanced command post, and boat-control communications did not function as intended. Telephone wires were laid on the first day, and these provided the major link between command posts, beach masters, and division.[33]

D Day Logistics

The 3rd Division's headquarters and most of its remaining combat troops came ashore during the balance of the 8th. The 30th/3rd BLT landed between 0830 and 1030, mostly on the Red Beaches. The 7th/3rd BLT began disembarking at 0930 on Red 3, "an operation which continued for a considerable period because of the shortage in serviceable landing craft." At noon Patton decided to land the 15th Regiment, a process that stretched on until after dark. The 3rd Division's Maj. Gen. Jonathan Anderson reached shore at 1030 and Patton at 1320, getting wet in the process. The vast majority of troops used either Red or Blue Beach, but there were several outliers. Four landing craft from *William P. Biddle* loaded with 113 men of a military police company set out for Yellow Beach and got lost. Two of them ended up hailing a French patrol boat off Casablanca, thinking anything afloat was friendly. The vessel sank both of the landing craft and took the survivors prisoner. On the extreme far side of the landing zone three amphtracs bound for Blue 2 broke down and drifted northeast. A scout boat was sent to bring them back along the coast and land at the first available beach. Two other stray landing craft joined and the miniflotilla finally beached at 0945 at a cove halfway to Rabat. Besieged by French troops they held out two days before running out of ammunition and surrendering. Thus, a span of twenty-five miles separated the southwestern-most from the northeastern-most landing points.[34]

Around 1500 the transports moved farther inshore and by 1542 *Wood* was anchored six thousand yards north of Cape Fédala. Unloading continued and by 1700, 39 percent of the troops had landed. The transports *Wood, Jefferson, Carroll, Dickman,* and *Hewes* had all discharged at least 90 percent of their troops, and *Bliss* and *Scott* had discharged 25 and 10 percent, respectively. The rest of the transports remained fully loaded. Sixteen percent (270 of 1,701) of vehicles had landed, mostly from the four assault transports. However, only 1.1 percent (165 of 15,000 tons) of supplies was ashore. The Americans captured Fédala intact, and the port's daily capacity of four hundred tons could be expanded to a thousand using lighters. Much unloading remained to be done.[35]

The Bombardment of Casablanca

On the evening of 7 November a major convoy had just arrived at Casablanca from Dakar, with another from Dakar and two more from Oran expected. The fates of Convoys R 41 and R 42 from Oran have been described. D 61 from Dakar—*Porthos, Savoie, Lipari, Fort de Douaumont, Vendome,* and *Ville du Havre* escorted by the sloop *La Grandière*—began docking at 0650 on 7 November and the last ship tied up at 2330.

At 0520 Vice Admiral Michelier dispatched five submarines to patrol off Casablanca. *Méduse* was under way at 0550 followed by *Orphée* at 0553, *Amazone* at 0613, *Antiope* at 0630, and *La Sibylle* at 0704. As *Antiope* emerged from the harbor her captain saw "the horizon to the north-east . . . suddenly lit-up with the blinding flashes of large naval guns." Reports from *Lorrain,* from Safi, from *Victoria,* and from Pont Blondin began flooding Michelier's headquarters. At 0630 he ordered the warships of the 2nd Light Squadron to raise steam and attack enemy forces off Fédala. Dawn was still twenty minutes away and a thick haze smothered the shoreline.[36]

While the French mustered a naval response, Rear Admiral Giffen's TG 34.1 was fifteen miles off Casablanca with *Massachusetts* in the lead followed by *Tuscaloosa* and *Wichita*. The destroyers *Wainwright* and *Mayrant* screened to starboard and *Rhind* and *Jenkins* to port. Farther out sailed McWhorter's Air Group TG 34.2. At 0615 the carriers started launching eighteen F4F Wildcats assigned to suppress Rabat's Salé airfield. At 0635 seventeen SBDs followed. Their mission was to strike hostile submarines, then surface ships, and finally shore batteries. At 0700 eighteen F4Fs lifted off to strafe Casablanca's Cazès airfield. Sixteen F4Fs assigned to support the Fédala landings followed. *Suwannee* put eight F4Fs

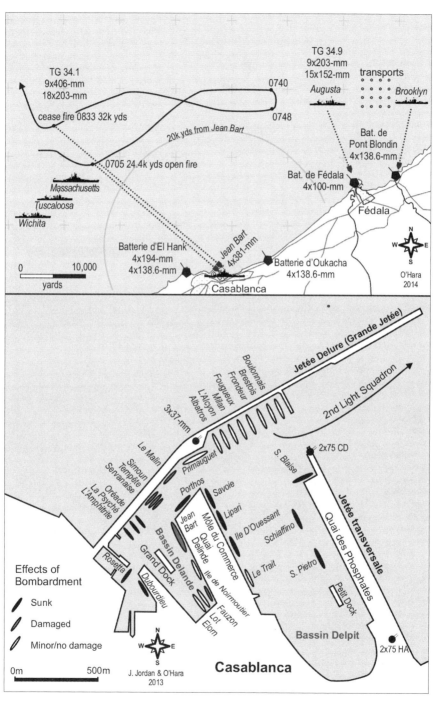

MAP 11.2 *Bombardment of Casablanca*

over the task group at 0635 as combat air patrol, and at 0700 eight TBFs armed with four 500-pound bombs soared into the sky to attack submarines and hostile shipping. One TBF crashed taking off.[37]

Even before the carrier fighters and bombers roared off flight decks the ships of TG 34.1 started launching their own aircraft. At 0610 *Tuscaloosa* catapulted four and *Wichita* three Seagulls for spotting and antisubmarine patrol. *Massachusetts* launched Vought OS2U-3 Kingfisher spotters at 0618 and 0620. As the planes circled over the city, several warned that submarines and destroyers were standing out of the harbor. Heavy flak assailed one that buzzed the port. Then French Hawk 75As out of Cazès attacked. Four went after two *Tuscaloosa* Seagulls over the city. One Seagull escaped with a spiraling plunge into the clouds while the other dove toward the cover of friendly flak. As they fled, the rear gunner helped the pilot avoid French bullets. "[He] would say 'NOW' . . . and I would do a vertical turn to whichever side seemed best. As we turned [he] would open up with the free gun." This spotter claimed it sent one attacker off in smoke.[38]

French fighters also harassed floatplanes from *Wichita* and *Massachusetts*. At 0659 one of the Kingfishers radioed to *Massachusetts*, "Am coming in on starboard bow with couple hostile aircraft on my tail. Pick them off—I am the one in front." The battleship obliged with thirty-five 5-inch rounds and other ships joined in. *Wainwright* fired eighty 5-inch rounds out to 13,000 yards "before the planes maneuvered away." Beginning at 0701 *Wichita* expended 215 5-inch rounds against fighters that chased her SOCs to within four thousand yards of the cruiser's battery. The Americans believed they downed one fighter while French gunfire wounded the pilot of a *Wichita* SOC-1 and forced it to make a hard landing off Casablanca. A fishing vessel rescued the crew. Following these attacks Rear Admiral Hewitt broadcast the order, "Play Ball as to planes."[39]

At 0705 the Batterie d'El Hank loosed a four-gun 194-mm salvo at *Massachusetts* (0703 by the battleship's clock) near the limit of the battery's 25,000-meter range. The green gouts of water that splashed nearby made it clear that French resistance off Fédala was no anomaly. *Massachusetts* immediately turned 40 degrees from due east to northeast and a minute later opened fire on *Jean Bart* from 24,400 yards. *Tuscaloosa* targeted the submarine berthing area, range 28,000 yards, while *Wichita* answered El Hank from 21,800 yards.[40]

At 0708 *Jean Bart*'s four-gun 15-inch turret entered the fray. Her first two-round salvo—fired from 22,000 meters and marked by yellow dye—dropped six hundred yards off *Massachusetts*'s starboard bow. The next, fired at 0711, splashed close to port. El Hank's aim was also good. The battleship's chronology recorded "very large" yellow and green splashes falling "close aboard" to starboard at 0711 and to port at 0713. However, the French could barely discern their maneuvering targets and the battleship fired only two more salvos: one at 0716 of two rounds and the last of one round at 0719.[41]

The Americans had targeting problems of their own. The harbor was curtained in smoke and after the third salvo a tube failure caused *Massachusetts*'s fire control FC Mk 3 radar to blink out. It was not repaired until that afternoon forcing her to fight the entire day—save her last two salvos—without this radar. Then the massive concussion from the second nine-gun main battery salvo blew the fuses on two FD Mk 4 (antiaircraft fire control) radars. Air spot was initially unavailable as her Kingfishers were busy dodging unfriendly fighters. For the first fifteen minutes the battleship, using indirect fire based on a bearing obtained from the El Hank light, shot ineffectively. When the aircraft did begin to spot, smoke over the harbor hampered their observations. They reported range accurately but not deflection. However, seventeen SBDs were now orbiting Casablanca loaded with 500-pound bombs and at 0710 they struck.[42]

The first vessels hit in this aero-naval barrage were a small tug holed by a bomb, and *Saint Blaise,* an ex-Danish steamer being used as a prison hulk, flooded after a shell cracked her hull. The captain of the submarine *Le Tonnant,* rushing orders for his boat and *Sidi-Ferruch* to put to sea, had just arrived at the jetty when a blast killed him and seriously wounded *Sidi-Ferruch*'s skipper. The executive officers of the two submarines cast off immediately after witnessing this tragedy. The submarine *Conquérant* got under way at 0800 shortly before a 16-inch round pulverized the dock where she had been berthed, but bombs sank her sisters *L'Amphitrite, Oréade,* and *La Psyché* at their moorings. SBDs also hit *Jean Bart* at 0718 with a 500-pound bomb that detonated on the battleship's port catapult mounting. This ignited a small fire and caused minor flooding. A second bomb exploded alongside the battleship and holed the hull plating aft abreast Boiler Room No. 2. American gunfire did not register until 0725 when a 2,700-pound 16-inch projectile bashed the battleship aft on the shelter deck, slicing through two armored decks before exploding in an empty 152-mm magazine. Despite the rain of shells El Hank fought back. From the decks of *Massachusetts,* it seemed to one participant that "throughout this action, heavy stuff was whizzing over . . . and splashing in the water close aboard."[43]

The incomplete French battleship *Jean Bart* at Casablanca. Only one of her two four-gun turrets had been fitted before her 1940 flight from France. It was, however, fully operational and on 10 November fired nine salvos at USS *Augusta*, causing the heavy cruiser to break off an action against a French warship and flee out of range. (U.S. Naval Institute Photo Archive)

The destroyers of the 2nd Light Squadron were berthed in the line of fire, but remarkably, as they raised steam and recalled men and officers, the operational vessels escaped damage. Nearest the exit, *Boulonnais* cast off her aft mooring buoy prematurely and fouled the jetty, but *Brestois* was in the roadstead by 0737, followed by *Frondeur*. The ships masked their movement with smoke, but aircraft repeatedly warned *Massachusetts* and the cruisers that destroyers were getting under way.

While the French destroyers hastened to sea, *Massachusetts* continued hitting. At 0735 a 16-inch shell clipped *Jean Bart*'s bow and a minute later another struck the quay, sweeping the battleship's deck with a shower of stone fragments that damaged the 90-mm mounts and breeched the hull. A minute later a round passed through the funnel and angled down into the hull before exiting at the main armored deck, and another plowed through the quay wall and hit the main armor belt. The belt deflected the shell down and it exited without exploding.

At 0740 *Massachusetts* checked fire. *Jean Bart* had been quiet for twenty minutes and smoke made it difficult for spotters to assess her damage. At 0748, after receiving a report that the French ship was on an even keel and appeared unharmed, *Massachusetts* opened up again.

The flyers reported the antiaircraft fire as intense. By the time *Suwannee's* seven TBFs appeared overhead three SBDs had been damaged. A bomb hit the auxiliary *Dubourdieu* at 0745 followed by a pair of shells that caused her to slowly sink at her mooring. Meanwhile, a tug freed *Boulonnais* and the destroyer joined her sisters in the roadstead at 0750 followed by *Fougueux* five minutes later. They anchored there under a long-distance shelling from *Wichita* awaiting the rest of the squadron. Because the cruiser *Primauguet* was more than an hour from being able to sail, Rear Admiral Raymond Gervais de Lafond, the 2nd Light Squadron's commander, transferred his flag to the *contre-torpilleur Milan*. *Milan* reached the outer harbor at 0759 followed by the destroyer *L'Alcyon* at 0806 and the *contre-torpilleur Albatros* at 0813. The destroyers *Tempête* and *Simoun* were repairing hull damage suffered in an 8 September collision and could not sail. *Malin,* which had been detached from Dakar for a refit, had no hope of getting under way. In any case, at 0806 a 16-inch shell landed between *Malin* and the jetty. The impact riddled the vessel with enormous splinters, killing seven and wounding five. The projectile's cap traveled eighty feet, flooding the boiler and engine rooms and causing a 13.5-degree list.[44]

The 16- and 8-inch shells along with the bombers destroyed or damaged much of the commercial shipping in the harbor as well. The newly arrived passenger ships *Porthos, Savoie,* and *Lipari* were still crowded with civilian evacuees from Dakar. They had started disembarking at 0545, and when the first shells came screaming into the harbor hundreds of passengers fled the docks. At 0736 a 16-inch projectile smacked *Porthos,* which was tied to the head of the commercial môle. She capsized, suffering twenty-four dead and ten wounded. *Lipari, Savoie,* and the tanker *Ile d'Ouessant* were moored along the Delpit Basin's commercial môle. At 0750 an 8-inch shell gouged a ten-foot hole in *Lipari* near the waterline, killing six and sparking an intense fire that took days to burn itself out. *Savoie* absorbed two 16-inch rounds at 0752, followed by several near misses. At 0820 a shell exploded in her engine room. The battered liner ultimately capsized with three killed and thirteen wounded. A pair of 16-inch rounds smashed *Ile d'Ouessant* at 0755 and she sank rapidly with one killed. *Fauzon* and *Ile de Noirmoutier* were moored behind *Jean Bart* along the Delande Quay. Sixteen-inch shells passed through *Fauzon* at 0800 and 0815, but the ship remained afloat. A

192 | Chapter 11

16-inch round ripped *Ile de Noirmoutier* at 0810 and caused major flooding. The bombardment also sank the Italian freighter *San Pietro* along with two trawlers and four fishing boats. Several shells fell alongside the tankers *Elorn* and *Lot,* both moored at the end of the Delande Bassin, but did little harm.[45]

At 0806 a 16-inch round ricocheted off *Jean Bart*'s operational turret, carrying away a 90-mm gun mounted alongside. The shell did not explode, but it pushed the glacis plate down and jammed the turret in place. Another shell from the same salvo struck Turret No. 2's barbette and broke up. It ricocheted off the main armored deck and penetrated several compartments before stopping. Four minutes later a projectile pierced *Jean Bart*'s starboard quarterdeck. After ripping through a 100-mm armored deck, the shell exploded in a ballast tank beneath the steering gear. Fragments punched through the ship's bottom. At 0818 and again at 0830 aircraft hit *Tempête* and *Simoun.* In the first attack a bomb ignited a fire in *Simoun*'s crew's quarters and disabled No. 1 Mount. Fragments from a bomb falling alongside *Tempête* killed the destroyer's captain.

Up through 0835 *Wichita* fired 225 rounds of 8-inch HC ammunition and 369 rounds of AP. *Tuscaloosa* discharged 300 rounds of 8-inch HC and 172 AP shells. Their targets are shown in Table 11.1 on p. 193.

The Batterie d'El Hank and Batterie d'Oukacha remained fully operational, losing just one man killed by a burst of shrapnel at 0800. A major reason was the use of AP ammunition, the effects of which a subsequent analysis called disappointing. El Hank's gunnery was deliberate but inflicted no damage. The position fired on *Massachusetts* for the most part, although it also targeted the cruisers at 0725, 0825, and 0835 at ranges out to 23,000 meters.[46]

At 0830 Giffen overheard a TBS message that there was no resistance ashore and that the bombardment was killing townspeople. He wrote, "Although it was doubted whether this message referred to Casablanca . . . I was not desirous of causing wanton destruction and ordered cease firing at 0833." This order came at a good time for *Massachusetts* because during Salvo 45 fired at 0812 a shell being loaded into Turret 1 tipped and fell through the hoist, jamming the turret, which was training to port at the time. This casualty required thirty-five minutes to correct. Minor problems with shell supply or mechanics caused one or more guns to miss salvos during Salvos 4, 5, 6, 25–28, and 42–50.[47]

The Air Battle

The Americans sought to gain air superiority by striking the French airfields in the Rabat/Casablanca area. These included Rabat Ville, the base of nineteen

TABLE 11.1

Task Group 34.1 Gunnery, Bombardment of Casablanca, 8 November 1942

Ship	Time	Target	Range (yards)	Salvos
Wichita	0706–0723	El Hank	21800	25
	0727–0740	Submarines	27000	14
	0751–0804	Oukacha	24800	11
	0806–0820	Harbor	23500	18
	0828–0835	Harbor	26300	3
Tuscaloosa	0705–0719	Submarines	28000	15
	0720–0740	Oukacha	27000	32
	0759–0806	Submarines	22500	10
	0810	El Hank	24100	1
	0815	Destroyer	28000	1
	0821	Destroyer	30450	1
Massachusetts	0704–0717	*Jean Bart*	24400	9 (6 to 9 guns)
	0717–0740	*Jean Bart*	23700	13 (3 to 6 guns)
	0720–	El Hank	22900	5 (1 to 3 guns)
	0748–	*Jean Bart*	26000	24 (3 to 6 guns)
	0803–	El Hank	24000	11 (1 to 3 guns)
	0828–0833	El Hank	27600	3 (6 to 9 guns)

operational Curtiss Hawk 75A fighters, Rabat Salé with thirteen LeO 45 bombers, and Cazès outside of Casablanca with twenty H75A and thirteen D.520 fighters and eleven operational Douglas DB-7s.

The sixteen-plane strike against Cazès did not catch the French napping. The D.520s and H75As began lifting off as early as 0630. There was a patrol over the field when the first Americans arrived shortly after 0700, and other fighters were chasing the U.S. spotters. However, the Douglas DB-7s were in the process of arming and F4Fs incinerated five of them on the ground. *Ranger*'s air group struck again at 1305 and destroyed two more DB-7s. The Salé attack arrived at 0630 and caught the bombing group on the open ground. It damaged or destroyed all thirteen LeO 45s. At Rabat Ville American fighters strafed the field four times between 0655 and 0800, destroying three Hawks on the ground.[48]

Throughout 9 November, *Ranger*'s aircraft made 203 sorties and expended 61 500-pound bombs, 105 100-pound bombs, and 72 incendiary bombs. *Ranger* lost one F4F and one SBD that crashed on takeoff. French fighters and flak downed

The liner *Porthos* capsized in Casablanca Harbor. She had arrived the morning of 8 November carrying refugees from Dakar who fled when the shelling started. (U.S. Naval Institute Photo Archive)

seven F4Fs and one SBD. *Ranger's* aircraft claimed the destruction of fifty-two French aircraft.[49]

TG 34.2 pilots flew a variety of missions. For example, Lt. E. W. Wood operated an F4F for VGF 41. On the 8th he participated in the initial strike against Cazès and fought two separate dog fights with D.520s and damaged a DB-7 on the ground. His second mission that day found him above Port Lyautey, where he strafed an antiaircraft battery that was firing on landing craft. On the 9th he flew patrol over Port Lyautey and *Ranger* and ended the day above Fédala where he strafed French troops and the Sidi Yahia airfield and claimed one French fighter shot down. On the 10th and 11th he flew combat air patrol over *Ranger* and attacked an enemy submarine. In four busy days he flew eight missions, engaged in three aerial combats, and strafed troops, airfields, artillery batteries, and a submarine.[50]

12

THE NAVAL BATTLE OF CASABLANCA

If circumstances force us to fire upon the French, once our victorious
ally, let it be done with the firm conviction that we are striking not at the
French people, but at the men who prefer Hitler's slavery to freedom.
—CAPT. F. E. M. WHITING, USS *MASSACHUSETTS*, 7 NOVEMBER 1942

The Naval Battle of Casablanca was the largest surface, air, and subsurface naval action fought in the Atlantic Ocean during World War II. From first shot to last, the battle lasted more than six hours. During that time the U.S. Navy deployed a battleship, four cruisers, ten destroyers, and a minesweeper supplemented by carrier fighters and bombers. On the French side, participants included one immobile battleship, three shore batteries, a light cruiser, two *contre-torpilleurs*, seven destroyers, two sloops, a patrol boat, and three submarines.

The 2nd Light Squadron Sorties: 0815

At 0815 the 2nd Light Squadron's immediately serviceable units, two *contre-torpilleurs* of the 11th DCT (Division de Contre-Torpilleurs, or *contre-torpilleur* division) and five destroyers of the 2nd and 5th DT started up the coast at eighteen knots led by Rear Admiral Gervais de Lafond on board *Milan*. The sortie occurred despite the great force deployed to prevent it. French warships had been gathering outside the harbor for nearly an hour. Aircraft reported their presence, but the information did not reach the officer responsible for containment, Rear

Admiral Giffen on the flag bridge of *Massachusetts*. As the French squadron got under way, he was fifteen miles off, leading his task group in the opposite direction, trading slow salvos with El Hank. *Massachusetts*'s chronology notes that at 0817 two submarines were observed leaving Casablanca but says nothing about destroyers. *Tuscaloosa,* the second ship in the column of American heavies, targeted a destroyer at 0815 and again at 0821 when a heel to starboard elevated her guns enough to fling a salvo nearly 30,000 yards. After that, though, there was "a lull in the action." The third cruiser, *Wichita,* shelled the harbor blindly because smoke rendered spotting impossible.[1]

Giffen's report does not address his failure to contain the French squadron. Perhaps the intensity of the bombardment and the smoke roiling up from the harbor made him believe the surface threat had been eliminated. What is certain is that the absence of TG 34.1 presented Gervais de Lafond with a golden opportunity. The French admiral had battled the Italians in June 1940 (after service as naval attaché in Rome from 1936 to 1939) and had been decorated for leading a pair of *contre-torpilleurs* to victory over a division of four British destroyers off Syria in June 1941—one of several successful actions he fought in the eastern Mediterranean. His plan was to head up the coast with the rising sun behind him and strike enemy transports reported off Fédala. It was just a thirty-minute sail.

At 0818 the leader of a group of F4Fs orbiting Fédala waiting a call to action spotted the French column and radioed, "There are four destroyers and two cruisers . . . heading for our transports. The destroyers are laying smoke. I am going to attack them with four planes." Both Rear Admiral Hewitt and Captain Emmet entered this report in their logs. *Augusta* noted "number and disposition of enemy ships uncertain because of haze and smoke screen."[2]

Meanwhile, five miles up the coast *Milan* spotted two destroyers off her port bow, which her lookouts identified as cruisers. Gervais de Lafond signaled his squadron to form columns by division with divisions in echelon. The 11th DCT (*Milan, Albatros*) was inshore leading the 5th DT (*Brestois, Boulonnais*) by three thousand meters and the 2nd DT (*Fougueux, Frondeur, L'Alcyon*) fifteen hundred meters behind the 5th. As the French deployed, F4Fs roared up the columns from down-wind. The flight leader remembered, "I could see the Tricolor on the stern of the last ship growing larger. . . . I started firing at about four thousand feet. . . . I could see the tracers were squirting on the decks and bouncing off. I almost felt that I was running into my own ricochets." His target was *Boulonnais,* and his bullets fatally wounded her captain, Lieutenant Commander Martinant

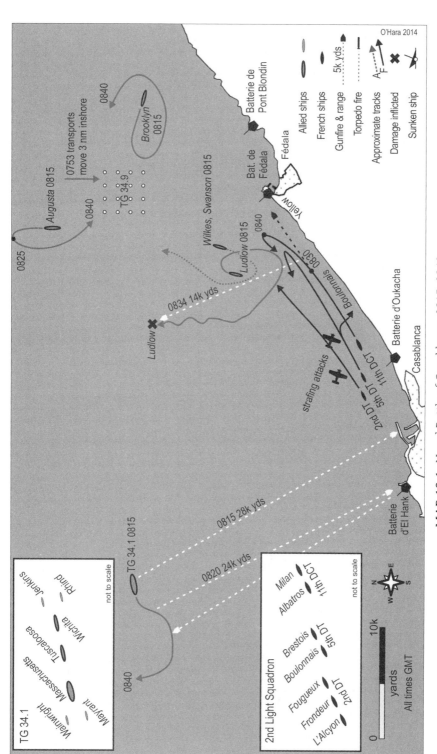

MAP 12.1 *Naval Battle of Casablanca, 0815–0840*

TG 34.1

Wainwright
Mayrant
Massachusetts
Tuscaloosa
Wichita
Rhind
Jenkins

not to scale

2nd Light Squadron

Milan
Albatros — 11th DCT
Brestois
Boulonnais — 5th DT
Fougueux
Frondeur
L'Alcyon — 2nd DT

not to scale

yards
10k
All times GMT

Allied ships
French ships
Gunfire & range — 5k yds
Torpedo fire
Approximate tracks
Damage inflicted
Sunken ship

O'Hara 2014

TG 34.1 0815
0840
0815 28k yds
0820 24k yds

Batterie d'El Hank
Casablanca
Batterie d'Oukacha
strafing attacks
2nd DT
5th DT
11th DCT
Boulonnais
0830
0840
Ludlow
0834 14k yds
Ludlow 0815
Wilkes, Swanson 0815
TG 34.9
0840
0815 transports move 3 nm inshore
Augusta 0815
0825
0840
Brooklyn 0815
Bat. de Fédala
Fédala
Yellow
Batterie de Pont Blondin

de Préneuf. One shot damaged the tiller control, causing the destroyer to lurch to starboard and come dangerously close to shore. On *Milan* the .50-caliber barrage sickled through bridge personnel and wounded Gervais de Lafond; some ready ammunition caught fire, the forward magazine had minor flooding, and bullets pierced two oil bunkers. F4Fs also hit *Albatros* and roughed up *Brestois*, killing her executive officer and damaging her antiaircraft director.[3]

The ships *Milan* had spotted were *Wilkes, Swanson,* and *Ludlow.* These destroyers disengaged from Cape Fédala at 0811 to begin patrolling west of the transports. *Ludlow* had just repaired a steering casualty caused by a near miss, and *Swanson's* men were fixing two mount failures. At 0820 Cdr. Edward R. Durgin, the squadron commander, logged what appeared to be two cruisers and three destroyers standing out of Casablanca. At 0825, despite harassment from the strafing Wildcats, the 11th DCT opened fire from 14,500 meters. *Wilkes* noted, "Visibility toward enemy very poor with only gun flashes discernible." She and *Swanson* retreated north at flank speed. *Ludlow* zigzagged after them as pink, green, blue, and uncolored geysers spouted around her and a few splinters rattled on board.[4]

At 0825 Hewitt's flagship, *Augusta,* turned south to intercept the French ships threatening the transports. The admiral also jumped on the radio and informed Giffen that there were enemy warships off Casablanca. *Brooklyn's* log indicated that Hewitt ordered her to attack "French cruisers" at 0834 and she turned west at thirty-three knots to join the action.[5]

At 0830 *Milan* trained her battery on landing craft off Yellow Beach loaded with troops of the 7th Regiment's much-delayed Company L. Gunfire sank one boat and damaged others. This was the only occasion during World War II when American landing craft came under fire at sea from a major enemy warship.[6]

At 0834 a 138.6-mm round from *Albatros* struck *Ludlow's* forecastle deck at a steep angle of fall, plowed into the officer's quarters, and detonated against the main deck, sparking several large fires. One sailor remembered, "Paint and red deck linoleum were burning like tar paper. Damage control organized a human chain to pass ammunition out of the handling room and magazine because the bulkheads were getting too hot." *Ludlow* retired northeast and the fires burned until 0950.[7]

By 0840 *Milan* was within five miles of *Leonard Wood.* A French account asserts that poor visibility led Gervais de Lafond to confuse the transports for Cape Fédala. But he did see *Augusta* heading in his direction 18,000 yards north.

At the same time another flight of F4Fs was strafing his flagship, as well as *Albatros* and *Frondeur.* The admiral signaled a 180-degree turn by divisions hoping to lure the cruiser within range of *Jean Bart* and El Hank. The 11th DCT and *Brestois* came about but *Fougueux,* embroiled in clouds from the oil tank fire on Cape Fédala, missed the signal and continued leading the 2nd DT northeast.[8]

At 0843 *Augusta* shot the first of six nine-gun salvos at *Fougueux* from 19,000 yards. At 0845, with still no word from Giffen, Hewitt radioed his subordinate, "French Cruisers standing up coast from Casablanca to Fedala. Cover Transports." *Brooklyn,* meanwhile, engaged the 11th DCT at 0848 from 18,000 yards while *Wilkes* and *Swanson* reversed course and added their rapid salvos to the cruisers' measured fire. Red and green splashes from the *contre-torpilleurs*, shooting at near their maximum effective range, fell about *Brooklyn.* "Several passed so close to our superstructure that you could hear them go by. One hit the water about 8 yards behind our fantail." The warships maneuvered radically to confuse French aim and submarines reported in the area. At the same time, Wildcats buzzed *Fougueux,* killing a navigation officer, the helmsman, and signals personnel. At 0845 *Ranger* started launching fifteen SBDs "to intercept submarines and light craft."[9]

At 0850 an 8-inch salvo fired from 16,700 yards landed alongside *Fougueux,* causing minor flooding. Commander Louis S. Sticca, the division commander, realized he was facing the enemy alone and at 0852 he reversed course. This opened range and at 0857, now thirteen miles from the enemy, *Augusta* turned west. Hewitt's flagship held this course for eight minutes before turning southeast at 0905. During this period *Brooklyn* sailed west, firing as visibility permitted.

At 0900 the light cruiser *Primauguet* got under way, and at 0915 she joined the 11th DCT northeast of Oukacha. Thus reinforced, Gervais de Lafond turned back toward the transports, but he was having trouble communicating: *Milan's* shortwave radio had been disabled and smoke obscured flag signals. Moreover, strafing had decimated the squadron's navigation, signals, and gunnery personnel. According to a French historian, the situation forced "each division commander, each captain to maneuver according to his own inspiration."[10]

Enter Task Group 34.1: 0918–0940

At 0834, with American warships and landing craft under fire, *Massachusetts* ceased fire against El Hank but continued steering north by northwest. At 0848 Giffen radioed Hewitt, asking if he desired assistance after observing "what

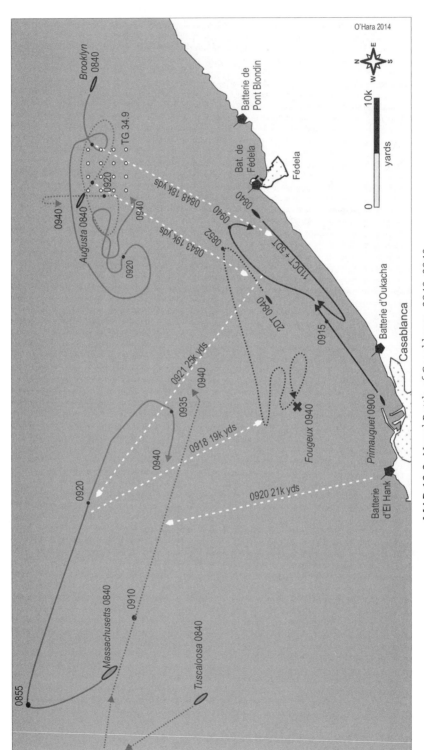

MAP 12.2 *Naval Battle of Casablanca, 0840–0940*

O'Hara 2014

Brooklyn 0840

TG 34.9

0920

0940

Augusta 0840

0920

0940

0920

0940

0848 18k yds

0843 19k yds

0940

0652

2DT 0840

0921 25k yds

0935

0940

0918 19k yds

0920

0940

11DCT + 3DT

0940

0840

Bat. de
Fédela

Batterie de
Pont Blondin

Fédela

0915

Batterie d'Oukacha

Casablanca

Fougeux 0940

Primauguet 0900

0920 21k yds

Batterie
d'El Hank

Massachusetts 0840

0910

0855

Tuscaloosa 0840

10k

yards

0

N
W E
S

appeared to be two destroyers standing out of Casablanca harbor." He was beyond sight of the harbor at this time and it was likely that staff alerted the admiral to radio chatter about the French sortie. In any case, this query is Giffen's first acknowledgement that French warships were in action. Shortly thereafter Hewitt's 0845 order arrived. This answered Giffen's question and at 0855 he came about and set course at twenty-seven knots, the battleship's maximum speed, for Fédala thirty-five miles away.[11]

At 0916, after sailing east-southeast for twenty-one minutes (covering 19,000 yards) *Massachusetts* spotted ships making smoke off her starboard bow. "It was difficult to ascertain the exact number . . . or to identify them accurately." Nonetheless, she opened fire two minutes later, range 19,400 yards. "More than one or two ships were rarely visible. . . . Consequently it was necessary to shift [fire] from ship to ship as they emerged from the smoke." *Massachusetts*'s targets were destroyers of the 2nd DT. The battleship noted return fire at 0921. Giffen reported that the enemy's "fire control was excellent and numerous splashes of various colors were observed, many within 50 yards of various ships of this group."[12]

Tuscaloosa entered action at 0925, range 22,000 yards. Her targets "maneuvered radically against shore line background and made heavy white smoke. Targets bore directly into the sun causing terrific glare." *Wichita* in the rear was still out of range. She resorted to bombarding the harbor, firing 204 shells in twenty-seven salvos from 0919 to 0939. At 0942 she finally zeroed in on *Primauguet* from 24,000 yards. *Mayrant* and *Wainwright* preceded *Massachusetts* three thousand yards off either bow while *Rhind* and *Jenkins* followed *Wichita* an equal distance off each quarter. The commander of Destroyer Squadron 8, Capt. Don P. Moon, noted that "it was a temptation to leave formation to become more closely engaged with enemy destroyer leaders." He did keep his flagship, *Wainwright*, on the near side so she could open fire as the range closed. *Mayrant* discharged her first salvo toward the 5th DT at 0922 from 16,000 yards. Return fire forced the destroyer to employ "a very radical zig-zag" to avoid being hit.[13]

Primauguet dueled *Massachusetts* while, starting at 0920, El Hank targeted the cruisers from 21,000 yards. Poor visibility and equipment failures affected American gunnery. *Massachusetts* relied on optical spotting because the main battery director's FC Radar 1 had blown a fuse and FC Radar 2's ranges varied so greatly from optical spots that the gunners discounted its output. At 0930 the concussion from a main battery salvo jumped a circuit breaker and all four FD

Gleaves-class destroyer firing to port during the Naval Battle of Casablanca as she executes a high-speed turn. (U.S. Naval Institute Photo Archive)

Mk 4 and FC Mk 3 radars lost power "with a consequent loss of target pips." "Shooting was 'from the hip' with application of spots in range and deflection when salvo landed." Nonetheless, the French situation was dire and, as TG 34.1 closed, it grew worse. From *Augusta* it seemed to Hewitt that Giffen had taken control and the French were retreating. Moreover, Hewitt had Major General Patton pacing beside him, anxious to get ashore. Thus *Augusta* ceased fire at 0920 and headed north of the transport area. *Brooklyn* logged the order to break off at 0932 and swung east to rejoin the transports.[14]

Even with the withdrawal of *Augusta* and *Brooklyn* it seemed it would take a miracle for the 2nd Light Squadron to survive, but this is what happened. At 0935, having reached a point ten miles north of Casablanca and only 11,500 yards from the nearest enemy ship, *Massachusetts* came about. The battleship's log states this was done to avoid "restricted waters." Giffen's report only notes, "Range varied from 11,500 yards at 0935 to 30,000 yards at 1016." This perplexing maneuver at least gave *Wainwright* a chance to fight. She obtained a line of fire from 14,000 yards on "enemy destroyer leaders which were circling and laying smoke screens off Casablanca." She fired 112 rounds from 0940 until 0953 when the range widened once again.[15]

0940–1000

When Giffen turned away, *Primauguet, Milan,* and *Albatros* were approaching Cape Fédala. Sticca's 2nd DT was 11,000 yards north of Casablanca. *Boulonnais* had repaired her steering casualty and rejoined *Brestois.* This division was following *Albatros* at a distance. All French ships were belching smoke and skillfully using concealment, at least in the opinion of frustrated American gunners.

As *Primauguet* neared Cape Fédala only destroyers opposed her. *Bristol,* which had been patrolling northwest of the cape, turned southeast at 0925 to meet the enemy. She engaged at 0938 from 12,000 yards while steaming northwest of the French column on a reciprocal course. Captain Emmet learned of the renewed threat at 0939 and ordered his formation inshore "to a position 10,000 yards from Cape Fédala." Heavy smoke blowing offshore hid the enemy from his sight.[16]

At 0940 *Primauguet* reversed course. At the same time *Wilkes* and *Swanson,* which had been patrolling west of the transports, intervened and opened fire at 0946, closing to 12,000 yards. However, after six minutes they veered away and formed up on *Bristol* because "enemy ceased fire and disappeared in haze and smoke, apparently retiring toward Casablanca." *Brooklyn,* which had just reached station east of the transports, received word of the new French thrust at 0941. This was followed a minute later by an order from Emmet to suppress the Batterie de Fédala while the transports moved inshore.[17]

As American destroyers skirmished with the French warships northwest of Fédala, TG 34.1 steamed away, stern turrets engaging *Fougueux, Frondeur,* and *L'Alcyon* to the south. At 0940 a 16-inch round fired from 12,000 yards crashed into *Fougueux.* This, the first direct hit obtained by an American warship, crumpled the destroyer's bow up to the quarterdeck, drove the stem underwater, and set the bridge afire. *Fougueux* rapidly flooded and Commander Sticca ordered the crew to abandon ship. *Frondeur* maneuvered to assist and came under *Tuscaloosa's* fire from 15,000 yards. At 0946 an 8-inch round slammed through *Frondeur's* bridge from the port side, spraying the area with splinters, killing the gunnery officer and wounding six men. Another round fell near the stem without exploding and a few large fragments pierced the hull. Nonetheless, *Frondeur* held steady toward *Fougueux,* which was drifting to a halt. However, when Sticca signaled that he did not require assistance, *Frondeur* followed *L'Alcyon* to join the 5th DT three miles east.[18]

Using plane spots *Wichita* meanwhile lofted three salvos toward *Primauguet* from 24,000 yards between 0942 and 0946 before losing her target in the smoke. At 0947 *Wichita* turned her guns against *Frondeur* and *L'Alcyon* from 17,000 yards and thereafter engaged whatever targets were visible.[19] *Massachusetts* delivered some telling blows despite her radar and spotting difficulties. At 0956 *Milan* was twenty-seven hundred yards north-northwest of Oukacha steaming southwest when ships nearby saw her disappear in a giant green geyser. A 16-inch shell fired from the impressive distance of 28,000 yards smashed through the *contre-torpilleur,* exploding in the No. 2 crew's quarter and rupturing the hull to starboard at the waterline. Splinters wreaked havoc, destroying the radio room and cutting through the sick bay. Some penetrated all the way to the bow. Fires erupted and spread rapidly. With more than a hundred casualties *Milan* turned into the wind to contain the flames and slowly drifted toward Roches Noires while survivors jettisoned ammunition and torpedoes. Meanwhile, *Primauguet* and *Albatros* came about and headed back toward Fédala.[20]

El Hank engaged as TG 34.1 passed to the north. *Tuscaloosa* reported shells "whizzing around" and splashes within fifty yards. Rear Admiral Giffen remarked, "There were many instances of enemy overs landing within 50 feet of the disengaged side, in some cases as close as 10 or 15 feet." The stately progress of *Massachusetts* and her attendant cruisers across the battle zone had also attracted French submarines. At 0930 *Antiope* sighted a cruiser 11,000 meters away and began an approach, helped when her target turned toward her some minutes later and held to a steady course. At 0954 the submarine fired six torpedoes from two thousand meters. On *Tuscaloosa* two sailors on the signal bridge simultaneously reported tracks off the cruiser's port bow, and Capt. Norman C. Gillette immediately ordered a hard turn to port. "Men at exposed battle stations crouched in the lee of the bridge wings and gun shields, fully expecting an explosion." One torpedo ran "within 50 feet along the port side." These details suggest that *Antiope* had a poor target angle and that the range was greater than estimated.[21]

Minutes later *Massachusetts* was 28,000 yards northwest of El Hank steering course 250 at twenty-seven knots when "a shower of wooden splinters so stunned [her] executive officer . . . that it took him a few seconds to realize the ship had been hit." A 194-mm projectile had struck opposite of No. 2 turret on the port side, penetrated a deck and detonated against the second, protective deck, gouging an inch-deep hole. The main deck planking caught fire. There were no casualties, although one sailor's "locker yielded thirty shell fragments varying from the size of a pea to that of a match box." The executive officer, who was conning the battleship from a catwalk, then spotted torpedo wakes. Overriding Capt. Francis Whiting's orders, he maneuvered *Massachusetts* between a spread of four torpedoes launched by *Méduse* at 1003 from a range of thirty-eight hundred meters. One torpedo reportedly passed five yards down the battleship's starboard side.[22]

While French submarines narrowly missed, American aircraft continued their deadly harassment of French warships. A strafing attack at 0948 against *Boulonnais* and *Brestois,* which were several miles north of *Primauguet,* seriously wounded the 5th DT's commander, Mariani, causing him to order *Boulonnais's* captain, Lieutenant Commander Martinant de Préneuf, to assume the division's command. But because Martinant de Préneuf was already mortally wounded, this duty devolved on his executive officer, Lieutenant Commander Chazereau. At 0955 SBDs bracketed *L'Alcyon* with a pair of 500-pound bombs, wounding a dozen men and causing minor flooding. SBDs also dropped on *Milan* from two thousand feet. The aircraft reported that heavy smoke and contrary winds made them miss, although even under the best conditions destroyers were difficult targets.[23]

After Lieutenant Commander Chazereau took over the 5th DT, he saw the American battleship disappearing to the west and fires raging on *Milan* and *Fougueux.* He ordered *Brestois* to form on his lead. Thinking "to inflict on the enemy the most damage possible and to try and open a route for the 2nd Light Squadron," he steered his two-ship column toward Fédala at twenty-eight knots. It was already too late for *Fougueux.* She blew up and sank at 1000.[24]

The Decisive Phase: 1000–1130

In a hundred minutes of action the 2nd Light Squadron had circled between Casablanca and Cape Fédala. It had moderately damaged *Ludlow* and foiled a minor landing, but failed to exploit two opportunities to attack the transports. It had been subjected to sustained fire from a vastly superior naval force as well as dive-bombing and strafing attacks. However, with the effective use of smoke and light it had suffered the loss of only *Fougueux,* the crippling of *Milan,* and moderate damage to *Frondeur.* These losses had come at the end of the period; the rest of the squadron, one light cruiser, one *contre-torpilleur,* and three destroyers, remained effective.

By 1000 Hewitt had returned to supporting transports and Giffen to his duel with El Hank and guarding against the appearance of the Dakar squadron.

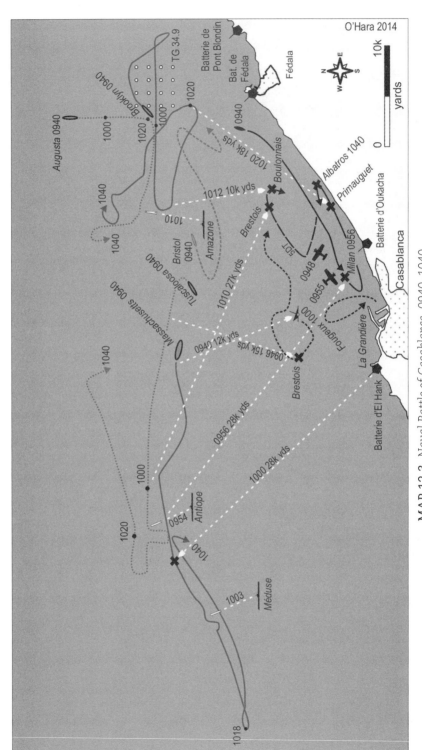

MAP 12.3 *Naval Battle of Casablanca, 0940–1040*

Giffen wrote, "It is believed that severe losses were suffered by the enemy during this phase." In fact, both admirals exaggerated the damage their gunnery inflicted. This was understandable: it was their first surface combat, and spotters and lookouts tended to see in every puff of smoke a hit, or ships rolling over and bows projecting from the water. Consequently, they embraced victory prematurely.[25]

Gervais de Lafond, on the other hand, refused to embrace defeat. By prolonging the action he gave his potential equalizers—shore batteries and submarines—opportunities to inflict a telling blow on the American force. The French remembered how, two years before, the British attack on Dakar had been defeated on the operation's third day when a submarine torpedoed the battleship *Resolution*. While the hope of repeating such a victory off Casablanca was slim, it was the second-best hope the French had. The best hope was to sink transports and at 1000, with *Boulonnais* and *Brestois* forming up for an attack, the Americans were allowing French warships another chance to do exactly that.

TG 34.1 had vanished over the western horizon as the two destroyers neared Fédala. At 0951 Hewitt overrode Emmet's orders for *Brooklyn* to engage shore batteries and instructed *Wilkes, Swanson,* and *Bristol* to stand by. *Brooklyn,* which had taken position east of the transports and north of the Batterie de Pont Blondin, circled to port and headed due west to close distance as rapidly as possible.[26]

At 1008 when she was 13,000 yards northwest of Cape Fédala the cruiser's executive officer reminded Capt. Francis C. Denebrink that he had been steering a straight course for "some time" (actually twelve minutes) and recommended a course change. Denebrink ordered the wheel over 25 degrees left and at that instant saw five torpedoes streaking toward his ship. *Amazone* had just launched a spread of six (one got stuck in the tube) from 2,500 meters. *Brooklyn* swung 90 degrees left as tracks ran down the starboard side—the closest seventy-five yards away. At the same moment *Boulonnais* and *Brestois* opened fire and straddled the light cruiser. At 1012 *Brooklyn* radioed Rear Admiral Hewitt, "Am engaging two enemy cruisers." The flagship was north of the transports refueling a plane and preparing to put Patton ashore, but the general had to wait. Hewitt radioed at 1015, "*Augusta* coming to your assistance."[27]

At 1010, with *Boulonnais* and *Brestois* spewing clouds of white and black smoke, Chazereau ordered a torpedo attack estimating the range as 11,800 meters. However, a transmission failure prevented execution, and as the division turned to starboard, an 8-inch shell plunged into *Brestois*'s forecastle. This exploded in the crew's quarters and flooded the galley and *cale à vin* (wine locker). This was before *Augusta* engaged and while *Tuscaloosa* was shelling *La Grandière,* which at 1006 had ventured from the smoke shrouding the harbor to rescue *Fougueux's* men. *Wichita* was targeting "whichever of 3 DD's [destroyers] or *Primauguet* could best be seen in the smoke" and was likely the source of this blow, which, if so, was delivered from nearly 27,000 yards.[28]

At 1012, before *Boulonnais* could assume her new course, *Brooklyn's* rapid-firing 6-inch guns staggered the destroyer with a crippling broadside. One shell exploded in boiler room No. 1, a second hit a boiler room's ventilators and destroyed a fuel pump, a third traversed boiler alley No. 2 and a splinter perforated a fuel bunker, a fourth hit the port engine room and exploded against a turbine causing serious flooding, a fifth punched into the mechanics' mess, and a sixth struck the commander's quarters and caused more flooding. *Boulonnais* shuddered to a stop and started to sink. *Brooklyn's* report does not mention this success. Instead it complains that "enemy destroyers were continually dodging in and out of a very effective and extensive smoke screen. This ship was never able to continue firing on a given target more than a minute or two before losing it again in the smoke screen."[29]

Meanwhile, at 1000 a single 100-mm gun from Batterie de Fédala began heaving pot shots at landing craft on the beach. The destroyer-minesweeper *Palmer* was searching for mines reported nearby when at 1005 a French shell "passed through two after engine room hatch doors and a garbage can," while another carried away the vessel's commission pennant. *Palmer* retired at high speed, pumping out twenty-four 3-inch rounds at a mean range of 4,700 yards. *Bristol,* meanwhile, engaged the battery from 1005 to 1016 from eight thousand yards. *Wilkes* and *Swanson* formed column on *Bristol* and briefly participated, but *Swanson* suffered two gun casualties (again) and dropped out. Next *Boyle* and *Edison* made a pass and shelled the battery between 1012 and 1018 from ten thousand yards, expending thirty-five and seventy-four rounds, respectively. The fact that *Bristol* aimed several rounds "to burst 25 feet above ground in hope of neutralizing personnel" dismayed the American soldiers who were, at that time, gathering to storm the position.[30]

At 1025 *Augusta* joined the fight, forcing Patton to witness more naval action. He recalled, "I was on main deck just back of number two turret leaning on the rail when one [shell] hit so close that it splashed water all over me. . . . Some of the people got white but it did not seem very dangerous to me—sort of impersonal."[31]

During this period *Primauguet* remained pressed against the coast zigzagging at high speed in an area four thousand yards wide. *Massachusetts* ceased fire at 1016 when she was eighteen miles west-northwest of El Hank. She reversed course to the east at 1018. As the battleship returned toward Casablanca she could observe "4 cruisers and 4 destroyers at the entrance to the harbor" with "2 cruisers badly afire." She had expended 580 16-inch rounds. *Tuscaloosa* was leading *Wichita* fifteen miles north-northwest of El Hank. The heavy cruisers, now widely separated from the battleship, reached the apogee of their western swing and at 1017 began heading east.[32]

At 1020 three rounds struck *Primauguet*—one at the stem, another amidships, and a third on the military mast. All failed to explode. *Brooklyn* was 18,000 yards away just south of the transports. *Bristol* observed a hit on an enemy cruiser at 1026 just before she turned back into the smoke. "Size of closest splashes indicated six or possibly eight inch shells had made the hit." *Brooklyn* also saw *Primauguet* duck back into the smoke (at approximately 1030) and the impact of a hit "in the vicinity of her #1 turret forward by a *Brooklyn* green salvo." Destroyers were also engaging *Primauguet*, but the evidence suggests that *Brooklyn,* or *Brooklyn* and a destroyer, inflicted these blows. *Tuscaloosa* targeted *Primauguet* at 1030, firing nine salvos using plane spot and experiencing "visual difficulties with glare, haze and smoke." The range was more than 30,000 yards. *Jenkins* and *Wainwright* advanced from TG 34.1's screen to support Hewitt's cruisers and at 1020 Capt. John B. Hefferman, head of Destroyer Squadron 13, assessing the opposition as two cruisers and two destroyers, ordered *Bristol* and *Edison* to suspend their shore bombardment and help out. *Edison* fired just twenty rounds while *Bristol* complained that the "volume of fire from our forces [was] so great that it was impossible to identify our own splashes."[33]

Massachusetts opened fire at 1030 from a range of 30,000 yards. She went to rapid-fire five minutes later at a destroyer. Even though her gunners complained of the smoke and difficulty in acquiring targets, they claimed four hits. In fact, *Massachusetts* was shelling the immobile *Boulonnais* and sank a boat that had embarked the body of *Boulonnais*'s captain.

At 1040 a shell exploded off *Albatros*'s bow, causing minor flooding and a steam leak, but the *contre-torpilleur* could still make twenty knots. At this time *Augusta* and *Brooklyn* were within a few thousand yards of each other due north of *Albatros* and firing at ranges just above 21,000 yards. *Tuscaloosa* had checked fire at 1036 after Giffen sent an order to conserve ammunition and she turned to starboard to close range.[34]

At 1045 the tug *Lavandou* reached *Milan* and began rescue operations. Gervais de Lafond transferred to the nearby sloop *Commandant Delage*. At the same time *Albatros* tagged *Brooklyn* on No. 1 5-inch mount. The 138.6-mm round wounded five men before bouncing over the starboard side without exploding. A *Brooklyn* sailor later wrote, "At the first sight of the vicinity where we were hit, I got sick! . . . because where the disabled gun stood was a mass of red, which I thought to be blood. It covered the bulkhead . . . and was all over the decks. However, [an] officer told me it was a red dye from the French shell." Also at 1045 a near miss astern shook *Primauguet* severely, killing two and causing minor flooding.[35]

At 1052 *Massachusetts,* steaming north-northwest at twenty-seven knots with ranges to *Primauguet* at 22,000 yards, reported shells splashing twenty-five yards off the starboard beam. At 1057 a plunging 155-mm round ricocheted off battleship's starboard quarterdeck and burst over a 20-mm mount, igniting small fires. From 1050 to 1114 *Wainwright* sparred with *Frondeur* and *L'Alcyon* and expended a torpedo at 1107 at very long range. *Jenkins* opened fire at 1054 from 14,700 yards on a destroyer "of the Le Terrible Class" but after a few rounds her target vanished in the smoke. *Rhind* squeezed in ten salvos between 1100 and 1140 and claimed success against a destroyer leader.[36]

As long-range salvos crisscrossed the smoky sky, *Brestois* steamed past *Boulonnais* and joined *Frondeur* and *L'Alcyon.* Commander Mariani had regained consciousness and, wounded through he was, took command of the ad hoc formation. The ships, however, could only twist and circle amid a forest of geysers. From *Brooklyn* it seemed "they were darting all over the ocean like squirrels. They were very fast; our guns would lay a barrage down on them and they would slip into a smoke screen. At that we would figure they were hit, and about the time we had figured, they would dash at us from the screen from somewhere else."[37]

At 1103, after shooting twenty-three six- to nine-gun salvos during the previous half hour, *Massachusetts* ceased fire. Giffen explained that the battleship "had expended 60% of her 16" ammunition and the preservation of the remainder was considered essential against a possible sortie of the *Richelieu*." At 1105, after discharging five salvos at ranges up to 17,000 yards at a destroyer on the edge of the smoke screen, *Augusta*'s guns also fell silent and she headed east toward the transports. Patton commented, "We had lunch—naval war is nice and comfortable."[38]

At 1050 Giffen ordered the heavy cruisers to stay out of range of the shore batteries, but twelve minutes later he had *Tuscaloosa*'s Captain Gillette take

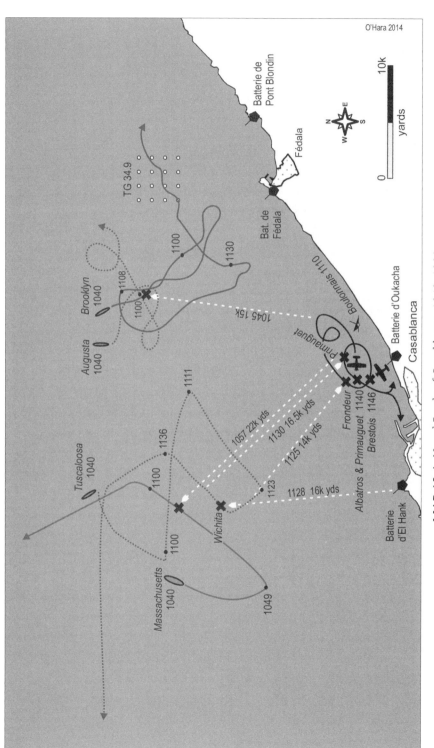

MAP 12.4 *Naval Battle of Casablanca, 1040–1200*

command of Cruiser Division 7 to "move closer to the enemy." At this time *Tuscaloosa* was 25,000 yards north-northwest of Casablanca. Screened by *Rhind* and under El Hank's fire, the two cruisers continued east for nine minutes roughly ten miles offshore. *Wichita* recorded the battery's bombardment as "very deliberate, resulting in many straddles." At 1111 they turned southwest, firing broadsides to port at the 2nd Light Squadron. At 1123 when the cruisers were 13,000 yards north of El Hank they turned northeast to open range. *Brooklyn* likewise remained in the fight. At 1108 she looped to port and began running southeast, shooting at the destroyers. At 1138 she ceased fire and headed back to the transports because all targets had disappeared.[39]

Boulonnais sank by the stern at 1110 four miles northeast of the harbor entrance. At the same time the patrol boat *La Servannaise,* which had been moored outside of the destroyers *Tempête* and *Simoun,* got under way. This allowed the tug *Phosphate 2* to tow *Tempête* to the Delpit Basin. *Simoun,* which had nearly completed her repairs, maneuvered to a mooring buoy in the outer harbor to act as a floating battery.

At 1125 an 8-inch shell struck *Frondeur* astern, causing serious flooding, disabling an engine, bursting oil drums, and blowing out a magazine wall. Listing heavily, *Frondeur* dropped out of formation and anchored eight hundred meters off the port's entrance. *Wichita* probably delivered this strike from 14,000 yards. Three minutes later a round from El Hank punched through *Wichita* from port to starboard nine feet above the main deck and traveled fifty-four feet before detonating on the starboard side and blowing a hole in the deck. It wounded fourteen men. Fires filled several compartments with smoke and fumes. These were quickly extinguished and the ship's fighting ability remained intact. Two minutes later a shell—probably delivered by *Tuscaloosa*—penetrated *Primauguet's* boiler room. It did not explode, but the impact destroyed a boiler and cut the ship's speed by four knots.[40]

At 1136 when she was 23,000 yards north of Casablanca *Tuscaloosa* ceased fire and turned 90 degrees from northeast to northwest. Three minutes later *Wichita* made an emergency turn to port to dodge three torpedoes. She judged that two passed a ship's length ahead while one probably ran deep under the bow. No French submarines attacked at this time, so whatever the cruiser saw, they were not torpedoes. *Wichita* ceased fire at 1142, having expended 380 rounds in fifty-seven salvos since 0946. Between 0925 and 1136 *Tuscaloosa* fired more than six hundred rounds in eighty-six salvos. Captain Gillette of *Tuscaloosa* decided to terminate the action because he believed that every French ship was beached or sunk with the exception of one destroyer that was immobilized and because the "fire from shore batteries [had] become so accurate as to seriously threaten our group."[41]

Although all ships had now ceased fire, the U.S. Navy continued to harry the French. At 1140 twelve SBDs struck *Primauguet* and *Albatros*. Five dived on the light cruiser and landed a 500-pound bomb astern. The other seven hit *Albatros* twice: one bomb toppled No. 3 funnel and the other exploded in an oil bunker. Fumes forced the evacuation of the forward engine and aft boiler rooms and flames erupted near the bridge. After the bombers departed, F4Fs lined up to strafe the gravely damaged vessel. The crippled *contre-torpilleur* limped toward the coast on one engine and at 1155 anchored north-northeast of Oukacha.[42]

More SBDs zeroed in on *Brestois* and *L'Alcyon* as they circled *Primauguet* to wrap her in smoke. At 1146 a bomb burst just a yard to port of *Brestois*. The shock opened her hull to an onrush of water. As his ship began listing dangerously, Commander Mariani steered to join *Primauguet*. The light cruiser hove to at 1152 to let Rear Admiral Gervais de Lafond board, but he found conditions little better than on *Milan*. *Primauguet* and *Brestois* anchored off Roches Noires shortly thereafter.

Battle's End

By noon *Fougueux* and *Boulonnais* were sunk. *Primauguet* and *Albatros* were anchored with major damage. In the outer harbor *Milan* burned fiercely. *Frondeur* was slowly flooding, and *Brestois* was in danger of capsizing. Of the 2nd Light Squadron, only *L'Alcyon* remained in service.[43]

At 1152 Giffen, reacting to an unconfirmed report, radioed *Tuscaloosa* and *Wichita* that there was a "cruiser laying smoke screen southwest of Casa Blanca and heading down coast. Intercept and sink her." *La Gracieuse* used this opening to reach *Fougueux*'s survivors. With TG 34.1 again absent, Hewitt kept a careful eye on the collection of cripples congregated around the harbor entrance and aircraft continued to harass them.[44]

At 1212 *L'Alcyon* spotted rafts crowded with *Boulonnais*'s men and steamed to succor them. *La Servannaise* joined her while the large colonial sloop *La Grandière* (that from a distance had a cruiser-like profile) headed for a group of *Fougueux* survivors. All this activity alarmed Hewitt. At 1258 *Augusta* began heading south to launch spotters and intercept while *Brooklyn*, overhearing TBS chatter about a cruiser and two destroyers standing out of Casablanca, queried Captain Emmet,

"Have you any orders for me?" As the cruisers deployed, Hewitt radioed Giffen at 1301 that the French warships still needed containing.[45]

L'Alcyon's whaler had rescued twenty men when, at 1312, *Brooklyn*'s 6-inch shells—fired from 17,200 yards—began dropping nearby. The destroyer accelerated to twenty-five knots, returned fire, and laid a smoke screen. Behind the smoke *La Servannaise* picked up several raft-loads of men that she ferried to the steamer *Vendome* anchored offshore. *Brooklyn,* however, was running low on ammunition. Turret No. 2 had expended its entire supply and only by transferring rounds from No. 3 could it keep one gun in action. *Brooklyn* fired her last salvo of the day at 1335 and retired east of the transport park.[46]

Augusta launched spotters at 1319 and 1324 and then during the next six minutes aimed ten salvos at *La Gracieuse,* initially from 18,000 yards. The sloop responded with heavy black smoke, which an aircraft reported as "direct hits." *Augusta* then sent four salvos at *La Grandière* from 15,000 yards while *La Grandière* returned fire from a range she estimated as 16,000 meters. At 1338 the sloop engaged aircraft buzzing *Primauguet. La Gracieuse* made port at 1350. Her motor launch joined her at 1425, but her dingy and whaler were sunk.[47]

Commandant Delage also rescued survivors and was the target of nine *Augusta* salvos between 1351 and 1356. During the next hour bombers made several runs on the 630-ton sloop. One bomb opened the hull and riddled her deck with splinters, killing one man and wounding eight. *Suwannee*'s report noted that three TBFs dropped a dozen 325-pound depth charges on a heavy cruiser in the outer harbor and that a fourth plane dropped four depth charges on a light cruiser or destroyer leader. The pilots claimed two hits, one probable hit, and nine near misses.[48]

Augusta returned to the transport area at 1400. TF 34 had expended huge amounts of ammunition, considering the operation was still in its first day. Hewitt had expected Giffen to contain the French flotilla, but *Richelieu* and El Hank preoccupied the admiral all day. For example, even though *Massachusetts* had withdrawn from the surface battle to preserve ammunition should *Richelieu* appear, she exchanged fire with El Hank from 1345 to 1351, firing seven nine-gun salvos. The battery fired back. As one participant recorded, "Every few seconds, intermingled between the shocking blast from our own guns, could be heard the ominous rumble of the approaching French shells and their sharp whine as they splashed a few feet on either side of the big ship or directly ahead or astern. . . . Why we were not hit dozens of times no one will ever know." Plainly running short on patience, Hewitt radioed Giffen again at 1340: "Light forces Casa Blanca making reported sorties. Destroy them before nightfall."[49]

Wichita and *Tuscaloosa,* their magazines depleted to 20 percent capacity, broke off their search for the phantom cruiser and at 1444 engaged *Primauguet* from 25,000 (*Tuscaloosa*) and 17,000 (*Wichita*) yards. *Wichita* fired sixty-three rounds through 1505, reporting, "Excellent spotting coupled with improved visibility resulted in effective fire." *Tuscaloosa* loosed twelve salvos and "obtained several straddles and quite certainly some hits." In fact, all shells missed. El Hank, in return, was straddling frequently and at 1450 the cruisers began opening range.[50]

Recap

Throughout the battle, including the initial shore bombardment, *Augusta* fired 794 rounds in 104 salvos. *Brooklyn* shot 2,691 6-inch rounds. *Massachusetts* expended 798 16-inch rounds, *Wichita* 1,263 8-inch rounds in 170 salvos and 350 5-inch, and *Tuscaloosa* nearly 1,300 8-inch. *Wainwright* fired 710 rounds, *Mayrant* 670, *Rhind* 144, and *Jenkins* 110.

For the French, *Jean Bart* fired just seven main battery rounds: *Primauguet* 512, *Milan* 300, *Albatros* 420, *Fougueux* 120, *Frondeur* 300, *L'Alcyon* 180, *Brestois* 120, *Simoun* 30, and *La Grandière* 113. *Fougueux* and *Boulonnais* sank offshore while *Primauguet, Milan, Albatros, Frondeur,* and *Brestois* were heavily damaged. From Gervais de Lafond's original force only *L'Alcyon* remained effective. On the American side *Massachusetts* was hit twice with minor consequences. Her own gun blasts caused more damage. After the action "heavy steel fixtures were torn loose from their fastenings. . . . Steel doors in some cases stood swinging idly on their hinges, bent and useless." *Brooklyn* absorbed one glancing hit. *Wichita* took one heavy hit. A 138.6-mm shell knocked the destroyer *Ludlow* out of the battle.[51]

Shore batteries and submarines were potential equalizers for the outgunned French, but American aircraft proved more damaging. Incessant strafing killed or wounded many officers and navigation, communications, and gunnery personnel. Dive bombing attacks damaged a cruiser, two destroyers, and a sloop. French aircraft, on the other hand, completely failed their navy. The Armée de l'Air concentrated on attacking the beaches and made little effort to protect friendly warships or attack enemy vessels. Even though their crews were all long-term veterans, it is remarkable that the French ships performed and shot as well as they did, given their lack of routine training and the unexpectedness of the attacks.

Massachusetts was a new ship in her first combat. Nineteen of her eighty-four officers had more than two years' experience while twenty-two had no prior sea

French *contre-torpilleur Milan* (partially visible, right), *contre-torpilleur Albatros* (center), and light cruiser *Primauguet* (upper center) anchored off Casablanca on 11 November 1942. All had been badly damaged during the Naval Battle of Casablanca. (U.S. Naval Institute Photo Archive)

service at all, and 1,417 enlisted personnel were raw recruits. Generally shooting at ranges beyond 15,000 yards and hampered by radar failures and the enemy's use of smoke, her gunners shot well. The same was true of the cruisers and destroyers. On the other hand, American tactics led to some dangerous moments. Hewitt, Giffen, and Emmet had conflicting priorities and failed to coordinate their activities. Hewitt had overall responsibility for all three landings, but the command arrangements put him in the middle of a battle on the bridge of a heavy cruiser while the army commander hovered impatiently at his side. Captain Emmet, even though he was on board a transport, had tactical responsibility for *Augusta, Brooklyn,* and Destroyer Division 26 as shore bombardment vessels. His main concerns were securing the beachhead, unloading the transports, and battling the shore batteries, although that would have changed in a hurry had French destroyers burst through the smoke to confront him. Giffen was tasked with suppressing *Jean Bart* and El Hank, watching for *Richelieu,* and containing the French warships at Casablanca. These proved two jobs too many. The fact that a battleship

TABLE 12.1

Gunnery Damage on Warships during Bombardments and Surface Action,
Casablanca, 8 November 1942

Time	Range*	shell	Fired by	Target	Damage
0643	6	138-mm	Pont Blondin	*Murphy*	moderate
0725	23	16-in	*Massachusetts*	*Jean Bart*	moderate
0735	25	16-in	*Massachusetts*	*Jean Bart*	minor
0736	25	16-in	*Massachusetts*	*Jean Bart*	moderate
0737	25	2x16-in	*Massachusetts*	*Jean Bart*	minor
0803	10	100-mm	Fédala	*Ludlow*	minor
0806	26	16-in	*Massachusetts*	*Malin*	severe
0806	26	2x16-in	*Massachusetts*	*Jean Bart*	severe
0810	27	16-in	*Massachusetts*	*Jean Bart*	severe
0834	14	138-mm	*Albatros*	*Ludlow*	moderate
0940	12	16-in	*Massachusetts*	*Fougueux*	sunk
0946	15	8-in	*Tuscaloosa*	*Frondeur*	moderate
0956	28	16-in	*Massachusetts*	*Milan*	severe
1000	28	194-mm	El Hank	*Massachusetts*	minor
1005	6	100-mm	Fédala	*Palmer*	minor
1010	26.5	8-in	*Wichita*	*Brestois*	moderate
1012	10	6x6-in	*Brooklyn*	*Boulonnais*	sunk
1020	18	3x6-in	*Brooklyn*	*Primauguet*	moderate
1040	21	8-in (?)	*Augusta* (?)	*Albatros*	near miss/moderate
1045	15	138-mm	*Albatros*	*Brooklyn*	minor
1045	17	8-in (?)	*Augusta* (?)	*Primauguet*	near miss/minor
1057	22	155-mm	*Primauguet*	*Massachusetts*	minor
1125	14	8-in	*Wichita*	*Frondeur*	severe
1128	16	194-mm	El Hank	*Wichita*	moderate
1130	16.5	8-in	*Tuscaloosa*	*Primauguet*	moderate
1235	?	5-in	*Tillman*	*Estafette*	severe

*Thousands of yards.

based thousands of miles away received consideration while a French squadron snuck out of port and attacked transports fifteen miles away is testimony to the deep respect battleships inspired in those with the job of potentially facing them, but speaks poorly of Giffen's priorities.

Rear Admiral Gervais de Lafond, perhaps recognizing that a thin margin decided many naval actions, was persistent. Every ship in his force fought until it could fight no longer. Even though communication difficulties quickly degraded the squadron's cohesion and effectiveness, junior officers stepped up and fought aggressively, and French gunnery impressed the Americans, although it achieved relatively few hits. Nevertheless, when Gervais de Lafond had the opportunity to lead his united squadron around Cape Fédala into the transport park, he failed to take it.

During World War II major warships tried to break up an amphibious landing nearly a dozen times. The U.S. Navy found itself on the defensive in many such engagements, including Savo Island, Empress Augusta Bay, and Leyte Gulf. Japanese warships never brought American landing craft under fire like the French did at Casablanca. The Naval Battle of Casablanca was more than a futile expression of false Gallic pride, which is how much of the literature portrays it. Had Gervais de Lafond reached the transports, had French submarines disabled *Massachusetts* or one or more of the cruisers, the consequences could have materially affected the outcome of the landings.

13

THE FALL OF CASABLANCA

If the [German] armistice commission had been more understanding
of our defense needs, the French air force would have been in
better condition to fulfill the task entrusted to it.
—COMMANDER MEKNÈS, 11 NOVEMBER 1942, RESPONDING TO
CRITICISMS OF GERMAN ARMISTICE COMMISSIONER

9 November

On 9 November the 3rd Division consolidated its beachhead around Fédala—a process impeded by the loss of 242 of 378 landing craft on the 8th. High surf did not help. On Red 2 the beach master watched a loaded LCPR attempt to land. "The boat started in on the back of a wave which, I estimated, was 12 to 15 feet high. The boat's speed was a little too great and it crossed the crest of the wave while still about a hundred yards from shore. The boat was thrown end over end and swamped." Because of this and similar incidents, he suspended beach landings and diverted boats into Fédala Harbor. To cut turnaround time the transports moved inshore at 1130. Patton himself, after spending the night at the Hôtel Miramar, complained in his diary, "The beach was a mess and the officers were doing nothing." He spent several hours kicking and cursing and took credit for the beach master's decision to use Fédala Harbor.[1]

Large vessels also crowded into the small port. During the morning *Arcturus* entered with the aid of a French pilot and several LCMs acting as tugs and discharged her cargo of tanks directly onto the quay. By 1700 (D+36) TG 34.9 had offloaded 55 percent of personnel, 31 percent of vehicles, and 3.3 percent of supplies.[2]

Ground Operations

On the 9th the 3rd Division started toward Casablanca. The 7th/3rd Battalion deployed on the coast with the 2nd on its left flank and the 1st in reserve. The 15th/2nd and 1st Battalions comprised the left wing with the 3rd in reserve. The 30th Regiment held the beachhead's eastern and southern perimeter and deflected several probes by the 1 RCA moving down from Rabat.

The two American regiments advanced against scattered resistance, reaching a line approximately midway between Fédala and Casablanca. Then Major General Anderson decided his men were not receiving the supplies they required and at 1400 he called a halt to bring up materiel from Fédala.[3]

For the most part, French troops awaited the Americans in positions surrounding Casablanca and did not conduct the aggressive counterattacks that marked the fighting at Port Lyautey. Division General Raymond Desré, who had relieved Béthouart, commanded five infantry battalions: the III/6 RTS to the east covering Oukacha and the principal highway to Fédala, the II/6 RTM to the southeast, the III/6 RTM to the south, the II/RICM to the southwest, and the I/6 RTM to the west. Supporting these units were three artillery battalions: the III/64 RAA, the II RACM (Régiment d'Artillerie Coloniale du Maroc, or colonial artillery regiment of Morocco), and the IV RACM. Desré also deployed elements of the 1 RSM (Régiment de Spahis Marocains, or Moroccan Spahis regiment), an ad hoc naval battalion formed by 334 survivors of the 2nd Light Squadron, and a mobile reserve group.

Air Attacks

At dawn five fighters swooped over Fédala and strafed landing craft. At 0715 a formation of six LeO 451s, three DB-7s, and a pair of Glenn Martins, escorted by fifteen fighters, bombed the beach at Fédala. Six Wildcats tangled with the escort and shot down four.[4]

One aircraft overflew the transport area at 0733 and drew fire from "practically every ship in the area." A solitary DB-7 bomber dropped four bombs on *Brooklyn* at 0737. The nearest fell a hundred feet away and splinters slightly wounded three men. Aircraft also flew reconnaissance missions. However, attrition continued and by the end of the day the Armée de l'Air's 11th Mixed Group could deploy only five bombers and nine fighters.[5]

10 November

Major General Anderson planned a large attack against Casablanca to start at dawn on the 10th. The 7th and 15th regiments packed extra loads of ammunition and moved out for their start lines at midnight. Almost immediately patrols from the 15th stumbled on elements of the 1 RSM holding Tit Mellil, a village southeast of the city. Rather than bypass the position, both battalions halted to wait for dawn so they could take it before the general attack. In the ensuing action, supported by the regiment's entire resources, the 15th drove the Spahis from Tit Mellil at the cost of only eleven wounded; this success delayed the main blow by ten hours, however.

To the north the 7th/3rd Battalion captured an antiaircraft battery southwest of Oukacha, but thereafter the Batterie d'Oukacha and *Commandant Delage,* which was offshore supporting the army, started shelling the American troops. *Commandant Delage* opened fire at 1100 from under two thousand meters with her main battery and machine guns and expended fifty 100-mm rounds. This drove the battalion to cover and it lost touch with regimental headquarters for several hours. On their left the 2nd Battalion, advancing along the Rabat-Casablanca highway, reached the departure line on schedule, only to be disrupted by French artillery fire. Elements led by Lieutenant Colonel Salzmann moved south to reach high ground while the remainder dug in. At 1045 the 1st Battalion moved up to reinforce the 2nd. The two battalions attempted to reach the French military barracks at Camp de la Jonquière, but by 1700 they were still four hundred yards shy of their objective. The regiment lost twenty-seven men killed and seventy-two wounded in the day's fighting.

Naval Actions

The submarine *Le Tonnant* attacked *Ranger* at 0900, firing four torpedoes from nine hundred yards. All missed, but the escort's counterattack was equally unsuccessful. At 1010 the sloops *La Servannaise, La Gracieuse,* and *Commandant Delage* sortied to support French troops along the coast and forestall any attempt to land behind French lines. Once again aircraft reported their movements and in

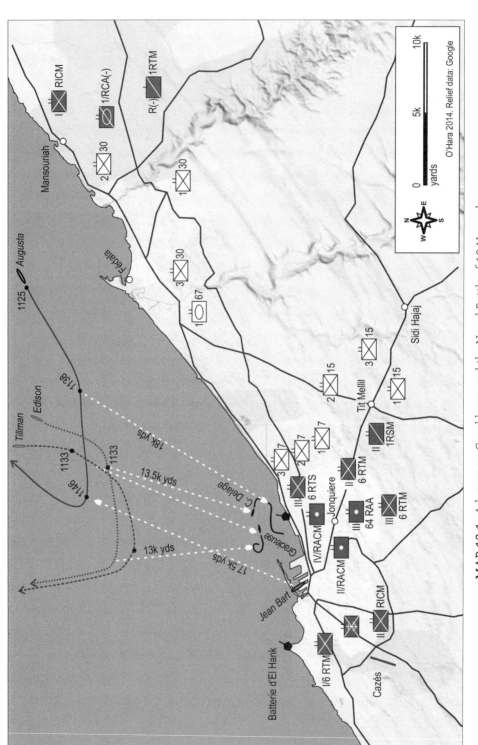

MAP 13.1 *Advance on Casablanca and the Naval Battle of 10 November*

response *Augusta,* accompanied by *Edison, Boyle, Tillman,* and *Rowan,* headed southwest. Making thirty-five knots and well in the van *Edison* engaged *Commandant Delage* at 1133 from 13,500 yards. She rapidly expended two hundred rounds and reported, "Observed accuracy of gunfire and the volume of gunfire undoubtedly resulted in hits." She also claimed that the sloop was burning as it "proceeded at high speed and with radical zigs toward Casablanca." Next *Edison* shifted her guns to *La Gracieuse* and expended sixty-eight rounds against that target. *Tillman* engaged *La Gracieuse* at 1135 but took on the Batterie d'Oukacha five minutes later after the battery started dropping shells close by. At 1144 *Tillman* turned to open range. She fired 180 rounds and claimed that she forced a destroyer leader aground.[6]

At 1137 *Augusta* entered the fray from 18,000 yards. Within minutes a pair of 8-inch shells struck *Commandant Delage.* The first killed five men near the bridge. The second landed forward of the main gun and exploded, killing one and wounding five. A third shell sliced an antenna and detonated close aboard. The French vessels made smoke and zigzagged toward port. *Rowan* chipped in some long shots at 1140 from 17,900 yards, but *Boyle* was "unable to range on the target while being under fire from the shore batteries. Numerous salvos were observed falling close to *Augusta* and a number fell very near *Boyle*."[7]

By 1144 *Augusta* had discharged twenty-four rounds in seven salvos. Meanwhile, *Jean Bart's* crew had cleared the turret jammed two days before, but left it trained in the same position so the Americans would not suspect it had been repaired. *Jean Bart's* captain later told Hewitt, "When you ran down the coast after our little corvettes the gunnery control officer sat up in the top beckoning and saying 'Come a little closer! Come a little closer!'" At 1146 the battleship's main battery arched a salvo 17,500 yards toward *Augusta.* Hewitt recalled, "Suddenly, two huge orange splashes rose, so close alongside the bridge of the *Augusta* that I and others on the flag bridge were doused with the spray." The cruiser spun around spewing smoke as *Jean Bart* fired eight more two-gun salvos, chasing *Augusta* out to 29,000 yards. The cruiser's war diary complained, "We returned to the transport area feeling very fortunate that no damage had been sustained and indignant at the falsity of the report that the *Jean Bart* had been 'gutted by fire.'" American aircraft retaliated with strikes on the battleship and strafing attacks against the docks and stranded destroyers. Nine SBDs armed with 1,000-pound bombs dived on *Jean Bart* shortly before 1500; two struck, disabling her for good.[8]

The transports off Fédala continued unloading. *Procyon* replaced *Arcturus* in Fédala. At noon *New York* reported from Safi to relieve *Massachusetts* of bombardment duties. *Howard* and *Hamilton* escorted the old battleship; *Howard* continued north and joined TG 34.8. *Cleveland* replaced *Brooklyn* in the firing line because *Brooklyn* was low on ammunition. TG 34.1 retired west to refuel Destroyer Squadron 8 from *Chemung* and *Housatonic*.

On the 10th Lieutenant General Eisenhower telegrammed Patton, "Algiers has been ours for two days. Oran defense crumbling rapidly. . . . The only tough nut left is in your hands. Crack it open quickly." The embarrassed general took this request at face value and readied a grand offensive to commence at 0730 on the 11th. It was to include air attacks, naval bombardments, and a renewed assault by the 3rd Division, hopefully aided by Combat Command B of the 2nd Armored Division, which was hurrying north from Safi. Hewitt received Patton's plan at 0130 that morning and *New York, Augusta,* and *Cleveland* moved up to take on El Hank and support the troops.[9]

The Armistice

At 1105 on the 10th Admiral Darlan issued orders in the marshal's name to cease fighting throughout North Africa. Vice Admiral Michelier received the news by radio at 1430 and General Noguès an hour later. Because Algiers was occupied by the Americans, both wanted confirmation that Darlan was acting freely. In the meanwhile, Noguès ordered Michelier and the divisions at Casablanca and Marrakech to suspend hostilities and wait for instructions. Michelier, who had just witnessed *Jean Bart* being bombed and his wrecked warships strafed, was suspicious, and at 1706 he sought guidance directly from Vichy.[10]

Several telephone conversations satisfied Noguès that Darlan's order was authentic, and at 2000 he telephoned Michelier and told him so. Michelier still hesitated and at 2008 dispatched another message to Vichy. The capital was nonresponsive, in part because Laval was still meeting with Hitler. Finally at 2140 Rear Admiral Auphan answered Michelier's first query, saying that Pétain's orders were to continue "hostilities for as long as possible." It was clear that Noguès was going to honor the cease-fire, and the admiral, who had seen his command fight so hard and suffer such losses, reluctantly concluded that further resistance was impossible. At 0300 he issued orders to all naval units in Morocco to immediately suspend hostilities. Michelier communicated his decision to the admiralty in

Vichy forty-five minutes later. Auphan replied at 0750 on the 11th: "I agree with your decision . . . and bow before the painful heroism of the navy in Morocco whose sacrifices will allow the marshal to save France." At 1100 on the 11th Noguès telegraphed to Vichy a long explanation of his decision to accept the cease-fire, but this did not arrive until 0700 on the 12th.[11]

At 0200 Noguès dispatched a party from Rabat to inform the Americans that he would accept Darlan's cease-fire call and to carry appropriate orders to Casablanca. This was accomplished just in time to avoid Patton's offensive. At 1400 that day the American commander hosted Noguès, Lascroux, Division General Auguste Lahoulle of the Armée de l'Air, and Vice Admiral Michelier at the Hôtel Miramar. Accounts of this meeting vary. Patton arranged a formal honor guard and in a letter to his wife written that evening stated, "Gen. Nogues and Adm. Michelier came to treat for terms. . . . Nogues is a crook—a handsome one. Michelier is a man and a very mad one at the moment. . . . I opened the conference by congratulating the French on their gallantry. . . . I closed the conference with champagne and many toasts." In between the congratulations and the champagne Patton granted generous terms. In a subsequent letter to Stimson explaining his actions the general noted that French Morocco was a protectorate and its security depended on maintaining the French army's prestige. For this reason he allowed the French to retain their arms and administration. He obtained acknowledgement that American troops had the right to occupy any areas required for security, but not the release of Brigade General Béthouart or his adherents who had all been arrested. Darlan and Clark would determine the final terms. According to a French historian, Patton, as the victor, wished to apply harsh terms that amounted to unconditional surrender, but Noguès, who knew the deal granted in Algiers, complained that Patton's terms were worse than those imposed by the Germans. "Patton softened, impressed by the firm and dignified attitude of Noguès, and above all by the possibility that fighting might renew."[12]

Patton was criticized for allowing the administration to retain power, and many Frenchmen were likewise displeased by the outcome. Béthouart barely escaped execution for treason. When Hewitt paid a courtesy call on Michelier on 13 November, he was a little bemused to see two unexploded 16-inch shells mounted on either side of the entrance to naval headquarters. It was, he later wrote, "a truly French touch."[13]

Logistics and Submarines

At 1400 on the 11th *Oberon* replaced *Procyon* in Fédala. By 1700 on the 11th (D+84) all combat troops were ashore and only a few vehicle drivers and some working details remained on the transports. Sixty-eight percent of all vehicles (1,156) had landed, but the discharging of supplies continued to lag, with only 24 percent offloaded.[14]

There were fifteen transports and cargo vessels anchored in rows close off Fédala, and Hewitt was sensitive to the threat submarines poised to this concentration. It appeared that the day began with a success when, at 0710, TBFs from *Suwannee* sighted a submarine "of the German 740 ton type" sailing on the surface twelve miles west of Casablanca. Three of the aircraft approached from astern and dropped twelve depth charges and observed as many as eight explode within lethal range as the submarine was submerging. "A large oil slick appeared and bubbles persisted . . . for about 30 minutes." The submarine was sunk, but unfortunately it was the French *Sidi-Ferruch*. She had transferred two wounded men to a Spanish vessel at 2200 the night before and had presumably intercepted the signal regarding the cease-fire and was making for Casablanca. However, this is not certain as there were no survivors.[15]

U 173, the first German submarine to reach the scene, evaded patrolling destroyers and at 1948 on the 11th fired torpedoes into the crowded anchorage. One caught *Joseph Hewes* on her port bow, flooding three holds. The transport settled by the bow at 2032, taking the captain and several other men along with 90 percent of her cargo down with her. A second torpedo slammed into the tanker *Winooski* amidships, blasting a hole twenty-five feet wide in a tank ballasted with sea water. However, counterflooding easily corrected the list, and by discharging 4,830 barrels of oil the tanker maintained buoyancy. The next day she refueled two destroyers from her undamaged forward tanks and ultimately unloaded her entire cargo. A third torpedo from the same salvo struck the destroyer *Hambleton* on the port beam, nearly breaking the ship in two. *Hambleton* immediately assumed a 12-degree list to starboard, but strenuous damage control efforts reduced this to 5 degrees and the destroyer stayed afloat. On the 12th the tug *Cherokee* towed her into Casablanca. She went on to serve in the Normandy landings.[16]

At 2027 *Bristol* picked up a radar contact as *U 173* headed north to escape. The accelerating destroyer illuminated a minute later and steered to ram as the starboard ready 20-mm gun rattled into action. The forward 5-inch mount fired moments later. The flash temporarily blinded the gunnery officer and the 20-mm crew and a shell hoist malfunction prevented the gun from firing rapidly as ordered. By the time a second round had been hand-loaded, the submarine had vanished. *Bristol* dropped depth charge patterns at 2030 and 2047, but *U 173,* on her second war patrol under a rookie captain, escaped for the time being.[17]

12 November

By this date Rear Admiral McWhorter was growing anxious about the submarine threat to his carriers. Early that morning he cautioned Hewitt that carrier aircraft were "entirely inadequate" to protect against the submarine threat and that "retention of carriers [was] not considered justified." According to the report of the ship's captain, there followed that morning "an intensive attack by a wolf pack of submarines which assumed the proportions of a sea battle." Lookouts reported periscopes, submarines, or torpedo wakes at 0643, 0806, 0812, 0912, and 0916. *Brooklyn* noticed torpedo wakes coming from a pair of Spanish fishing boats, and, worried they might be sheltering a submarine beneath them, *Ranger* and her aircraft machine gunned the vessels. The escorting destroyer *Woolsey,* after dropping depth charges, investigated. Her boarding party found frightened fishermen and holds full of fish and ice but no radio apparatus or fueling gear (for supplying submarines). At 1059 *Ranger*'s port batteries opened fire at another sighting and at 1123 the starboard guns joined in. The ship expended sixty-eight 5-inch and nearly three thousand 20-mm and 1.1-inch rounds. Her aircraft dropped depth charges and strafed wakes and conning towers. Finally, at 1225 McWhorter got his wish and the *Ranger* and her screen shaped course for North America. Despite the fuss and fury, no French or German submarines sighted the carrier that day.[18]

While *Ranger* fought a phantom wolf pack, Hewitt chaired a conference ashore to decide how to continue unloading the task force, given the extreme shortage of landing craft and the fact that most cargo remained on board. One group believed that the transports would be sitting ducks for submarines and that unloading should continue in Casablanca Harbor as berths became available. The rest of the ships would form a convoy that would periodically pass Casablanca, allowing vessels to be detached as berths were available. Another opinion held that Casablanca Harbor was seriously obstructed by sunken and damaged vessels and that using it would delay clearing these in time to receive the follow-up convoy expected on the 15th. This group recommended that transports should continue offloading at Fédala—instantly ready to sail should submarine attacks develop. Hewitt selected the Fédala option and the Germans quickly tested his decision.[19]

U 130, skippered by a Knight's Cross holder, had left France on 29 October. She spent the day approaching Fédala from the east close inshore, scraping her bottom several times. At 1730 the submarine fired four torpedoes from her bow tubes and a fifth from astern. This salvo hit *Hugh L. Scott* with one torpedo on the starboard side. The transport burst into flames and quickly sank, losing 65 percent of her cargo. Two torpedoes struck *Edward Rutledge* on the starboard side. The first one caused "a heavy jar" but the second "a terrific explosion. . . . Debris of all kinds, including bedding rolls, broken hatch boards, cement, and other gear, was thrown into the air at least twice as high as the mainmast." *Rutledge* rapidly listed to starboard and sank at 1848 with the loss of fifteen men and 97 percent of her cargo. Finally, two torpedoes simultaneously struck *Tasker H. Bliss.* "Flames, smoke, and a great column of oil, water, and debris were thrown up abreast of the stack to a height of about 200 feet. . . . The ship heeled sharply to port and then rolled immediately to starboard. . . . She then rolled sharply back, and finally settled to a list of about 30° to starboard." Within a half hour violent fires erupted in the holds storing ammunition and gasoline. "Although cries for help could be heard from the interior of the ship, it was . . . entirely enveloped in smoke and flames." Thirty-three men and 65 percent of the cargo went down with *Bliss.* Following this triple blow Hewitt ordered the transports to get under way.[20]

On 13 November the support forces started to disperse. *New York* and two destroyers were ordered back to the United States. At 1645 *Thomas Jefferson, Wood, Stanton, Charles Carroll,* and *Thurston* entered Casablanca. A U.S. Navy Catalina sank the French submarine *Le Conquérant* en route to Dakar. There were no survivors.

On the 14th Hewitt sent *Susan B. Anthony* and *Algorab* to Safi to unload. *Electra* was ordered to Fédala, and the balance of TG 34.8 with *Sangamon, Jefferson, Carroll, Stanton,* and *Thurston* sailed for the United States at 0915 on the 15th. Meanwhile, *U 173* torpedoed *Electra* at 0630, as related. The waters outside the harbor were clearly too dangerous, and at 1030 *Biddle, Arcturus, Procyon, Dickman,* and *Ancon* entered Casablanca to unload.

On the 16th *U 173*'s luck ran out. The destroyer *Woolsey* was on antisubmarine patrol off Casablanca awaiting her turn to refuel because heavy weather prevented her from so doing at sea when, at 1135, she picked up a "sharp and firm" sound contact only seven hundred yards away. Turning hard she fired two depth charges with her starboard throwers. Black oil bubbled to the surface and

Edward Rutledge at the moment of being torpedoed by *U 130* off Fédala on 12 November 1942. This photo was taken from the deck of *Hugh L. Scott*, which herself had just been torpedoed by the same submarine. *U 130* also sank *Tasker H. Bliss* in this most effective attack. (U.S. Naval Institute Photo Archive)

the destroyer dropped four more depth charges at 1149 and another pattern of four at 1214. "Violent bubbling resulted and continued as long as the area was in sight." She then headed for Casablanca "to obtain urgently needed fuel" as *Swanson* and *Quick* took over, dropping more patterns to ensure the kill. Also that day a protective minefield was laid off the harbor, and five and a half hours later the British hospital ship *Newfoundland* was mined entering port, an "accident entirely due to excessive communication delays."[21]

On 17 November TG 34.9 departed for the United States. In assessing the operation Captain Emmet rated the transports as well-trained (*Biddle* and *Arcturus*), fairly well-trained (*Wood, Dickman, Rutledge, Hewes, Oberon*), well-converted but inexperienced (*Carroll, Jefferson, Procyon*), and poorly converted and inexperienced (*Bliss, Scott, Ancon, Stanton,* and *Thurston*). He noted that *Carroll* and *Jefferson* were used to embark assault troops, but his two biggest complaints were, first, that Major General Patton had devised a landing plan that was too complicated and, second, that he had not been consulted. "Each of the Assault APs was expected to load and put on the Line of Departure for the Assault over

TABLE 13.1

Landing Craft Losses in Initial Assault, Fédala Area, 8 November 1942

Type	Total	Losses in Initial Assault
LCPR and LCPL	156	103
LCV	165	107
LCS(S)	13	4
LCM(3)	44	28
Totals	378	242

fifty (50) landing craft of various types. None of them could have done so, even though HPYP Hour was delayed a total of forty-five (45) minutes, at the request of the Commanding General." Regarding the high loss of landing craft he also blamed the surf that was "*much* higher and more destructive in its effect than any experienced . . . during Drill and Training Exercises." The fact that the initial landings were made on a falling tide and that the landing beaches were under enemy artillery and air fire attack contributed to the high losses. He also faulted the training of the transports and the troops while noting that well-trained ships lost fewer boats than the inexperienced ones.[22]

The beach master in his report also analyzed the high losses of landing craft. He gave the reasons, in order of importance, as the following:

1. Overloading. They took longer to unload and thus, "With large seas breaking over the sterns, the boats soon became helpless."
2. Bombardment of beaches, particularly Red 3 Beach and Blue Beach. "There was nothing the crews of the boats could do . . . except to get into a fox hole to escape destruction. As soon as they left their boats for shelter, the surf soon smashed the boats." Also, shell fire destroyed many boats.
3. Strafing of beaches by French aircraft.
4. Lack of salvage equipment.[23]

Summary

Capturing a strongly held major port with forces from across the Atlantic Ocean was a breathtaking accomplishment. American daring in conducting the undertaking in the first place was rewarded not only by success but also by the opportunity to learn hard lessons at little relative cost—at least compared to an operation like Dieppe. Examined in detail, there were many things to improve. A short list includes the fact that so many landing craft were lost, supplies were unloaded too slowly, submarines sank so many transports after the landings had succeeded, troops fought ineffectively, and enemy forces, particularly naval forces, were not properly contained. The butcher's bill for the fighting in Morocco reflected the human cost of these errors. U.S. forces lost 337 killed, 637 wounded, and 122 missing. The French navy had 457 killed and 624 wounded; the army, 490 killed and 969 wounded; the air force, 13 killed, 20 wounded; and the merchant marine, 39 killed, 31 wounded. Thus, total U.S. casualties were 1,096 compared to 2,643 for the French.[24]

14

SAFI

The landing craft into which we dropped looked like a miniature
toy boat bobbing in a tub of bath water.

—Duane D. Olson, 47th Infantry Regiment

Plans and Objectives

The 47th RCT of the 9th Infantry Division and Combat Command B of the 2nd Armored Division conducted the southernmost of the Moroccan landings at the small phosphate-exporting harbor of Safi, a town of 25,000 inhabitants 135 miles southwest of Casablanca. The planners selected this out-of-the-way objective because it was lightly held and harbor facilities included large cranes that could unload medium tanks directly onto the quay. The plan called for the 47th to hold the port and block interference from the Marrakech Division while the armor sped north to reinforce the 3rd Division's attack on Casablanca.

The 47th's BLTs were each 1,420 men strong: the transport *Harris* carried the 1st BLT, which would come ashore at three beaches around the town designated Red, Blue, and Green Beaches, while the 2nd BLT embarked on *Dorothea L. Dix* would use Yellow Beach south of the city. *Lyon* carried the 3rd BLT, half of which would assault the port directly from two cut-down destroyer-transports while the other two companies formed a reserve. The M3 Stuarts of the 2nd Armored Landing Team of the 67th Armored Regiment carried in *Titania* would also land at Yellow. The railroad transport *Lakehurst* carried a cargo of fifty-four medium

M4 Sherman tanks of the 3rd Battalion, 67th Armored Regiment. *Lakehurst* would dock at the port's large quay once the port was captured.[1]

Red Beach, objective of Company A (elements) and Company B, was a sandy cove 250 yards wide backed by "a weathered cliff 50 feet high." It was nine hundred yards north of the Jetée Transversal, the long jetty that formed one of the two barriers protecting Safi's artificial port. The planners believed that for at least six hours each tide there was a usable beach and that troops could scramble up the cliffs before high tide submerged the area. The rest of the 1st BLT would land on Blue Beach, a strip of sand six hundred yards long, separated from Red by a headland. The same cliffs loomed behind it, but there was a vehicle exit on the southern end beside the jetty. Green Beach was a cove 125 yards wide within the harbor where fishing craft beached. Five LCMs each carrying a Stuart and troops of the 47th's reconnaissance platoon were scheduled to land there immediately behind the destroyer transports to stiffen their attack on the harbor. Yellow Beach was eight miles south near the fishing village of Jorf el Houdi. It was rocky, but the planners considered a six-hundred-yard stretch "apparently an excellent beach for both vehicles and troops," at least in mild weather. If the landings around the port failed, troops and tanks advancing from the south could still secure the objective.[2]

French Dispositions

The Safi-Mogador sector was under Division General J. Henry-Martin, commander of the Marrakech Division headquartered in that city, ninety-five miles east of Safi.[3] American intelligence believed that Safi was occupied by about a thousand men, but in fact there were only 450 from the 104th Coastal Defense Company, the 5th Company of the 2 RTM, the 3rd Battery of the 2 REI with two 75-mm guns, and a platoon of Renault FT-17 tanks. A battery of three 155-mm guns of the 3 GPF was emplaced south of the city. Shore batteries, all army manned, included the Batterie de la Railleuse with modern fire control and two 130-mm guns (and two more that were disarmed) salvaged from the destroyer of that name, perched on a cliff overlooking the ocean several miles north of the harbor; and the Front de Mer, just inland from Blue Beach with two 75-mm guns. Pairs of machine guns were perched on the Jetée des Phosphates and at the yacht club near Green Beach. The head of the Safi subsector was a naval officer, Captain François Deuve.

On the night of the 7th an emissary from Brigade General Béthouart contacted Henry-Martin and advised that American troops would be arriving the next day. Trying to decide how to react to this startling news, the general tele-phoned army command in Rabat and was flabbergasted to learn they knew nothing about it. The general tried to reach Béthouart, but was told he had left Casablanca. Finally, checking with Noguès, Henry-Martin learned that Béthouart had attempted to imprison the resident-general. "Outraged by this method, Henry-Martin decided to implement the plan of defense" and issued an alert at 0225. Captain Deuve had already received a warning from Marine au Maroc at 0225 on the 8th and a full alert followed at 0325.[4]

Approach and Landings

TG 34.10 separated from TF 34 at 0653 on 7 November and headed south. Nearly four hundred men of Companies L and K transferred from the transport *Lyon* to destroyer-transports *Cole* and *Bernadou.* The task group then formed a column led by *New York* with destroyers screening the flanks. The carrier *Santee* and oiler *Merrimack* followed well astern. Rear Adm. Lyal A. Davidson, the task group commander flying his flag on light cruiser *Philadelphia,* maneuvered to the landing zone, eight miles off the coast, and the transports came to a stop at 2345 on the 7th, fifteen minutes behind schedule. The night was partly cloudy and very dark with a smooth sea, moderate swell, and a light offshore breeze. "Scattered city lights were visible."[5]

    Harris embarked 1,861 men of the 1st BLT and assorted support units. Capt. O. M. Forster ordered boats away at 2355 and all twenty-eight landing craft were afloat by 0039—longer than it took in practice but a credible performance none-theless. Eight LCPRs and ten LCVs from *Lyon* and one LCS and two LCPRs from *Calvert* completed the numbers required to lift the assault troops ashore. The *Lyon* contingent did not locate *Harris* until 0200, which caused "anxious wait-ing but contributed slightly in the subsequent delay of H-hour." At 0300 Maj. Gen. Ernest N. Harmon and Capt. Wallace B. Phillips, commander of Transport Division 7, decided to postpone H hour to 0430. The problem, according to Cap-tain Forster, was "extreme slowness of the combat teams in arriving at the debarka-tion nets" and their caution in climbing down the nets. It took some boats an hour to load. This was a function of lack of practice and the overloading of the troops with equipment. The 47th Regiment's Col. Edwin H. Randle described his own descent:[6]

> His feet pushed the net toward the ship and there was nothing to resist the
> push. . . . The tommy gun crashed into his side, then swung out, the sling

Light cruiser USS *Philadelphia* off Safi. She and her sister ships *Brooklyn* and *Savannah* proved valuable vessels in the bombardment and surface combat roles. (Jody Mishan Collection)

sliding off his shoulder. He caught it in the crook of his elbow and managed to keep it there the rest of the way down. Map case, musette bag, gas mask, and pouch of magazines all alternately swung out then banged into him. The descent seemed interminable, but he kept on, a step at a time, feeling with his feet for each lower strand, hearing the black water surge below, but not looking down. . . . Finally, when the water sounded awfully close he did look down. Directly under him the boat was rising and falling and hands were reaching to help him. He jumped and the hands caught and steadied him. "Boy!" he breathed, "I should have practiced that more."[7]

The colonel did not carry the sixty pounds of equipment that burdened his troops in addition to their arms and ammunition.

Another problem was that the ship had not been properly combat loaded. "It was necessary to go down several decks for some of the equipment when actually loading boats." Nonetheless, the Tank Lighter Wave for Green Beach and the first three waves for Red and Blue Beaches arrived at the debarkation line in time to meet the revised schedule.[8]

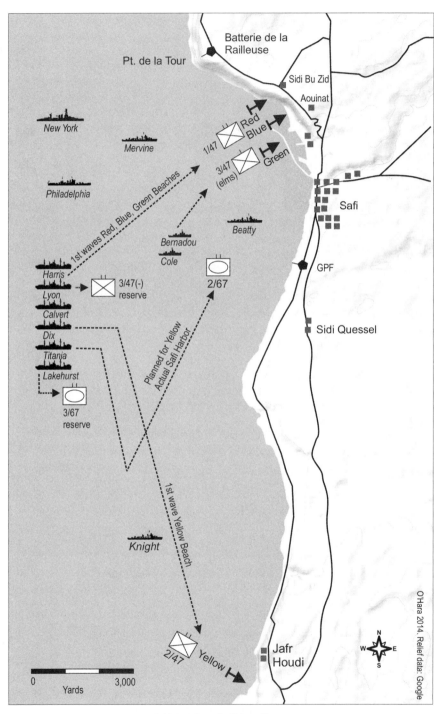

MAP 14.1 *Safi Landings*

Barb, the beacon submarine, was to launch a rubber boat that would proceed to a station off the outer jetty and guide in the assault destroyers and first landing waves with an infrared light. Although she was off Safi for forty-eight hours *Barb* launched the boat at 2200 on 7 November so far away the crew paddled six hours, only to reach the jetty behind the first waves. Once arrived, machine-gun fire drove them into the water where they clung to the gunwale as bullets whizzed overhead. Fortunately, when Captain Forster could not locate *Barb* he ordered an LCS skippered by Ens. J. J. Bell to proceed to the end of the jetty and mark the harbor entrance—just in case. Bell's boat shoved off at 0200. The ensign found *Bernadou* and *Cole* and conferred with their captains for several minutes regarding communications. He then motored toward shore at low speed. He cut the engine every fifteen minutes to listen and veered slightly off course to go through the submarine rendezvous area, flashing his infrared light but seeing nothing. At 0400 Bell reached the jetty's tip.[9]

The Harbor Assault

Bernadou left the disembarkation area at 0345. *Cole* followed fifteen minutes later leading two waves from *Harris* and the Tank Lighter Wave. At 0410 a light from shore challenged *Bernadou,* and her captain, Lt. Cdr. Robert E. Braddy Jr., recalling a similar instance in the Pacific, replied with the same letters. Because nothing happened, he assumed this ruse worked. In fact, a lookout had reported *Bernadou* to Captain Deuve ten minutes earlier. Thinking this might be a fishing vessel whose arrival was expected, he ordered the signal and—if a satisfactory reply was not received—a warning shot. However, after receiving the wrong answer, the battery lost track of *Bernadou* and so held fire.[10]

At 0428 *Bernadou* approached the Jetée Principale. Ensign Bell pointed the infrared light in her direction. "She came in without hesitation, passed the North of the breakwater and got as far as the mouth of the Harbor before anything happened." Then there was a muffled boom as the Batterie Front de Mer opened fire. At the same moment machine guns on both jetties erupted into action. The destroyer's weapons—ready with ranges and deflections predetermined—responded immediately. A volley of quarter-pound 20-mm rounds silenced the machine gun on the Jetée des Phosphates. Two grenade launchers on the fire control bridge took out another machine gun on the Jetée Principale. For good measure the destroyer also fired an American flag flare, but this did not properly deploy and her gunnery, with that of the supporting destroyers *Mervine* and *Beatty,* did far more to cool the hot reception. *Mervine* clocked her first salvo at 0430, aiming at gun flashes between Red Beach and Safi. "The problem was already set up on the computer, tracking having been done on a light leak in what afterwards proved to be the shore emplacement rangefinder shed." *Beatty* fired two minutes later, hesitating until her captain determined that the boat waves were on the line of departure: the news that H hour had been delayed had never been clearly communicated to him. It also helped that the French 75-mm guns "experienced many misfires and their fire was ineffective."[11]

With the harbor flickering in the light of gun flashes Batterie de la Railleuse entered the fray lobbing 130-mm shells at *Mervine.* The destroyer captain wrote that the projectiles "appeared as a white luminous glow whipping toward us, whistling overhead and then smacking the water." *Mervine* replied, followed by *Philadelphia* at 0438 and *New York* at 0441. The battleship lofted nine 5-inch star shells in three salvos, but the illumination was ineffective. At 0445 one main turret engaged from 14,000 yards ranging on the enemy's gun flashes. The first salvo was over, the second salvo, of one round, was under, and observers believed they inflicted damage with the third, likewise of one round, which appeared to start a small fire on the cliff top. La Railleuse ceased fire and so did *New York.* By 0500 *Mervine,* having expended 121 rounds, noted, "All batteries on the shore had been silenced."[12]

Bernadou increased speed as she steamed down the fairway and set course for the quay beyond the Jetée des Phosphates. Lieutenant Commander Braddy wanted to "effect landing as quickly as possible and to prevent sinking in the harbor should the ship suffer a fatal hit." However, he had to swerve to avoid a small steamer and moments later the destroyer piled onto rocks near the Petite Jetée just west of Green Beach. The impact knocked men off their feet and flooded four compartments, but according to the destroyer's report the assault troops began swarming down a cargo net draped over the starboard bow onto the rocks below within four minutes of impact. Remarkably, no one was hurt. The ship expended fifty-seven 3-inch and 750 20-mm rounds during her short run up harbor.[13]

Sailing at eight knots *Cole* left the transport area at 0400 followed by the boats heading for Red, Blue, and Green Beaches. Her skipper, Lt. Cdr. G. G. Palmer, doubted the accuracy of the given heading to the breakwater (063 degrees true) because the beacon submarine had not confirmed it, and so he followed 083 degrees true based on his own observations. He lost sight of *Bernadou's*

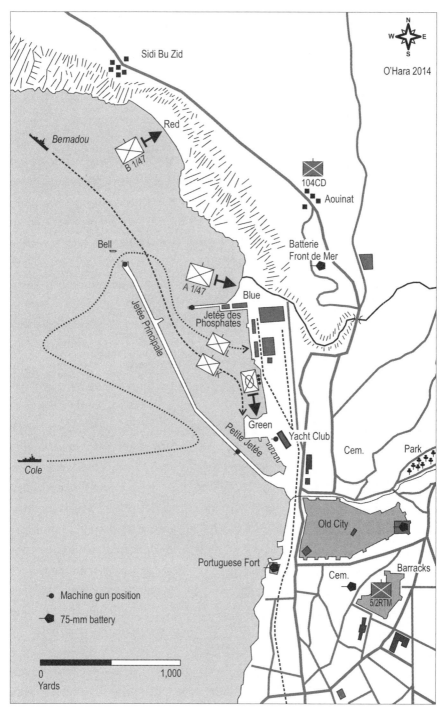

Sidi Bu Zid

Red

Bernadou

B 1/47

104CD

Aouinat

Bell

A 1/47

Batterie
Front de Mer

Blue

Jetée des
Phosphates

Jetée Principale

L

K

Green

Petite Jetée

Yacht Club

Cem.

Park

Cole

Old City

Portuguese Fort

Cem.

Barracks

5/2RTM

● Machine gun position

⬟ 75-mm battery

0   1,000
Yards

O'Hara 2014

MAP 14.2 *Attack on Safi Harbor*

infrared light after a few minutes and then picked up a silhouette on the port bow that was, as he later wrote, "in the approximate position at which the *Bernadou's* Infra-Red Beacon disappeared. This silhouette gave every indication of being the *Bernadou,* inasmuch as all assisting personnel on the bridge agreed that the shape of the silhouette was mastless and identically that of the *Bernadou.*" In fact, he had sighted *Mervine* and followed her, in the process unintentionally veering away from the entrance.[14]

Cole reported that shells fell close aboard to starboard within a minute of the bombardment's start at 0428 and that she returned fire with her No. 1 3-inch gun. *New York's* star shells burst overhead. Lieutenant Commander Palmer recorded, "The effectiveness of fire from the heavy ship's [*sic*] was very noteworthy." To the level-headed Ensign Bell, however, the "shots seemed to be quite wild and were landing all over the place." Meanwhile, still shadowing *Mervine, Cole* approached the outer jetty. Palmer wrote, "The shoreline was becoming very prominent and I felt that I might be going aground . . . [then] at about 0455 a white light flashing 3 dashes was sighted on the port bow. It was realized that this was Bell's signal." Bell was more emphatic: "At about 0450 I caught the first glimpse of the *Cole,* she was off her intended course and was . . . heading directly for the center of the breakwater." *Cole* veered to port, narrowly avoiding disaster, and then cut between Bell's boat and the end of the jetty, turning hard to starboard into the port. *Cole* reported the time as 0517, but it was earlier as Captain Deuve radioed Casablanca at 0457, saying, "Two enemy destroyers have entered the port."[15]

As *Cole* approached the Jetée des Phosphates a small ship blocked her path. Palmer attempted to come in behind and ease his stern against the quay. This proved difficult, so he maneuvered clear and shot a line and snagged a rail track. When a sailor ran to the line to warp the ship in, he discovered a soldier cutting it with his knife, "thinking that in some way he was doing the ship a service." Finally, at 0545, according to *Cole's* chronology, after much backing and filling, Palmer positioned the destroyer's bow alongside the dock and the troops stepped out onto dry land.[16]

The 1st Battalion Hits the Beach

One of the five LCMs in the Tank Lighter Wave was delayed and one broke down, but three followed *Cole* until shortly before 0500 when, "due to difficulty experienced by the *Cole* in making the harbor entrance [it] passed ahead of the *Cole* at the breakwater and landed three tanks on Green Beach at about 0505." The delayed craft arrived at 0530. Wave 1 with 213 men of the 47th's Reconnaissance Platoon in six LCPRs left the rendezvous area behind *Cole* and the LCMs. In the dark it lost contact but navigated by compass to the breakwater and picked up Bell's light. For the men motoring shoreward crouched in the small craft, the journey seemed interminable. Colonel Randle's boat followed the first waves. For him, "the speeding boat was still wrapped in a blackout curtain, getting nowhere, or so it seemed." He kept pestering the ensign at the helm and even directed him to change course. When the jetty finally came into sight the boat had to turn sharply to avoid piling onto the rocks. The colonel admitted to the ensign, "Guess I was wrong changing your course more to starboard." The ensign replied, "You have to trust your compass."[17]

Wave 1 hit Blue Beach at 0500. The men unloaded lethargically and sporadic rifle fire from the cliffs caused ducking and scurrying but harmed no one. Wave 2, 205 men in six LCPRs, hit Red Beach at 0520. They likewise navigated by compass the eight miles to their destination. Wave 3, 205 men in six LCPRs, also lost contact but reached the breakwater by compass bearing and, greatly assisted by Ensign Bell's signals, landed at 0520. Two boats had trouble retracting due to the falling tide and one boat was damaged by machine-gun fire rounding the breakwater on the way out. The men at Red Beach quickly scrambled up the cliff (they had been briefed that their beach would disappear in the rising tide), but it took the Blue and Green contingents nearly an hour to begin their advance.[18]

The fourth and fifth waves were delayed because *Harris* stood out to sea when the shore battery opened fire. She did not dispatch Wave 4 until 0650. The boats were straddled twice en route and sniped at from the cliff tops but landed at Blue Beach at 0745 without casualties. Wave 5 followed at 0905. Thereafter, vehicles, personnel, equipment, and supplies to the total of 368 boat loads came ashore without regard to waves, through 1220 on 11 November. *Harris* accomplished this without casualty or loss of a single landing craft.

The 2nd Battalion

Dorothea L. Dix began lowering her boats at 0001. These were supplemented by eight LCVs from *Calvert* and two LCMs, ten LCVs, three LCPRs, and two LCPLs from *Titania* and *Lyon*. All were in the water by 0130. The scout boat left at 0135 and arrived off Yellow Beach by 0355. The rest were to rendezvous around *Knight*, the designated control destroyer. Each wave consisted of four boats except the Tank Wave, which had six. However, the plan quickly disintegrated. *Dix* rolled

5 to 7 degrees in the slight swell, and this slowed loading and damaged two boats as they were being lowered. One soldier lost his grip on the net and fell into the sea. Capt. Leo B. Schulten blamed the lack of stability on improper ballasting. As on *Harris,* needed vehicles were stored below other materiel. Lack of training was also a problem. "This vessel was placed in commission on September 17 prior to completion of conversion and fitting out. No drill or exercise at unloading was held."[19]

Once the landing craft were finally manned they could not find *Knight* because the destroyer took station on *Harris.* This error emerged at 0400 when *Knight* signaled *Harris,* asking "Where are your babies?" In reply *Harris* "directed" *Knight* to find *Dix.* At 0430, a half hour behind schedule, *Dix's* five waves were ready and *Dix* was in contract with *Knight.* Finally, at 0515 the view from *Dix* was, "*Knight* appeared headed for Yellow Beach with the . . . waves following her." They were "not well assembled and had difficulty in seeing the destroyer." *Knight,* however, stated that only six landing craft had shown up. Her report does not mention that she had confused transports.[20]

Meanwhile, at 0530 a half-ton truck slammed against *Dix's* hull as it was being lowered, rupturing a five-gallon gasoline container. Fuel sprayed the LCV below and was ignited by the boat's engine. The boat exploded and the truck caught fire. *Dix's* crew deployed hoses and extinguished the blaze, but in the pre-dawn dark it seemed to *Knight* that the transport had been torpedoed. The destroyer turned away from the beach at high speed, leaving the landing craft behind her "lost and confused." *Merrimack* had just finished launching two crash boats that were supposed to act as dispatch and utility craft. They had the misfortune to appear at this moment and *Lyon* mistook them for enemy torpedo boats. In the words of *Lyon's* report, "At the same time what appeared to be a submarine or 'PT' boat crossed the stern from starboard to Port at high speed as if to gain position for firing on the Port beam." *Lyon* went to seventeen knots and opened fire with her 4-inch and 20-mm guns. Fortunately, her fire was wild.[21]

In this commotion the Yellow Beach waves returned to *Dix.* They did not again form up behind *Knight* until 0810. The first boats landed at 0928 and the last at 1100. The consensus was that the delay was actually fortunate as uncharted rocks would have made Yellow a dangerous destination to tackle in the dark. It proved dangerous even in the light because, as the morning progressed, three LCMs, three LCVs, and two LCPRs broached and were stranded. The troops began trekking north just before noon and linked up with elements of the 1st Battalion south of

Off Safi. Red Beach is on the left below the cliff. Blue Beach is to the right with the Safi breakwater farther to the right. (Jody Mishan collection)

Safi at 1600. They encountered no resistance. The rest of the battalion landed in Safi Harbor. High surf defeated an attempt to salvage the beached craft and the Navy abandoned them when it evacuated Yellow on the night of the 9th.

Battery Fire

At 0640, with enough light for effective spotting, the Batterie de la Railleuse began sniping at *Harris*. While the transport got under way *New York* intervened, firing one two-gun salvo every seventy seconds from ranges out to 18,000 yards. In response Railleuse switched targets. The first shots fell short, but straddles at a steady rate of four rounds a minute followed, forcing *New York* to make radical course and speed changes. Shell fragments from near misses struck the ship but caused no damage. *Philadelphia* shot eighty-nine 6-inch rounds at Railleuse between 0645 and 0710. *Mervine* and *Beatty* likewise pitched their 5-inch shells up onto the tableland. *Mervine's* captain noted, "The fire control problem of effective fire upon a shore battery situated on a five hundred foot cliff was similar to firing on an aircraft, speed zero." The two destroyers expended 184 and 260 5-inch rounds, respectively, during the morning bombardment.[22]

At 0710, after shooting fifty-six rounds, *New York's* spotter observed smoke and debris and Railleuse fell silent. In fact, a 14-inch shell struck just short of the battery's control tower and splinters ricocheted through the observation slot, demolishing the director and killing the battery commander and another man. The guns continued in action at a reduced rate of fire, but the dust raised by the bursting shells made accurate shooting impossible. *Mervine* recorded the last shells from the battery at 0730, and at 0850 the crew evacuated the position.[23]

The Capture of Safi

After unloading from *Bernadou,* K Company was joined by the 47th Reconnaissance Platoon and they infiltrated toward their objectives in the dark. The machine gun at the yacht club fired briefly and then fell silent. The Americans overran the waterfront and scattered a platoon of Moroccan *tirailleurs* that was advancing from its barracks in the town. Meanwhile, L Company ascended the heights overlooking the port. It was still dark when they debouched onto the plateau and surrounded the Batterie Front de Mer.[24]

The three Stuarts that landed on Green Beach proved an early disappointment. Engine and battery problems kept them inactive for several hours. The Renault FT-17s did little better. They clanked forward from a position near the public park, but at 0615 American troops took the unit commander prisoner and forced the two surviving tanks to retreat to the barracks.

Company A, most of which landed at Blue Beach, advanced slowly, especially after dawn as French gunfire increased and repeatedly drove the inexperienced soldiers to cover. Nonetheless, elements gained the heights where they joined Company L. The 104th Company, less a detachment at the Batterie de la Railleuse, was concentrated at the village of Aouinat two hundred yards north of the Front de Mer. Companies A and L attacked and overran Aouinat although snipers continued to harass the Americans.

The 155-mm battery south of Safi bombarded the landing craft at 0720, 0910, and 0930. Colonel Randle watched a wave bringing men of Company D and the headquarters platoon to Blue Beach. "When about two hundred yards from the beach shells began falling among the boats. . . . There was no panic. . . . The coxswains brought them to the beach perfectly aligned, though shells had been throwing up geysers between boats close in front and behind the waves." However, "the troops that had just landed were understandably nervous. It was their baptism of fire. . . . At each rifle crack officers and men dropped to the cinders." The colonel ordered them to advance, and "cautiously and with some reluctance the men got up and moved on." The tanks had solved their problems by this time. They motored around the town blasting snipers and by 1130, in conjunction with B Company, had taken the Batterie de la Railleuse. Combat engineers subsequently fused the breeches and blasted the muzzles.[25]

Tactical surprise and overwhelming force were key to the quick American success, but resistance remained. One house, perched on the slope above Blue Beach, sheltered a nest of snipers. At 1000 *Cole* shifted position to bring No. 6 gun to bear and fired four rounds at the house, hitting with the last two and "making stucco and chunks of masonry fly." That stopped the potshots for a while. The Moroccan 5th Company withdrew to positions in the Portuguese Fort, the command post, and the women's prison. They contested the Americans' advance, but ammunition was in short supply.[26]

After the first Yellow Beach wave Major General Harmon ordered the rest of the armored landing team to head for Green Beach, and it began landing at 0900, harassed by a 25-mm gun firing from the Portuguese Fort. A spotter called down a naval bombardment that quickly silenced the weapon. The newly landed tanks then investigated the fort and found it abandoned.

At 1025 Harmon requested naval fire to suppress the 155-mm battery. *Philadelphia* sent a ranging salvo to the location indicated, but the SOC overhead radioed that there were no targets there. The plane then undertook a low altitude search and spotted the battery, "cleverly camouflaged" about eight hundred yards away. At 1110 the light cruiser tried again but failed to hit with 109 rounds. However, six SOCs dropped four 325-pound depth charges and a pair of 100-pound fragmentation bombs and obtained a direct hit. By this time the crews had already spiked their guns and abandoned the position.[27]

In the town the barracks and women's prison continued to resist. The prison fell at 1400. Most of the troops escaped east although some retreated to the barracks. "Civilian employees, soldiers on leave and stragglers from the 5th and 104th companies" held the walled barracks south of the old city. Company I, which landed at 0903 with Company M, attacked this position from the north to support Company K, which was assaulting from the south. According to an observer, Maj. James Y. Adams, I Company's advance was stopped by "overs from K Company firing from house tops directly across the Barracks." The position's thirty-one defenders surrendered at 1500 after a twenty-minute bombardment by Company M's mortars. The commander of the 5th Company along with twenty-five men escaped and rallied to the 2 RTM at Tetla.[28]

The Shermans Come Ashore

At 1350 the sea train *Lakehurst,* loaded with the Shermans of the 3rd Battalion, 67th Armored Regiment, eased its way into the harbor and berthed at the Jetée des Phosphates. Shortly thereafter *Titania* with the rest of the 2nd Armored Battalion joined her. A *Lakehurst* officer noted, "There was continuous rifle firing between snipers and Army troops . . . in the waterfront streets from 1430 to 1530." A typical incident occurred when landing craft disgorged armored troops at Blue Beach. Snipers still occupied a house on the hillside above. A few rifle shots broke the afternoon stillness. As Harmon and Randle watched, "every tanker dropped to the sand and three hundred trigger-happy tommy-gunners poured out streams of 45s as fast as magazine would empty. Not a man knew what he was firing at." It took the two commanding officers, shouting and waving their arms, ten minutes to halt the fusillade. Randle estimated that the episode used more ammunition than that expended in taking the town. The house was captured shortly thereafter and seventeen prisoners taken, including the 104th Company's commander.[29]

Lakehurst began to discharge cargo at 1610, but a jammed derrick took five hours to repair while on *Titania* a broken cable required seven hours to splice. The critical Major Adams observed that the unloading "seemed haphazard and utterly confused . . . [and] resulted in chaotic conditions on beaches and docks where supplies and equipment were piled high without regard to segregation in dumps or safe-keeping." The lieutenant commanding *Lyon's* beach party corroborated this observation, noting that when his men arrived at Blue Beach on the afternoon of the 9th the beach "was covered with vehicles waiting to be driven or hauled away. One ambulance and one jeep were in the water almost wholly submerged." There were also two broached LCMs. *Lyon's* men cleared the chaos, working until 0500 on the 10th. Just before dark armored units moved to Bouguedra twelve miles east on the Marrakech highway and established a blocking position to guard against French counterattacks.[30]

Air Operations 8 November

The escort carrier *Santee* had been operational for less than a month and had only five veteran aviators. Rear Admiral Davidson intended the flattop's air group to provide reconnaissance, antisubmarine, and combat air patrols. He also had his battleship and cruiser aircraft. French air assets at Marrakech consisted of twenty-six LeO 451 and Potez 63 bombers, and at Agadir thirteen Douglas DB7 light

Safi from the north. The house that sheltered snipers for much of the 8th is prominent at the bottom center of the photo. (Jody Mishan Collection)

bombers and a pair of naval Glenn Martins. The Americans believed that Division General Henry-Martin would not order hostilities unless provoked, so orders specified that French aircraft with engine and cockpit covers on (i.e., not prepared for flight) would not be attacked.[31]

At first light *New York* and *Philadelphia* catapulted eight SOC Seagulls, three for spotting and five for antisubmarine patrol. Operating forty miles out to sea *Santee* started launching fourteen F4Fs, eight TBFs, and four SBDs before dawn. Six F4Fs were armed with 100-pound bombs and incendiary clusters in case it was necessary to attack Marrakech, while the others flew combat air patrol. The TBFs were assigned armed reconnaissance and the SBDs antisubmarine duties. Five SBDs stayed in reserve and one F4F and one TBF performed photoreconnaissance.

A TBF reported a submarine at 1145 and expended the only weapon used that day. French sources do not record any attacks. Unfortunately, seven F4Fs and two TBFs from the initial launching were lost. At 0745 a Wildcat developed an oil leak and disappeared. At 0830 another could not locate the carrier and had to ditch. The pilot was rescued. At 0920 four F4Fs landed at Mazagan, having run out of fuel. The carrier's flight commander attributed these losses to communication difficulties, poor navigation, and "lack of recent and general flight experience." The Avengers and one Wildcat crashed on takeoff. There was hardly any French air activity—a DB-7 out of Agadir overflew the transports at 1545, drawing heavy flak, and crashed east of the city. Boats from *Dix* complained that they were strafed by a French aircraft while conducting their landing. The planes at Marrakech were inactive because it had rained and the field was too muddy for bombers to take off.[32]

Communications between Rear Admiral Davidson and his air commander, Capt. William D. Sample of *Santee,* were poor, and the admiral complained that the results of the reconnaissance missions, particularly the fact that there were an estimated thirty-five French aircraft at Marrakech, were not received until 2300 on the 8th, although the missions were completed in the early morning.[33]

9 November

The weather on 9 November was cloudy with light rain. Davidson received intelligence from ashore that the French would mount an air raid, so the destroyer screen was drawn in around the harbor as an antiaircraft umbrella. Friendly aircraft were warned to stay clear. The expected dawn attack duly arrived, but only one aircraft penetrated the overcast to attack the harbor. At 0650 it dropped a bomb that exploded in an ammunition dump, killing five men, wounding ten, and destroying two vehicles. This courageous effort was greeted with a storm of antiaircraft fire and the plane crashed in flames a half mile after releasing its bomb.[34]

Unloading continued with the priority being to get the tanks off the ships so they could start the advance against Casablanca. However, Combat Command B's (CCB's) combat elements did not finish landing until 1800. Another air raid could have seriously delayed this process and the Americans were fortunate one did not develop.

The day's carrier operations consisted of fifty-two flights. At 0845 a *Philadelphia* SOC sighted the submarine *Méduse* off Cape Blanc. A strafing attack by Wildcats off Casablanca on the 8th (after her attack on *Massachusetts*) had seriously wounded three of the submarine's men and her captain intended to put in to Safi to repair damage, not knowing that the port was also under attack. The Seagull dropped a depth charge that fell close by and cracked the submarine's starboard ballast tank.[35]

At 1000 French guns fired on a F4F scouting the airfield at Marrakech and in response the pilot dropped two 325-pound bombs, but too low for them to arm. Captain Sample dispatched a strike force against the airfield without clearing it with Davidson, who had not approved the reconnaissance mission either. The admiral recalled the strike at 1400 because he believed the French had not demonstrated hostile intent.

At 1350 three Wildcats strafed a powerful French column on the Safi-Marrakech road consisting of the II/2 RTM, the 2 REI, and the 11 RCA. The flight leader radioed, "found fourteen trucks and destroyed same." At 1457, Davidson changed his mind about the Marrakech attack upon being informed that French fighters were warming their engines. At 1635 seven SBDs escorted by three F4Fs strafed and bombed the Marraskech airfield. The Americans claimed three French aircraft destroyed and seven damaged. In fact, this strike destroyed or damaged six operational and twenty stored aircraft. The returning fighters buzzed the same column previously strafed and claimed "20 trucks badly shot up."[36]

At the same time Stuarts from the 67th Armored Regiment set out to intercept the French column, which had nearly reached Bouguedra only fifteen miles away. The regiment's first Shermans followed. They encountered the enemy at 1700 outside Bouguedra. After securing a bridge east of the town the battalion bivouacked for the night.

10 November and After

At 1900 Combat Command B began a night march toward Casablanca. The first objective was Mazagan forty miles south of the city. Because there were not enough trucks to transport gasoline from Safi, *Cole* and *Bernadou,* each loaded with three hundred tons of supplies, along with six LCMs would establish a base in Mazagan once the port was taken. The 47th Regiment remained to defend Safi.

Air activities consisted of twenty-four carrier flights. Shortly after dawn three F4Fs and one TBF machine gunned French troops outside Bouguedra. However, enemy artillery frustrated an American attempt to advance past the town into the foothills. Bad weather forced four SBDs sent to scout Marrakech to turn back and so they used their ordnance on the same troops. Seven Dauntlesses and five Avengers strafed and bombed the same position shortly after noon. Just before dark three Wildcats attacked the airfield at Chichauoa. They claimed a dozen aircraft damaged or destroyed. These results came at a high price.[37]

TBFs crash-landed as the result of enemy gunfire at 0930 and 1200. During the afternoon three F4Fs landed at Safi, two as "as a matter of convenience to the ship which was fueling the USS *Philadelphia* at the time." Both were badly damaged. After that, Safi, a small, sloping, and muddy field, was considered unusable. Nonetheless, three Dauntlesses and two Avengers had to land there later that day "as the result of the Pilots' failure to locate the Carrier." All five were damaged. An SBD and a TBF ran out of fuel in the air. Finally, on the 12th a TBF crash-landed on *Santee*. Overall, the carrier air group suffered the destruction of twelve aircraft with another ten damaged and lost to service. By the end of the day on the 10th the *Santee* had three SBDs, four F4Fs, and one TBF operational. The U.S. Navy's air assets were further reduced when *New York* departed for Casablanca to replace *Massachusetts* on the firing line.[38]

After being bombed, *Méduse* proceeded south and landed a reconnaissance party off Pointe de la Tour. By the time the submarine learned that Safi had been captured she was listing 20 degrees to starboard and was short of options. She turned north and, at 0640 on the 10th, beached herself off Cape Blanc. One of *Santee*'s aircraft spotted her there and bombed the wreck at 1055. At 1120 a destroyer arrived and scored three hits in four salvos.[39]

Wrap Up

The armor reached Mazagan's outskirts at 0430 on the 11th. The plan was to attack at 0630, but news of an impending armistice arrived and the town surrendered at 0745. Overall, the French had 239 men taken prisoner, twenty-seven killed, and forty-four wounded.[40]

The attack on Safi was the smallest and most successful of the five major landings. The paucity of opposition was a major reason, but other factors also applied. Of particular note was that the destroyer harbor-forcing attack succeeded. In contrast to Oran and Algiers, the Safi raiders fired the operation's first shots and were immediately reinforced. Destroyers close offshore provided critical fire support. The army leadership, Major General Harmon and Colonel Randle, had combat experience, and in contrast to the Port Lyautey and Casablanca landings, and despite their personal Francophile leanings, they did not treat with the enemy. The use of naval firepower was more effective than at Port Lyautey as evidenced by the greatly different ways *Texas* and *New York* were employed. Navigation was simpler, with fewer beaches to worry about, but the fact that every soldier was landed at the right location was nonetheless an accomplishment no other task group could claim. Harmon believed this was because he had a silhouette of the Safi coast and landscape painted on the walls of the wardrooms of each ship. Landing craft losses were low compared to the other zones. Eight craft were lost to the surf on Yellow Beach on the first day and two LCMs broached on Blue Beach. Transports were unloaded more rapidly than elsewhere, with all cargo discharged by the 13th—a period of five days and eighteen hours. The fact that a port was captured so quickly was a factor, but the use of Arab stevedores was another. This was made possible because the Army quickly established positive relations with the local pasha who helped organize work parties.[41]

The positive results make it easy to overlook several serious problems with the Safi operation. One of the two BLTs came ashore nearly five hours behind schedule. If Safi had been better defended the whole operation could have depended on the landings at Yellow Beach. In that case, the huge delay in coming ashore because of the mishap on *Dix* and *Knight*'s failure to find her boats may have been disastrous. Air power played a minor role. French aerial resistance was insignificant but American losses were major. Aircraft did not provide effective reconnaissance. This was a consequence of sending a brand new carrier into action with an inexperienced air group. Communication problems were another shortcoming. Rear Admiral Davidson complained that there was a "total lack of security and discipline on the UHF (TBS/TBY) circuit during the passage," that it got worse during the operation, and that it "reached its peak on the combat air patrol and direct support aircraft frequencies." He also pointed out that there were too many circuits and too few competent operators and that the adoption of British procedure and publications stifled communications. "No ship of the southern Attack Group was able to break the 'Jig' series messages from Gibraltar until D+1 day."[42]

Nonetheless, success is magnanimous. Had Casablanca resisted another two days the tanks of the 67th Armored Regiment could have intervened. Davidson and Harmon accomplished their mission.

15

AXIS REACTION

The Struggle in the Mediterranean has reached its climax. . . . I demand
that every man should surpass himself and that the attacks . . . should
not be surpassed even by our Japanese comrades of the air.
—REICHSMARSCHALL HERMANN GÖRING

A t 0910 on 8 November the American chargé d'affaires in Vichy delivered a letter to Marshal Pétain from President Roosevelt. This asserted
that the Americans were landing in Africa to preempt an Axis invasion
and denied any designs on French territory. The text had actually arrived several
hours earlier, allowing Laval to draft a reply while the marshal slept. The reply
began, "It is with stupor and grief that I learned during the night of the aggression of your troops against North Africa." It went on to say that France's honor
was at stake and that it would defend itself.[1]

Germany offered air support almost immediately. Rear Admiral Auphan
radioed Darlan at 0500 (GMT), asking him, "In what form and in what area
would you welcome this support?" Darlan replied four hours later, suggesting
that the Germans bomb the transports off Algiers from Sicilian airfields, "something," Auphan later wrote, "for which they manifestly needed no permission."
Meanwhile, Laval conferred with the German foreign ministry representative in
Vichy and suggested that the German government should guarantee the integrity of France's territory and empire, with the exception of Alsace-Lorraine. He
explained this would short-circuit the dissidence movement in Africa.[2]

The French cabinet considered the landings at 1100. They unanimously endorsed Pétain's order to resist and Laval's call for German guarantees. The question of German air support, however, provoked debate. Laval was reticent to accept, saying it would "call down the thunderbolt," but ultimately the cabinet concluded it had little choice.[3]

There were others more enthusiastic about military collaboration with the Axis. Admiral de Laborde ordered the Forces de Haute Mer (high seas fleet) at Toulon to raise steam. At 1255 he asked the French armistice commissions at Wiesbaden and Turin to see if Axis fighters would cover the fleet, "which was ready to sail in an hour," and whether French warships could use Italian bases. The Germans were reluctant but the Italians enthusiastic, and Comando Supremo asked for French liaison officers to fly to Rome to coordinate operations. When Auphan did not issue the anticipated orders, de Laborde telephoned and asked permission to sail that night. He had all the necessary fuel and stated, "My cruisers can cause decisive havoc on this armada." Auphan told him to wait. He explained that Darlan was in Algiers and the cabinet was considering its options.[4]

And in Berlin

Hitler and OKW always considered Africa a secondary theater. Torch changed that. As one OKW staff officer recalled, "With sudden violence interest was focused on Africa which now became a main theatre of war for the German high command." The landings confronted OKW with two choices: abandon Africa or reinforce it. Abandonment meant the loss of the German-Italian army in Egypt, the potential establishment of a second front, and dire political consequences, especially in Italy and France. Rushing troops to Tunisia and stabilizing the Egyptian front was Germany's only practical option. In fact, Hitler regarded the invasion as an opportunity and envisioned German panzers sweeping the inept Americans back to Morocco. The biggest uncertainty facing Hitler and Mussolini was France's attitude.[5]

After Hitler received Laval's request for a guarantee he sought Mussolini's opinion. The duce told Hitler that he preferred collaboration. However, "it seems to me requisite that France should not only break off diplomatic relations with America but also declare war both on England and the United States." Otherwise, "I think it is essential to occupy immediately the rest of France and Corsica." He also called for the immediate occupation of Tunisia. Although deeply skeptical, Hitler agreed to consider French cobelligerency.[6]

At 1400 the German Wiesbaden Commission formally asked for access to Tunisian bases. At 1450 the German representative at Vichy presented Hitler's response to Laval's request for guarantees. The führer, he said, wished to know whether France was prepared to fight at Germany's side and declare war against the Anglo-Americans. Because the representative did not address the matter of guarantees, Laval politely refused to answer Hitler's question. When the cabinet met again at 1815 Laval reported that Germany was pressing France to break relations with the United States, but he omitted to mention Hitler's call for a declaration of war. The cabinet agreed to proclaim that by its actions the United States had de facto severed relations. They also agreed to accept Axis air support as long as the German and Italian planes used their own fields, but balked on granting basing rights.[7]

On the night of 8 November Germany's foreign minister, Joachim von Ribbentrop, telephoned Galeazzo Ciano, his Italian counterpart, to arrange a meeting in Munich between the Axis heads of state. Because Mussolini was in poor health, Ciano traveled in his stead. Ribbentrop also summoned Laval so that he could clarify France's position. With the exception of de Laborde's eagerness to fling his cruisers against the Anglo-American fleet (and the conduct of the navy in general) the Axis considered the French reaction to the invasion half-hearted. At 1720 Wiesbaden declared, "Among the delegation, the impression remains that there is no readiness on the part of the French government for unconditional military collaboration with the Axis." Accordingly, at 0015 on the 9th the German high command gave Vichy one hour to permit the basing of German air forces at Constantine and Tunisia or face invasion. Moreover, Laval still had to speak to Hitler. He had departed Vichy early that morning by automobile hoping to secure the territorial guarantees he considered crucial to France's future.[8]

As Operation Torch's second day dawned the political situation seemed to be changing hourly. At OKW a general wrote, "The attitude of the French government was not transparent." Eisenhower's diary entry for 9 November states, "Just how the French angle will develop only the future will tell." In fact, the Allied invasion exposed the deeply fractured nature of the French State—a regime conceived in defeat, heir to a contentious political tradition, and sustained by a fetish for legitimacy that served to disguise the collective responsibility for that defeat behind the facade of absolute loyalty to Marshal Pétain. It was a regime impotent in the face of crisis. While Darlan was dealing with Clark, Laval was traveling to see Hitler in pursuit of an empty guarantee, and Pétain was making decisions based on his last conversation. While some ministers like Rear Admiral Auphan saw the Allied invasion as an opportunity to escape German bondage, others wanted to declare war to defend Europe from the Anglo-Saxon menace.[9]

AIR AND SUBMARINE ATTACKS

On the afternoon of the 8th nearly a hundred aircraft lifted off from Sardinian airfields to attack shipping around Algiers, but only sixty located a target and these accomplished little. Ju 88s damaged the British destroyer *Cowdray* and the American transports *Exceller* and *Leedstown*. Allied gunners downed six aircraft.[10]

German submarines spent the day chasing shadows. The Kriegsmarine's Mediterranean command considered Bougie the logical spot for an Allied landing and sent seven boats there. As late as noon on the 8th, the war diary of Captain Leo Kreisch, commander U-boats, recorded that aerial reconnaissance had "still not proved that the enemy is not in Bougie, which is very suitable for a landing. . . . It is therefore better to wait for more definite reconnaissance information before leaving Bougie." Not until 1730 did Kreisch determine that the landings were occurring at Oran, Algiers, east of Cherchell, and at Mostaganem. However, two hours later *U 593* reported no traffic off Algiers, and at midnight *U 605* radioed that the bay was empty although there were fires in the harbor. This led Kreisch to direct three boats off Algiers to start searching west.[11]

On the 9th Kreisch deployed fourteen submarines, including two that had just slipped through the Strait of Gibraltar. He organized them into Group Hai of six vessels, which he instructed to concentrate around Algiers, and the eight-strong Group Delphin, which he assigned to Oran. He then reinforced Delphin with three of Hai's boats because intelligence indicated that "Algiers is in enemy hands; fighting is taking place around Oran. Therefore valuable targets for U-boats may rather be expected there. The sea area off Algiers is at present free from the enemy." Even as the Luftwaffe was launching heavy attacks against massed shipping at Algiers, Kreisch still believed Algiers was free of enemy units until he received a 2103 report from OB Süd that Algiers was, in fact, crowded with twenty large transports and fifteen cruisers and destroyers. On the 10th he took five boats from Delphin and two from Hai to create a Group Wal to strike reinforcement convoys east of Gibraltar. The Regia Marina meanwhile had twenty-one submarines deployed in the western Mediterranean, concentrated mainly in the Strait of Sicily and east of Oran.[12]

On 9 November the North African political situation remained obscure. There was an armistice in Algiers, but fighting continued in Oran and Morocco. Darlan had advised the government that the Americans wanted to negotiate a cease-fire for all of North Africa. Ciano detrained in Munich that morning and Laval was scheduled to arrive that night. OB Süd had already sent two air units to Tunisia along with several companies of airborne infantry. Pétain persistently ordered resistance, but the cease-fire in Algiers inflamed Hitler's skepticism of French intentions.

Hitler met with Ciano that evening and shared his thoughts in a "ranging monologue." He regarded the situation as less dangerous than in the winter of 1940–41 and said that if the landings in Africa were indeed the long-heralded Second Front, then the military situation was improved, "especially true if the French really defended themselves against the Americans." He clarified that his attitude toward France had not changed. He knew that the "French loved neither Germany nor Italy," but in accordance with Mussolini's position, he was ready to reward loyal collaboration. In any case, he told Ciano that "Laval must take a clear stand tomorrow" and that German troops were moving up to the armistice line to occupy the Free Zone if need be. He invited Italy to make similar preparations.[13]

As the Axis leadership conferred, their forces continued to attack. A night raid against Allied shipping off Algiers by ten He 111 and sixteen Ju 88s was followed by fifty Ju 88s during the day of the 9th and then by a strike of forty bombers after dark. The crews reported that they had targeted several naval units, including some warships, but the only ship damaged was the British antiaircraft auxiliary *Tynwald*. Spitfires, newly arrived at Maison Blanche, opposed the raids, and throughout the day the Germans lost ten aircraft. *U 331* finished off the American transport *Leedstown* and *U 605* reported an "escort vessel sunk" but in fact missed her target.[14]

COOPERATION OR OCCUPATION

Laval arrived in Munich at 0400 on the 10th after a journey much delayed by fog. His conference with Hitler was scheduled for noon, but first he met Ribbentrop who sounded out the French leader about a military alliance. Ribbentrop had prepared a draft treaty that called for France to "take an active part, and with all the resources at her disposal, in the Axis war against England and the United States." In return France would maintain her 1914 boundaries and her African territories— or be compensated for any adjustments. These were the guarantees Laval so desperately sought, but Ribbentrop never presented this document, probably because of Darlan's negotiations with the Americans, the obvious coolness of French leaders in Tunisia to the arrival of German and Italian units, and Laval's evasiveness. This displeased the führer, who postponed the meeting. Then news arrived that at 1105 Darlan had ordered a cease-fire throughout North Africa.[15]

Auphan and General Weygand, who had been recalled to advise Pétain, urged the marshal to support Darlan's action "with all our strength." According to Auphan, Pétain agreed and they drafted orders to send the fleet to Algeria and to resist the Germans in Tunisia. However, before these orders could be sent, Laval telephoned the foreign ministry "in a panic." With the Germans eavesdropping, he stated, "I shall be received presently by Hitler: therefore do nothing for the moment. Everything will be broken off and I shall resign, if you negotiate with the Americans without my having got back." In the face of this ultimatum Pétain backed down. At 1625 an "Extreme Urgent" message arrived in Algiers from the marshal, affirming the order to resist the Anglo-Saxon aggressors. The adamancy of Pétain's orders caught the French leaders in Algiers off guard. In Vice Admiral Moreau's words, "This complete repudiation was even stronger than I expected. After Rear Admiral Auphan's telegram saying that the Marshal's inner thoughts corresponded to [Darlan's] advice I assumed we would have just a formal disclaimer, an official approval obviously being out of the question. But this was an absolute. . . . Officially the armistice with the Americans was violently rejected." Darlan, "visibly shaken," immediately telegraphed that he would annul his cease-fire order, but he was a prisoner and could not follow the marshal's order to resist. However, this volte-face came too late to help Laval.[16]

When finally admitted after two hours in the anteroom, the French president "found Hitler in a glacial mood." The führer stated that France could either rely on the Axis or lose its empire. Laval mustered his eloquence and spoke of how he had promoted better relations with Germany, how he had persuaded the marshal to disavow Darlan's cease-fire order, how the leadership in Morocco and Tunisia were loyal. He portrayed Darlan's action as a misunderstanding. He acknowledged the need for "very great and urgent counter-measures against the danger in North Africa." At this point Hitler interrupted and demanded port access in Tunisia. Laval, according to Ciano's account, wanted to discuss it "like a good Frenchman." He stated that only the marshal could make this decision but he would support the German request. Behind Laval's stall was a fear that Italian territorial demands would quickly follow for access to French bases. Laval claimed great admiration for Mussolini but complained of Italian support for subversive movements in Tunisia. He professed his passion for the struggle against Bolshevism and his belief in a Europe "organized for peace." He climaxed with a plea for German help in creating the "moral conditions in France in favour of collaboration with Germany." In other words, he still sought a guarantee of French territorial integrity.[17]

Hitler wanted to hear none of this. After dismissing Laval he issued orders to occupy the Free Zone and instructed Ribbentrop to tell the French president the next morning. Laval "had never in his career played so hard for time, nor from such a position of weakness," but the only thing he could give Hitler that the führer could not take for himself was a French declaration of war. Although Laval was resolved to help Germany in the struggle against Bolshevism and did not trust the Anglo-Saxons, he was not going to commit France to war against the Allies without major guarantees in advance.[18]

AIR AND SUBMARINE STRIKES CONTINUE

On 10 November twenty-six Ju 88s struck the British carriers. They scored one hit on the edge of *Argus's* flight deck and several near misses. Six S.79s torpedoed and sank the sloop *Ibis*. Nine Cant Z.1007 bis bombers raided Maison Blanche that night.[19]

On 10 November the first follow-up convoys entered the Mediterranean. *U 81* sank the collier *Garlinge* from Convoy TE 1 early that day. The ship went down in just sixty seconds and only fourteen of her forty-man crew survived. The antisubmarine trawler *Lord Hotham* reported she was missed by a torpedo. *U 431* torpedoed and sank the destroyer *Martin* from Force H at 0258. One of the few survivors recalled, "When I heard the first explosion which was aft the ship shook and it was then I realized we had been torpedoed. But within seconds there was a second and a third explosion and all I saw looking through my gun layers screen was this terrific blinding red flash go across and the whole of the bows disappeared. So everyone that was below didn't know what happened, they died instantaneously." Only sixty-three men survived to be rescued by *Quentin*. The submarine claimed a light cruiser.[20]

Later that day the trawler *Lord Nuffield* detected a contact west of Algiers and was preparing to attack when the Italian submarine *Emo* surprised her by surfacing nearby. The submarine immediately dived, but depth charges brought her back to the surface whereupon the trawler scored a series of quick hits. The Italian boat's forward gun fired a few rounds in reply, but "these shells did little damage." *Emo* sank shortly thereafter. *Lord Nuffield* rescued forty-nine survivors. *U 458* attacked a large destroyer and missed ("because of sea reflections"); *U 561* missed the aircraft carrier *Argus* at 1108; *U 77* missed the aircraft carrier *Furious* at 2310, although she claimed success; and at 1925 *U 73* missed the battleship *Rodney* with a fan of four torpedoes from five thousand meters. Bad intelligence continued to confuse the U-boat command. For example, at 1135 on 10 November aerial spotters reported a convoy of thirty transports and twenty-three escorts just east of Gibraltar. Kreisch sent submarines from Group Wal against this target "by altering the orders already issued." However, by the next morning he ruefully noted that the giant convoy had disappeared.[21]

11 NOVEMBER

On the 11th there were seventeen German submarines along the Algerian coast. The Germans continued to adjust their deployments, sending five boats to blockade Algeria, five to patrol off Oran, and seven boats to plug the passage into the Mediterranean. They made six attacks that day and had three successes: *U 407* sank the troopship *Viceroy of India.* Four men were lost but 454 were rescued. *U 380,* newly arrived from the Atlantic, dispatched the Dutch troopship *Nieuw Zeeland,* killing fifteen. *U 595* took out the freighter *Browning* at 0200 as the ship was following a minesweeper into Oran. The submarine suffered sixteen hours of depth-charge attacks as a consequence. *U 73* missed the LSI *Otranto.* Depth charges foiled *U 755*'s attempt against a larger steamer. *U 617* reported that she suffered seven hours of continuous depth-charge attack from a position thirty miles northwest of Oran. During this day German signals intelligence units intercepted twelve British sighting reports of German submarines.[22]

At 0700 on 11 November ten German and six Italian divisions invaded the French Free Zone and elements of two Italian divisions disembarked in Corsica. The deployment of the 10th Panzer Division demonstrated the speed of the German advance. On 9 November this unit was concentrated at Amiens. It moved into Burgundy and then on the morning of the 11th motored to Lyon. It left there at 1500 and, "rushing ahead toward the south, without any rest, proceeding along both banks of the Rhone," the division's advanced elements arrived at Marseille the next morning at 0230—a movement of 220 miles in eleven and a half hours. This was possible because Pétain ordered l'Armée de l'Armistice's eight divisions to stand down rather than take to the hills and resist and limited himself to a solemn radio protest. The Germans, in turn, preserved the fiction of an armistice by stating they would respect the Vichy administration.[23]

The fate of the fleet at Toulon was a major issue arising from the German occupation. Auphan issued orders to de Laborde and Vice Admiral André Marquis, commander of the Toulon Naval District, that they were to peacefully oppose occupation of the naval base and attempt to reach an arrangement with the Germans. Otherwise, the ships were to scuttle. When the German command, which feared the fleet would sail, agreed to respect the base if de Laborde and Marquis guaranteed to defend it against attacks from the Allies and French dissidents, the admirals, with Auphan's blessing, agreed. Accordingly, the German army stopped fifteen kilometers short of the base, leaving Toulon (and the city of Vichy itself) the only unoccupied French enclave. Grand Admiral Erich Raeder endorsed this policy and urged that Berlin encourage Vichy cobelligerency against the Allies.

In Algiers the German occupation of Vichy presented Giraud a golden opportunity, but despite the urging of Mast and members of the Group of Five, he failed to step forward. According to Murphy, he and Clark met with Giraud late at night on the 10th. Giraud, he said, had been amazed to learn that most French officials considered him a dissident and refused to recognize his authority. He "seemed appalled by the complexities of civil authority" and, to Clark and Murphy's amazement, "went on to say that Darlan obviously was essential to the success of our enterprise and that he would be content to serve under him."[24]

At 0800 on the 11th, before news of the Axis invasion of the Free Zone arrived, Pétain designated General Noguès the supreme commander in North Africa. This weakened Darlan's position, and when Clark visited a few minutes later he "found the admiral in an ugly mood, obviously worried." But Auphan softened the blow at 1120 with a message in the secret admiralty code that the marshal had taken this action because he believed Darlan was a prisoner, not because he had lost confidence in him. Another reason Clark refrained from elevating Giraud was a growing conviction that only Darlan could deliver the cooperation needed. Clark remembered, "I was also impressed with the way his [Darlan's] orders were received and carried out by subordinate Frenchmen."[25]

Conclusion

During the crucial first three days after the invasion the French government in Vichy tried to maintain its neutrality and failed to take a decisive stand either with the Axis or with the Allies. The Axis powers could not deploy enough naval or air forces to seriously discomfort much less defeat the Allied invasion—even at its most exposed points. However, there was still Tunisia: every mile east the vulnerable transports ventured brought them that much closer to the cluster of German and Italian airbases in Sardinia and Sicily.

Deal makers. Top: Admiral François Darlan shaking hands with Maj. Gen. Mark Clark on 12 November 1942 after concluding their agreement. Marshal Pétain, in the photo at the far right, seems to be looking over Clark's shoulder. Bottom: Corps General Alphonse Juin and Robert Murphy (left) posing after the agreement. (U.S. Army Signal Corps)

16

THE ALLIES MOVE EAST

French war-time psychology is completely inexplicable.
—Rear Adm. Ernest McWhorter

The occupation of Algiers brought the Allies to within four hundred air miles of Tunis. The initial plan to cross this distance envisioned the 78th Division's floating reserve, the 36th Brigade Group, occupying Bougie a hundred miles east of Algiers and the airfield at Djidjelli thirty miles beyond on 12 November. Meanwhile, Commandos and paratroopers would seize Bône, Bizerte, and Tunis on the 11th, 12th, and 13th, respectively. This bold concept, however, required French cooperation and on 9 November, with battles raging everywhere save Algiers, such cooperation was obviously not forthcoming. More-over, the American airborne component had been roughly handled and most of the Commandos were still engaged. Consequently, Eisenhower scrapped the Tuni-sian coup de main but retained the amphibious thrust against Bougie.

The Situation in Tunisia

Vice Admiral Jean-Pierre Estéva was resident-general of Tunisia. Division General Georges Barré commanded the Tunisia Division while the Bizerte maritime dis-trict was the responsibility of Rear Admiral Edmond Derrien, who reported to Vice Admiral Moreau in Algiers.

Early on 8 November the U.S. consul-general in Tunis gave Estéva a letter from President Roosevelt that declared American troops were landing in Algeria and Morocco, and requested unopposed passage into Tunisia. In response Estéva ordered an alert and implemented the defensive plan. Air units withdrew west and arrangements were made to block Sousse and Gabès Harbors. At 1225 news arrived that the government was accepting German air support from units flying out of Sardinia. At 2200 Barré learned that Darlan had given him command of the Constantine Division and responsibility for everything east of Algiers.[1]

9 November

Shortly after midnight Laval notified Estéva that the government was allowing German access to Tunisian airfields while Auphan telegrammed the news to Barré and Derrien at 0523. That same morning Field Marshal Kesselring sent envoys to Tunis. The French leaders reluctantly listened to German requirements and tried to delay by claiming they needed to consult with their government. After receiving a coded message that a German landing would probably be unopposed, Kesselring ordered General Bruno Loerzer, head of Fliegerkorps II, to dispatch a fighter unit to Tunis. The first German aircraft landed at 1230. A tense standoff ensued as French armored cars covered the planes. However, Ju 52s and glider-towing Ju 88s followed the fighters, bringing the troops of Kesselring's headquarters company. As Junkers continued to stream in carrying elements of the 5th Paratroop Regiment, Barré pulled his troops back. Within four and a half hours 103 planes had landed, including twenty-five Bf 109s, twenty-five Ju 87s, and fifty Ju 52s.[2]

The Tunisian leaders protested this development. At 1330 Barré radioed the cabinet: "I have a duty to report the emotion that has arisen because of this occupation of our field of El Aouina by Axis air forces and the disturbing comments it has caused in the majority of officers whose loyalty I soon will not be able to answer for." Estéva urged "that this whole matter be reexamined." Derrien addressed similar complaints to the admiralty.[3]

Auphan responded that evening, sympathizing but clarifying: "It is impossible, given the Anglo-Saxon aggression to prevent German aircraft from coming to North Africa. It is not us or the Germans who have begun war in French Africa. We can only endure. I ask you to trust me." Laval was on his way to see Hitler in Munich, and the government wanted to stall and to keep the Germans out of the Free Zone if that was still possible.[4]

Barré, for one, was not reassured. He ordered the Chasseurs of the 1st Reserve Group to cordon off El Aouina airfield. Meanwhile, General Loerzer had arrived to confer with Estéva and Barré. The German armistice commissioner, who picked him up, reported the situation as doubtful. Loerzer observed machine guns trained on the airfield and Barré was absent when he arrived at army headquarters. An "extremely correct and reserved" staff general received him and responded to every query by stating he had no instructions. After "a cool leave taking," Loerzer called on Estéva, whom he described as an "old gentleman with a white goatee [who was] more friendly by far." The admiral assured him that he had received instructions from Vichy and would "do everything in his power to fulfill Loerzer's requests and to establish a good understanding."[5]

10 November

Admiral Darlan's 10 November suspension of hostilities against American forces and their allies hit Tunisia like a bombshell, especially since Vichy continued to order cooperation with the Germans. At 1630 British Beaufighters attacked El Aouina as German fighters were landing. The four German 20-mm guns there did not yet have ammunition and French antiaircraft held its fire. The low-level strafing attack destroyed two aircraft and damaged several others. British Ultra decryptions indicated that the German naval command considered Axis-French cooperation doubtful in Tunis and that "a possibility even existed of hostile action." This was encouraging. However, at 1935 Auphan confirmed Derrien's instructions to allow German troops to land, consoling him that "I am thinking of the final good of France."[6]

The Landings at Bougie

Hart Force, an ad hoc motorized formation from the 11th Infantry Brigade, departed Algiers for Tunisia on 11 November. The 36th Brigade sailed for Bougie in four groups. A ten-knot convoy left Algiers at 1600 on 10 November. It consisted of the transports *Glenfinlas, Stanhill, Urlana,* and *Ocean Volga,* escorted by the monitor *Roberts,* the destroyer *Blyskawica,* the corvettes *Samphire* and *Penstemon,* and the armed trawlers *Hoy, Incholm,* and *Rysa.* Refueling duties delayed the tanker *Dewdale* and she sailed separately at 1800 escorted by the trawler *Mull.* At 2000 a fifteen-knot assault convoy followed. This consisted of the LSIs *Karanja* (Captain N. V. Dickinson landing force commander), *Marnix,* and *Cathay* loaded with the brigade's three infantry battalions. The escort included the light cruiser *Sheffield,* the antiaircraft vessel *Tynwald,* the Hunt destroyer *Bramham,* fleet minesweepers *Cadmus* and *Albacore,* and the corvettes *Rother* and *Spey.* Finally, the LSI

Awatea with an RAF support group and supplies and gasoline for the Spitfires to be based at Djidjelli sailed at 2310. The Hunt destroyers *Bicester* and *Wilton* accompanied her.

Several hours before the force sailed Vice Admiral Moreau issued an order to Commander Théry, chief naval officer at Bougie, that stated, "American landings will take place tonight in your ports. Stop. You are not to oppose." He then assured Vice Admiral Burrough, commanding the operation, "of a friendly reception." However, when Pétain repudiated Darlan's armistice, the French chain of command in Africa started to splinter. While Moreau was conferring with Darlan, the naval commander in Bône, disturbed by the contradiction in orders emanating from Algiers and Vichy, telephoned Moreau's headquarters seeking an explanation. Moreau's staff instructed him to disregard previous orders to allow the American landing. Moreau was horrified to further learn that his staff had taken the initiative and telegraphed the same instructions to Bougie and Philippeville. He got on the telephone and tried to undo the damage by telling the commanders that they had to follow the lead of the army, which was not going to fight. As he later commented, though, "Some officers seemed dangerously excited." Consequently, Moreau advised Clark that Marshal Pétain's orders were to continue resistance, adding, "I cannot answer for the execution of the armistice agreement by the forces under my command." Clark forwarded this bad news to Captain Dickinson who elected to land on a beach outside the range of Bougie's shore batteries rather than within Bougie Bay as planned.[7]

The convoy arrived at the new disembarkation point four miles westnorthwest of Cape Aokas at 0445 on 11 November. *Karanja*'s landing craft picked up troops from *Cathay* while *Marnix* used her own boats. Her first wave departed at 0530 while those from *Cathay* were under way by 0600. Four landing craft foundered in the strong surf, but rumors of heavy resistance proved false. One officer recalled, "We went in as dawn broke. There was a destroyer on either side of us, with their guns trained on the shore, it was a very eerie feeling, we duly landed, rushed up the beach and the only sign of anybody were two men in rubber swim suits."[8]

At dawn on 11 November the carrier *Argus,* the cruisers *Scylla* and *Charybdis,* and the destroyers *Vanoc* and *Wrestler* took station to support the landing. *Argus* had only seven Seafires serviceable of the eighteen she had carried into battle three days before. She was to remain in the area until noon, by which time a fighter group would have supposedly occupied Djidjelli. The slow convoy arrived at 0547 and closed the LSIs. *Awatea,* meanwhile, headed for Djidjelli but encountered such a heavy swell that she aborted landing the RAF service troops and joined the main force instead. As British transports congregated west of Bougie, returning boats reported unsafe conditions. Accordingly, Captain Dickinson suspended operations and dispatched *Wilton* and *Bramham* to determine the French attitude.[9]

Fortunately for the British, Théry had decided to follow the chain of command and obey Moreau's orders rather than Pétain's. Upon hearing this, the LSIs hoisted landing craft and at 1000 *Urlana, Glenfinlas,* and *Stanhill* entered port while the others anchored in Bougie roadstead where they continued unloading in better conditions. Djidjelli remained unoccupied and thus there were no land-based Spitfires to assume protection of the fleet. Burrough nonetheless ordered *Argus* to withdraw as scheduled.

Axis forces had anticipated an Allied move east from Algiers. Five S.79 bombers attacked Bougie at 1345. Their torpedoes missed and the defenders shot down the commander's aircraft. By 1625 *Awatea* had finished discharging, but as she was getting under way fifty Ju 88s and three He 111 torpedo bombers swooped down through the fading light. Four bombs smashed into the large ex-liner; one ignited a fire in No. 2 Hold and another blasted through the hull in the engine room. An *Awatea* crewmember witnessed a "great wall of water under tremendous pressure shooting straight into the engine room and splashing with great force off everything it hit." *Penstemon* and *Bicester* stood alongside, but the fire proved uncontrollable, and, attracted by this beacon, the Italian submarine *Argo* torpedoed *Awatea,* sinking her seven miles off Bougie with the loss of 150 men. In the same raid, two bombs stuck *Roberts,* causing flooding and knocking the monitor's boiler room fans out of action. One bomb fell through *Cathay*'s galley but did not explode. More damaging were several near misses. Many of the twelve hundred troops embarked panicked and took to boats and landing craft clustered around her. *Cathay* was prematurely abandoned and fires burned out of control. A Reuter's correspondent wrote, "Bougie's first blackout was rent by huge flames bursting from the listing liner *Cathay* in the centre of the bay. Gradually the whole superstructure merged into one fiery inferno topped by the shimmering incandescence of the white hot funnel." She burned throughout the night and eventually sank.[10]

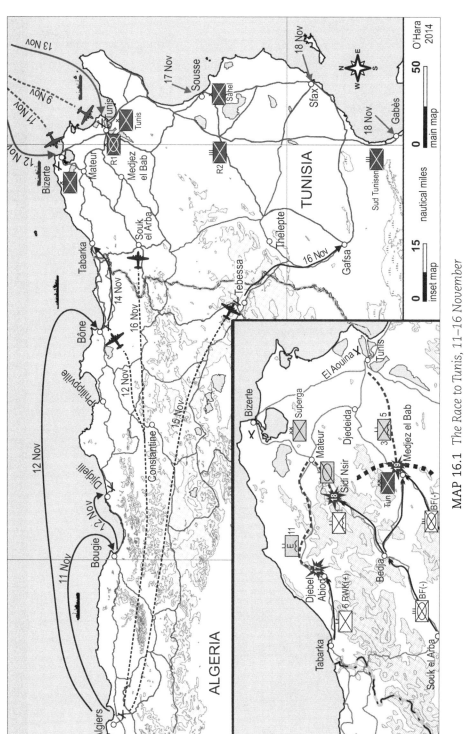

MAP 16.1 *The Race to Tunis, 11–16 November*

Also on 11 November

On the 11th confusion intensified in Tunisia. That morning, upon learning that Pétain had elevated Noguès to supreme commander, Derrien warned Auphan that Barré was following Juin's orders and adopting a policy of neutrality. He asked the admiralty to take immediate measures. Auphan, however, was preoccupied with the ongoing Axis invasion of the Free Zone and the threat to Toulon. Noguès himself was confused and dispatched a private messenger to Vichy to clarify what was expected of him. Laval arrived in Vichy at noon, his mission to Hitler clearly a failure. However, the Council of Ministers was not scheduled to convene until that evening and their attitude remained unclear.

While the landings at Bougie were under way, while Laval was in transit, and while Axis troops violated the Free Zone, Clark reopened talks with Darlan in Algiers. The Axis invasion allowed Darlan to claim that Pétain's orders were invalid because the marshal was under duress. One of the major points of discussion was the French fleet. Eisenhower's naval aide called it "the biggest prize of the war," and the Allies were concerned that the Germans would seize it. Darlan thought this unlikely, but at 1547 he obliged Clark by issuing a call that the German violation of the armistice allowed Frenchmen to act freely and remain loyal to the captive marshal. He invited the fleet to sail for Dakar and conveyed American guarantees there would be no opposition. He did not mention to Clark that bad blood between him and Admiral de Laborde made this extremely unlikely. The two admirals communicated only in writing, even during Darlan's review of the fleet, and Darlan had been planning to replace de Laborde upon his return from Africa. Predictably, de Laborde refused to sail the fleet. Darlan also invited Noguès to a conference in Algiers to clarify the chain of command. That same evening Juin radioed Tunisia that "the position of neutrality vis-a-vis the Axis has ended. Any action of Axis forces in North Africa should be repulsed by force." Meanwhile, Noguès' envoy to Vichy had returned carrying instructions from Pétain (given before Laval's return from Munich) to negotiate the best deal possible with the Americans and preserve the overseas empire.[11]

At 1600 Auphan finally replied to Derrien shortly after the Tunisian admiral had received Juin's instructions to fight the Axis. Auphan personally endorsed neutrality but cautioned that no official government position would be immediately forthcoming. From this Derrien concluded that Juin's orders were valid and at 1622 he informed his command that "after two long days of talk and confusion the order has arrived explicitly designating our enemy: Germany and Italy.

Our path is fixed, revenge is coming. Long Live France." Army and naval forces in Bizerte received this news enthusiastically: men sang the Marseillaise and officers toasted the order with champagne.[12]

While this event unfolded, the Council of Ministers met to learn about Laval's mission to Munich and to consider the next step. Although he had failed to secure any guarantees, the president urged genuine collaboration with the Axis and stated that cease-fire in Africa was the same as open fire in France. Rear Admiral Auphan dissented and argued that to continue to fight was to fight for Germany, not France. "This argument provoked a general outcry and encountered vehement opposition from nearly all the ministers." Auphan recalled, "Many . . . still believed in German supremacy. The majority were fascinated by Laval's oratory." Pétain, clearly exhausted, was passive. The outcome was a communiqué praising the army in Africa for its loyalty and bravery and ordering it to fight in the interest of France and the empire to the limits of its forces against the Anglo-Saxon invaders.[13]

Even before this communiqué reached Tunisia, Vice Admiral Estéva telephoned Derrien. When he learned that Derrien was going to fight the Germans, he told the Bizerte commander that he had lost his mind and that his action would have disastrous consequences. Although Derrien did not report to Estéva, this admonishment, coupled with Vichy's just-arrived instructions, caused Derrien to reverse himself at 2352, provoking consternation and confusion among the troops in Bizerte. Meanwhile, Division General Barré definitively quit Tunis at 2200 and continued concentrating his men east of Tunis around Tabarka, Medjez el Bab, and Gafsa while maintaining strict neutrality with Axis forces.[14]

That night Juin annulled his order to Tunisia to resist Axis forces. This followed a midnight visit to Juin's residence by generals Koeltz and Mendigal. Rousting their superior from bed, the generals expressed concern that Juin lacked the authority to issue such an order after Pétain's elevation of Noguès. Worried about being considered a dissident, Juin agreed, pending a meeting with Noguès scheduled for the next afternoon. Juin planned to reinstate the call for resistance at that time, but Major General Clark was furious when the news reached him. At 0600 on the 12th Clark met with Juin and Darlan. Unmoved by their legalistic arguments, he demanded that Juin's anti-Axis orders be reinstated before General Noguès's arrival, going so far as to accuse Juin of treachery and weakness and threatening to arrest everyone and putting Giraud in command. After a prolonged argument Juin called Barré and afterward told Clark that he had agreed to resist German landings on Tunisian airfields. This satisfied Clark, who agreed to wait until that afternoon for Juin to formally reinstate his order.[15]

The Axis Forces Establish Themselves

The first Axis formations to arrive in Tunisia were cautious, aware that they faced vastly superior French forces. According to Kesselring's memoirs he feared that the French would refuse to cooperate if Italian troops appeared and so secured Mussolini's promise not to act unilaterally. Kesselring recalled, "To begin with relations between the French and German troops were excellent. Our parachutists went out on patrol against the enemy in French armoured cars. But all of a sudden the situation changed when an Italian fighter squadron . . . landed near Tunis. At once our friends became foes." He was referring to an Italian unit of twenty-two MC.202 fighters that arrived on 10 November and departed the next day after Kesselring pressed Marshal Ugo Cavallero, the Italian chief of staff, to withdraw it. French histories, however, do not mention this incident and are very specific that there were no interactions between French and German troops, much less joint patrols. Objection to an Italian presence was just another stalling tactic.[16]

Italian participation in the occupation was a given from the start. Supermarina quickly organized the first convoy—the motor ships *Caterina Costa* and *Città di Napoli* escorted by four destroyers and a torpedo boat—and it weighed anchor at 1600 on the 11th, arriving in Bizerte twenty-four hours later. Ultra dispatches alerted Malta and accurately forecast the convoy's composition and time of arrival with an attack window of eight hours, but Torch preparations had not included provisions for striking Axis shipping from Sicily to Tunisia, and Malta was short of aviation fuel. While the Italian convoy was in transit, Malta's Beaufighters and long-range Spitfires were flying sorties "to protect arrival of friendly cruiser bringing food and supplies from Egypt." Air forces from Malta attacked transport aircraft on the 14th and claimed the downing of two transports and three escorts at the cost of four of their own. For the next three days, however, bad weather kept the British planes grounded, and the next offensive action was an attack by seven Wellingtons on El Aouina field on the 18th.[17]

During this period six Italian transports docked in Bizerte or Tunis and delivered 3,682 men, 2,827 tons of supplies, and 450 vehicles, mostly from the Superga Division. On the 11th and 14th destroyers brought another 975 men and on the 15th the San Marco Regiment landed in Corsica. Although aircraft delivered in

Italian Fiat G.12 transport aircraft unloading troops at Tunis. (Storia Militare)

November 15,000 men and 581 tons of supplies, Italian convoys did the heavy lifting, transporting without loss 176 tanks, 131 artillery pieces, 1,152 vehicles, and 13,000 tons of materiel. Throughout the month only one ship engaged in this traffic was lost, *Città di Napoli,* which was mined on the 28th while returning to Italy.[18]

On the night of 11/12 November German paratroopers occupied the city of Tunis. The German navy sent the 3rd S-Boote Flotilla consisting of *S 30, 35, 54, 56, 57,* and *60* and two R-Boats of the 6th Minesweeper Flotilla to Bizerte from Palermo on 11 November, ferrying a battalion of the 10th Bersaglieri Regiment.

12 November

Spitfires of 154th Squadron arrived at Djidjelli early on the 12th, but there was no gasoline there. It was not until noon that laden landing craft began crossing Bougie Bay to the airfield, and they did not finish unloading until past midnight. Meanwhile, after sinking *Awatea, Argo* stalked shipping in the anchorage and at 0515 the Italian submarine torpedoed *Tynwald.* This important antiaircraft escort quickly capsized with the loss of ten men. Twenty-five minutes later six Ju 88s, diving out of the overcast, bombed *Karanja.* Two explosions ignited fuel fires, causing men to abandon ship without orders. By 0830 *Karanja* was a total loss. At 0630 the transport *Strathnaver* arrived, escorted by *Bramham* and *Blyskawica,* and anchored in the outer harbor. At 1000 fifty-two Ju 88s attacked. Most targeted *Marnix* and *Dewdale*, but intense antiaircraft fire kept them high and they only near-missed *Blyskawica. Marnix* left for Algiers an hour later as soon as the attack ended, although she had not finished unloading. At 1240 six S.79s struck.

Their torpedoes missed and they lost one aircraft. Ten Cant Z 1007 bis followed at 1330 and four more at 1430. Near misses damaged *Blyskawica* and the destroyer departed for Algiers at 1600. Two Italian aircraft failed to return. Ju 88s escorted by Me 210s attacked next and hit *Wilton,* but the bomb passed through the ship without exploding. Finally, fifteen He 111s and six Ju 88s armed with torpedoes lined up on *Wilton.* The destroyer splashed two aircraft and avoided all torpedoes. Overall, it was a deadly day for Axis airmen. The Italians lost the three aircraft mentioned and the Germans two Me 210s, two He 111s, three Ju 88s, and one Do 17, the last shot down by a Spitfire from Maison Blanche. The short range of the Spitfires meant that those based at Algiers could spend only twenty minutes over Bougie, and all but one of the Axis air attacks occurred during gaps in their coverage.

On 12 November the seventeen German submarines operating in the western Mediterranean were poorly placed to affect the Bougie landings. *U 77* torpedoed the sloop *Stork* at 0305 west of Algiers as she was escorting the follow up convoy KMS.1 along the coast. Although severely damaged, *Stork* was towed to Gibraltar and returned to service the next year.

At 1030 on the 12th Clark informed Eisenhower that he would be meeting with Darlan, Juin, and Noguès that afternoon. Noguès reached Algiers at 1700 and, as feared, wanted nothing to do with Giraud. Reportedly when Giraud approached Noguès with outstretched hand, the other put his own hands behind his back saying, "'I will not talk to a rebel general.' However, he finally muttered, 'hello' adding between his teeth the word 'traitor.'" The Moroccan leader preferred to maintain strict neutrality rather than collaborate with the Allies and he was anxious to maintain Pétain's authority. Darlan and Juin knew that neutrality was unrealistic, but the French commanders could not hammer out a compromise regarding Giraud, even though Juin was willing to serve under him. Ultimately Clark had Giraud brought in and demanded a solution before Eisenhower arrived the next day or he would arrest everyone and give Giraud supreme power. A French historian noted, "This touched a responsive chord because it was what [Noguès and Darlan] most feared. They preferred to let Giraud play a part and the conversation took a more practical turn." At 0130 on the 13th Noguès wired Pétain that Darlan was not a prisoner and recommended that he be restored to command to sidetrack Giraud and avoid Franco-German war in Tunisia.[19]

On the morning of the 13th, after a few hours of sleep, the French leaders continued their discussions. Juin finally broke the deadlock with "a masterful harangue" that convinced Noguès to abandon neutrality and accept Giraud as army commander. The principals shook hands just in time for Eisenhower's visit. Darlan's position was strengthened when Auphan dispatched a private message to the admiral that read, "Intimate agreement of the marshal and the president, but before answering you, they are consulting the occupation authorities." Darlan made sure this message "fell" into American hands because it gave the impression that Vichy was blessing Darlan's deal with Clark. In fact, it referred to Noguès's earlier message regarding restoring Darlan to command.[20]

Tunisia: More Orders

Accord in Algeria did not resolve confusion in Tunisia. Darlan, Juin, and Moreau telephoned Derrien and urged him to resist the Germans. Although such a course was clearly Derrien's preference, he perceived in these calls something worse than German occupation: French dissidence. At 1805 he wired Auphan, stating, "There is a high probability of a movement against the directives of the marshal erupting this night in North Africa by high military personalities. I refuse to take part but it is urgent that General Noguès asserts his authority." Auphan, who later described Derrien as politically naïve, replied that Noguès had Pétain's confidence and that Derrien should follow his orders. At 2030 Juin telephoned Division General Barré and ordered him to immediately start operations against the Germans. Barré replied that as long as hostilities had not started in Bizerte he preferred to wait until he had concentrated his troops in better positions. Just twenty minutes later Vichy instructed Barré in the name of Pétain that his mission was to defend Tunisia against the Anglo-Saxons. The general, however, had made up his mind. At 0200 on the 13th he telephoned Juin and affirmed that he would follow orders from Algiers.[21]

On to Bône

On 12 November the 8th/Argyll and Sutherland Highlanders occupied the airfield at Sétif south of Bougie. That same day 6th Commando reinforced by half the 3rd/RWK transported in the destroyers *Lamerton* and *Wheatland* arrived at Bône 125 miles east of Bougie. A company commander wrote that as *Wheatland* entered the harbor "the Stukas arrived and we were dive-bombed. . . . Stukas are very frightening things and were to become the evil genies of the campaign." More than three hundred men of the British 3rd Battalion, 1st Parachute Regiment, landed on a small airfield near Bône. They barely forestalled a German landing at the same field. Local French forces watched.[22]

On 13 November Axis air forces continued to pound Bougie. Although there were now fighters at Djidjelli, fuel shortages limited their effectiveness. At 1210 twenty-two Ju 88s (of thirty-two that took off) attacked and sank *Glenfinlas*. They also bombed and damaged the French freighters *Alcina, Koutoubia,* and *Florida,* forcing the last two to scuttle. That night *Ocean Volga, Stanhill,* and *Dewdale,* along with five French steamers, upped anchor for Algiers.

Although most Italian submarines had been pulled back into defensive positions off Tunisia, *Platino* torpedoed *Narkunda* near Bougie at 0326 on 14 November. A raid by thirty-six Ju 88s at 1800 finished off the British transport with the loss of thirty-one men. Eight Ju 87s bombed the two destroyer transports at Bône but missed. One was shot down by antiaircraft fire, two others collided, and a Spitfire downed an escorting Bf 109.[23]

The four days, 11 through 14 November, provided a sharp lesson, if one was indeed needed, of the danger of risking ships beyond the range of effective fighter cover. Four transports and two freighters, displacing 62,287 GRT, were lost, along with three French freighters. Aircraft damaged two destroyers and a monitor. Italian submarines also sank one antiaircraft ship and shared in the sinking of two transports.

The Choices of Rear Admiral Derrien

On the 13th Rear Admiral Derrien needed to adopt a policy. Darlan had ordered him to resist the Axis in the name of the marshal, but he had already permitted Italian transports to dock in Bizerte and Tunis. Estéva, meanwhile, had made up his mind: in a meeting with Derrien at 1830 he declared that the option of opposing the Germans no longer existed.[24]

On the 14th Barré ordered his troops to fall back in the face of Axis advances, thereby delaying an outbreak of hostilities. Derrien wrote the general that it was impossible for him to resist the Axis without reinforcements. In reply Barré told Derrien to avoid a fight in Bizerte; he promised assistance once he was reinforced, presumably by the Americans. Vice Admiral Moreau, meanwhile, was instructing Derrien to scuttle shipping and to send, if possible, the torpedo boats of the 12th Division and the two 630-ton sloops to Algiers. Then at 1130 an open telegram from Pétain arrived that generated a final fracture between Darlan/Juin/

Barré on one side and admirals Derrien and Estéva on the other. This message stated that Darlan's decision to collaborate with the Allies violated the marshal's direct orders and instructed Derrien to cooperate with Axis forces in defending North Africa against American aggression.

At 2025 Derrien informed Moreau that his orders were contrary to Pétain's explicit instructions and that he would follow the marshal's orders. The confusion suited the Axis. Kesselring concluded he could secure complete control over both Tunis and Bizerte "in spite of the extraordinary numerical inferiority of the German forces" and gave instructions to prolong negotiations with Estéva "as much as possible, without coming to a decision." He judged Estéva to be "manifestly loyal to Vichy" and Barré ambivalent or anti-German. Kesselring was uncertain how far Marshal Pétain's authority extended as he kept issuing orders for cooperation with the Germans that many authorities seemed to disregard.[25]

Into Tunisia

Elements of the 36th Brigade Group moved east from Bône on 14 November along the coastal highway and reached Tabarka the next day. The U.S. 2nd Battalion, 503rd Paratroop Regiment, which had concentrated at Maison Blanche, dropped near Tébessa at Youks-les-Bains on the 15th and advanced to Gafsa in requisitioned buses. Delayed by bad weather the British 1st Paratroop Battalion landed at Souk el Arba a day later. Thus, one week after the initial landings Allied forces had entered Tunisia at three locations. To reinforce these penetrations the 11th Brigade Group and Blade Force, the 17th/21st Lancers armored regiment of the 6th Armored Division, departed Algiers on the 15th.

The RAF supported these advances by aggressively pushing fighter squadrons forward. By the 14th Djidjelli was hosting aircraft of the 154th and 242nd Squadrons while Spitfires of the 81st and 111th Squadrons had leapfrogged to Bône. C-47s ferried in ground crews, ammunition, gasoline, and antiaircraft guns.

On the 15th Rear Admiral René-Charles Platon, the ex-colonial secretary and current minister without portfolio, arrived in Africa to enforce Pétain's shaky writ. Platon was one of the more pro-German members of the French government and one of those who "had declaimed the loudest against the 'traitors' of Algiers." Estéva summoned Barré to Tunis to meet with Platon, but the general refused to leave his troops and instead invited Platon to Medjez el Bab. Platon went partway, but when he saw French troops manning a front line that faced east he turned back, fearing that if he crossed he would be unable to return.[26]

Italian M 14 tanks of the Centauro Armored Division being unloaded in Bizerte from the ferry *Aspomonte* on 24 November 1942. Italian, German, and French personnel are all visible in this photograph. (Rivista Marittima)

On the 16th Estéva and Derrien met with General Walther Nehring, former head of the Afrika Korps, who had just arrived to command German forces in Tunisia. Nehring found Estéva "an old, distinguished gentleman, whom the events seemed to have taken completely by surprise. He considered Derrien a man of honor struggling against his fate, which forced him to fulfill a duty contrary to his own inclinations." Nehring questioned Estéva about the reliability of French troops, and Estéva answered that his men would obey orders to fight British, American, or Gaullist troops, but he could not guarantee that they would fight Barré's men. Estéva suggested that the best way to avoid incidents would be to create a defense sector in Bizerte exclusively manned by French forces. Nehring was reluctant, but needing French cooperation he agreed. Thus, Kesselring noted with regret, "it happened that in the area of the Bizerte fortress with its large subterranean installations a French strong point continued to exist which was closed to the examination of the German authorities."[27]

By 15 November Nehring's forces included two battalions of the 5th Paratroop Regiment, the 11th Paratroop Engineer Battalion, one replacement infantry battalion, an artillery battery with four 88-mm guns, and an armored reconnaissance company. Italy had three battalions including marines at Bizerte and elements of the Superga Division concentrating at Mateur southwest of Bizerte. Formations slotted to reinforce the bridgehead included the Hermann Göring Division, the 10th Panzer Division, the 344th Infantry Division, the rest of Superga, the Imperiali Brigade, and nondivisional Italian formations including some self-propelled gun units. An armored battalion was arriving to supplement the reconnaissance company. This was not much, but still impressive considering just a week before there had been no Axis troops in Tunisia. By 10 November Fliegerkorps II had 445 aircraft, up from 283 a month earlier, and 673 transport aircraft. These had established a ferry service that was delivering men at the rate of 750 a day.[28]

The naval forces supporting Operation Torch continued to suffer losses. On the 15th at 0342 the Italian submarine *Ascianghi* torpedoed and sank the British fleet minesweeper *Algerine* off Bougie. There were only eight survivors, the death toll being so great because the sweeper's depth charges had detonated while she sank, killing many men in the water. Even worse was the loss of the carrier *Avenger*. She had departed Algiers on 12 November and on the 15th was just west of Gibraltar when *U 155* hit her with one torpedo. This caused a sympathetic detonation in the carrier's bomb room, sending her quickly to the bottom. Only 12 of 528 men survived.

First Ground Contacts

Elements of the 78th Division pushed east in widely separated columns along the two main roads from Algeria into Tunisia. German battle groups motored west along the same routes, seeking to expand their bridgehead. On 17 November, the tenth day of Anglo-American operations in Africa, the adversaries clashed east of Djebel Abiod. Two companies of the 11th Parachute Engineer Battalion, fifteen tanks, a 105-mm battery, and Italian armored cars cut off Hart Force and forced it to abandon its vehicles and retreat cross country. Then the Axis column ran into three reinforced companies of the 6th/RWK. After two days of back-and-forth action, the paratroopers began to slowly retreat. In other contacts a company of the British 1st Parachute Battalion ambushed a German reconnaissance unit near Sidi Nsir on 18 November.[29]

Open fighting between Axis forces and elements of Division General Barré's Tunisia Division finally erupted at Medjez el Bab on 19 November. General Nehring sent an officer to Barré on the 17th seeking permission for his paratroopers to advance through French lines. This "request" was reinforced by an order from Pétain forbidding Barré to engage the Germans. Nehring noted that "until now reconnaissance had been prevented from passing through, and had, in certain instances, even been disarmed." His envoy was denied access to Barré and returned complaining of rude treatment. Still, Nehring hesitated to force the issue, "a necessity partly based on our own weakness, and partly on the desire not to burn bridges and to make additional enemies." But when aircraft reported American vehicles among the French force, elements of the 5th Parachute Regiment and Italian infantry attacked. The French, supplemented by an American field artillery battalion and a small British detachment from Blade Force, fought tenaciously for a day before withdrawing west. Lieutenant General Kenneth Anderson, commander of the newly activated British First Army, withheld reinforcements because he wanted to "avoid frittering away Allied strength and to conserve all possible means for the final push eastward in a few more days." Not only was Medjez el Bab the first occasion when Vichy French units fought the Germans, but it was also the first battle between German and American troops.[30]

While Anderson hoarded his strength for his final push, Nehring expanded his small bridgehead, and both sides waged an aggressive campaign against the enemy lines of communication. On the 20th German bombers raided Maison Blanche, destroying or damaging nineteen aircraft, including all the photoreconnaissance Spitfires in Algeria. Eleven Ju 88s hit Algiers Harbor and severely damaged the LSG *Dewdale*. A bomb struck the light cruiser *Delhi* on her quarterdeck and blew away her stern structure. Bombers also jumped a supply convoy between Philippeville and Bône and badly damaged the destroyer *Bramham,* which had to be towed back to Algiers. On the 21st Ju 88s raided Bougie, Philippeville, Algiers, and Bône. In the first attack the freighter *Ocean Vista* was lightly damaged and two LCPs lost. In the last, ten Spitfires were damaged or destroyed. On the 23rd Ju 88s and He 111s attacked convoy KMF.3 and badly damaged the liner *Scythia* (19,761 GRT) with a torpedo. On the 24th Ju 88s hit the same convoy and sank the transport *Trentbank*. In a raid on Philippeville the Dutch steamer *Aurora* was sunk in the harbor after she had unloaded. Eight ships from KMS.3 docked at Bône on the evening of the 25th, after an unsuccessful air raid.

On 25 November 1942 French prisoners are being taken to Italy in the destroyer *Ardente*, which had escorted the ferry *Aspomonte* to Tunisia. (Storia Militare)

The British, meanwhile, raided Tunis on the 18th and 19th and Bizerte on the 21st, 23rd, and 24th. Beaufighters dropped mines off Bizerte on the 24th and Wellingtons unsuccessfully attacked shipping in the Strait of Sicily on several occasions.

On the 18th an Italian column entered Tunisia from the south and occupied Gabès. Detachments sparred along the Tunisian Dorsal as the Axis acted to maintain communications with Libya. Allied intelligence overestimated enemy forces (which by the 25th consisted of about 15,500 German and 9,000 Italian troops), causing Anderson to delay his offensive another four days to bring up more units and fine-tune his meticulous plan. Finally, on the 24th Axis forces took the defensive to await Anderson's blow, which fell on the 25th.

The 78th Division's 11th and 36th Brigade Groups along with Blade Force, all supplemented by American artillery and armored units, advanced in three widely separated columns. In the north the Axis withdrew before contact. In the south the Allies suffered greatly before retaking Medjez el Bab. By 28 November the British had reached Djedeida, just fifteen miles west of Tunis. Unfortunately for Anderson, his spearheads were dangling at the end of a long supply line while the

Axis had air superiority and was growing stronger every day. The 10th Panzer Division's first armored elements docked on the 29th and rushed into action, pushing the British back. Eisenhower suspended the offensive 30 November. This was supposed to be a temporary suspension, but in fact he had lost the race to Tunis.

The crux of the matter proved to be the two weeks from 11 to 25 November. The Allied forces did not advance fast enough to offset a rapid enemy buildup in Tunisia that flew in the face of what they considered military logic. They were not aggressive in exploiting French help when they finally got it, and they had inadequate resources to discomfort Axis reinforcements arriving by sea despite the advantages Ultra intelligence gave them. Surface strike forces consisting of three light cruisers and three destroyers were formed in Malta (Force K) and Bône (Force Q) on 26 and 27 November, respectively. Six Swordfish advanced to Bône on the 25th. In a report on that date Admiral Cunningham noted that it was vital to reinforce Malta's air striking forces and that "quick action will lead to quick results and the dividend will be enormous." However, it was already too late. Axis forces were established and five months of hard fighting would follow before Allied troops marched into Tunis.[31]

17

FINAL ROUNDUP

Every possible vessel must be pressed into the supply service to Tunisia,
and I have ordered the operation of German forces accordingly.
As long as there is still a single soldier of the Axis powers fighting
in North Africa we must not leave him in the lurch.
—GRAND ADMIRAL KARL DÖNITZ, 8 MAY 1943, TO ADMIRAL RICCARDI

Toulon

Two major military events occurred in the Mediterranean in the closing days of November. One was the repulse of the British 78th Division just miles from Tunis, and the other was the mass scuttling of the French fleet at Toulon.

Hitler's distrust of French intentions precipitated his 19 November order for Operation Anton—the occupation of the naval base and the seizure of the warships therein. He decided on this despite the strong objections of Grand Admiral Raeder who well realized that a fleet was not just a collection of ships: it was crews, bases, resources, an industrial infrastructure, and a specialized and willing workforce. He appreciated that the French navy could immediately benefit the Axis only as a cobelligerent, and then only if sufficient fuel could be gathered to permit routine operations as opposed to a one-time sortie.

At 0425 on 27 November German armored columns forced the gates on either side of the extensive base area, which measured four kilometers east to west and up to a kilometer and a half deep. However, by the time the first troops had navigated the labyrinthine complex and reached *Strasbourg,* the flagship of Admiral de Laborde, he had already sent out the signal to scuttle. When a German officer called for the apparently undamaged battleship to surrender, the admiral replied, "The ship is sunk."[1]

The materiel consequences of de Laborde's action were tremendous: lost were three battleships, four heavy cruisers, three light cruisers, sixteen *contre-torpilleurs,* eleven destroyers, three torpedo boats, four sloops, a seaplane carrier, a minelayer, and ten submarines. Only the submarine *Vénus* escaped. Forty-five hundred Kriegsmarine personnel, optimistically dispatched to man captured warships, returned to Germany before they reached Toulon. Italy immediately commenced salvage operations and got as far as assigning names to two cruisers, four *contre-torpilleurs,* seven destroyers, and two torpedo boats. Of these, however, only four destroyers entered service under Italian colors between April and August 1943 and proved of limited value. Germany salvaged two of the 750-ton sloops.[2]

The scuttling deprived the Allies of a potential reinforcement and removed an ongoing worry because as long as the French fleet remained intact, it was a wild card that had to be accounted for. Moreover, had it rallied to North Africa, Darlan's position would have been uncontestable. On the Axis side, Hitler, for one, was happy to see it gone and Mussolini was right behind. Pétain and Laval were the big losers. With the fleet went the last of their military strength, the last shred of independence, and the last barrier between France and the full brutality of unrestrained German occupation.

The End of Darlan

The agreement between Major General Clark and Admiral Darlan negotiated on 12 November made Darlan high commissioner in French Africa and called for "the closest cooperation" between French armed forces and the U.S. Army. It also confirmed the "status, command, functions, employment, rights and privileges" of French forces and guaranteed French authority, and gave the Americans access to all required facilities and bases. The French were required to disclose all people detained as a consequence of their "dealings or sympathies with the United Nations," and to release the detainees when so directed. In short, the agreement confirmed French sovereignty under the old administration and required its cooperation against the Axis.[3]

The agreement provoked a storm of protest in the British and American press, in part instigated by the Fighting French movement. Some critics called the

North African administration Vichy South. Darlan was characterized as a "stinking skunk" or a "notorious Quisling." Many commentators accused the Allies of betraying the very cause they were fighting to uphold. This, and a protest from Churchill, who characterized Darlan's record as odious, drove Roosevelt to issue a statement on 17 November that the agreement with Darlan was only a temporary military expedient. His prestige staggered by this announcement, the admiral bitterly characterized himself as "a lemon which the Americans will drop after they have squeezed it dry." In any case, despite Roosevelt's qualifications, the howling of de Gaulle's faction, Churchill's sanctimonious condemnations, and the lashing of public opinion, the CCS endorsed the deal and it was formally executed in Algiers on 22 November 1942.[4]

Darlan proved loyal and effective, bringing French West Africa and the Dakar squadron into the Allied camp, and gradually the controversy became yesterday's news, at least as far as the American public was concerned. In Algiers, however, it was a different matter. By December the political scene was boiling as the various French factions vied for power, retribution, or survival. Even though Roosevelt had excluded the Fighting French from Operation Torch, de Gaulle remained a force irreconcilable to the course events had taken. According to a report filed by an American diplomat, "De Gaulle himself could not forget the fact that it was Darlan who, as prime minister, had had General de Gaulle tried and had condemned him to death as a traitor for supporting the Allies. . . . If there was anything certain in life, it was that the Free French could not strike hands with Darlan."[5]

A young Frenchman assassinated Darlan on 24 December 1942. The culprit was apprehended, secretly tried, and executed within two days. The group immediately responsible was a small faction with the unlikely agenda of bringing de Gaulle and Giraud into a royalist government led by Henri d'Orleans, the count of Paris and pretender to the French throne. The ultimate responsibility has never been undisputedly fixed. Admiral Leahy, however, sitting as head of the JCS, noted, "I had received from many sources information that the British might make an effort to get Darlan out of the picture and put de Gaulle in." Certainly de Gaulle was the greatest beneficiary. A Gaullist staff member, who also happened to be the brother of one of the monarchist group's leaders, visited Algiers immediately before the assassination and delivered $40,000 to Fighting French partisans.[6]

For his part, Eisenhower noted that despite Darlan's reputation "of a notorious collaborator with Hitler," during his time as high commissioner "he never once . . . violated any commitment or promise." Admiral Cunningham wrote, "He acted absolutely squarely with us, and was the only man who could have brought North and West Africa in with us." At Darlan's funeral, according to Cunningham's description, "All the leading figures attended, and French, American and British officers filed slowly past the coffin. It was a colourful and impressive display with the mass of different uniforms." Giraud knelt at the coffin and briefly cried.[7]

General Noguès, Darlan's designated successor, declined the job, and Girard became high commissioner, as well as military chief, mostly due to American pressure. When General de Gaulle finally landed in Algiers on 30 May 1943 he and Giraud became copresidents of the Comité Français de Libération Nationale. This arrangement lasted from May to October 1943. De Gaulle gradually squeezed Giraud first from his post as commissioner and then even from his lofty military position, and forced the general's retirement on 8 April 1944.

For the most part the other principal French leaders fared poorly. Noguès resigned in June 1943 and fled to Portugal to avoid arrest. In 1947 the French government sentenced him to twenty years' imprisonment for collaboration; he was arrested in 1957 when he returned to France, but was soon released. Vice Admiral Michelier became leader of French naval forces in Africa under Giraud until 16 July 1943 when the Comité Français de Libération Nationale accused him of collaboration with the Axis. Admiral Jean-Pierre Estéva was arrested in 1944, tried for treason, and condemned to life imprisonment, a sentence Admiral Cunningham called "cruelly vindictive." He was released in 1950 and died in 1951. Rear Admiral Derrien was likewise sentenced to life on 12 May 1944. He received a suspended sentence in 1946 due to blindness and died that same year. Marshal Pétain, Pierre Laval, and Rear Admiral Auphan were all arrested. Auphan was sentenced to life imprisonment for treason but released in 1955. Laval was executed in 1945, and Pétain's death sentence was commuted due to his age. He died in 1951, age ninety-five, still in prison. Corps General Alphonse Juin became resident-general of Tunisia in 1943 and then commanded French troops in Italy in November 1943. In 1944 he became chief of staff for national defense. Division General Charles Mast took command of the Casablanca Division in December 1942 and replaced Juin as resident-general of Tunisia in May 1943, a post he held until 1947. Brigade General Antoine Béthouart was released from imprisonment on 14 November and served in the French military mission to

Washington. From September 1944 to the end of the war he commanded the French I Corps.[8]

The Last Roundup

The campaign in Tunisia lasted six months and contained some perilous moments for Allied forces, particularly the Battle of Kasserine Pass in February 1943 when German and Italian forces routed the U.S. 1st Armored Division and advanced fifty miles through American lines. Nonetheless, given the Allied ability to interdict Axis supply lines, the result was inevitable and the last Axis forces in Africa surrendered on 13 May 1943. The British anticipated an evacuation attempt and every night from 9 May Royal Navy destroyers patrolled the Strait of Sicily in an operation named by Admiral Cunningham: Operation Retribution. However, the Axis partners never contemplated a maritime withdrawal because they lacked the means and, until the very end, the German command remained convinced that resistance had to be maintained as long as possible—even planning to hold out on Cape Bon after Tunis fell and ordering extra submarines into the Mediterranean to serve as underwater transports. As late as 1 May Grand Admiral Dönitz replied to objections raised by local German and Italian commanders to the use of warships to supply Tunisia with the admonition, "*Everything* must be done to hold Tunis. Days and weeks might count. To sacrifice the [Italian] fleet for this task would be of greater benefit than to save it for tasks to come."[9]

Thus when Axis resistance collapsed, it was rapid and confused and no one tallied the troops captured. Historians have advanced overstated claims. "A human deluge of 130,000 German and 120,000 Italian soldiers—more prisoners than the Russians had taken at Stalingrad," or "The Germans could ill afford to lose nearly a quarter million crack troops." The reality was somewhat less. In March Allied intelligence estimated that 150,000 men would become prisoners when Tunisia finally fell. But this count failed to include "the number of extra administrative troops and civil and military officials in Tripolitania who had nothing to do with the final battle but headed east into the last bridgehead." The official British history states, "The closest Allied record is that of the unwounded prisoners actually held on 25th May." This numbered 101,784 Germans, 89,442 Italians, and 47,017 men nationality unspecified (Arab auxiliaries and volunteers and some French). However, even if a quarter million prisoners had been taken, this would not have offset Torch's failure to achieve its original goal. Had Tunisia fallen in December, the vast majority of the 40,000 Italians and Germans in Tunisia and the 133,000 Italian, 70,000 German, and 26,000 native troops in Tripolitania would have certainly been captured anyway. An early victory would have avoided more than 75,000 Allied (including French) casualties, saved much shipping, opened the Mediterranean far earlier; subsequent campaigns, be they in Sicily or France, would have started earlier. There is little question that the maintenance of an Axis bridgehead in Tunisia for so many months was Torch's worst failure.[10]

CONCLUSION

I can assure you that the hour when the United States took action
in Europe and Africa seemed very slow to come to us Frenchmen
who were under the conqueror's boot.
—Admiral François Darlan to Admiral William D. Leahy,
27 November 1942

Operation Torch required five months to conquer French North Africa, a process that was supposed to take three weeks. Many benefits advanced by Roosevelt, Churchill, and the British chiefs to justify the operation did not materialize. It gave a few American troops some seasoning against the German foe, but only because of the need to fight an unplanned campaign. It did not relieve German military pressure on the Soviet Union—the Soviet victory at Stalingrad did that (and not even Stalingrad and Torch together were enough to prevent the Germans from launching a renewed Russian offensive in 1943). Torch did not open the Mediterranean to traffic or save shipping—instead, the need to support the Tunisian front cost shipping. The fact that the campaign lasted well into 1943 killed any hope General Marshall and the American chiefs harbored for avoiding a Mediterranean commitment and invading northwestern Europe that year. In the end, the conquest of Africa proved a life-or-death matter for the Vichy French State, but not for Italy or Germany. For these reasons, some have argued that Torch prolonged the war. If Torch thus failed to achieve its primary military goal and its strategic implications are unclear, and if it failed to gain the benefits expected by its authors, what then did it accomplish? Some answers lie in the realms of politics, policy, and doctrine.

A delayed European invasion was a good thing, according to the strategic concepts of Great Britain's Churchill-dominated War Cabinet and the British chiefs. On 3 October 1942 staff wrote, "It is too early to see exactly where Torch may lead us. If it is successful it will certainly pay us to reinforce that success and concentrate on wearing down the Axis in the Mediterranean." The pros and cons of the British Mediterranean and "wear-down" policies versus the thrust-to-the heart strategy espoused by the American JCS has inspired a literature that eloquently argues both sides. The fact remains, however, that every major victory in the Mediterranean, starting with the British Empire's rout of the Italian 10th Army in Libya in December 1940, through Torch in November 1942, the Italian Armistice in September 1943, the capture of Rome in June 1944, and even the crossing of the Po River in April 1945, failed to materially degrade Germany's ability to wage war. In northwestern Europe, on the other hand, it took American and British armies only four months from the time they landed in Normandy to enter Germany. It was the occupation of German territory and nothing else that ended the war.[1]

Nonetheless, perhaps a delayed invasion of northwestern Europe was indeed a good thing. The British appreciated better than the Americans how difficult it would be to land an amphibious force—not to mention an army—against a strong and determined foe. They were probably right that a major landing against France in 1942 had little chance of success and that Roundup in spring 1943 was only marginally more likely to succeed. But even if these military reasons were disregarded, the Allies reaped other benefits by delaying their invasion of northwestern Europe.

From the perspective of the early twenty-first century it is easy to forget that in 1941 the United States had only twice fought a war as part of a coalition: in the Revolutionary War and in World War I. The experiences of 1783 were too distant to matter, while those of 1917–1918 caused much disillusionment and contributed to the popular rejection of military alliances and the isolationism of the 1930s. Operation Torch gave the Anglo-Americans a platform to practice two critical processes necessary to their eventual victory: it taught them how to conduct combined warfare on the strategic level and it taught them how to fight joint warfare on the operational level. It established effective mechanisms for the planning, training, and execution of a risky and complicated operation in a setting where—as high as the stakes may have been—the consequence of failure was not absolute German victory. Even better, Torch forced them to do this quickly.

Torch sharpened a doctrine of amphibious warfare that was next practiced eight months later in Operation Husky off Sicily where an Anglo-American armada of 154 major warships, 243 minor warships, 221 transports and freighters, 1,734 landing craft, and 86 miscellaneous vessels landed 180,000 men in eight divisions on twenty-one separate beaches. Inevitably some things went wrong: shipping arrived at disembarkation points late, boats navigated to the wrong beaches, paratroopers were squandered. Nonetheless, the Allied partners applied many of the lessons learned in Operation Torch. They organized beaches, moved materiel forward more rapidly, and lost far fewer landing craft than in North Africa. Warships delivered effective gunfire support and the landings succeeded at comparatively small cost in men and ships. This doctrine was further refined in mainland Italy before being put to the absolute test in Normandy. There were a few close calls, particularly at Omaha Beach, but after Torch every Anglo-American amphibious landing, be it large or small, succeeded, whereas before Torch the majority had failed. The experience gained in North Africa was fundamental to this record of success.[2]

There were other, less apparent benefits that came out of the process of fighting in North Africa. General Charles de Gaulle's courage and vision is beyond question. However, it was Darlan and not his Fighting French movement that brought France back to the Allied camp. If this seems of marginal importance to the reader, the excitement of Italy's Marshal Cavallero at the prospect of French partnership with the Axis should be kept in mind. Learning that the French fleet at Toulon was raising steam to intervene against the British off Oran, he exclaimed, "I do not dare to hope, but if this collaboration comes off, we have won the war." Perhaps Cavallero exaggerated, but consider the impact of a French declaration of war against the Allies: forty or fifty French divisions, easily raised from trained men still languishing in German prison camps, would, in conjunction with German forces, have rendered an amphibous invasion of northwestern Europe practically impossible.[3]

These benefits of Operation Torch were all significant, and perhaps they were the minimum prerequisites for the victory the western Allies won in 1945. If that is true, then Torch played a crucial role in that victory and must be judged a success.[4] If, in the end, the Allies had lacked the ability to insert an army over heavily defended beaches, if they lacked the ability to supply and quickly expand that army, if they lacked the ability to effectively set joint priorities and fight as more or less true partners, they probably would have still emerged victorious from World War II, but it would have been as junior partners to a triumphant Soviet Union. To picture this one must remember that the British War Cabinet's original Grand Strategy, conceived in September 1940 and affirmed in the December 1941–January 1942 Arcadia Conference between American and British military and political leaders, was for British (or Allied) armies to return to the continent as the consequence of a "wear-down" policy that consisted of erecting a blockade around Germany; attrition, carried out particularly by strategic bombing; subversion and sabotage; and a landing in force only when Germany was at the point of collapse. Events proved that blockade, conventional bombing, and subversion would never have caused Germany's collapse. A Russian army in Berlin was a different matter, and if the Allies had landed in France after a Soviet-induced German collapse, it would have been a far different postwar world.

APPENDIX I
Abbreviations

COMPARATIVE NAVAL RANKS

United States	Great Britain	France
Fleet Admiral	Admiral of the Fleet	Amiral de la Flotte
Admiral	same	Vice Amiral d'Escadre
Vice Admiral	same	Vice Amiral
Rear Admiral	same	Contre Amiral
Commodore	same	none
Captain	same	Capitaine de Vaisseau
Commander	same	Capitaine de Frégate
Lieutenant Commander	same	Capitaine de Corvette
Lieutenant	same	Lieutenant de Vaisseau
Lieutenant (jg)	Sub-Lieutenant	Enseigne de Vaisseau 1ère Classe
Midshipman	same	Enseigne de Vaisseau 2ème Classe

CONVERSIONS

1 nautical mile = 2,205 yards, 1,852 meters, or 1.151 statute miles

1 knot = 1.852 kilometers/hour or 1.151 statute miles/hour

1 meter = 1.094 yards

1 yard = 0.9144 meters

1 centimeter = 0.3937 inches

1 inch = 2.54 centimeters

1 kilogram = 2.205 pounds

1 pound = 0.4536 kilograms

1 tonne = .9842 long tons

1 long ton = 1.016 tonnes

ABBREVIATIONS
General Abbreviations

a/c: aircraft

AP: armor-piercing

Aux: auxiliary

Bdg: brigade

Be: Belgium

BLT: battalion landing team

BR: British

CCS: Combined Chiefs of Staff

COHQ: Combined Operations
  Headquarters

CSC: Chiefs of Staff Committee

Du: Dutch

FC: fire control

GE: German

GMT: Greenwich Mean Time

GRT: gross registered tons

HE: high-explosive (or high effect)

HMCS: His Majesty's Canadian Ship

HMS: His Majesty's Ship

in: inch

JCS: Joint Chiefs of Staff

JIC: Joint Intelligence Committee

k: kilometer

LF: Lancashire Fusiliers

mm: millimeter

na: not available

OB Süd: Oberbefehlshaber Süd

OKW: Oberkommando der
  Wehrmacht

PO: Polish

RAF: Royal Air Force

RCT: regimental combat team

RN: Royal Navy

RWK: Royal West Kents

SFCP: Shore Fire Control Party

SIS: Servizio Informazioni Speciali
  della Regia Marina (Italian naval
  intelligence)

TBS: talk between ships VHF radio

TG: task group

TT: torpedo

USN: U.S. Navy

Ship Types

AAS: antiaircraft ship

ACV: auxiliary aircraft carrier

AD: auxiliary minesweeper

AK: attack cargo ship

AM: minesweeper

AMT: auxiliary minesweeper (trawler)

AO: oiler

AP: attack transport

AVP: seaplane carrier

BB: battleship

BC: battle cruiser

BM: monitor

CA: heavy cruiser

CL: light cruiser

CM: minelayer (large)

C/S: cable ship

CT: *contre-torpilleur*

CV: aircraft carrier

CVE: escort carrier

CVL: light aircraft carrier

DC: corvette

DD: destroyer

DE: destroyer escort or Hunt-type
    destroyer

DMS: destroyer minesweeper

DS: sloop

GB: gunboat

LC: landing craft

LCA: landing craft assault

LCM: landing craft mechanized

LCP: landing craft personnel

LCPL: landing craft personnel, large

LCPR: landing craft personnel, ramped

LCS: landing support craft

LCV: landing craft vehicle

LSC: landing ship carrier

LSG: landing ship gantry

LSH: landing ships headquarters

LSI: landing ship infantry

LSI (H): landing ship infantry
    (hand-hoisting)

LSI (L): landing ship infantry (large)

LSI (M): landing ship infantry
    (medium)

LSS: landing ship stern-chute

LST: tank landing ship

MGB: motor gun boat

ML: motor launch

MS: minesweeper

MTB: motor torpedo boat

PB: patrol boat

SC: submarine chaser

SS: submarine

TB: torpedo boat

Tran: transport

trwl: trawler

U-boat: *Unterseeboot,* or German
    submarine

VP: *Vorpostenboot,* or German
    patrol boats

Army Types

AAB: antiaircraft battalion

AB: artillery battery

CCB: Combat Command B

Cdo: Commando

Coy: company

CR: cavalry regiment

CS: cavalry squadron

EB: engineer battalion

elms: elements

IB: infantry battalion

Icoy: infantry company

MB: motorized battalion

McB: mechanized battalion

McCR: mechanized cavalry regiment

Mcoy: mechanized company

MotB: motorized battalion

French Abbreviations

DCA: défense contre avions (antiaircraft)

DCT: Division de Contre-Torpilleurs (*contre-torpilleur* division)

DT: Division de Torpilleurs (torpedo division)

GACA: Groupe d'Escadrons Autonome Portés de Chasseurs d'Afrique (chasseurs mobile squadron group of Africa)

GB: Groupement de Bombardement (bomber group)

GC: Groupement de Chasse (fighter group)

GPF: *grande puissance de feu* (heavy firepower)

GR: Groupement de Reconnaissance (reconnaissance group)

GT: Groupement de Transport (transport group)

RA: Régiment d'Artillerie (artillery regiment)

RAA: Régiment d'Artillerie d'Afrique (artillery regiment of Africa)

RACM: Régiment d'Artillerie Coloniale du Maroc (colonial artillery regiment of Morocco)

RCA: Régiment de Chasseurs d'Afrique (chasseurs regiment of Africa)

REC: Régiment Étranger de Cavalerie (foreign cavalry regiment)

REI: Régiment Étranger d'Infanterie (foreign infantry regiment)

RG: Régiment de la Garde (guard regiment)

RIC: Régiment d'Infanterie Coloniale (colonial infantry regiment)

RICM: Régiment d'Infanterie Coloniale du Maroc (colonial infantry regiment of Morocco)

RMZT: Régiment Mixte de Zouaves et de Tirailleurs (mixed Zouave and rifleman regiment)

RSA: Régiment de Spahis Algériens (Algerian Spahis regiment)

RSM: Régiment de Spahis Marocains (Moroccan Spahis regiment)

RST: Régiment de Spahis Tunisiens (Tunisian Spahis regiment)

RTA: Régiment de Tirailleurs Algériens (regiment of Algerian riflemen)

RTM: Régiment de Tirailleurs Marocains (regiment of Moroccan riflemen)

RTS: Régiment de Tirailleurs Sénégalais (regiment of Senegalese riflemen)

RTT: Régiment de Tirailleurs Tunisiens (regiment of Tunisian riflemen)

RZ: Régiment de Zouaves (Zouave regiment)

SA: Sapeurs Annamites (Annamite sappers)

APPENDIX II
French Order of Battle, North Africa, 8 November 1942

The Armée d'Afrique was organized into eight divisions with an authorized strength of 137,000 men. Effective strength was approximately 120,000. It also clandestinely maintained about 60,000 men in isolated areas and planned to mobilize 109,000 more men in the event of hostilities. As of 1 October 1942 ground forces had 358 artillery pieces (with an additional 157 in hidden depots), 335 armored fighting vehicles (plus 53), 3,014 machine guns (plus 1,511), 340 81-mm mortars (plus 210), and 253,000 rifles (plus 57,500). There were 600 rounds per rifle and 3,350 shells per tube on hand.[1]

HIGH COMMAND
Armed Forces: Corps Gen. Alphonse Juin
Navy: 4th Maritime District: Vice Adm. Jacques Moreau
Army: 19th Military Region: Corps Gen. Louis-Marie Koeltz
Air Force: 1st Air Region: Div. Gen. Jean Mendigal

ALGIERS
Navy: Marine Alger (Vice Adm. Marcel Leclerc)
9th Submarine Division
- *Caïman* (1927, 974 tons, 1x100-mm, 10x550-mm TT, 15/9 k) (Lt. Cdr. Mertz)
- *Marsouin* (as given in the last ship described in line above; hereafter "as above") (Lt. Minne)

26th Auxiliary Minesweeper Section
- *AD 244 Angèle Pérez*, *VP 14 Marsouin* (unarmed), *VP 107 Colonel Casse* (inactive)

Patrol Boats
- *Ch 3* (1933, 148 tons, 1x75-mm, 20 k)
- *Engagante* (1917, 315 tons, 2x100-mm, 14 k)
- *La Boudeuse* (1940, 630 tons, 1x100-mm, 20 k) (Lt. Cdr. Mayer)
- *Sergent Gouarne* (refit) (1928, 1,131 GRT, 3x100-mm, 11 k) (Lt. Puech)

Coastal Batteries
- Batterie du Lazaret (Cape Matifou): 4x194-mm (two armed)
- Batterie Duperré (Pointe Pescade): 3x194-mm (two armed)
- Batterie de l'Amirauté (Algiers): 4x120-mm
- Batterie du Musoir Nord (Algiers): 2x75-mm
- Batterie du Musoir Sud (Algiers): 2x75-mm
- Batterie des Arcades (Algiers): 3x95-mm
- Batterie Sidi-Ferruch (Sidi-Ferruch): 4x75-mm (disarmed)

Naval Air Force
- 4th Squadron (Maison Blanche): BR. Potez 63.11x22 (6 operational)

Army (Corps Gen. L. M. Koeltz)
Algiers Division (Div. Gen. C. E. Mast)
- 1 RZ (Algiers, Fort National): 3xIB
- 1 RTA (Blida): 3xIB
- 5 RTA (Fort National): 3xIB
- 9 RTA (Orléansville): 3xIB
- 13 RTS (Algiers): 3xIB
- 29 RTA (Koléa): 3xIB
- 65 RAA: 4xAB
- 5 RCA (Algiers and Maison Carreé): McCB
- 1 RSA (Médéa, Bou Saada, and Teniet el-Had): CR
- III/7 Guard (Algiers): CR
- II/411 (Algiers): AAB
- 1 SA (Beni Messous and Bene Mansour): EB

Constantine Division (Div. Gen. M. J. E. Welvert)
- 15 RTS (Philippeville): 2xIB
- 3 RTA (Bône): 3xIB
- 3 RZ: 2xIB
- 7 RTA (Setif): 3xIB
- 67 RAA (Constantine): 3xAB
- 3 RCA (Constantine): MB

- 3 RSA (Batna): CR
- 6 RSA (Aunale): CR
- 7 Guard Legion: 4xCoy.

Air Force
- GC II/3 (Maison Blanche): D.520x22
- GC III/6 (Maison Blanche): D.520x25
- GB I/19 (Blida): DB-7x13
- GB II/61 (Blida): DB-7x13, LeO 451x2
- GT II/15 (Blida): Potez 540x17, Potez 650x3

ORAN
Navy: Marine Oran (Vice Adm. A. G. Rioult)
- *Contre-torpilleur: Epervier* (1934, 2,441 tons, 5x138-mm, 6x550-mm TT, 36 k) (Cdr. J. Laurin)

7th Torpedo Division (Cdr. A. de Féraudy)
- *Tramontane* (1927, 1,319 tons, 4x130-mm, 6x550-mm TT, 33 k) (Cdr. de Féraudy)
- *Typhon* (1928, as above) (Lt. Cdr. G. Abgrall)
- *Tornade* (1928, as above) (Lt. Cdr. R. Parès)

Sloops and Patrol Boats
- *La Surprise* (1940, 647 tons, 1x100-mm, 20 k) (Lt. Cdr. J. Lavigne)
- *La Bônoise* (1937, 590 tons, 1x102-mm, 10 k) (Lt. Denis)
- *L'Ajaccienne* (1936, 738 tons, 1x102-mm, 10 k) (Lt. Lazennec)
- *La Toulonnaise* (1934, as above, in dock) (Lt. Lavolay)
- *La Sétoise* (as above, at sea escorting convoy K 39)

3rd Patrol Division (Tugs/Minesweepers)
- *Tourterelle* (1918, 680 tons, 11 k) (in dock)
- *Pigeon* (as above)
- *Chêne* (1918, 360 tons, 1x90-mm, 9 k)

27th Patrol Division (Tugs/Minesweepers)
- *VP 88 Jean Argaud, VP 77 Nadal, Joos, Anna, D 275 Lilias* (unavailable)

12th Submarine Division
- *Argonaute* (1932, 630 tons, 1x75-mm, 6x550-mm, 2x400-mm TT, 14/9 k) (Lt. Véron)
- *Diane* (1932, 651 tons, as above, in dock)

5th Submarine Division
- *Actaéon* (1931, 1,570 tons, 1x100-mm, 9x550-mm, 2x400-mm TT, 17/10 k) (Lt. Clavières)
- *Fresnel* (as above) (Lt. Saglio)

Submarines in Reserve and Unavailable
- *Ariane* (1929, 626 tons, 1x75-mm, 7x550-mm TT, 14/7.5 k)
- *Danaé* (as above)
- *Pallas* (1939, 662 tons, 1x75-mm, 6x550-mm, 3x400-mm TT, 14.5/9 k)

Shore Batteries
- Canastel (Pointe du Canastel): 3x240-mm
- Santon (Mers el-Kébir): 4x194-mm
- Batterie du Nord (Arzew): 4x105-mm

Antiaircraft Batteries
- 2nd, 8th each 4x90-mm, 54th: 14x37-mm

Land Batteries
- 31st, 32nd, 124th, 125th, 157th, 160th, each 4x75-mm and 2x20-mm
- 158th, 159th, each 4x75-mm

Naval Air Force
- Flotilla 4F (Latigue): LeO 451x13
- 5th Flotilla (Arzew): Lat 298x13

Army
Oran Division (Div. Gen. R. Boisseau)
- 2 RZ (Oran): 3xIB
- 2 RTA (Mostaganem): 3xIB
- 6 RTA (Tlemcen): 3xIB
- 16 RTA (Oran): 3xIB
- 66 RAA (Oran): 3xAB
- 2 RSA (Tlemcen): CR
- 2 RCA (Oran): McCR
- 9 RCA (Mascara): MB
- 411 RAA: AAB

Air Force
3rd Mixed Group
- GC III/3 (La Sénia): D.520x26
- GB I/11 (La Sénia): LeO 451x13

- GR II/52 (La Sénia): Bloch 175x9, Bloch 174x2
- GR I/36 (Sétif): Po63.11x6

MOROCCO: GENERAL AUGUSTIN NOGUÈS, RESIDENT-SUPERIOR
Navy: Marine au Maroc (Vice Adm. François Michelier)
- *Jean Bart* (BB, 35,000 tons, immobile, 4x380-in, 4x90-mm) (Capt. E. Barthes)
- *Malin* (under repair) (CT, 1935, 2,569 tons, 5x138-mm, 7x550-mm TT, 38 k) (Cdr. M. de Vignaux)

2nd Light Squadron (Rear Adm. R. G. de Lafond)
- *Primauguet* (CL, 1926, 7,250 tons, 8x155-mm, 4x75-mm, 12x550-mm TT, 33 k) (Capt. L. J. M. Mercier)

11th Contre-Torpilleur Division (Cdr. F. Costet)
- *Milan* (1934, 2,440 tons, 5x138-mm, 6x550-mm TT, 36 k) (Cdr. Costet)
- *Albatros* (1931, as above) (Cdr. Périès)

2nd Torpedo Division (Cdr. L. S. Sticca)
- *Fougueux* (1930, 1,378 tons, 4x130-mm, 7x75-mm, 6x550-mm TT, 29 k) (Cdr. Sticca)
- *L'Alcyon* (1929, as above) (Lt. Cdr. De Bragelongne)
- *Frondeur* (1931, as above) (Lt. Cdr. Begouën-Demeaux)

5th Torpedo Division (Cdr. Mariani)
- *Brestois* (1928, as above) (Cdr. Mariani)
- *Boulonnais* (as above) (Lt. Cdr. Martinant de Préneuf)

6th Torpedo Division (Cdr. Delplanque)
- *Tempête* (1926, 1,319 tons, 4x130-in, 7x75-mm, 6x550-mm TT, 29 k) (Cdr. Delplanque)
- *Simoun* (as above) (Cdr. O'Neil)

6th Escort Squadron (sloops) (Capt. Tranier)
- *Commandant Delage,* (1939, 630 tons, 2x100-mm, 14 k) (Lt. Cdr. Rochette)
- *La Gracieuse* (1940 as above) (Lt. Cdr. Mounier)
- *La Grandière* (1940, 1,969 tons, 3x138-mm, 15.5 k) (Cdr. Le Hagre)

6th Patrol Squadron (Patrol Boats)
- *La Servannaise* (738 tons, 2x100-mm, 9 k)
- *L'Algéroise* (inactive, as above)

- *La Sablaise* (inactive, as above)
- *Chasseur 2* (1933, 148 tons, 1x75-mm, 20 k) (Lt. Nadillac)

4th Submarine Division
- *Sidi-Ferruch* (1939, 1,570 tons, 1x100-mm, 9x550- and 2x400-mm TT, 17/10 k) (Lt. David)
- *Le Tonnant* (1935, as above) (Lt. Corre)
- *Le Conquérant* (as above) (Lt. Lefevre)

16th Submarine Division
- *La Sibylle* (1934, 651 tons, 1x75-mm, 6x550- and 2x400-mm TT, 14/9 k) (Lt. Cdr. Corre)
- *Amazone* (1933, as above) (Lt. Verdavaine)
- *L'Amphitrite* (as above) (Lt. Rotti)
- *Antiope* (1932, as above) (Lt. Mille)

17th Submarine Division
- *La Psyché* (1933, as above) (Lt. Guittet)
- *Oréade* (as above) (Lt. Loiseau)
- *Orphée* (as above) (Lt. Cdr. Le Gall)
- *Méduse* (1932, as above) (Lt. Roy)

Fédala
- *Abbé Desgranges* (Aux MS 1939)

Port Lyautey
- *Ailette* (DS, 1918, 492 tons, 4x100-mm, 20 k)

At Sea
- *Victoria* (Aux PB, 1928, 849 GRT, 3x100-mm, 11.9 k) (Lt. Lacaze) (Convoy R 41)
- *Estafette* (Aux PB, 315 tons, 2x47-mm, 10 k) (Convoy R 42)

Shore Batteries
- Batterie Ponsot (Mehdia): 2x138-mm Mle 1923
- Batterie de Fédala (Fédala): 3x100-mm Mle 1897/1917
- Batterie de Pont Blondin (Fédala): 3x138-mm Mle 1910
- Défense des Passes (Fédala): 2x75-mm
- Batterie d'Oukacha (Casablanca): 4x100-mm Mle 1897/17
- Batterie du Poste d'Entrée de Rade (Casablanca): 2x75-mm
- Batterie d'El Hank (Casablanca): 4x194-mm Mle 1902, 4x138-mm Mle 1910
- Batterie de la Railleuse (Safi): 4x130-mm Mle 1924

- Batterie du Port (Safi): 2x75-mm
- Agadir: Batterie de Brougham: 4x100-mm Mle 1897/1917

Naval Air Force
- Flotille 1F (Port Lyautey): De.520x27
- Flotille 3F (Port Lyautey): GM 167 Fx11
- Flotille 3F (Agadir): GM 167 Fx2

Army: (Corp Gen. Georges Lascroux)
Fez Division (Brig. Gen. M. M. Salbert)
- 4 RTM (Taza and Boured): 2xIB
- 5 RTM (Oudjda and Guercif): 2xIB
- 11 RTA (Fez and Gafsai): 2xIB
- III/3 REI (Fez and Ksar el Souk)
- I/6 RTS (Fez): MB
- 1 REC (Fez, Oujda, and Guercif): McB
- IV/9 RG: 2xCoy
- 63 RAA: 4xAB

Meknès Division (Div. Gen. A. M. F. Dody)
- 7 RTM (Meknès and Midelt): 2xIB
- 8 RTM (Meknès and Ouezzan): 2xIB
- 3 REI (Meknès, El Hajeb, and Kenifra): 2xIB
- 3 RSM: CB
- 10 GACA: 2xMCoy
- III/9 RG: 2xCoy
- 64 RAA: 3xAB

Casablanca Division (Brig. Gen. M. E. A. Béthouart)
- 1 RTM (Port-Lyautey and Souk el Arba): 3xIB
- 6 RTM (Casablanca, Kasbah Tadla, Mediouna): 3xIB
- RICM (Casablanca, Rabat, Mazagan): 3xIB
- III/6 RTS (Casablanca): MotB
- 1 RCA (Rabat): McB
- 3 RSM (-) (Rabat): CR
- I/9 RG: 2xCoy
- RACM: 2xAB

Marrakech Division (Div. Gen. J. J. M. Henry-Martin)
- 2 RTM (Marrakech, Mogador, Agadir): 3xIB
- 2 REI (Marrakech, Ouarzazat, Agadir): 3xIB

- II/6 RTS (Marrakech): CR
- 4 RSM (Marrakech, Tiznit): CR
- II/9 RG: 1xCoy
- RACM: 2xAB

Air Force: (Div. Gen. Auguste Lahoulle)
11th Mixed Group (Col. Labaurie)
- GC I/5 (Rabat Ville): Curtiss H-75x26 (19 operational)
- GC II/5 (Cazès): Curtiss H-75x20; D.520x13
- GB I/23 (Marrakech): LeO 451x13
- GB II/23 (Meknès): LeO 451x13
- GB I/32 (Cazès): DB-7x13 (11 operational)
- GB II/32 (Agadir): DB-7x13
- GR I/22 (Rabat-Salé): LeO 451x13
- GR I/52 (Marrakech): Potez 63.11x13
- GT I/15 (Rabat-Salé): Potez 29x18, F222.x5, F224x1
- GT III/15 (Oujda): Amiot 143x4, LeO 451 (na)

TUNISIA: VICE ADM. JEAN-PIERRE ESTÉVA, RESIDENT-GENERAL
Navy: Rear Adm. Edmond Derrien
12th Torpedo Division
- *La Pomone* (1935, 610 tons, 2x100-mm, 2x550-mm TT, 34.5 k)
- *L'Iphigénie* (as above)
- *Bombarde* (1936, as above)

3rd Escort Squadron
- *Commandant Rivière* (1939, 630 tons, 1x100-mm, 14 k)
- *La Batailleuse* (as above)

1st Mine Section (Auxiliary Minesweepers)
- *Canard, AD 167 Goeland, AD 283 Grondin, AD 166 Héron I, AD 242 Pen Men*

2nd Mine Section
- *Fracas, AD 256 Gascogne, AD 279 Ravignan, AD 271 Penfret II*

25th Mine Section
- *Chasseur 81, AD 268 Saint Antoine, AD 190 L'Afrique, AD 280 Madone de Pompei, AD 272 Méduse*

Police Boats
- *VP 74 Chien de Mer, VP 87 Aigle de Mer, VP 89 Loup de Mer*

Laid Up
- *Contre-torpilleur: L'Audacieux* (1934, 2,569 tons, 5x138-mm, 9x550-mm TT, 37 k)
- Minelayer: *Castor* (1916, 3,150 tons, 4x100-mm, 14.5 k)

Submarines
- *Circé* (1925, 615 tons, 1x75-mm, 7x550-mm TT, 14/7.5 k)
- *Calypso* (1926, as above)
- *Turquoise* (1928, 761 tons, 1x75-mm, 5x550-mm, 6x400-mm TT, 12/7.5 k)
- *Saphir* (as above)
- *Nautilus* (1925, as above)
- *Phoque* (1926, 974 tons, 1x100-mm, 10x550-mm TT, 15/9 k)
- *Espadon* (as above)
- *Dauphin* (1925, as above)
- *Requin* (1924, as above)

Shore Batteries
- El Meltline (Bizerte): 2x340-mm
- Cap Bizerte (Bizerte): 4x164-mm
- Sidi Bou Said (Tunis): 4x138-mm
- Batterie de Sousse (Sousse): 4x138-mm
- Tyna (Sfax): 4x138-mm

Antiaircraft Batteries
- Ben Negro, Djebel Abiod, Ras Charaa, Sidi Yahia, Wadi Guenine, each 4x75-mm

Naval Air Force
- Flotte 1 (Karouba): Bréguet 521x3, LeO H.257 bis x3

Army Tunisia Division (Div. Gen. Georges Barré)
Bizerte Group (Rear Adm. Derrien)
- 43 RIC: 2xIB
- III/4 RMZT
- III/8 RG II: CR
- II/62 RAA
- Fusiliers-Marins: 1xIB

Tunis Group (Col. Bergeron)
- I/, II/4 RMZT
- II/4 RCA: CR

- I/8 RG: CR
- I/62 RAA
- I/412 RA

Sahel Group (Brig. Gen. Trémeau)
- II/4 RTT: 2xCoy
- III/4 RTT: 2xCoy
- III/ 4 RCA: CR
- I/4 RST: CR
- II/412 RA

South Tunisian Group (Lt. Col. Nussard)
- I/4 RTT: IB
- II 4 RST: CR

1 Reserve Group (Tunis) (Col. Le Coulteux)
- III/43 RIC: IB
- I/4 RCA: McB
- VII/4 RCA: McB
- II/8 RG: MB
- III/62 RAA

2 Reserve Group (Col. Lecourtier)
- II/4 RTT: 2xICoy
- III/4 RTT: 2xICoy
- V/8 RG: MCoy
- III/62 RAA(-)

Air Force
8th Mixed Group
- Sidi Ahmed: GC II/7: D.520x26
- 3/13 (Gabès): Potez 631x8
- GB I/25 (El Aouina): LeO 451x13
- GB II/25 (El Aouina): LeO 451x13
- GB II/33 (El Aouina): Bloch 174x11

APPENDIX III
Allied Order of Battle as of 0100, 8 November 1942

MEDITERRANEAN TASK FORCES (ADM. ANDREW B. CUNNINGHAM)
Force R (Refueling Force H)
- *Brown Ranger* (AO, 1940, 6,000 tons, 1x4-in)
- *Dingledale* (AO, 1940, 8,145 tons)
- *Coreopsis* (DC, 1940, 1,015 tons, 16.5 k, 1x4-in) (Lt. Cdr. A. Davies)
- *Loch Oskaig* (AMT, 1937, 534 tons, 12 k, 1x4-in) (Lt. G. Clampitt)
- *Imperialist* (AMT, 1939, 520 tons, 12 k, 1x4-in) (Lt. A. Peling)
- *Arctic Ranger* (AMT, 1937, 493 tons, 12 k, 1x4-in) (Lt. J. Banks)
- *St. Nectan* (AMT, 1937) (Lt. J. Proby)

Force H (Vice Adm. Edward N. Syfret)
- *Duke of York* (BB, 1941, 35,900 tons, 28 k, 10x14-in, 16x5.25-in) (Capt. G. Creasy)
- *Renown* (BC, 1916, 32,000 tons, 29 k, 6x15-in, 20x4.5-in) (Capt. C. Daniel)
- *Victorious* (CV, 1941, 23,200, 30.5 k, 16x4.5-in, 46 a/c) (Capt. H. Bovel)
    809 Sqd: 6xFulmar IIP; 882 Sqd: 18xMarlet IV; 884 Sqd: 6xSeafire IIB;
        817 Sqd: 8xAlbacore; 832 Sqd: 8xAlbacore
- *Formidable* (1940, as above) (Capt. C. Talbot)
    885 Sqd: 6xSeafire IIB; 888 Sqd: 12xMarlet IV; 893 Sqd: 12xMarlet IV;
        820 Sqd: 12xAlbacore
- *Bermuda* (CL, 1942, 8,525 tons, 31 k, 12x6-in, 8x4-in, 6x21-in TT) (Capt. T. Back)
- *Argonaut* (CL, 1942, 5,600 tons, 30k, 10x5.25-in, 6x21-in TT) (Capt. E. Longley-Cook)
- *Sirius* (as above) (Capt. P. Brooking)
- *Eskimo* (DD, 1938, 1,960 tons, 32 k, 6x4.7-in, 2x4-in, 4x21-in TT) (Lt. Cdr. W. Whitworth)

- *Ashanti* (as above) (Cdr. R. Onslow)
- *Tartar* (1939, as above) (Cdr. St. J. Tyrwhitt)
- *Meteor* (DD, 1941, 1,920 tons, 32.5 k, 6x4.7-in, 1x4-in, 4x21-in TT) (Lt. Cdr. D. Jewitt)
- *Milne* (as above) (Capt. I. Campbell)
- *Martin* (1942, as above) (Cdr. C. Thomson)
- *Lookout* (as above) (Lt. Cdr. A. Forman)
- *Quentin* (as above) (Lt. Cdr. A. Noble)
- *Quality* (DD, 1942, 1,692 tons, 32 k, 4x4.7-in, 8x21-in TT) (Lt. Cdr. G. Farnfield)
- *Quiberon* (as above) (Cdr. H. Broning)
- *Pathfinder* (as above) (Cdr. E. Gibbs)
- *Opportune* (as above) (Cdr. J. L. Barber)
- *Penn* (as above) (Lt. Cdr. J. Swain)
- *Panther* (as above) (Lt. Cdr. V Jocelyn)
- *Ithuriel* (DD, 1942, 1,360 tons, 31.5 k, 4x4.7-in, 4x21-in TT) (Lt. C. H. M. M. Crichton)
- *Isaac Sweers* (DD, 1940, 2,228 tons, 37 k, 6x4-in, 8x21-in TT) (Cdr. W. Harmsen)

Rodney, Boreas, Bulldog, and *Beagle* were part of Force H but detached to the Center Naval Task Force.

Eastern Naval Task Force (Vice Adm. Harold H. Burrough)
(Maj. Gen. Charles W. Ryder, USA)

Naval Support Force
- *Sheffield* (CL, 1937, 9,400 tons, 30.5 k, 12x6-in, 8x4-in, 6x21-in TT) (Capt. A. Clarke)
- *Scylla* (CL, 1942, 5,580 tons, 30 k, 10x5.25-in, 6x21-in TT) (Capt. J. MacIntyre)
- *Charybdis* (1941, as above) (Capt. G. Voelcker)
- *Argus* (CVL, 1918, 14,555 tons, 20.5 k, 2x4-in, 18 a/c) (Capt. G. Philip)
  880 Sqd: 18xSeafire IIB
- *Avenger* (CVE, 1942, 12,150 tons, 17 k, 1x5- 2x3-in, 14 a/c) (Cdr. A. Colthurst)
  802 Sqd: 6xSea Hurricane II; 883 Sqd: 8xSea Hurricane II
- *Vanoc* (DD, 1917, 1,090 tons, 32 k, 2x4-in, 3x21-in TT) (Cdr. C. Churchill)
- *Wrestler* (DD, 1918, 1,100 tons, 32 k, 2x4-in, 3x21-in TT) (Lt. R. Lacon)
- *Clare* (DD, 1920, 1,190 tons, 35 k, 3x4- 1x3-in, 6x21-in TT) (Lt. Cdr. L. Landman)
- *Stork* (DS, 1936, 1,190 tons, 18 k, 4x4.7-in) (Lt. G. Brewery)

- *Enchantress* (1935, as above) (Lt. Cdr. A. Christie)
- *Ibis* (DS, 1941, 1,300 tons, 18.5 k, 6x4-in) (Cdr. H. Darell)
- *Spey* (DC, 1942, 1,370 tons, 18 k, 2x4-in) (Cdr. H. Boys-Smith)
- *Marigold* (DC, 1940, 940 tons, 16 k, 1x4-in) (Lt. J. Halcrew)
- *Convolvulus* (1941, as above) (Lt. Churston)
- *Samphire* (as above) (Lt. Cdr. F. Renny)
- *Pentstemon* (as above) (Lt. Cdr. J. Byron)

A (Apples) Sector Landing Support Force
- *Pozarica* (AAS, 1940, 4,540 tons, 16 k, 6x4-in) (Capt. L. Hill)
- *Rysa* (AMT, 1941, 545 tons, 12 k, 1x12-pdr) (Lt. J. Cooper)
- *Juliet* (as above) (Lt. L. Moffatt)
- *Stroma* (as above) (Lt. J. Harper)
- *Rother* (DC, 1942, 1,370 tons, 18 k, 2x4-in) (Cdr. R. Cas)
- *Bicester* (DE, 1942, 1,050 tons, 25 k, 6x4-in) (Lt. Cdr. S. Bennetts)
- *Bramham* (as above) (Lt. E. Baines)
- *ML 283, 336, 338* (ML, 1941, 70 tons, 11.5 k, 1x3-pdr)
- *Cadmus* (MS, 1942, 850 tons, 16.5 k, 1x4-in) (Lt. Cdr. J. Temple)
- *P 221* (SS, 1941, 842 tons, 14.75/9 k, 7x21-in TT) (Lt. M. Ainslie)

A (Apples) Sector Landing Force
- *Karanja* (LSI [L], 9,890 GRT, 17 k, 1x6-in) (9xLCA, 1xLCS, 2xLCM)
- *Viceroy of India* (LSI [L], 19,627 GRT, 19 k) (13xLCP)
- *Marnix Van Sint Aldegonde* (Du) (LSI [L]), (19,355 GRT, 17 k) (12xLCP)
- *Dewdale* (LSG, 14,500 GRT, 11.5 k, 1x4.7-in) (14xLCM)
- *Manchester Port* (Tran, 7,071 GRT, 13.5 k) (2xLCM)
- *Lalande* (Tran, 7,453 GRT, 12.5 k) (11th Bdg; 2xLCM)
- *Ocean Wanderer* (Tran, 7,178 GRT, 11 k) (2xLCM)
- *Ocean Viceroy* (Tran, 7,174 GRT, 11 k)

78th British Division (Maj. Gen. V. Evelegh)
- 11th Infantry Brigade Group (Brig. E. Cass)
  2/Lancashire Fusiliers (Lt. Col. L. A. Manly)
  5/Northamptonshire Regiment
  1/East Surrey Regiment
- 36th Infantry Brigade Group (Brig. A. L. Kent-Lemon)
  5/The Buffs
  6/Royal West Kent Regiment
  8/Argyll and Sutherland Highlanders
- 17th, 132nd, 138th Field Regiments, Royal Artillery

- 84th Light Antiaircraft Battery, Royal Artillery
- 214, 237, 256 Field Companies, Royal Engineers
- 56th Reconnaissance Regiment
- 64th Anti-Tank Regiment

B (Beer) Sector Naval Support Force
- *Roberts* (BM, 1941, 7,973 tons, 23 k, 2x15-in, 8x4-in) (Capt. J. Loveband)
- *Blyskawica* (PO) (DD, 1936, 2,144 tons, 39 k, 8x4-in) (Lt. Cdr. L. Lichodzie-jewski)
- *Lamerton* (DE, 1941, 1,050 tons, 25 k, 6x4-in) (Lt. Cdr. C. Purse)
- *Wheatland* (as above) (Lt. Cdr. R. Brooke)
- *Wilton* (as above) (Lt. A. Northey)
- *Palomares* (AAS, 1940, 4,540 tons, 16 k, 6x4-in) (Capt. J. Jauncely)
- *Acute* (MS, 1942, 850 tons, 16.5 k, 1x4-in) (Cdr. D. Lempen)
- *Alarm* (as above) (Lt. Cdr. R. Patterson)
- *Albacore* (as above) (Lt. Cdr. J. Williams)
- *Hoy* (AMT, 1941, 545 tons, 12 k, 1x12-pdr) (Lt. G. McNair)
- *Incholm*(as above) (Lt. A. Whitcombe)
- *Mull* (as above) (Lt. J. Plomer)
- *ML 444, 238, 307* (ML 1941, 70 tons, 11.5 k, 1x3-pdr)
- *P 48* (SS, 1941, 630 tons, 11/10 k, 4x21-in) (Lt. M. Faber)

B (Beer) Sector Naval Landing Force (Capt. R. J. Shaw, RN)
- *Bulolo* (HQ ship, 9,111, 15 k, 2x6-in) (Capt. R. J. Shaw)
- *Keren* (LSI [L], 9,890 GRT, 17 k, 1x6-in) (9xLCA, 2xLCP, 1xLCS, 2xLCM)
- *Winchester Castle* (LSI, 20,012 GRT, 20 k) (9xLCA, 2xLCP, 1xLCS, 2xLCM)
- *Otranto* (LSI, 20,026 GRT, 18 k) (10xLCA)
- *Awatea* (LSI, 13,482 GRT, 23 k) (10xLCP, 1xLCM)
- *Strathnaver* (Tran, 22,283 GRT, 20 k) (14xLCP)
- *Sobieski* (Po) (Tran, 11,030 GRT, 17 k) (10xLCP, 1xLCM)
- *Cathay* (Tran, 15,225 GRT, 16.5 k)
- *Ennerdale* (LSG, 14,500 GRT, 11.5 k, 1x4.7-in) (14xLCM)
- *Sobo* (Tran, 5,124 GRT, 12.5 k) (2xLCM)
- *Jean Jadot* (Be) (Tran, 5,895 GRT, 13 k) (2xLCM)
- *Tiba* (Du) (Tran, 5,293 GRT, 13 k) (3xLCM)
- *Loch Mona* (Tran, 9,412 GRT, 12.5 k) (3xLCM)
- *Urlana* (Tran, 6,852 GRT, 12 k) (2xLCM)
- *Glenfinlas* (Tran, 7,479 GRT, 13.5 k) (2xLCM)
- *Stanhill* (Tran, 5,969 GRT) (4xLCM)
- *City of Worcester* (Tran, 5,469 GRT, 10.5 k)

- *Ocean Volga* (Tran, 7,174 GRT, 11 k)
- *Ocean Rider* (as above)

B (Beer) Sector Landing Force
- 168th Regimental Landing Team/34th Infantry Division (Col. J. W. O'Daniel)
  - 1/168 (Lt. Col. E. J. Doyle)
  - 2/168 (Lt. Col. D. H. Baer)
  - 3/168 (Lt. Col. S. T. Vincent)
- 1 Commando (-) (Lt. Col. T. H. Trevor)
- 6 Commando (Lt. Col. I. F. McAlpine)

C (Charlie) Sector Naval Support Force
- *Cowdray* (DE, 1941, 1,050 tons, 25 k, 6x4-in) (Lt. Cdr. C. North)
- *Zetland* (as above) (Lt. A. Wickham)
- *Tynwald* (AAS, 1941, 3,650 tons, 21 k, 6x4-in) (Capt. P. Walehouse)
- *Algerine* (MS, 1941, 850 tons, 17 k, 1x4-in) (Lt. Cdr. W. Cooke)
- *Hussar* (as above) (Lt. R. Biggs)
- *Speedwell* (as above) (Lt. Cdr. T. William)
- *Cava* (AMT, 1941, 545 tons, 12 k, 1x12-pdr) (Lt. R. Petty-Mayor)
- *Othello* (as above) (Lt. S. Dickson)
- *ML 273, 295* (ML, 1941, 70 tons, 11.5 k, 1x3-pdr)
- *P 45* (SS, 1941, 630 tons, 11/10 k, 4x21-in) (Lt. H. Turner)

C (Charlie) Sector Naval Landing Force (Capt. C. D. Edgar, USN)
- *Samuel Chase* (US) (APA-26, 11,760 tons, 18 k, 1x5- 4x3-in) (24xLCP, 2xLCM)
- *Thomas Stone* (US) (APA-29, 11,760 tons, 17 k, 1x5- 4x3-in) (24xLCP, 2xLCM) (torpedoed on 7 November and did not participate in landings)
- *Leedstown* (US) (AP-73, 9,135 tons, 18 k, 1x5- 4x3-in) (26xLCP 2xLCM)
- *Almaack* (US) (AK-27, 8,600 tons, 18.5 k, 1x5- 4x3-in) (10xLCP, 4xLCM)
- *Exceller* (US) (Tran, 6,597 GRT) (2xLCM)
- *Dempo* (Du) (Tran, 17,024 GRT, 18 k)
- *Macharda* (Tran, 7,998 GRT, 14.5 k) (5xLCM)
- *Maron* (Tran, 6,487 GRT, 14 k) (5xLCM)

C (Charlie) Sector Landing Force
- 39th RCT/9th Infantry Division (Col. B. F. Caffey Jr.)
  - 1/39 (Lt. Col. A. H. Rosenfeld)
  - 2/39 (Maj. W. M. Oakes) (did not participate in landings)
  - 3/39 (Maj. F. O. Griggs)
- 1 Commando (elms) (Maj. K. R. S. Trevor)

Algiers Harbor Assault Force (Capt. H. L. St. J. Fancourt, RN)

- *Broke* (DD, 1925, 1,480 tons, 32.5 k, 2x4.7-in, 6x21-in TT) (Lt. Cdr. A. Layard)
- *Malcolm* (DD, 1919, 1,530 tons, 32 k, 5x4.7-in, 6x21-in TT)(Cdr. A. Russell)
- 3rd Battalion/135th Regiment/9th Division (Lt. Col. E. T. Swenson)

Central Task Force (Commodore Thomas Troubridge)
(Maj. Gen. Lloyd R. Fredendall)
Naval Support Force

- *Rodney* (BB, 1927, 33, 900 tons, 23 k, 9x16-in, 12x6-in) (Capt. J. Rivett-Carnac)
- *Furious* (CV, 1917, 22,450 tons, 29.5 k, 12x4-in, 32 a/c) (Capt. T. Bulteel)
    Sqd 801: 12xSeafire IC; Sqd 807: 12xSeafire IIB; Sqd 822: 8xAlbacore
- *Biter* (CVE, 1942, 10,366 tons, 16.5 k, 3x4-in, 15 a/c) (Capt. E. Abel-Smith)
    Sqd 800: 15 Sea Hurricane II
- *Dasher* (as above, 12 a/c) (Cdr. C. Lentaignes)
    Sqd 804: 6xSea Hurricane II; Sqd 891: 6xSea Hurricane II
- *Jamaica* (CL, 1942, 8,525 tons, 31 k, 12x6- 8x4-in, 6x21-in TT) (Capt. J. Storey)
- *Boreas* (DD, 1931, 1,360 tons, 32 k, 3x4.7-in, 4x21-in TT) (Lt. Cdr. E. Jones)
- *Bulldog* (as above) (Cdr. M. Richmond)
- *Beagle* (as above) (Cdr. R. Medley)
- *Boadicea* (as above) (Lt. Cdr. F. Brodrick)
- *Amazon* (DD, 1927, 1,352 tons, 32 k, 3x4.7-in, 3x21-in TT) (Lt. Cdr. Teynham)
- *Achates* (DD, 1930, 1,350 tons, 32 k, 2x4.7-in, 3x21-in TT) (Lt. Cdr. A. Johns)
- *Antelope* (DD, 1930, 1,350 tons, 32 k, 3x4.7-in, 3x21-in TT) (Lt. Cdr. E. Sinclair)
- *Wescott* (DD, 1918, 1,100 tons, 32 k, 4x4-in) (Cdr. I. Bockett-Pugh)
- *Farndale* (DE, 1941, 1,050 tons, 25.5 k, 6x4-in) (Cdr. D. Trentham)
- *Calpe* (as above) (Lt. Cdr. H. Kirkwood)
- *Avon Vale* (as above) (Lt. Cdr. P. Withers)
- *Puckeridge* (as above) (Lt. J. Cartwright)
- *Alynbank* (AAS, 1940, 8,635 tons, 12 k, 8x4-in) (Capt. H. Nash)
- *Brixham* (MS, 1942, 673 tons, 16 k, 1x12-pdr) (Lt. G. Simmers)
- *Bude* (1941, as above) (Lt. F. Andrew)
- *Felixstowe* (as above) (Lt. L. Moffatt)
- *Rhyl* (1940, as above) (Cdr. L. Ede)
- *Stornaway* (as above) (Lt. C. Fraser)
- *Clacton* (MS, 1941, 656 tons, 16 k, 1x12-pdr) (Lt. Cdr. L. Shaw)

- *Rothesay* (as above) (Cdr. A. Martin)
- *Polruan* (1942, as above) (Lt. Cdr. J. Landers)
- *Fluellen* (AMT, 1941, 545 tons, 12 k, 1x12-pdr) (Lt. B. Hampson)
- *Shiant* (as above) (Lt. A. Elton)
- *Ronaldsay* (as above) (Lt. A. Stirling)
- *ML 280* (ML, 1941, 85 tons, 20 k, 1x3-pdr)
- *HDML 1127* (ML, 1941, 70 tons, 11.5 k, 1x3-pdr)
- *P 54* (SS, 1942, 540 tons, 11.25 k, 4x21-in TT) (Lt. C. Oxborrow)
- *Ursula* (as above) (Lt. R. Lakin)

Z Sector Naval Support Group
- *Delhi* (CL, 1919, 4,850 tons, 27 k, 5x5-in) (Capt. A. Peachey)
- *Vansittart* (DD, 1919, 1,090 tons, 32 k, 2x4-in, 3x21-in TT) (Lt. Cdr. T. Johnston)
- *Aberdeen* (DS, 1936, 990 tons, 16 k, 4x4-in) (Lt. Cdr. H. Day)
- *Exe* (DC, 1942, 1,370 tons, 20 k, 2x4-in) (Cdr. N. Biddulph)
- *Swale* (as above) (Lt. Cdr. J. Jackson)
- *Deptford* (DS, 1935, 990 tons, 16 k, 2x4.7-in) (Lt. Cdr. R. Jenkins)
- *Rhododendron* (DC, 1940, 976 tons, 16 k, 1x4-in) (Lt. Cdr. L. Sayers)
- *Violet* (1941, as above) (Lt. G. Stewart)

Z Sector Naval Landing Force
- *Ulster Monarch* (LSI [H],3,791 GRT, 18 k) (5xLCA)
- *Royal Ulsterman* (LSI [H], 3,244 GRT, 16 k) (5xLCA)
- *Royal Scotsman* (LSI [H], 3,288 GRT, 16 k) (5xLCA)
- *Reina del Pacifico* (LSI [L], 17,702 GRT, 18 k) (12xLCA, 1xLCS)
- *Ettrick* (LSI [L], 11,279 GRT, 15 k) (18 RCT; 10xLCA)
- *Tegelberg* (Du) (Tran, 14,150 GRT, 17 k) (10xLCA)
- *Duchess of Bedford* (LSI [L], 20,123 GRT, 17.5 k) (11xLCA)
- *Warwick Castle* (LSI [L], 20,107 GRT, 20 k) (12xLCA, 1xLCM)
- *Durban Castle* (LSI [L], 17,382 GRT, 18.5 k) (18xLCA)
- *Derwentdale* (LSG, 14,500 GRT, 11.5 k) (14xLCM)
- *Misoa* (LST, 6,455 GRT, 10 k)
- *Tasajera* (LST, 5,679 GRT, 8.25 k)

Z Sector Slow Convoy
- *Recorder* (Aux [C/S])
- *Alcinous* (Du) (Tran, 6,189 GRT, 13.5 k)
- *Charles H. Cramp* (US) (Tran, 6,220 GRT, 12 k)
- *Chattanooga City* (Tran, 5,687 GRT, 11 k)

- *Delilian* (Tran, 6,423 GRT, 12 k)
- *Derbyshire* (Tran, 11,660 GRT, 16 k)
- *Edward Rutledge* (US) (Tran, 7,177 GRT, 11 k)
- *Empire Confidence* (Tran, 5,023 GRT, 14.5 k)
- *Empire Mordred* (Tran, 7,024 GRT, 11 k)
- *Havildar* (Tran, 5,401 GRT, 11.5 k)
- *Letitia* (Tran, 13,595 GRT, 15. 5 k)
- *Lycaon* (Tran, 7,350 GRT, 13.5 k)
- *Mootian* (Tran, 20,952 GRT, 17 k)
- *Nieuw Zeeland* (Du) (Tran, 11,069 GRT, 15 k)
- *Pacific Exporter* (Tran, 6,734 GRT, 13 k)
- *St. Essylt* (Tran, 5,634 GRT, 12 k)
- *Theseus* (Tran, 6,527 GRT, 13 k)
- *William Floyd* (US) (Tran, 7,176 GRT,11 k)
- *William Wirt* (US) (Tran, 7,193 GRT, 11 k)
- *Zebulon B. Vance* (US) (Tran, 7,177 GRT, 11 k)

Z Sector Landing Force (1st Infantry Division) (-) (Maj. Gen. T. Allen)
- 18th RCT (Col. F. U. Greer)
- 16th RCT (Col. H. B. Cheadle)
- CCB/1st Armored Division (-) (Brig. Gen. L. E. Oliver)
    1st Battalion/1st Armored Regiment (Lt. Col. J. K. Waters)
    2nd Battalion/13th Armored Regiment
    2nd Battalion/6th Armored Infantry Regiment
    27th Armored Field Artillery Regiment
- 1st Ranger Battalion (Lt. Col. W. Darby)

X Sector Naval Support Force
- *Aurora* (CL, 1937, 5,270 tons, 31 k, 6x6-in, 8x4-in, 2x21-in TT) (Capt. W. Agnew)
- *Wivern* (DD, 1919, 1,190 tons, 24 k, 3x4.7-in, 6x21-in TT) (Cdr. M. Mayrick)
- *Gardenia* (DC, 1940, 976 tons, 16 k, 1x4-in) (Lt. C. Jackson)
- *Vetch* (1941, as above) (Lt. Cdr. H. Beverley)
- *Horatio* (AMT, 1940, 545 tons, 12 k, 1x12pdr) (Lt. C. Lemkey)
- *HDML 1139* (ML, 1941, 70 tons, 11.5 k,1x3pdr)

X Sector Naval Landing Force (Capt. G. R. G. Allen, RN)
- *Batory* (PO) (LSI [L], 14,287 GRT, 18 k) (14xLCP, 1xLCM)
- *Queen Emma* (LSI [M], 4,136 GRT, 23 k) (5xLCA, 1xLCS, 2xLCM)

- *Princess Beatrix* (as above) (5xLCA, 1xLCS, 2xLCM)
- *Benalbenach* (Tran, 7,153 GRT, 13.5 k) (4xLCM)
- *Mary Slessor* (Tran, 5,027 GRT, 12.5 k)
- *Mark Twain* (US) (Tran, 14,245 GRT, 11 k) (2xLCM)
- *Walt Whitman* (US) (as above) (2xLCM)
- *Bachaquero* (LST, 6455 GRT, 10 k)

X Sector Landing Force
- Combat Command B/1st Armored Division (elms) (Col. P. M. Robinett)
    1st Battalion/6th Armored Infantry Regiment
    1st Battalion/13th Armored Regiment

Y Sector Naval Support Force
- *Brilliant* (DD, 1931, 1,360 tons, 32 k, 3x4.7-in, 4x21-in TT) (Lt. Cdr. A. Poe)
- *Verity* (DD, 1919, 1,190 tons, 24 k, 2x4-in) (Lt. C. Adams)
- *Eday* (AMT, 1941, 545 tons, 12 k, 1x12-pdr) (Lt. W. Surtees)
- *Inchmarinock* (as above) (Lt. Cdr. S. Darling)
- *Kerrera* (as above) (Lt. R. Slater)
- *Coriolanus* (1940, as above) (Lt. N. Hunt)
- *ML 458, 463, 469, 471* (ML, 1941, 85 tons, 20 k, 1x3-pdr)

Y Sector Naval Landing Force (Capt. E. V. Lees)
- *Glengyle* (LSI [L] 9,919 GRT, 18 k) (11xLCA, 1xLCS, 3xLCM)
- *Monarch of Bermuda* (LSI [L] 22,424 GRT, 20 k) (12xLCA)
- *Llangibby Castle* (LSI [L] 11,951 GRT, 16.5 k) (10xLCP, 1xLCM)
- *Clan Mactaggart* (Tran, 7,622 GRT, 12 k) (5xLCM)
- *Salacia* (Tran 5,445 GRT, 14 k) (2xLCM)

Y Sector Landing Force (Brig. Gen. T. Roosevelt Jr.)
- 26th RCT (Col. A. N. Stark Jr.)
- 33rd Field Artillery Battalion
- 531 Engineer Shore Regiment

Oran Harbor Attack Force
- *Walney* (DS, 1930, 1,546 tons, 13 k, 1x5-in, 1x3-in) (Lt. Cdr. P. Meyrick)
- *Hartland* (as above) (Lt. Cdr. G. P. Billot)
- 3/6th Armored Infantry, Coys G & H (Lt. Col. G. F. Marshall)

Paratroop Task Force (Col. W. C. Bentley Jr.)
- 2nd Battalion/503rd Paratroop Regiment

MOROCCO INVASION FORCE MAJ. GEN. GEORGE F. PATTON
TASK FORCE 34 (REAR ADM. H. KENT HEWITT)

Task Group 34.1 Covering Force (Rear Adm. Robert C. Giffen)

- *Massachusetts* (BB-59, 1942, 38,000 tons, 27.5 k, 9x16-in, 20x5-in) (Capt. F. Whiting)
- *Wichita* (CA-45, 1939, 10,589 tons, 33 k, 9x8-in, 8x5-in) (Capt. F. Low)
- *Tuscaloosa* (CA-37, 1934, 10,136 tons, 32.7 k, 9x8-in, 8x5-in) (Capt. N. Gillette)
- *Chemung* (AO-30, 1941, 7,470 tons, 15 k, 2x5-in) (Capt. J. Twomey)

Destroyer Squadron 8 (Capt. D. Moon)

- *Wainwright* (DD-419, 1940, 1,764 tons, 35 k, 4x5-in, 5x21-in TT) (Lt. Cdr. R. Gibbs)
- *Mayrant* (DD-402, 1939, 1,637 tons, 38.5 k, 4x5-in, 5x21-in TT) (Lt. Cdr. E. Walker)
- *Rhind* (DD-404, 1940, as above) (Cdr. H. Read)
- *Jenkins* (DD-447, 1942, 2,325 tons, 38 k, 5x5-in, 10x21-in TT) (Lt. Cdr. H. Miller)

Task Group 34.2 Air Group (Rear Adm. Ernest D. McWhorter)

- *Ranger* (CV-4, 1934, 14,810 tons, 29 k, 72a/c, 8x5-in) (Capt. C. T. Durgin)
  VF 9: 27xF4F; VF 41: 27xF4F; VS 41: 18xSBD
- *Suwanee* (ACV-27, 1942, 10,494 tons, 18 k, 38a/c, 2x5-in) (Capt. J. Clark)
  VGF 27: 11xF4F; VGF 28: 12xF4F; VGS 30: 6xF4F; VGS 27: 9xTBF
- *Cleveland* (CL-55, 1942, 11,744 tons, 32.5 k, 12x6-in, 12x5-in) (Capt. E. Burrough)
- *Winooski* (AO-38, 1942, 21,850 tons, 16.7 k, 1x4-in, 2x3-in) (Cdr. J. Murphy)

Destroyer Squadron 10 (Capt. J. Holloway)

- *Ellyson* (DD-454, 1941, 1,839 tons, 35 k, 4x5-in, 5x21-in TT) (Cdr. J. Rooney)
- *Corry* (DD-463, as above) (Lt. Cdr. E. Burchett)
- *Forrest* (DD-461, 1942, as above) (Capt. T. Wattles)
- *Fitch* (DD-462, as above) (Lt. Cdr. H. Crommelin)
- *Hobson* (DD-464, as above) (Lt. Cdr. R. McFarlane)

Submarines

- *Gunnel* (SS-253, 1942, 1,526 tons, 20 k, 10x21-in TT, 1x3-in) (Lt. Cdr. J. McCain)
- *Herring* (SS-233, as above) (Lt. Cdr. R. Johnson)

Task Group 34.8. Northern Attack Group (Rear Adm. Monroe Kelly)
- *Texas* (BB-35, 1914, 27,000 tons, 23 k, 10x14-in, 16x5-in) (Capt. R. Pfaff)
- *Savannah* (CL-42, 1937, 9,767 tons, 32.5 k, 15x6-in, 8x5-in) (Capt. L. Fiske)

Destroyer Squadron 11 (Cdr. D. L. Madeira)
- *Roe* (DD-418, 1940, 1,764 tons, 35 k, 4x5-in, 5x21-in TT) (Lt. C. R. Nolan)
- *Livermore* (DD-429, 1940, 1,839, 35 k, 4x5-in, 5x21-in TT) (Cdr. V. Huber)
- *Kearny* (DD-432, as above) (Cdr. A. Oswald)
- *Ericsson* (DD-440, 1941, as above) (Lt. C. C. Jensen)
- *Parker* (DD-604, 1942, as above) (Lt. C. J. Bays)

Air Group
- *Sangamon* (CVE-26, 1942, 10,494 tons, 18 k, 30xa/c, 2x5-in) (Capt. E. MacGregor)
     VGS 26: 9xTBF, 9xSBD; VGF 26: 12xF4F
- *Chenango* (CVE-28, 1942, 10,494 tons, 18 k, 76xP-40, 2x5-in) (Capt. B. Wyatt)

Destroyer Division 19 (Capt. C. Wellborn)
- *Hambleton* (DD-455, 1941, 1,839 tons, 35 k, 4x5-in, 5x21-in TT) (Cdr. F. Close)
- *Macomb* (DD-458, as above) (Cdr. W. Duvall)

Special Units
- *Dallas* (DD-199, 1920, 1,190 tons, 32.5 k, 6x3-in) (Lt. Cdr. R. Brodie)
- *Eberle* (DD-430, 1940, 1,839 tons, 35 k, 4x5-in, 5x21-in TT) (Lt. Cdr. K. Poehlmann)
- *Raven* (AM-55, 1940, 810 tons, 18 k, 2x3-in) (Lt. Cdr. C. Rucker)
- *Osprey* (AM-56, as above) (Lt. Cdr. C. Blackwell)
- *Barnegat* (AVP-10, 1941, 2,040 tons, 20 k,2x5-in) (Cdr. J. Briggs)
- *Kennebec* (AO-36, 1942, 6,013 tons, 16.7 k, 1x5-in, 4x3-in) (Cdr. S. Reynolds)
- *Shad* (SS-235, 20 k, 1,526 tons, 1942,10x21-in TT, 1x3-in) (Lt. Cdr. E. MacGregor)

Transport Division 5 (Capt. A. Gray)
- *Henry T. Allen* (AP-30, 21,300 tons, 16.7 k, 4x3-in) (35 LC) (LCV, LCPL, LCPR)
- *George Clymer* (AP-57, 11,760 tons, 18.4 k, 1x5-in, 4x3-in) (13xLCV, 2xLCM, 10xLCPL)
- *Susan B. Anthony* (AP-72, 8,193 tons, 18 k, 1x5-in, 4x3-in) (27 LCPL and LCV, 2 LCM)

- *John Penn* (AP-51, 14,250 tons, 16 k, 1x5-in, 4x3-in) (approx. 20xLC)
- *Florence Nightingale* (AP-70, 7,980 tons, 18 k, 1x5-in, 4x3-in) (approx. 20xLC)
- *Anne Arundel* (AP-76, 14,400 tons, 18.4 k, 4x3-in) (12xLCV, 7xLCPR, 1xLCPL, 2xLCM)
- *Electra* (AK-21, 13,910 tons, 16.5 k, 1x5-in, 4x3-in) (approx. 20xLC)
- *Algorab* (AK-25, as above) (9xLCV, 2xLCPR, 7xLCM)

Landing Force (Maj. Gen. L. Truscott)
- 60th RCT/9th Infantry Division (Col. F. J. de Rohan)
     1/60 (Maj. P. McCarley)
     2/60 (Maj. J. H. Dilley)
     3/60 (Lt. Col. J. J. Toffey)
- 1/66 Armored Battalion (Col. H. H. Semmes)
- 1/540 Engineer Battalion,
- XII Air Support Command

Task Group 34.9 Central Attack Force (Capt. R. M. Emmet)
- *Augusta* (CA-31, 1931, 9,006 tons, 32.5 k, 9x8-in, 8x5-in) (Capt. G. Hutchins)
- *Brooklyn* (CL-40, 1937, 9,767 tons, 32.5 k, 15x6-in, 8x5-in) (Capt. F. Denebrink)

Destroyer Squadron 25 (Cdr. E. Durgin)
- *Wilkes* (DD-441, 1940, 1,839 tons, 35 k, 4x5-in, 5x21-in TT) (Lt. Cdr. J. McLean)
- *Swanson* (DD-443, 1941, as above) (Cdr. L. Markham)
- *Ludlow* (DD-428, as above) (Lt. Cdr. L. Creighton)
- *Murphy* (DD603, 1942, as above) (Lt. Cdr. L. W. Bailey)

Destroyer Squadron 13 (Capt. J. B. Hefferman)
- *Bristol* (DD-453, 1941, 1,839 tons, 35 k, 4x5-in, 5x21-in TT) (Cdr. J. Glick)
- *Woolsey* (DD-437, as above) (Cdr. B. Austin)
- *Edison* (DD-439, as above) (Lt. Cdr. W. Headden)
- *Tillman* (DD-641, 1942, as above) (Cdr. F. McCorkle)
- *Boyle* (DD-600, as above) (Lt. Cdr. E. Karpe)
- *Rowan* (DD-405, 1940, 1,637 tons, 38.5 k, 4x5-in, 8x21-in TT) (Lt. Cdr. R. Ford)

Mine Squadron 7
- *Palmer* (DMS-5, 1919, 1,090 tons, 32.5 k, 3x3-in) (Lt. Cdr. J. Cooper)
- *Hogan* (DMS-6, as above) (Lt. Cdr. U. Sharp)

- *Stansbury* (DMS-8, as above) (Lt. Cdr. J. Maher)
- *Miantonomah* (CM-10, 1938, 2,870 tons, 14 k, 2x4-in) (Lt. Cdr. R. Edwards)
- *Auk* (AM-57, 1942, 890 tons, 18 k, 1x3-in) (Lt. Cdr. W. Ryan)
- *Terror* (CM-5, 1942, 5,875 tons, 20 k, 4x5-in) (Cdr. H. Fitch)

Naval Landing Force (Capt. R. M. Emmet)
- *Leonard Wood* (AP-25, 21,900 tons, 17.5 k, 4x3-in) (4xLCPL, 8xLCPR, 13xLCV, 2xLCS, 2xLCM)
- *Thomas Jefferson* (AP-60, 11,760 tons, 18.4 k, 4x3-in) (13xLCPL, 1xLCPR, 15xLCV, 2xLCS, 2xLCM)

Transport Division 3 (Capt. R. G. Coman)
- *Charles Carroll* (AP-58, 8,409 tons, 16 k, 4x3-in) (2xLCPL, 10xLCPR, 14xLCV, 2xLCS, 2xLCM)
- *Edward Rutledge* (AP-52, 14,330 tons, 16 k, 1x5-in, 4x3-in) (1xLCPL, 4xLCPR, 8xLCV, 1xLCS, 2xLCM)
- *Hugh L. Scott* (AP-43, 12,579 tons, 16 k, 4x3-in) (16xLCPR, 13xLCV, 1xLCS, 2xLCM)
- *Joseph Hewes* (AP-50, 14,100 tons, 15 k, 1x5-in, 4x3-in) (1xLCPL, 6xLCPR, 7xLCV, 1xLCS, 2xLCM)
- *Joseph T. Dickman* (AP-26, 21,900 tons, 17.5 k, 4x3-in) (1xLCPL, 14xLCPR, 16xLCV, 2xLCS, 2xLCM)
- *Tasker M. Bliss* (AP-42, 12,568 tons, 16.5 k, 4x3-in) (1xLCPL, 15xLCPR, 16xLCV, 1xLCS, 2xLCM)
- *William P. Biddle* (AP-15, 14,450 tons, 16.5 k, 1x5-in, 4x3-in) (3xLCPL, 8x LCPR, 11xLCV, 1xLCS, 2x LCM)

Transdiv 9 (Capt. W. Quigley)
- *Ancon* (AP-66, 14,150 tons, 18 k, 2x5-in) (1xLCPL, 8xLCPR, 5xLCV)
- *Arcturus* (AK-18, 14,225 tons, 16.5 k, 1x5-in, 4x3-in) (1xLCPL, 6xLCPR, 6xLCV, 7xLCM)
- *Elizabeth C. Stanton* (AP-69, 7,980 tons, 18 k, 4x3-in) (1xLCPL, 9xLCPR, 10xLCV, 2xLCM3)
- *Oberon* (AK-56, 7,391 tons, 16.5 k, 1x5-in, 4x3-in) (2xLCPL, 14xLCV, 8xLCM3)
- *Procyon* (AK-19, 14,225 tons, 16.5 k, 1x5-in) (6xLCPL, 7xLCV, 7xLCM3)
- *Thurston* (AP-77, 13,910 tons, 16.5 k, 4x3-in) (8xLCPR, 10xLCV, 2xLCM3)

3rd Infantry Division (+), (Maj. Gen. J. Anderson)
- 7th RCT (Col. R. Macon)
    - 1/7 (Lt. Col. R. Moore)

2/7 (Lt. Col. R. Salzmann)

3/7 (Lt. Col. A. H. Manhart)

- 30th RCT (Col. A. H. Rogers)

  1/30 (Lt. Col. F. Sladen)

  2/30 (Lt. Col. L. W. Bernard)

  3/30 (Maj. C. E. Johnson)

- 15th RCT (Col. T. Monroe)

  1/15 (Maj. A. W. Gardner)

  2/15 (Maj. W. H. Billings)

  3/15 (Maj. E. H. Cloud)

- 1st Battalion/67th Armored Regiment (Maj. R. E. Nelson)
- XII Air Support Command
- 436rd Coastal Artillery Battalion
- 2nd Battalion/20th Engineer regiment

Task Group 34.10 Southern Attack Group (Rear Adm. Lyal A. Davidson)

- *New York* (BB-34, 1914, 27,000 tons, 23 k, 10x14-in,16x5-in) (Capt. S. Umsted)
- *Philadelphia* (CL-41, 1937, 9,767 tons, 32.5 k, 15x6-in, 8x5-in) (Capt. P. Hendren)

Destroyer Squadron 15 (Capt. C. C. Hartman)

- *Mervine* (DD-489, 1942, 1,839 tons, 35 k, 4x5-in, 5x21-in TT) (Lt. Cdr. S. Willingham)
- *Knight* (DD-633, as above) (Lt. Cdr. R. Levin)
- *Beatty* (DD-640, as above) (Lt. Cdr. F. Stelter)

Destroyer Division 30 (Cdr. H. C. Robinson)

- *Cowie* (DD-632, 1942, 1,839 tons, 35 k, 4x5-in, 5x21-in TT) (Lt. Cdr. C. Whiting)
- *Quick* (DD-490, as above) (Lt. Cdr. R. Nickerson)
- *Doran* (DD-634, as above) (Lt. Cdr. H. Gordon)
- *Cole* (DD-155, 1919, 1,090 tons, 30 k, 6x3-in) (Lt. Cdr. G. Palmer)
- *Bernadou* (DD-153, as above) (Lt. Cdr. R. Braddy)

Landing Force (Capt. W. B. Phillips)

- *Harris* (AP-8, 13,529 tons, 17 k, 4x3-in) (2xLCPL, 10xLCPR, 9xLCV, 1xLCS, 6xLCM)
- *Calvert* (AP-65, 8,889 tons, 16 k, 1x5-in, 4x3-in) (6xLCPL, 3xLCPR, 15xLCV, 1xLCS, 2xLCM)

- *Titania* (AK-55, 13,910 tons, 16.5 k, 1x5-in, 4x3-in) (4xLCPL, 4xLCPR, 8xLCV, 8xLCM)
- *Dorothea L. Dix* (AP-67, 11,625 tons, 16 k, 1x4-in, 4x3-in) (11xLCPR, 2xLCPL, 18xLCV, 6xLCM)
- *Lyon* (AP-71, 7,954 tons, 18.4 k, 4x3-in) (1xLCPL, 8xLCPR, 10xLCV, 2 LCM)
- *Lakehurst* (AP-49, 7,450 tons, 16 k, 1x5-in, 4x3-in)

Minecraft
- *Monadnock* (CM-9, 1938, 3,110 tons, 17.5 k, 2x3-in) (Cdr. F. Goldsmith)
- *Howard* (DMS-7, 1919, 1,090 tons, 32.5 k, 3x3-in) (Lt. Cdr. C. Zondorak)
- *Hamilton* (DMS-18, as above) (Lt. Cdr. R. Sampson)
- *Barb* (SS-220, 1942, 1,810 tons, 20/9 k, 1x3-in 10x21-in TT) (Lt. Cdr. J. Waterman)

Air Group
- *Santee* (ACV-29, 1942, 10,494 tons, 18 k, 2x5-in, 31a/c) (Capt. W. Sample)
   VGF 29: 14xF4F; VGS 29: 8xTBF, 9xSBD
- *Rodman* (DD-456 1942,1,839 tons, 35 k, 4x5-in, 5x21-in TT) (Cdr. W. Michelet)
- *Emmons* (DD-457, as above) (Lt. Cdr. H. Heming)

Auxiliaries
- *Housatonic* (AO-35, 1942, 21,825 tons, 17 k, 4x3-in) (Cdr. A. Boileau)
- *Merrimack* (AO-37, 1942, 21,850 tons, 16.7 k, 1x5-in, 4x3-in) (Capt. W. Hilbert)
- *Cherokee* (AT-66, 1940, 1,240 tons, 16 k, 1x3-in) (Lt. J. Lawson)

Landing Force (Maj. Gen. E. N. Harmon)
- 47th RCT/9th Infantry (Colonel E. H. Randle)
   1/47 (Maj. F. C. Feil)
   2/47 (Maj. L. Gershenow)
   3/47 (Lt. Col. J. B. Evans)
- CCB 2nd Armored Division (Brig. Gen. H. J. Gaffey)
   2/67th Armored Regiment
   3/67th Armored Regiment

Submarine Deployments
Off Toulon
- *P 222* (Lt. Cdr. A. J. Mackenzie), *P 51* (Lt. M. L. C. Crawford), *P 217* (Lt. E. J. D. Turner)

Off Messina
- *Una* (Lt. C. P. Norman), *Utmost* (Lt. J. Coombe), *P 35* (Lt. S. L. C. Maydon), *P 37* (Lt. E. T. Stanley), *P 43* (Lt. A. C. Halliday)

Strait of Sicily
- *P 44* (Lt. T. E. Barlow), *Unruffled* (Lt. J. S. Stevens), *P 211* (Cdr. B. Bryant), *P 212* (Lt. J. H. Bromage), *P 247* (Lt. M. G. R. Lumby)

Off Cagliari
- *Parthian* (Lt. M. D. St. John), *Turbulent* (Cdr. J. W. Linton)

APPENDIX IV
Ships Sunk in Operation Torch

ALLIED SHIPS

8 November
- *Broke* (BR/DD). Sunk by French shore batteries Algiers Harbor.
- *Hartland* (BR/DS). Sunk by French warships and shore batteries Oran Harbor.
- *Walney* (BR/DS). Sunk by French warships and shore batteries Oran Harbor.

9 November
- *Leedstown* (US/AP 9,135 tons). Torpedoed by German He 111 off Algiers 8 November. Torpedoed by *U 331* next day.
- *Gardenia* (BR/DC). Collided with HMS *Fluellen* off Oran.

10 November
- *Martin* (BR/DD). Torpedoed by *U 431* eighty miles northwest of Algiers.
- *Ibis* (BR/DS). Torpedoed by Italian S.79 ten miles north of Algiers.
- *Garlinge* (BR/Tran 2,012 GRT). Torpedoed by *U 81*.

11 November
- *Awatea* (BR/LSI 13,482 GRT). Hit by four bombs from German Ju 88s off Bougie. Torpedoed by Italian submarine *Argo* and sunk seven miles off Bougie.
- *Cathay* (BR/Tran 15,225 GRT). Hit by one bomb from German Ju 88 off Bougie.
- *Joseph Hewes* (US/AP 14,100 tons). Torpedoed by *U 173* off Fédala.
- *Nieuw Zeeland* (Du/Tran 11,069 GRT). Torpedoed by *U 380* east of Gibraltar.
- *Viceroy of India* (UK/LSI 19,627 GRT). Torpedoed by *U 407* north of Oran. Taken in tow and foundered.

12 November
- *Tynwald* (BR/AAS). Torpedoed by Italian submarine *Argo* off Bougie.
- *Karanja* (BR/LSI 9,890 GRT). Bombed by German Ju 88s off Bougie.
- *Edward Rutledge* (US/AP 14,330 tons). Torpedoed by *U 130* off Fédala.
- *Hugh L. Scott* (US/AP 12,579 tons). Torpedoed by *U 130* off Fédala.
- *Tasker H. Bliss* (US/AP 12,568 tons). Torpedoed by *U 130* off Fédala.
- *Browning* (BR/Tran 5,332 GRT). Torpedoed off Cap Ferrat west of Oran by *U 593*.
- *Hecla* (BR/Aux). Torpedoed in Atlantic by *U 515*.

13 November
- *Isaac Sweers* (Du/DD). Torpedoed by *U 431* fifty-five miles northwest of Oran.
- *Glenfinlas* (BR/Tran 7,479 GRT). Bombed by German Ju 88s in Bougie Harbor.
- *Maron* (BR/Tran 6,487 GRT). Torpedoed by *U 81* 220 miles east of Gibraltar.

14 November
- *Warwick Castle* (BR/LSI 20,107 GRT). Torpedoed by *U 413* returning to United Kingdom.
- *Narkunda* (BR/Tran 16,632). Torpedoed by Italian submarine *Platino,* then bombed by German Ju 88s off Bougie.
- *Electra* (US/AK 13,910 tons). Torpedoed by *U 173* en route to Casablanca.

15 November
- *Avenger* (BR/CVE). Torpedoed by *U 155* west of Gibraltar.
- *Algerine* (BR/MS). Torpedoed by Italian submarine *Ascianghi* off Bougie.
- *Ettrick* (BR/LSI 11,279 GRT). Torpedoed by *U 155* returning to United Kingdom.

16 November
- *Clan Mactaggart* (BR/Tran 7,622 GRT). Torpedoed by *U 91* returning to United Kingdom.

24 November
- *Utmost* (BR/SS). Depth-charged by Italian TB *Groppo* southwest of Sicily.
- *Trentbank* (BR/Tran 5,060 GRT). Torpedoed by German He 111 north of Cape Tenes.

25 November
- *Aurora* (Du/Tran 1,695 GRT). Bombed by German Ju 88s at Philippeville.

28 November
- *Ithuriel* (BR/DD). Bombed by German Ju 88s at Bône.
- *Selbo* (NO/Tran 1,778 GRT). Torpedoed by Italian S.79s off Cape Cavallo in transit to Bône.

FRENCH SHIPS

8 November

Surface Combat off Casablanca with U.S. Warships

- *Albatros* (CT), *Brestois* (DD), *Boulonnais* (DD), *Fougueux* (DD), *Frondeur* (DD)

Air and Surface Bombardment in Casablanca Harbor

- *L'Amphitrite* (SS), *La Psyché* (SS), *Oréade* (SS)
- *Porthos* (Tran 12,692 GRT), *Savoie* (Tran 10,196 GRT), *Lipari* (Tran 9,954 GRT), *Ile d'Ouessant* (AO 6,187 GRT), *Schiaffino* (Tran 3,236 GRT), *Saint Blaise* (prison ship 1,778 GRT), *Rosetta* (trwl)*, Dubourdieu* (trwl)

Surface Combat off Oran with British Warships

- *La Surprise* (DS), *Tornade* (DD), *Tramontane* (DD)

Other Causes

- *La Sibylle* (SS). Cause unknown off Casablanca.
- *Actaéon* (SS). Depth-charged by British destroyer *Wescott* off Oran.
- *Argonaute* (SS). Depth-charged by British destroyer *Achates* off Oran.
- *St. Emile* (Tran 1,269 GRT), *Ste. Madeleine* (Tran 962 GRT). Scuttled at Port Lyautey.
- *Abbé Desgranges* (Aux MS). Scuttled at Fédala.

9 November

Scuttled at Oran

- Commercial vessels: *Gouverneur Général Laferrière* (3,353 GRT), *Chateau Pavie* (2,047 GRT), *Mitidja* (3,286 GRT), *Boudjemel, Spahi, Capitaine Saint Martin* (3,439 GRT), *Lorraine* (9,512 GRT), *Tidjitt, Minhir Braz, Mont Cassel, Sidi Bel Abbès* (4,392 GRT), *Forfait, Capitaine Tessier*
- Warships: *La Bônoise* (DS), *Pigeon* (MS) *Chêne* (MS), *Tourterelle* (MS), *Nadal* (MS), *Jean Argaud* (MS), *L'Ajaccienne* (DS) *La Toulonnaise* (DS), *Typhon* (DD), *Ariane* (SS), *Diane* (SS) *Cérès* (SS), *Pallas* (SS)

Other Causes

- *Saint Bertrand* (Tran 3,436 GRT). Scuttled at Bizerte.
- *Kramer* (Tran). Scuttled at Tunis.
- *St. Benoît* (Tran 1,595 GRT), *St. Hughes* (Tran 1,818 GRT). Scuttled at Port Lyautey.
- *Epervier* (CT). Sunk in surface combat off Oran with British warships.

10 November

- *Méduse* (SS). Bombed by SOC float planes from *Philadelphia* north of Safi.

Scuttled at Port Lyautey
- *Saint Bernard* (Tran 2,116 GRT), *Saint Sylvain* (Tran 1,140 GRT), *Nyhorn* (Tran 8,087 GRT), *Saint Edmond* (Tran 1980), *L'Alphée* (armed yacht 1,060 GRT), *Ailette* (DS)

11 November
- *Sidi-Ferruch* (SS). Bombed by U.S. TBFs west of Casablanca.

13 November
- *Le Conquérant* (SS). Bombed by U.S. Catalina off West Africa.

Scuttled at Bougie after Bomb Damage from German Aircraft
- *Koutoubia* (Tran 8,790 GRT), *Florida* (Tran 9,331 GRT)

14 November
- *Le Tonnant* (SS). Scuttled at Cadiz, Spain.

AXIS SHIPS
8 November
- *San Pietro* (IT/Tran 5,199 GRT). Sunk by U.S. bombardment Casablanca.

10 November
- *Emo* (IT/SS). Sunk in surface action with British trawler *Lord Nuffield*.

12 November
- *U 660* (GE/SS). Depth-charged by *Lotus* and *Starwort* north of Oran.

14 November
- *U 595* (GE/SS). Bombed by British Swordfish between Tenes and Oran.
- *U 605* (GE/SS). Bombed by British Hudsons north of Algiers.

15 November
- *U 259* (GE/SS). Bombed by British Hudsons north of Algiers.

16 November
- *U 173*. Depth-charged by U.S. destroyers off Casablanca.

17 November
- *U 331*. Bombed by British Hudsons off Algiers.

23 November
- *Fertilia* (IT/Tran 223 GRT). Torpedoed by British submarine *Porpoise* near Kerkennah Banks.

28 November
- *Città di Napoli* (IT/Tran 5,418 GRT). Mined in the Strait of Sicily.

Notes

INTRODUCTION

1. The État Français or French State is commonly referred to as Vichy France after the regime's temporary capital. Quotes: Marder, *Operation Menace,* 106; Churchill, *Their Finest Hour,* 437.
2. "There are very few Frenchmen who feel what amounted to a suicide mission by the French warships at Casablanca . . . in the early days in North Africa could have been avoided without a complete loss of 'honor' and self-respect." Leahy, *I Was There,* 139.

CHAPTER 1. SITUATION

1. Quotes: Ugaki, *Fading Victory,* 172–73; Ciano, *Diaries,* 509.
2. Quote: Danchev and Todman, *War Diaries,* 285.
3. Brooke noted in his diary (5 March 1942), "Eden apparently nervous lest Russia should make peace with Germans." Danchev and Todman, *War Diaries,* 236. For casualties, see Ellis, *World War II,* 254–55.
4. See Pugh, "Military Need and Civil Necessity," in Howarth and Law, *Battle,* 35–37.
5. Weir, "German Submarine Blockade," 10. Quote: Smith, *Conflict over Convoys,* 67–68.
6. Smith, *Conflict over Convoys,* 249.
7. Ibid., 75–76.
8. Lyon, "British Order of Battle," in Howarth and Law, *Battle,* 273; Morison, *Battle of the Atlantic,* 235.
9. Quote: *Fuehrer Conferences on Naval Affairs,* 288.
10. Quote: Leahy, *I Was There,* 29.
11. Quotes: Hastings, *Winston's War,* 47; Ismay, *Memoirs,* 139.
12. Quotes: Ismay, *Memoirs,* 140; Langer, *Vichy Gamble,* 19; Heckstall-Smith, *Fleet that Faced,* 15.
13. Jackson, *Dark Years,* 123. Quote: Langer, *Vichy Gamble,* 26–27.
14. Quote: Langer, *Vichy Gamble,* 43.
15. Warner, *Laval,* 242. Quotes: Paxton, *Vichy France,* 33.
16. Regarding Mers el-Kébir, Somerville wrote to his wife, "I *begged* the Admiralty not to go to the lengths of opening fire on the French as I felt sure it would be disastrous.

Besides, the idea of slaughtering our former allies (or being slaughtered by them) was most repugnant." Simpson, *Somerville Papers,* 108; emphasis in original. For calories, see Jackson, *Dark Years,* 249–50. The number 1,327 calories a day strikes this author as too precise (and too low), but the point is that there was widespread hunger, especially in the cities.

17. Quote: Lochner, *Goebbels Diaries,* 189.
18. Quote: ibid.
19. Quotes: Warner, *Laval,* 23; U.S. Department of State, Foreign Relations of the United States (hereafter FRUS), *France, 1942,* 181.
20. "His methods of working appeared slovenly to the Marshal's precise military mind and he showed a marked lack of deference, instanced by his habit of blowing cigarette smoke in Pétain's face." Warner, *Laval,* 258.
21. Quotes: FRUS, *France, 1940,* 490, 466. An American diplomat reported, "[Darlan] talked at length and with some feelings of the 'drunkard Churchill who had crawled to him on his knees during 10 months only to turn on him at Mers-el-Kebir.'" (FRUS, *France 1940,* 490)
22. Quotes: Melton, *Darlan,* 110, 109. See also FRUS, *France 1941,* 168; and Paxton, *Vichy France,* 116–18.
23. Quote: Melton, *Darlan,* 113. See Paxton, *Vichy France,* 118. Weygand is often given credit for scuttling the Paris Protocols. Other historians assert that the Protocols never went into effect because the Germans lost interest after invading the Soviet Union. Melton asserts that Germany's failure to make true concessions and intelligence about the forthcoming invasion convinced Darlan that the collaboration that seemed necessary in April was no longer such a good idea. Thus, the admiral deliberately used the political clauses to escape from the military clause that he considered too risky. See Jackson, *Dark Years,* 180–81, for a summary of various interpretations.
24. Quote: Melton, *Darlan,* 153.

CHAPTER 2. THE ART OF AMPHIBIOUS WARFARE

1. Quotes: Fergusson, *Watery Maze,* 35; Frank, "Amphibious Revolution," 20. "Combined operations" is the British term for what this chapter refers to as "amphibious operations."
2. Howcroft, *Amphibious Assaults,* 32. Quote: Millett, "Assault from the Sea," 64.
3. Quote: Fergusson, *Watery Maze,* 49. A Commando was a lightly armed, roughly battalion-sized infantry unit. Units of this type figured prominently in Operation Torch.
4. United Kingdom, Admiralty Series (hereafter ADM) 199/906, Part 5, 4–7; Marder, *Operation Menace,* 125–26.
5. Quote: *London Gazette,* 4 March 1948, 1606.
6. Quote: ADM 234/331, 41.
7. U.S. Navy, "Report on Fleet Landing Exercise No. 2," 2–3.
8. Dyer, *Amphibians,* 210; U.S. Navy, Action Reports and War Diaries, Commander Task Force (hereafter ComTF) 34, "Report," 1.
9. Quote: Frank, *Guadalcanal,* 60.
10. Quote: Playfair et al., *Destruction of Axis Forces,* 22.
11. Quotes: Dear, *World War II,* 299; Neillands, *Dieppe,* 124–26.
12. Friedman, *Amphibious Ships,* 67–86. Specifications vary in other sources.

CHAPTER 3. DECISION

1. Quotes: Weygand, *Recalled,* 360; Jackson, *Dark Years,* 177; Churchill, *Grand Alliance,* 490.
2. Quotes: Dorrel, *Office of Strategic Services,* 20.
3. Quotes: Murphy, *Diplomat,* 68; Leahy, *I Was There,* 443.
4. Quote: Beam, "Intelligence," 63. In August 1941, after Darlan informed Leahy that Germany had broken the State Department codes, he immediately switched to the more secure naval codes.
5. Quotes: FRUS, *France 1942,* 125; Leahy, *I Was There,* 43. See also Weygand, *Recalled,* 393–94.
6. Quotes: FRUS, *First Washington Conference,* 64, 71–72, 78.
7. Quotes: Leighton and Coakley, *Global Logistics,* 153; FRUS, *First Washington Conference,* 102.
8. Quote: Franklin Delano Roosevelt (hereafter FDR) Library, Arcadia Folder, "Memorandum by the U.S. and British Chiefs of Staff: American-British Grand Strategy," 31 December 1941. See also FRUS, *First Washington Conference,* 210.
9. Quote: United Kingdom Cabinet Series (hereafter CAB), W. P. (40), 362.
10. Quotes: FRUS, *First Washington Conference,* 208; Ben-Moshe, "Churchill and the 'Second Front,'" 509.
11. Quotes: CAB 79/56, 46, 91. See also Pogue, *Ordeal and Hope,* 315–17.
12. Quotes: Sherwood, *Roosevelt and Hopkins,* 538; Pogue, *Ordeal and Hope,* 318; Charmley, "Churchill and the American Alliance," 361; Ismay, *Memoirs,* 249.
13. For example, see CAB 79/56, 129, 166.
14. Quote: CAB 79/56, 179. See 159 for an example of Churchill's Norway obsession. For examples of the lack of confidence, see Strange, "British Rejection," 8–9.
15. Quote: Roberts, *Masters and Commanders,* 180. See Sherwood, *Roosevelt and Hopkins,* 582–83 for Mountbatten's summary.
16. CAB 79/21, 314.
17. Quote: FRUS, *Second Washington Conference,* 427.
18. Quotes: ibid., 467, 435. Stimson's opinion is given in ibid., 434. See also CAB 99/20, 18.
19. Quote: Ismay, *Memoirs,* 256.
20. Quote: Ferrell, *Eisenhower Diaries,* 62, 67. See also Clark, *Calculated Risk,* 25.
21. Quotes: Pogue, *Ordeal and Hope,* 340; Churchill, *Hinge of Fate,* 391–94; CAB 79/56, 227.
22. Quote: FDR Library, Marshall, "War Department Personal and Confidential," 23 July 1942. See also Pogue, *Ordeal and Hope,* 340; and George C. Marshall Foundation, Marshall interview, 5 October 1956, 588.
23. Leighton and Coakley, *Global Logistics,* 357–58; Friedman, *Amphibious Ships,* 219.
24. Quotes: FDR Library, Marshall, "Instructions for London Conference, July 1942"; FDR Library, "Memorandum to Hopkins, Marshall, King, July 16, 1942."
25. Pogue, *Ordeal and Hope,* 344.
26. See ibid., 345–47, and Roberts, *Masters and Commanders,* 245–55, for descriptions of these meetings. Quote: Danchev and Todman, *War Diaries,* 283.
27. Quotes: CAB 99/19, 7–9.
28. Quotes: CCS 94, reprinted in CAB 99/21, 12–13.
29. Quotes: Matloff, *Strategic Planning,* 282, 283.

CHAPTER 4. PLANNING AND PREPARATION

1. Quotes: Matloff, *Strategic Planning,* 286; Churchill, *Hinge of Fate,* 406; Danchev and Todman, *War Diaries,* 276; Ismay, *Memoirs,* 258; Bland and Stevens, *Papers of George Catlett Marshall,* 3-269. See also Pogue, *Ordeal and Hope,* 477, n84; and Sherwood, *Roosevelt and Hopkins,* 616.

2. CAB 79/57, 76–77. Quote: Matloff, *Strategic Planning,* 287–88.

3. The CCS defined "collaboration between two or more of the nations at war with the Axis powers as 'combined' and called inter-Service cooperation by one nation 'joint.'" Rearden, *Council of War,* 2.

4. Quotes: Pogue, *Ordeal and Hope,* 349; Bland and Stevens, *Papers of George Catlett Marshall,* 3-282.

5. Quote: Eisenhower, *Crusade,* 77.

6. Combined Chiefs of Staff, "CCS 103: Operation Torch" (hereafter CCS 103), "Enclosure S to Outline plan of 21 August."

7. Butcher, *My Three Years,* 67–68. Quotes: CCS 103, "Enclosure C to Outline plan of 21 August."

8. CAB 79/57, 58. Quotes: Matloff, *Strategic Planning,* 290; Bland and Stevens, *Papers of George Catlett Marshall,* 3-291.

9. Quote: Churchill, *Hinge of Fate,* 473. See also Kennedy, *Business of War,* 265; Danchev and Todman, *War Diaries,* 314; and CAB 79/57, 69.

10. Quotes: Churchill, *Hinge of Fate,* 475; CCS 103, "Enclosure C Telegram from the British Chiefs, 27 August 1942"; CAB 79/57, 84.

11. Quotes: Bland and Stevens, *Papers of George Catlett Marshall,* 3-327; Danchev and Todman, *War Diaries,* 315. See also CAB 79/57, 83.

12. Quotes: Bland and Stevens, *Papers of George Catlett Marshall,* 3-302.

13. Quotes: ibid., 3-316–17; CAB 79/57, 92; Danchev and Todman, *War Diaries,* 317.

14. Quote: CAB 79/57, 106.

15. See Churchill, *Hinge of Fate,* 475–86, for the text of the transatlantic exchange. The quoted material is on page 483. In his postwar history Churchill often paraphrased his wartime communications to make them look better in the light of subsequent events. For an example, compare Bland and Stevens, *Papers of George Catlett Marshall,* 3-302, and Churchill, *Hinge of Fate,* 476–77.

16. Quote: Matloff, *Strategic Planning,* 298.

17. For Portsmouth-Wales convoys, see Admiralty Staff, "War Diary" (hereafter "Admiralty War Diary"), 3 October 1942, 942. See also Roskill, *Period of Balance,* 214, November 1942; and Anti-Submarine Warfare Division Naval Staff, "Monthly Anti-Submarine Report," October 1942, 17. Quote: Matloff, *Strategic Planning,* 311–12.

18. Quotes: CAB 79/57, 117; CCS 103, "Outline Plan, Operation Torch, 20 September 1942."

19. Quote: CCS 103, "Policy with Regard to Vichy French Forces."

20. Langer, *Vichy Gamble,* 309.

21. Beck et al., *Engineers,* 62–63.

22. Quote: Blumenson, *Patton Papers,* 88. See also Kirkpatrick, "Joint Planning," 80–81.

23. Quote: CAB 79/58, 168. See also ibid., 171.

24. Quote: Cherpak, *Hewitt,* 127.

25. U.S. Navy, Action Reports and War Diaries, Commander Amphibious Forces Atlantic (hereafter ComAmpForLant), "War Diary," September 1942.

26. Quotes: U.S. Navy, Action Reports and War Diaries, Commander Transport Division (hereafter ComTranDiv) 11, "Action Report," 2; U.S. Navy, Action Reports and War Diaries, Commander Task Group (hereafter ComTG) 34.1, "Report: *Harris,*" 164, emphasis in original. See also ComTranDiv 11, "War Diary," September and October 1942.

27. Quotes: U.S. Navy, Action Reports and War Diaries (hereafter name of ship, e.g., *Charles Carroll*), *Charles Carroll,* "Report," 6; Harmon, *Combat Commander,* 76–77; ComTG 34.1, "Report: *Dorothea L. Dix,*" 225. See also ComAmpForLant, "War Diary," August, September, 1942.

28. Quotes: ComAmpForLant, "War Diary," October 1942; Cherpak, *Hewitt,* 143.

29. Quote: *Charles Carroll,* "Report," 2.

CHAPTER 5. OPPOSITION

1. Quotes: Playfair et al., *Destruction of Axis Forces,* 95; Hastings, *Inferno,* 364.

2. For Malta's situation, see CAB 79/57, 151, 166–68.

3. CAB 79/57, 52–53; Hinsley et al., *British Intelligence,* vol. 2, 464–65.

4. Hinsley et al., *British Intelligence,* vol. 2, 466, 480.

5. Quotes: Moreau, *Les derniers jours,* 40; Felmy, *German Air Force,* 537; Bragadin, *Italian Navy,* 222. See also Italy, Ministero della Marina, Servizio Informazioni Speciali della Regia Marina (hereafter SIS), "Intercettazioni," 26357.

6. Kahn, *Hitler's Spies,* 471–73. British intelligence had compromised most, if not all, German agents within the United Kingdom.

7. Ibid., 475; SIS, "Intercettazioni," 27302.

8. Kahn, *Hitler's Spies,* 474.

9. Quote: Deakin, *Brutal Friendship,* 60. See also Kesselring, *Soldier's Record,* 160.

10. Quotes: Bragadin, *Italian Navy,* 224; Kahn, *Hitler's Spies,* 477. See also Biagini and Franolillo, *Diario storico comando supremo,* vol. 8, 650, 657.

11. Quotes: FRUS, *France 1942,* 387, 402; CAB 79/58, 30; FRUS, *France 1942,* 408.

12. Quote: Moreau, *Les derniers jours,* 43.

13. Melton, *Darlan,* 161. Quote: FRUS, *France 1942,* 298.

14. Sadkovich, *Major Naval Combatants,* 97, n23; Funk, "Deal with Darlan," 94. Quote: FRUS, *France 1942,* 392–93; Melton (*Darlan,* 163–64) asserts, "Chrétien overstated Darlan's willingness to join the Americans in a North African adventure and that Darlan preferred cooperation in the mainland more than an Allied landing in North Africa."

15. Quotes: Murphy, *Diplomat,* 118; Funk, "Deal with Darlan," 96; Warner, *Laval,* 298. See also Danchev and Todman, *War Diaries,* 330–31; FRUS, *France 1942,* 392; and Mast, *Histoire,* 20, 24. An organization of thirty-four people, including Mast, helped Giraud escape. The Germans subsequently executed four of Giraud's helpers.

16. Quotes: Langer, *Vichy Gamble,* 325; Murphy, *Diplomat,* 119, 115.

17. Quote: Mast, *Histoire,* 99–100.

18. Ibid., 83.

19. Quotes: Funk, "Command of Torch," 106; Murphy, *Diplomat,* 119; Mast, *Histoire,* 79.

20. Langer, *Vichy Gamble,* 328. Quote: Clark, *Calculated Risk,* 70.

21. Quote: Funk, "Command of Torch," 106.

22. Quotes: Mast, *Histoire,* 106; Simpson, *Cunningham Papers,* 38. Murphy, *Diplomat,* 120, states that Mast's "reception of this news was far more agitated than I had expected." See also FRUS, *France 1942,* 409.

23. Caroff, *Les débarquements,* 16.
24. Quote: Funk, "Command of Torch," 107.
25. Quote: U.S. Navy, Action Reports and War Diaries, Commander Naval Forces Europe (hereafter ComNavEu), "Report on Operation Minerva," 3.
26. Quotes: Eisenhower, *Crusade,* 99 (first and fifth quotes); Clark, *Calculated Risk,* 82, 83 (second, third, and fourth quotes).

CHAPTER 6. MEDITERRANEAN CONVOYS

1. Quote: Pugh, "Military Need and Civil Necessity," in Howarth and Law, *Battle,* 37.
2. See appendix III.
3. Quote: Roskill, *Period of Balance,* 317.
4. Blair, *Hunted,* 88. Kahn, *Hitler's Spies,* 476. Quotes: Patch, "Fortuitous Endeavor," 83.
5. Roskill, *Period of Balance,* 320; Blair, *Hunted,* 69. Zimmerman, "Convoy SL-125," advances the deliberate sacrifice conspiracy.
6. SIS, "Intercettazioni," 79, 27589.
7. See appendix II.
8. SIS, "Intercettazioni," 79, 27968.
9. Nassigh, *Guerra,* 212–13. The boats were *Acciaio, Alagi, Aradam, Argento, Argo, Asteria, Avorio, Axum, Brin, Bronzo, Corallo, Dandolo, Diaspro, Emo, Mocenigo, Nichelio, Platino, Porfido, Topazio, Turchese,* and *Velella.*
10. Blair, *Hunted,* 96; Nassigh, *Guerra,* 214. Quote: "Admiralty War Diary," 7 November 1942, 247.
11. Santoni and Mattesini, *La partecipazione tedesca,* 291. Rohwer, *Axis Submarine Successes,* 237, credits *U 205* with this attack. The surrounding ships were definite that an aerial torpedo was the cause: "A plane glided in from the port quarter of the U.S.S. *Thomas Stone* dropping an aerial torpedo which hit her aft, likewise launching an aerial torpedo which missed the U.S.S. *Samuel Chase* by about 50 yards." *Samuel Chase,* "Report," 1. Captain Edger's report may account for the confusion. He wrote, "It was first believed that this plane had torpedoed the *Thomas Stone,* but the evidence now indicates that a submarine was responsible, and that the plane was a British Swordfish in pursuit of the submarine." ComTranDiv 11, "Report," 2.
12. Quotes: *London Gazette,* 23 March 1949, 1515.
13. Deakin, *Brutal Friendship,* 62; Blair, *Hunted,* 96.
14. Caroff, *Les débarquements,* 9; Auphan and Mordal, *French Navy,* 210–11. Quotes: FRUS, *France 1942,* 425; Moreau, *Les derniers jours,* 56–57.
15. Moreau, *Les derniers jours,* 57. Interestingly, Bergeret withheld this information from other members of the government.
16. Moreau, *Les derniers jours,* 59–63, 73–74. Quote: ibid., 62. Moreau believed the meeting occurred on 29 October just before Darlan's departure from North Africa. Murphy does not record a meeting with Darlan, but he did meet with General Juin on 2 November and assured him that "if we ever came here in force we would naturally expect a French invitation." He met with Chrétien on 5 November. See FRUS, *France 1942,* 425. See also Caroff, *Les débarquements,* 12–13.

CHAPTER 7. ALGIERS

1. Quote: U.S. Army Historical Division, "First Eisenhower Period," 208.
2. See appendix III.
3. See appendix II.

4. Quote: ADM 234/359, 26. Mast wrote, "In this poorly chosen sector the sea is shallow and, because of this fact, landing craft ran aground 600 to 800 meters from the shore." Mast, *Histoire,* 141.

5. U.S. Army Historical Division, "First Eisenhower Period," 208; ComNavEu, "Action Report," 78.

6. ComNavEu, "Action Report," 77.

7. Quotes: *London Gazette,* 23 March 1949, 1515; ADM 234/359, 24.

8. Quotes: Thompson, *War at Sea,* 196–98.

9. Morison, *North African Waters,* 205.

10. Caroff, *Les débarquements,* 25–26; Moreau, *Les derniers jours,* 113.

11. Mast, *Histoire,* 139. Quote: Bruce, *Invaders,* 50.

12. Caroff, *Les débarquements,* 25; Monsabert, *Hommage,* 5–6.

13. Quotes: Moreau, *Les derniers jours,* 97; Hoisington, *Dubreuil,* 62. See also Kammerer, *Du débarquement africain,* 253.

14. Quote: St. George Saunders, *Green Beret,* 130. See also Caroff, *Les débarquements,* 28.

15. Quote: *London Gazette,* 23 March 1949, 1517.

16. Quotes: Ryder, "Lessons," 3, 6.

17. Quote: Monsabert, *Hommage,* 8.

18. Quotes: ComNavEu, "Action Report," 2; U.S. Army Historical Division, "First Eisenhower Period," 210.

19. Quote: *Samuel Chase,* "War Diary," 6. See also *Almaack,* "War Diary," 9.

20. Quotes: *Samuel Chase,* "War Diary," 16; *Almaack,* "Report: Damage and Loss of Landing Boats," 1–3. See also ComNavEu, "Action Report," 4.

21. Caroff, *Les débarquements,* 27; Moreau, *Les derniers jours,* 108.

22. *Almaack,* "War Diary," 9; *Almaack,* "Report: Damage and Loss of Landing Boats," 8; *Samuel Chase,* "Report," 4.

23. Moreau, *Les dernier jours,* 115–16.

24. Quotes: *London Gazette,* 23 March 1949, 1517; Caroff, *Les débarquements,* 27.

25. Quotes: Bailey, "3rd Battalion," 9, 12.

26. Ibid., 12–13.

27. Quotes: "Admiralty War Diary," 8 November 1942, 287.

28. Quotes: ComNavEu, "Action Report," 14; Howe, *Northwest Africa,* 240fn; Monsabert, *Hommage,* 7.

29. Caroff, *Les débarquements,* 31; ComNavEu, "Action Report," 106.

30. ComNavEu, "Action Report: Appendix I," 7. Quote: "Admiralty War Diary," 8 November 1942, 270.

31. Quotes : Caroff, *Les débarquements,* 21; Murphy, *Diplomat,* 125. See also Mast, *Histoire,* 138–42; and Kammerer, *Du débarquement africain,* 258–59.

32. Quote: Murphy, *Diplomat,* 129. See also Kammerer, *Du débarquement africain,* 258–59.

33. Quotes: Kammerer, *Du débarquement africain,* 259; Murphy, *Diplomat,*129. See also Moreau, *Les derniers jours,* 87. Telegram text: Kammerer, *Du débarquement africain,* 262.

34. Kammerer, *Du débarquement africain,* 264.

35. Quotes: Caroff, *Les débarquements,* 79. Kammerer, *Du débarquement africain,* 269, writes, "It was consistent with his feelings so often expressed that 'I will do the English the most possible harm.'" See also Moreau, *Les derniers jours,* 105.

36. Melton, *Darlan,* 174.

37. Ibid. See also Moreau, *Les derniers jours,* 150.

38. Quotes: Kammerer, *Du débarquement africain,* 278; Murphy, *Diplomat,* 133.

39. *Almaack,* "Report: Damage and Loss of Landing Boats." Quotes: ADM 234/359, 31; Ryder, "Lessons," 7.

40. Quotes: *Leedstown,* "Report," 2; ADM 234/359, 31; "Admiralty War Diary," 8 November 1942, 300. See also *Samuel Chase,* "War Diary," 8 November 1942; and Santoni and Mattesini, *Partecipazione tedesca,* 291–92.

41. Santoni and Mattesini, *Partecipazione tedesca,* 292; "Admiralty War Diary," 9 November 1942, 340.

42. Quote: Clark, *Calculated Risk,* 87–88.

43. Quote: Kammerer, *Du débarquement africain,* 381.

44. Quote: Langer, *Vichy Gamble,* 351.

45. Kammerer, *Du débarquement africain,* 386–88; Mast, *Histoire,* 284; Moreau, *Les derniers jours,* 168.

46. Quote: "Admiralty War Diary," 9 November 1942, 338.

47. Quotes: Clark, *Calculated Risk,* 160. Vice Admiral Moreau never saw any U.S. troops and no one mentioned their presence to him. Moreau, *Les derniers jours* 168.

48. Quotes: Clark, *Calculated Risk,* 161; Moreau, *Les derniers jours,* 171.

49. Quotes: Caroff, *Les débarquements,* 83, 84. See also Warner, *Laval,* 330; Kammerer, *Du débarquement africain,* 389–92; Funk, "Deal with Darlan," 105–6; and Moreau, *Les derniers jours,*172–73.

50. Quote: Kammerer, *Du débarquement africain,* 277.

CHAPTER 8. ORAN

1. Quote: U.S. Army Historical Division, "First Eisenhower Period," 201.

2. Mayrock, *Air Phase,* 23.

3. Kammerer, *Du débarquement africain,* 314–17; Caroff, *Les débarquements,* 20; Mast, *Histoire,* 169–71.

4. Caroff, *Les débarquements,* 38.

5. Quote: Darby, *Darby's Rangers,* 23. The Batterie Sidi-Ferruch was disarmed according to the armistice terms and occupied by dissidents.

6. Caroff, *Les débarquements,* 39; Howe, *Northwest Africa,* 208.

7. Quote: Winton, *War at Sea,* 261.

8. Moreau, *Les derniers jours,* 134. Quote: Laiche, "Oran Operation," 19.

9. The column consisted of the 1/1st Armored Regiment (elements), Company E 6th Armored Infantry, a tank destroyer platoon, an armored engineer platoon, and a reconnaissance section. McDaniel et al., *Armored Division,* 11.

10. Quote: *London Gazette,* 23 March 1949, 1521.

11. Quotes: Cairns, "Employment of Armor," 4; Beck et al., *Engineers,* 76.

12. Caroff, *Les débarquements,* 51. Quote: ADM 234/359, 34.

13. U.S. Army, Headquarters, 1st Infantry Division, "Torch Field Orders, October 10, 1942."

14. Quote: Smith, "Anti Tank Platoon," 23.

15. Quotes: ADM 199/897, *Aurora,* "Report," 3; Smith, "Anti Tank Platoon," 28.

16. Quote: Caroff, *Les débarquements,* 56.

17. Quotes: Reardon, "Hands of Friends," 18; U.S. Navy, Action Reports and War Diaries, Commander Naval Operating Bases, Oran Area (hereafter ComNOBOA), "Report," 4.

18. Quotes : Reardon, "Hands of Friends," 19, 20. See also Caroff, *Les débarquements,* 40.

19. Passis, Disher, and Ault, *Springboard to Berlin,* 122–23.

20. Moreau, *Les derniers jours,* 127.
21. Quotes: Reardon, "Hands of Friends," 21; ComNOBOA, "Report," 75.
22. Quotes: ComNOBOA, "Report," 84.
23. Based on Caroff, *Les débarquements,* 43; and Moreau, *Les derniers jours,* 129.
24. Saibène, *Bourrasque,* 119n2. Caroff, *Les débarquements,* 44, gives 0445 as the time of *Tramontane*'s exit.
25. This account is based on the reports of *Aurora* and *Calpe* contained in ADM 199/897; Caroff, *Les débarquements,* 44–46; and Moreau, *Les derniers jours,* 129–132.
26. Quotes: ADM 199/897, *Aurora,* "Report," 6.
27. Quotes: Hawkins, *Destroyer,* 191; Moreau, *Les derniers jours,* 130. See also ADM 234/444, *Boadice,* 216.
28. Saibène, *Bourrasque,* 121–22. Quote: *Aurora,* "Report," 7.
29. Saibène, *Bourrasque,* 118–23; Caroff, *Les débarquements,* 43–47. Quote: Hawkins, *Destroyer,* 191.
30. Antier, *Les grandes batailles,* 1160.
31. Quote: "Admiralty War Diary," 8 November 1942, 271.
32. Moreau, *Les derniers jours,* 135; Mayrock, *Air Phase,* 63.
33. Quote: Mayrock, *Air Phase,* 58.
34. Craven and Cate, *Europe,* 71–73; Howe, *Northwest Africa,* 212–13.
35. Howe, *Northwest Africa,* 213.
36. Quote: Smith, "Anti Tank Platoon," 29.
37. Quote: Darrieus and Queguiner, *Historique,* 331.
38. Quote: Anon., *Silver Phantom,* 58. See also ADM 199/897, *Aurora,* "Report," 4; ADM 199/897, *Calpe,* "Report, 2."
39. Quotes: ADM 199/897, *Jamaica,* "Report," 1.
40. Ibid.; *Calpe,* "Report," 2; *Aurora,* "Report," 4.
41. Quotes: Darrieus and Queguiner, *Historique,* 331; ADM 199/897, *Jamaica,* "Report," 2. See also Caroff, *Les débarquements,* 49–50.
42. Caroff, *Les débarquements,* 50–53. See also appendix IV.
43. Caroff, *Les débarquements,* 69–70; Howe, *Northwest Africa,* 227; Reardon, "Hands of Friends," 23; Wilson, "Report," 66.

CHAPTER 9. ATLANTIC CONVOY

1. Quote: Truscott, *Command Missions,* 90.
2. Morison, *North African Waters,* 44.
3. Cherpak, *Hewitt,* 152.
4. Based on coordinates extracted from Rohwer, *Axis Submarine Successes.*
5. Quote: Cherpak, *Hewitt,* 152.
6. Quote: ibid., 155. See also "Admiralty War Diary," November 1942, 200.
7. Morison, *North African Waters,* 45; Tomblin, *Utmost Spirit,* 18.
8. Quotes: U.S. Army, Battlebook 3-A, 42; Tomblin, *Utmost Spirit,* 20; Moran, *Landings,* 16 (third and fourth quotes).
9. See appendix II.
10. Quote: Moran, *Landings,* 41fn.
11. Caroff, *Les débarquements,* 114–16; Howe, *Northwest Africa,* 93–94; Auphan and Mordal, *French Navy,* 228–29; Kammerer, *Du débarquement africain,* 334–49.
12. Quotes: Petit, *Mémoires.*
13. Quote: Howe, *Northwest Africa,* 94.

CHAPTER 10. PORT LYAUTEY

1. See appendix II.
2. Quotes: U.S. Navy, Action Reports and War Diaries, Commander Destroyer Squadron (hereafter ComDesron) 11, "Report," 2–3; *Shad,* "Report," 7 November 1942.
3. Quotes: Truscott, *Command Missions,* 92; *Shad,* "Report," 8 November 1942; Com TranDiv 5, "Report," 1–2.
4. ComTranDiv 5, "Report," 2.
5. The transports used metal or rope nets. *Clymer's* executive officer noted that the "chain nets are useless as they break easily, are slippery and cut the hands." However, "manila nets must be kept clear of the water. The nets stretched and fouled the propellers of many boats loading alongside." *Clymer,* "Report," Enclosure A, 2. See also *Anne Arundel,* "War Diary"; *Algorab,* "War Diary"; and *John Penn,* "War Diary."
6. Moran, *Landings,* 47.
7. Quotes: Truscott, *Command Missions,* 95; ComTranDiv 5, "Report," 2. See also *Clymer,* "Report," 2; and *Anthony,* "War Diary."
8. Quotes: Caroff, *Les débarquements,* 205; *Allen,* "Report," 3. See also *Parker,* "Report," 2.
9. Quotes: *Raven,* "War Diary," 8 November 1942; *Allen,* "Report," 1.
10. *Clymer,* "Report," 3.
11. Quotes: Morison, *North African Waters,* 122; *Clymer,* "Report," 3, "Report: Enclosure B," 4.
12. Quotes: *Osprey,* "War Diary," 8 November 1942; Morison, *North African Waters,* 122.
13. Caroff, *Les débarquements,* 134.
14. Ibid., 135; *Eberle,* "War Diary," 8 November 1942; *Savannah,* "Chronology," 8 November 1942, 2; ComAmpForLant, "Report," 45.
15. See Caroff, *Les débarquements,* 135, 138. According to *Savannah, Eberle, Roe, Ericsson,* and *Kearny* their guns were silent between 0635 (when *Roe* ceased fire) and 0701 (when *Roe* engaged Batterie Ponsot), but there are variations: *Eberle's* report indicated she opened fire at 0603. This was 0607 according to *Roe* and 0606 by the clocks of *Savannah, Ericsson,* and *Kearny.*
16. Quotes: ComDesron 11, "Report," 5; *Savannah,* "Report," 15; *Kearny,* "Report," 2.
17. Quote: *Clymer,* "Report," 4. See also *John Penn,* "Report," 1; and *Algorab,* "Report," 1.
18. *Kearny,* "Report," 3.
19. Quotes: *Sangamon,* "Report: Intelligence Report," 1–2; "Report: Air Operations Statistics." See also Caroff, *Les débarquements,* 138.
20. Cairns, "Employment of Armor," 125.
21. Quote: Howe, *Northwest Africa,* 156.
22. Quote: *Texas,* "Report," 1.
23. Quotes: Howe, *Northwest Africa,* 156; Mordal, *Casablanca,* 69; Cairns, "Employment of Armor," 143. Navy reports complained that the Army failed to fully utilize gunfire support: "The delay incident to the capture of the Kasba Fort and the coastal defense guns at Mehdia might have been avoided by having the early support of naval gunfire on these targets." See ComAmpForLant, "Comments and Recommendations," 1–2.
24. *Savannah,* "Chronology," 3; *Roe,* "War Diary," 3; *Ericsson,* "Report," 4; Caroff, *Les débarquements,* 136. Quote: Howe, *Northwest Africa,* 156.
25. Caroff, *Les débarquements,* 137. Quote: Mordal, *Casablanca,* 70.
26. *Dallas,* "Report," 1.
27. *Roe,* "War Diary," 3; *Texas,* "War Diary," 10. *Savannah,* "Chronology," 5; *Ericsson,* "Report," 6.

28. Howe, *Northwest Africa,* 157; Cardinell, *9th Infantry,* 144–45; Caroff, *Les débarquements,* 137.
29. Caroff, *Les débarquements,* 139.
30. *Savannah,* "Report," 3.
31. Quotes: Truscott, *Command Missions,* 111.
32. Quotes: ibid., 111, 113. See also *John Penn,* "Report," 2; *Anne Arundel,* "Report," 5; *Clymer,* "Report," 5; *Algorab,* "War Diary," 8 November 1942; and *Hambleton,* "War Diary," 8 November 1942.
33. Mordal, *Casablanca,* 242. These were elite Moroccan troops. A *goum* was roughly equivalent to a strong company and a *tabor* to a small battalion.
34. Quotes: Truscott, *Command Missions,* 117. See also Mordal, *Casablanca,* 243.
35. Quotes: Truscott, *Command Missions,* 82.
36. Quotes: Petit, *Mémoires.* See also Atkinson, *Army at Dawn,* 143.
37. Quotes: Truscott, *Command Missions,* 114; Mordal, *Casablanca,* 239. See also *Savannah,* "Chronology," 5; and Howe, *Northwest Africa,* 161. Caroff, *Les débarquements,* 140, tallies French losses as two tanks and American losses as four.
38. Quote: Mordal, *Casablanca,* 239.
39. Ibid., 244.
40. Quotes: Howe, *Northwest Africa,* 163; Truscott, *Command Missions,* 117.
41. Quotes: ComTranDiv 5, "Report," 4; *Allen,* "Report," 1; *Clymer,* "Report," 5.
42. Quote: *Clymer,* "Report," 5–6.
43. Quotes: Mordal, *Casablanca,* 246; Petit, *Mémoires.* See also Howe, *Northwest Africa,* 164.
44. Quotes: ComDesron 11, "Report," 9; *Dallas,* "Report," 2.
45. *Kearny,* "Report," 4; *Savannah,* "Report," 2; *Dallas,* "Report," 3.
46. Cardinell, *9th Infantry,* 155.
47. Quote: Howe, *Northwest Africa,* 164. See also Mordal, *Casablanca,* 246. The other ships were *St. Bernard* (2,116 GRT), *St. Gilbert, St. Edmond* (1,980 GRT), and *St. Sylvain* (957 GRT).
48. *Sangamon,* "Report: Intelligence Report," 1. This report does not state the time of the attack. The chronology of Destroyer Division 11 notes that they were bombing at 1008. Cairns, "Employment of Armor," says 1050.
49. Quotes: *Texas,* "War Diary," 10 November 1942; *Texas,* "Report," 3.
50. ComTranDiv 5, "Report," 4; *John Penn,* "Report," 2; *Clymer,* "Report," 6. Quote: *Clymer,* "Report," Enclosure A, 2.
51. Quote: ComDesron 11, "Report," 10. See also *Algorab,* "War Diary," 10 November 1942; *John Penn,* "Report," 2; and *Clymer,* "Report," 6.
52. Cairns, "Employment of Armor," 133. Quote: *Texas,* "War Diary," 10 November 1942.
53. *Allen,* "Report," 6.
54. *Anne Arundel,* "Journal," 8.
55. *Electra,* "Log," 15–16 November 1942; *Allen,* "Report," 3; *Clymer,* "Report," 7; Morison, *North African Waters,* 173.
56. *Clymer,* "Report: Enclosure B," 6; *John Penn,* "Journal"; *Arundel,* "Journal," 5–6; Morison, *North African Waters,* 173fn.

CHAPTER 11. CASABLANCA
1. Howe, *Northwest Africa,* 121.
2. Wilson, "Report," 1.
3. Ibid.

4. Quotes: *Charles Carroll,* "Report," 2; U.S. Navy, Action Reports and War Diaries, ComTG 34.9, "Report," 2; ComTranDiv 3, "War Diary," 7 November 1942.

5. *Boyle,* "War Diary," 7 November 1942.

6. See appendix II.

7. Caroff, *Les débarquements,* 148. Quote: *Murphy,* "Report," 2.

8. Quotes: ComTranDiv 3, "War Diary," 8 November 1942; *Dickman,* "Report," 5; *Carroll,* "Report," 3. See also *Oberon,* "War Diary," 8 November 1942; *Edward Rutledge,* "War Diary," 8 November 1942; *Ancon,* "War Diary," 8 November 1942; and *Arcturus,* "War Diary," 8 November 1942.

9. ComTranDiv 3, "War Diary," 8 November 1942; ComTG 34.9, "Report," 3.

10. ComTG 34.9, "Report," 3–4; U.S. Navy, Action Reports and War Diaries, Commander Destroyer Division (hereafter ComDesDiv) 26, "Report," 2.

11. Quotes: *Leonard Wood,* "Report," 7; Morison, *North African Waters,* 62.

12. Caroff, *Les débarquements,* 149.

13. Ibid. Quote: ComDesDiv 26, "Report," 3. See also *Ludlow,* "Report," 1; *Murphy,* "Report," 3; *Wilkes,* "Report," 2, 7; *Brooklyn,* "Report," 3; and *Leonard Wood,* "Report," 8.

14. Morison, *North African Waters,* 64. Quote: *Leonard Wood,* "Report," 7.

15. Quotes: ComAmpForLant, "Report," 73–74; Morison, *North African Waters,* 63–64. The Wave 1 commander implied that his boats came ashore somewhere west of Blue 2. The report of the Wave 2 commander stated his boat landed two miles east of Red 3 and the other five boats of this wave three miles east.

16. Quotes: ComAmpForLant, "Report," 76–82.

17. *Carroll,* "Report," 6. Quotes: *Carroll,* "Report," 8; Boyle, "Battle on the Beach."

18. *Dickman,* "Report," 5.

19. Quotes: *Hogan,* "Report," 1; Caroff, *Les débarquements,* 203–4.

20. *Tillman,* "War Diary," 8 November 1942; Caroff, *Les débarquements,* 204.

21. Caroff, *Les débarquements,* 205; *Tillman,* "War Diary," 8 November 1942.

22. ComDesDiv 26, "Report," 3; *Wilkes,* "Report," 8; Caroff, *Les débarquements,* 149.

23. Quote: *Brooklyn,* "Report," 3. See also *Swanson,* "Report," 2; *Ludlow,* "Report," 2; *Murphy,* "Report," 3; and *Wilkes,* "Report," 2.

24. Quote: *Wilkes,* "Report," 8. See also *Ludlow,* "Report," 2; and *Swanson,* "Report," 2.

25. Quote: *Brooklyn,* "Report," 6. See also *Brooklyn,* "Report," 4.

26. Quotes: *Murphy,* "Report," 4–6.

27. *Brooklyn,* "Report," 4.

28. Quotes: ComAmpForLant, "Report," 72, 73; *Leonard Wood,* "Report," 12, 13.

29. Quote: *Augusta,* "Report (A)," 3. See also Caroff, *Les débarquements,* 150.

30. Quote: Caroff, *Les débarquements,* 150.

31. Ibid., 152.

32. Shepherd says they were captured on a golf course trying to board a plane. U.S. Navy, Action Reports and War Diaries, Shepherd (hereafter Shepherd), "Report," 13. Quote: Cairns, "Employment of Armor," 71.

33. ComTG 34.9, "Report," 17.

34. Morison, *North African Waters,* 84–85. Quote: Howe, *Northwest Africa,* 131.

35. ComTG 34.9, "Report," 28–30.

36. Quote: Antier, *Les grandes batailles,* 1180–81.

37. *Ranger,* "War Diary," 8 November 1942, 5; *Suwannee,* "War Diary," 8 November 1942, 10.

38. ComTG 34.1, "Report: Action by Lt. Elliott," 217. Quote: ComTG 34.1, "Report: Operations Plane #6," 220.

39. Quotes: ComTG 34.1, "Report: *Massachusetts*," 86; ComTG 34.1, "Report: *Wainwright*," 276; ComTG 34.1, "Report," 7. See also ComTG 34.1, "Report: *Wichita* Anti-aircraft Battery Engagements," 251; and ComTG 34.1, "Report: Aircraft-Action with Enemy," 264.
40. ComTG 34.1, "Report," 9; ComTG 34.1, "Report: *Tuscaloosa*,"199.
41. Caroff, *Les débarquements*, 183; Darrieus and Queguiner, *Historique*, 338; Jordan and Dumas, *French Battleships*, 158. U.S. reports say the battleship opened fire at 0701. Quotes: ComTG 34.1, "Report: *Massachusetts*," 86.
42. ComTG 34.1, "Report," 9; ComTG 34.1, "Report: *Massachusetts*," 87. "These fire control sets are still too complicated and touchy for the concussion and shock they are subjected to. Whenever something goes out, too much time is lost in finding the failure. One thing such as loss of the range notch can be caused by [at] least three tube failures, with the consequent testing of three different circuits, to find the failure." ComTG 34.1, "Report: *Massachusetts*," 114. See also ComTG 34.1, "Report: *Tuscaloosa*, Aircraft Operations," 219.
43. Mordal, *Casablanca*, 112. Quote: Morison, *North African Waters*, 97. For damage to *Jean Bart*, see Jordan and Dumas, *French Battleships*, 160–61.
44. Cressman, *Ranger*, 220; Caroff, *Les débarquements*, 166.
45. Caroff, *Les débarquements*, 167.
46. ComAmpForLant, "Report: Torch Recommendations," 2, 30; Caroff, *Les débarquements*, 183.
47. Quote: ComTG 34.1, "Report," 13. See also ComTG 34.1, "Report: *Massachusetts*," 121.
48. Caroff, *Les débarquements*, 210.
49. U.S. Navy, Action Reports and War Diaries, ComTG 34.2, "War Diary," 24.
50. U.S. Navy, Action Reports and War Diaries, Commander in Chief Atlantic Fleet (hereafter CinCLant), "Aircraft Operations," 20.

CHAPTER 12. THE NAVAL BATTLE OF CASABLANCA
1. ComTG 34.1, "Report: *Massachusetts*," 88; ComTG 34.1, "Report: *Wichita*,"249. Quote: ComTG 34.1, "Report: *Tuscaloosa*," 200.
2. Quotes: ComTG 34.9, "Report," 5; *Augusta*, "Report," 6.
3. Mordal, *Casablanca*, 138. Quote: Wordell and Seiler, *Wildcats*, 96–97.
4. Quote: *Wilkes*, "Report," 3. See also ComDesDiv 26, "Report," 7, 4; *Wilkes*, "Report," 8; *Ludlow*, "Report," 2; and *Swanson*, "Report," 6. *Albatros* and *L'Alcyon* fired red dye–loaded shells; *Milan* and *Frondeur* used green. Mordal, *Casablanca*, 142.
5. Quote: *Brooklyn*, "Report," 7. See also *Augusta*, "Report (A)," 4.
6. Morison, *North African Waters*, 99. According to Cressman, *Ranger*, 222, there was a direct hit on one landing boat. *Brooklyn*, "Report," 7, mentions that a spotter saw the boats under fire. Shepherd, "Report," 12, remarks that a French destroyer or corvette sank at least one landing boat by gunfire. See also ComTG 34.9, "Report," 5.
7. Quote: Tomblin, *Utmost Spirit*, 34.
8. Mordal, *Casablanca*, 140.
9. Quotes: ComTG 34.1, "Report: Communications Log," 74; Dailey, "Cruiser USS *Brooklyn*: Action!"; *Ranger*, "War Diary," 5. See also *Brooklyn*, "Report," 7.
10. Saibène, *L'Adroit*, 140.
11. Quote: ComTG 34.1, "Report," 13.
12. Quotes: ComTG 34.1, "Report: *Massachusetts*," 90; ComTG 34.1, "Report," 14–15.

13. Quotes: ComTG 34.1, "Report: *Tuscaloosa,*" 201; ComDesron 8, "Report," 2; ComTG 34.1, "Report: *Mayrant,*" 297. See also ComTG 34.1, "Report: *Wichita,*" 246; and ComTG 34.1, "Report: *Tuscaloosa,*" 197. Captain Moon of Destroyer Squadron 8 was promoted to rear admiral and directed the landings on Utah Beach on 6 June 1944. He committed suicide on 5 August 1944 shortly before he was scheduled to lead a similar assault in southern France.

14. ComTG 34.1, "Report: *Massachusetts,*" 90. Taking *Massachusetts's* position based on her track chart and *Primauguet's* location based on French reports, the distance between the two at 0918 plots out to 25,000 yards. Quotes: ComTG 34.1, "Report: *Massachusetts,*" 113, 150. See also *Brooklyn,* "Report," 8; and *Augusta,* "Report (A)," 5.

15. Quotes: ComTG 34.1, "Report: *Massachusetts,*" 91; ComTG 34.1, "Report," 14; ComTG 34.1, "Report: *Wainwright,*" 277. See also Morison, *North African Waters,* 101n26. Morison, who never criticizes American admirals in this battle, did not understand what was meant by "restricted waters." The only report of a minefield was inshore east of Cape Fédala passed along by Captain Emmet to Hewitt at 0948, although there was TBS chatter about it earlier. The field proved to be floating life rings.

16. Quote: ComTG 34.9, "Report," 5–6.

17. Quote: *Swanson,* "Report," 3. See also *Bristol,* "Report," 3; *Wilkes,* "Report," 3; and *Brooklyn,* "Report," 8.

18. Saibène, *L'Adroit,* 140; Caroff, *Les débarquements,* 172.

19. Caroff, *Les débarquements,* 172; ComTG 34.1, "Report: *Wichita,*" 246, 250; ComTG 34.1, "Report: *Tuscaloosa,*" 201.

20. The battleship's report complained, "Our radars have held up beautifully in all drills, practice runs, and even during target practices . . . but when we commenced to shoot service velocity charges, it was entirely different as the radars failed." ComTG 34.1, "Report: *Massachusetts,*" 152–53. For *Milan* see Caroff, *Les débarquements,* 172–73; and Mordal, *Casablanca,* 148–49.

21. Quotes: ComTG 34.1, "Report: *Tuscaloosa,*" 232; ComTG 34.1, "Report," 15; ComTG 34.1, "Report: *Tuscaloosa,*" 197 (third and fourth quotes). See also Caroff, *Les débarquements,* 196.

22. Quotes: Tomblin, *Utmost Spirit,* 35; ComTG 34.1, "Report: *Massachusetts,*" 142. See also ComTG 34.1, "Report: *Massachusetts,*" 91. *Méduse* said she launched at 1012. See Caroff, *Les débarquements,* 194.

23. Cressman, *Ranger,* 228.

24. Quote: Caroff, *Les débarquements,* 173.

25. Quote: ComTG 34.1, "Report," 16.

26. *Brooklyn,* "Report," 8. This is an example of a confused command structure.

27. Quotes: *Brooklyn,* "Report," 8 (first two quotes); ComTG 34.1, "Report: Communications Log," 75. See also Caroff, *Les débarquements,* 196–97.

28. Caroff, *Les débarquements,* 173–74, 180; Saibène, *L'Adroit,* 140–41; ComTG 34.1, "Report: *Tuscaloosa,*" 233. Quote: ComTG 34.1, "Report: *Wichita,*" 251.

29. Caroff, *Les débarquements,* 173–74; Saibène, *L'Adroit,* 140–41. Quote: *Brooklyn,* "Report," 9. This report states that *Brooklyn* opened fire at 1015. There are many minor time discrepancies in French and American reports.

30. Quotes: *Palmer,* "Report," 3; *Bristol,* "Report," 3. See also *Wilkes,* "Report," 3; *Swanson,* "Report," 6; *Edison,* "Report," K1; ComDesron 13, "Report," 5; *Boyle,* "Report," 1; and Caroff, *Les débarquements,* 150.

31. Quote: Blumenson, *Patton Papers,* 103.

32. Quote: ComTG 34.1, "Report: *Massachusetts,*" 173.
33. Quotes: *Bristol,* "Report," 3; *Brooklyn,* "Report," 9; ComTG 34.1, "Report: *Tuscaloosa,*" 202; *Bristol,* "Report," 3. See also *Edison,* "Report," 2.
34. Caroff, *Les débarquements,* 175; ComTG 34.1, "Report: *Tuscaloosa,*" 202.
35. Quote: Dailey, "USS Brooklyn: Action!"
36. ComTG 34.1, "Report, *Massachusetts,*" 93; ComTG 34.1, "Report: *Wainwright,*" 277; *Rhind,* "Report," 1. Quote: *Jenkins,* "Report," 1.
37. Quote: Dailey, "USS Brooklyn: Action!"
38. Quotes: ComTG 34.1, "Report," 19; Blumenson, *Patton Papers,* 106. Patton's final report included the recommendation, "The necessity for a special command ship with adequate naval and military communication equipment is a paramount. . . . This ship must not be capable of engaging in battle." Allied Force Headquarters, "Lessons of Operation Torch," 31.
39. Quotes: ComTG 34.1, "Report: *Wichita,*" 250; ComTG 34.1, "Report: *Tuscaloosa,*" 197. See also *Augusta,* "Report," A6; and *Brooklyn,* "Report," 12.
40. ComTG 34.1, "Report: *Tuscaloosa,*" 202; ComTG 34.1, "Report: *Wichita,*" 246, 266; Caroff, *Les débarquements,* 175; Saibène, *L'Adroit,* 141–42. *Tuscaloosa* fired four salvos against a destroyer from 1119 to 1123, range 13,500 yards, and fourteen salvos against *Primauguet* from 1128 to 1136, range 16,400 yards. *Wichita* was engaging "enemy ships with both main and secondary batteries; range slightly under 14,000 yards" from 1118 to 1128. ComTG 34.1, "Report: *Wichita,*" 246.
41. ComTG 34.1, "Report: *Tuscaloosa,*" 198–201; ComTG 34.1, "Report: *Wichita,*" 247. Quote: ComTG 34.1, "Report: *Tuscaloosa,*"186.
42. Caroff, *Les débarquements,* 175–76; Cressman, *Ranger,* 232.
43. Caroff, *Les débarquements,* 176.
44. Quote: ComTG 34.1, "Report: Summary of Communications," 76.
45. Caroff, *Les débarquements,* 180–81. *Augusta,* "Report," 7. Quote: *Brooklyn,* "Report,"10.
46. *Brooklyn,* "Report," 11.
47. Caroff, *Les débarquements,* 181. Quote: *Augusta,* "Report," 7.
48. Caroff, *Les débarquements,* 180–81; *Augusta,* "Report," 8; *Suwannee,* "War Diary," 12.
49. Quotes: U.S. Navy, Action Reports and War Diaries, Commander Cruiser Division (hereafter ComCruDiv) 7, "War Diary," 8 November 1942, 58; ComTG 34.1, "Report: Communi-cations Log," 77.
50. Quotes: ComTG 34.1, "Report: *Wichita,*" 250; ComTG 34.1, "Report: *Tuscaloosa,*" 198, 203.
51. Quote: ComCruDiv 7, "War Diary," 8 November 1942, 59.

CHAPTER 13. THE FALL OF CASABLANCA

1. Quotes: ComTG 34.9, "Report," 47; Blumenson, *Patton Papers,* 108. See also ComTG 34.9, "Report," 41; and ComTF 34, "Report," 11.
2. ComTG 34.9, "Report," 28–30.
3. Howe, *Northwest Africa,* 139; Committee 25, "Armor in the Invasion," 76.
4. Caroff, *Les débarquements,* 213.
5. Quote: *Augusta,* "War Diary," 9 November 1942.
6. Caroff, *Les débarquements,* 192. Quotes: *Edison,* "Report," 3; *Tillman,* "War Diary," 11 November 1942.
7. Quote: *Boyle,* "War Diary," 36.
8. Quotes: Cherpak, *Hewitt,* 164, 163; *Augusta,* "War Diary," 7–8 November 1942.
9. Quote: Blumenson, *Patton Papers,* 109.

10. Caroff, *Les débarquements*, 224–25.
11. Quotes: ibid., 226. See also Warner, *Laval*, 335–36.
12. Quotes: Blumenson, *Patton Papers*, 111; Kammerer, *Du débarquement africain*, 458.
13. Cherpak, *Hewitt*, 171.
14. ComTG 34.9, "Report," 28–30.
15. Caroff, *Les débarquements*, 201. Quotes: *Suwannee*, "War Diary," 21.
16. *Joseph Hewes*, "Report," 1; *Winooski*, "Report," 1–2.
17. *Bristol*, "Report," 3–4.
18. Quotes: CinCLant, "Aircraft Operations," 69; *Ranger*, "War Diary." See also Cressman, *Ranger*, 286–88; and *Woolsey*, "War Diary."
19. Shepherd, "Report," 42–45.
20. Quotes: *Edward Rutledge*, "Loss of," 2; *Tasker H. Bliss*, "Loss of," 3.
21. Quotes: *Woolsey*, "War Diary," 28; ComTF 34, "Report," 18.
22. Quotes: ComTG 34.9, 23; emphasis in original.
23. ComTG 34.9, "Report," 23–24. Quotes: ComTG 34.9, 23, 53.
24. Howe, *Northwest Africa*, 174; Caroff, *Les débarquements* 233–34.

CHAPTER 14. SAFI

1. Wilson, "Report," 14.
2. Quotes: ComTG 34.10, "Report: Attack Order," 120–22.
3. See appendix II.
4. Quote: Mordal, *Casablanca*, 84.
5. ComTG 34.10, "Report," 10.
6. Quotes: ComTG 34.10, "Report: *Harris*," 153–54.
7. Quote: Randle, *Safi Adventure*, 29–30.
8. Quote: ComTG 34.10, "Report: *Harris*," 151.
9. Ibid., 141.
10. Ibid.; Report: *Bernadou*," 123; Caroff, *Les débarquements*, 154.
11. Caroff, *Les débarquements*, 154. The French opened fire at 0428 according to Davidson, *Harris*, and Destroyer Squadron 15. *Bernadou* reported the time as 0438 (eight minutes after she grounded!), and *Cole* at 0435. *Cole*'s captain noted that his chronology was approximate from memory as exact times were not recorded. See ComTG 34.10, "Report: *Cole*," 130; ComTG 34.10, "Report: Annex B Gunnery," 29; ComTG 34.10, "Report: *Harris*," 141. Quotes: ComTG 34.10, "Report: *Harris*," 141; ComTG 34.10, "Report: *Mervine*," 280; ComTG 34.10, "Report: *Beatty*," 291.
12. ComTG 34.10, "Report: ComDesron 15," 275; ComTG 34.10, "Report: Annex A," 30; ComTG 34.10, "Report: *Philadelphia*," 256; *New York*, "Report," B7. Quote: ComTG 34.10, "Report: *Mervine*," 280.
13. Quote: ComTG 34.10, "Report: *Bernadou*," 124–25. An Army observer, Maj. James Y. Adams, stated that the troops were dazed and took an hour to completely disembark. See Committee 25, "Armor in the Invasion," 93. Atkinson is much more dramatic: "[The troops] flopped back to the deck with each new shell burst until roused by their officers and shoved toward the single scrambling net now draped over the bow." Atkinson, *Army at Dawn*, 113.
14. Quote: ComTG 34.10, "Report: *Cole*," 133.
15. Quotes: ComTG 34.10, "Report: *Cole*," 134 (first and third quotes); ComTG 34.10, "Report: *Harris*," 142 (second and fourth quotes); Caroff, *Les débarquements*, 155fn (fifth quote).

16. Quote: ComTG 34.10, "Report: *Cole*," 135.
17. Quotes: ComTG 34.10, "Report: *Harris*," 161; Randle, *Safi Adventure*, 33–34.
18. ComTG 34.10, "Report: *Harris*," 162.
19. Quote: ComTG 34.10, "Report: *Dorothea L. Dix*," 227.
20. Quotes: ibid., 226; ComTG 34.10, "Report," 4; ComTG 34.10, "Report: *Knight*," 298.
21. Quotes: ComTG 34.10, "Report: *Dorothea L. Dix*," 226; ComTG 34.10, "Report: *Lyon*," 212.
22. *New York*, "Report," 2; ComTG 34.10, "Report: ComDesron 15," 274. Quote: ComTG 34.10, "Report: *Mervine*," 282.
23. ComTG 34.10, "Report," 13; ComTG 34.10, "Report: Annex B Gunnery," 30; *New York*, "Report," 7. The French say 0800. See Caroff, *Les débarquements*, 157.
24. Mordal, *Casablanca*, 87.
25. Quotes: Randle, *Safi Adventure*, 40.
26. Ibid., 38. Quote: ComTG 34.10, "Report: *Cole*," 136. According to *Cole's* report the whole second story was demolished. Randle says just a corner was destroyed, an observation supported by a photograph in his book.
27. Caroff, *Les débarquements*, 157; ComTG 34.10, "Report: *Philadelphia*," 258. Quote: ComTG 34.10, "Report: Air Operations," 67.
28. Caroff, *Les débarquements*, 156. Quotes: Mordal, *Casablanca*, 87; Committee of 25, "Armor in the Invasion," 97.
29. Quotes: ComTG 34.10, "Report: *Lakehurst*," 251; Randle, *Safi Adventure*, 58.
30. Quotes: Committee of 25, "Armor in the Invasion," 98; ComTG 34.10, "Report: *Lyon*," 213. See also ComTG 34.10, 218. Adams' report is scathing. Colonel Randle wrote that he and Adams did not hit it off, and the colonel later sought to bring charges against Adams for sending a platoon against a machine-gun nest and getting several men severely wounded. Randle, *Safi Adventure*, 50.
31. Morison, *North African Waters*, 150; ComTG 34.10, "Report: *Santee*," 41.
32. Quote: ComTG 34.10, "Report: *Santee*," 35. See also ComTG 34.10, 28–29; Caroff, *Les débarquements*, 213.
33. ComTG 34.10, "Report: Air Operations," 66.
34. Ibid., 67.
35. Ibid.; Caroff, *Les débarquements*, 194. The submarine's report also mentions an air attack at 0640.
36. Caroff, *Les débarquements*, 211; *Santee*, "War Diaries," 16–17. Quotes: ComTG 34.10, "Report: Air Operations," 68. Morison, *North African Waters*, 151–52, states that the reconnaissance flight dropped the unexploded bomb on the 8th and that this sparked the French retaliatory raid on the 9th. In fact, the French conducted the first air attack.
37. *Santee*, "War Diaries," 19–21.
38. Quotes: ibid., 30–31; ComTG 34.10, "Report: Air Operations," 69.
39. Caroff, *Les débarquements*, 195.
40. Ibid., 157; Wilson, "Report," 15.
41. ComTG 34.10, "Report," 4; Harmon, *Combat Commander*, 81.
42. Quotes: ComTG 34.10, "Report," 4, 26.

CHAPTER 15. AXIS REACTION
1. Quote: FRUS, *France 1942*, 431.
2. Quotes: Kammerer, *Du débarquement africain*, 269; Auphan and Mordal, *French Navy*, 220. See also Warner, *Laval*, 322.

3. Quote: Kammerer, *Du débarquement africain*, 300.
4. Quotes: Antier, *Les grandes batailles*, 644. See also Caroff, *Les débarquements*, 76–77.
5. Quote: U.S. Army Historical Division Europe, Foreign Military Studies (hereafter FMS), "OKW Reaction," 6.
6. Quote: Deakin, *Brutal Friendship*, 63–64. See also Warner, *Laval*, 323–24.
7. Langer, *Vichy Gamble*, 350; Warner, *Laval*, 324.
8. Auphan and Mordal, *French Navy*, 239. Quote: Warner, *Laval*, 326fn.
9. Quotes: FMS, "OKW Reaction," 8; Ferrell, *Eisenhower Diaries*, 81–82.
10. Santoni and Mattesini, *Partecipazione tedesca*, 292. See chapter 7, "Algiers," for more information.
11. Quote: Captain U-boats, Italy (hereafter U-boats), "War Diary," 444–46.
12. See Blair, *Hunted*, 96–97; U-boats, "War Diary," 450. Hai included *U 77, 205, 331, 431, 561,* and *660.* Delphin consisted of: U *73, 81, 458, 565, 593, 595, 605,* and *617. U 73, 81, 407, 565, 617,* and *660* were reassigned to a new group called Wai. The Italian boats were *Acciaio, Alagi, Aradam, Argento, Argo, Asteria, Avorio, Axum, Brin, Bronzo, Corallo, Dandolo, Diaspro, Emo, Mocenigo, Nichelio, Platino, Porfido, Topazio, Turchese,* and *Velella.*
13. Quotes: Deakin, *Brutal Friendship*, 65–66. See also Boog, Rahn, and Stumpf, *Global War*, 802.
14. U-boats, "War Diary," 451.
15. Quote: Deakin, *Brutal Friendship*, 67. See also Warner, *Laval*, 334.
16. Quotes: Weygand, *Recalled*, 399; Deakin, *Brutal Friendship*, 67; Moreau, *Les derniers jours*, 173. See also Melton, *Darlan*, 178; and Langer, *Vichy Gamble*, 353. Darlan, in fact, informed Clark first of Pétain's repudiation. Naturally Clark prohibited Darlan from issuing an official revocation of his orders.
17. Quotes: Jackson, *Dark Years*, 223; Deakin, *Brutal Friendship*, 69; Ciano, *Diaries*, 543; Warner, *Laval*, 333; Deakin, *Brutal Friendship*, 71.
18. Quote: Deakin, *Brutal Friendship*, 72.
19. Santoni and Mattesini, *Partecipazione tedesca,* 300.
20. Quote: Nye, *Memoirs: HMS* Martin *G44.*
21. Quotes: "Admiralty War Diary," 10 November 1942, 390; U-boats, "War Diary," 454, 456. See also *Trove*, "Trawler's Fight"; and U-boats, "War Diary," 459.
22. Blair, *Hunted*, 99; U-boats, "War Diary," 460–63, 465.
23. Quote: FMS, "Commitment of the 10th Panzer Division," 7. See also Auphan and Mordal, *French Navy*, 240.
24. Quotes: Murphy, *Diplomat*, 137.
25. Quotes: Melton, *Darlan*, 185; Langer, *Vichy Gamble*, 111.

CHAPTER 16. THE ALLIES MOVE EAST

1. Caroff, *Les débarquements*, 254; Kammerer, *Du débarquement africain*, 324–25.
2. Caroff, *Les débarquements*, 257; Kammerer, *Du débarquement africain*, 358; Kesselring, *Soldier's Record*, 168; FMS, "Missions of OB Sued," 9.
3. Quotes: Caroff, *Les débarquements*, 258; Kammerer, *Du débarquement africain*, 361.
4. Quote: Caroff, *Les débarquements*, 258.
5. Quotes: FMS, "Negotiations with the Representative of General Barré," 2–3.
6. Quotes: United Kingdom Ministry of Defence Series (hereafter DEFE), 3/373, QT 5848; Caroff, *Les débarquements*, 261.
7. Quotes: Moreau, *Les dernier jours*, 178–79. See also *London Gazette*, 23 March 1949, 1518; Caroff, *Les débarquements*, 71–72; and ADM 234/359, 43.

8. ADM 234/359, 43. Quote: Thompson, *Forgotten Voices,* 251.
9. *London Gazette*, 23 March 1949, 1519. These were supplemented by four Hurricanes from the carrier *Avenger,* which poked her nose out of Algiers where she was repairing an engine defect to fly off eight Hurricanes to *Argus.* Four were unable to locate their destination and turned back.
10. Quotes: Jackson, "His Majesty's Landing Ship Awatea, 22. See also *London Gazette*, 23 March 1949, 1519.
11. De Laborde's reply was *merde.* For Darlan and de Laborde, see Antier, *Les grandes batailles,* 635; Auphan and Mordal, *French Navy,* 242. Quotes: Butcher, *My Three Years,* 184; Caroff, *Les débarquements,* 86. For Noguès's instructions, see Kammerer, *Du débarquement africain,* 429–30.
12. Quote: Caroff, *Les débarquements,* 264. See also Auphan and Mordal, *French Navy,* 251.
13. Quotes: Auphan and Mordal, *French Navy,* 241–42. See also Kammerer, *Du débarquement africain,* 458–59.
14. Caroff, *Les débarquements,* 264–65; Kammerer, *Du débarquement africain,* 464–65.
15. Kammerer, *Du débarquement africain,* 453–54; Melton, *Darlan,* 187.
16. Quote: Kesselring, *Soldier's Record,* 168.
17. Quote: "Admiralty War Diary," 12 November 1942, 530. See also ibid., 14 November 1942, 634–35. See also DEFE, 3/783, QT 5931, and QT 5934.
18. Fioravanzo, *La difesa del traffico,* 137–38.
19. Funk "Deal with Darlan," 113; Melton, *Darlan,* 188–89. Quotes: Kammerer, *Du débarquement africain,* 474.
20. Quotes: Caroff, *Les débarquements,* 87; Melton, *Darlan,* 187.
21. Quote: Auphan and Mordal, *French Navy,* 252.
22. Quote: Thompson, *Forgotten Voices,* 82. See also Rolf, *Bloody Road,* 34.
23. Santoni and Mattesini, *Partecipazione tedesca,* 302.
24. Caroff, *Les débarquements,* 269.
25. Quote: FMS "Missions of OB Sued," 12.
26. Caroff, *Les débarquements,* 274. Quote: Auphan and Mordal, *French Navy,* 253.
27. Quotes: FMS, "Missions of OB Sued," 12, 23–24.
28. Boog, Werner, and Stumpf, *Global War,* 803; Playfair et al., *Destruction of Axis Forces,* 171.
29. In Lieutenant General Anderson's report, Hart Force "conducted a successful guerilla campaign against the enemy's rear." *London Gazette,* 5 November 1946, 5453. See also Howe, *Northwest Africa,* 284.
30. Quotes: FMS, "First Stage in the Battle for Tunisia," 10, 11; Howe, *Northwest Africa,* 288.
31. Quote: "Admiralty War Diary," 25 November 1942, 960.

CHAPTER 17. FINAL ROUNDUP

1. Quote: Antier, *Les grandes batailles,* 842.
2. See Cernuschi and O'Hara, "Toulon," 142–47.
3. Quotes: FRUS, *France 1942,* 453–57.
4. Quotes: Langer, *Vichy Gamble,* 370, 372–73; FRUS, *France 1942,* 445.
5. Quote: FRUS, *France 1942, 441.*
6. Quote: Leahy, *I Was There,* 140. There is a large and complicated literature surrounding this event. The summary in Melton, *Darlan,* 208–17 is clear and convincing.
7. Quotes: Eisenhower, *Crusade,* 129–30; Cunningham, *Odyssey,* 513–14.

8. Quote: Cunningham, *Odyssey*, 501.
9. Quote: German Naval Staff Operations Division, "War Diary," May 1943, 4; emphasis in original.
10. Quotes: Breuer, *Operation Torch*, 257; D'Este, *Mediterranean*, 37; Rolf, *Bloody Road*, 282; Howe, *Northwest Africa*, 666. For Axis strength in Libya in December 1942 correspondence with Enrico Cernuschi, 5 May 2014, taken from Canevari, *La Guerra Italiana*, vol 2. Playfair et al., *Destruction of Axis Forces*, 460, lists Allied casualties in the Tunisian campaign as 38,160 British, 18,221 American, and 19,439 French.

CONCLUSION

1. Quote: CAB 79/57, 236.
2. For ships participating in Operation Husky, the invasion of Sicily, see Roskill, *Period of Balance*, 121.
3. Quote: Biagini and Franolillo, *Diario storico comando supremo*, vol. 8, 670.
4. Another year of bloodletting on the Russian front, the 1943 defeat of Axis submarines in the North Atlantic, and the attrition of German air strength accomplished by the ongoing Mediterranean campaign and the accelerating bombardment of Germany and Axis-held territory are noted as other minimum prerequisites for victory.

APPENDIX II. FRENCH ORDER OF BATTLE

1. Vigneras, *Rearming the French*, 12, 18. The most important sources used for order of battle include Caroff, *Les débarquements*; Mordal, *Casablanca*; and Niehorster, *World War II Armed Forces*.

Bibliography

PRIMARY AND OFFICIAL SOURCES

Admiralty Staff. "War Diary." 1 October–31 October 1942. National Archives and Records Administration, Washington, DC.

———. "War Diary." 1 November–30 November 1942. National Archives and Records Administration, Washington, DC.

Allied Force Headquarters. "Lessons of Operation Torch." 19 January 1943. Combined Arms Research Library Digital Library.

Anti-Submarine Warfare Division Naval Staff. "Monthly Anti-Submarine Report, October 1942." 15 November 1942. The National Museum Royal Navy.

———. "Monthly Anti-Submarine Report, November 1942." 15 December 1942. The National Museum Royal Navy.

Biagini, Antonello, and Fernando Franolillo. *Diario storico comando supremo.* Vol. 8. Rome: Ufficio Storico dello Stato Maggiore dell'Esercito, 1999.

Bland, Larry I., and Sharon Ritenour Stevens. *The Papers of George Catlett Marshall.* Lexington, Ky.: George C. Marshall Foundation, 1981.

Captain U-boats, Italy. "War Diary." 1 July 1942–31 December 1942. Henry E. Eccles Library, U.S. Naval War College.

Combined Chiefs of Staff. "CCS 103: Operation Torch," 25 August 1942. Combined Arms Research Library Digital Library.

Combined Operations Headquarters. "Digest of Reports on Operation 'Husky.'" Combined Operations Headquarters, London, 1943. Combined Arms Research Library Digital Library.

Franklin Delano Roosevelt (FDR) Library. "Arcadia Folder." Safe Files, Box 1.

———. "Marshall." Safe Files, Box 4.

———. "Memorandum to Hopkins, Marshall, King." 16 July 1942.

Fuehrer Conferences on Naval Affairs, 1939–1945. London: Chatham, 1947. Reprinted 2005.

George C. Marshall Foundation. "Oral Histories, Collection Interview Notes: Torch Planning 1942." 5 October 1956.

"George C. Marshall's Report to U.S. Secretary of War, Mr. Henry L. Stimson: 7/1/41–6/30/43." Administrative Histories. National Archives and Records Administration, Washington, DC.

German Naval Staff Operations Division. "War Diary." April–May 1943. Henry E. Eccles Library, U.S. Naval War College.

Italy, Ministero della Marina. Servizio Informazioni Speciali della Regia Marina (SIS). "Intercettazioni estere e informazioni." No. 6, a 18 dal 24-5-1942 al 8-1-1943. Archivio Centrale dello Stato, Rome.

London Gazette. "The Capture of Diego Suarez." Supplement, 4 March 1948.

———. "The Landings in North Africa." Supplement, 23 March 1949.

———. "Operations in North West Africa from 8th November 1942 to 13th May 1943." Supplement, 5 November 1946.

Ryder, Charles W. "Lessons from Operation 'Torch.'" 26 December 1942. Combined Arms Research Library Digital Library.

Simpson, Michael, ed. *The Cunningham Papers.* Vol. 2, *The Triumph of Allied Sea Power 1942–1946.* Aldershot, UK: Ashgate, 2006.

———, ed. *The Somerville Papers.* Aldershot,UK: Ashgate, 1995.

United Kingdom Admiralty Series (ADM). 199/897. "HMS *Aurora:* 'Reports of Proceedings,' 13 November 1942." The National Archives, Kew, UK.

———. 199/906. "Operation Menace." The National Archives, Kew, UK.

———. 234/331. "Naval Operations at the Capture of Diego Suarez, May 1942." The National Archives, Kew, UK.

———. 234/359. "Operation 'Torch' Invasion of North Africa November 1942 to February 1943." The National Archives, Kew, UK.

———. 234/444. "H.M. Ships Damaged or Sunk by Enemy Action 3 Sept. 1939 to 2 Sept. 1945." The National Archives, Kew, UK.

United Kingdom Cabinet Series (CAB). 79/18–79/24. "War Cabinet Chiefs of Staff Committee Minutes of Meetings 31 January 1942–31 December 1942." The National Archives, Kew, UK.

———. 79/56–79/58. "Chiefs of Staff Committee Minutes of Meetings 9 January 1942–31 December 1942." The National Archives, Kew, UK.

———. 99/19–99/21. "Combined Staff Conferences Minutes of Meetings." The National Archives, Kew, UK.

———. 195/1–195/2. "War Cabinet Minutes (Transcriptions)." The National Archives, Kew, UK.

———. W. P. (40) 362. "Appreciation by the Chiefs of Staff on Future Strategy, 4 September 1940." The National Archives, Kew, UK.

United Kingdom Ministry of Defence Series (DEFE) 3/781–784. QT 4501–6500. "Ultra Dispatches, 27 October 1942–19 November 1942." The National Archives, Kew, UK.

U.S. Army. "Battlebook 3-A. Operation Torch." Combat Studies Institute, May 1984.

———. "Conference on Landing Assaults. 24 May–23 June, 1943." 1 July 1943. Combined Arms Research Library Digital Library.

———. Headquarters, 1st Infantry Division. "Torch Field Orders, October 10, 1942." Combined Arms Research Library Digital Library.

———. Headquarters, 1st Infantry Division. "Torch Operation G-3 Report." 24 November 1942. Combined Arms Research Library Digital Library.

———. "Intelligence Lessons from North Africa Operation 'TORCH' Up to 1st March 1943." 17 March 1943. Combined Arms Research Library Digital Library.

———. "Lessons Derived from Operations at Casablanca and Oran." 25 February 1943. Combined Arms Research Library Digital Library.

U.S. Army Historical Division. "First Eisenhower Period, ETO Monograph, 1941–43." n.d.

U.S. Army Historical Division Europe, Foreign Military Studies (FMS). A 952. "In Vichy nach der Amerikanischen Landung." National Archives and Records Administration, Washington, DC.

———. D017. "Luftwaffe Capabilities in the Mediterranean Theater after the Allied Landings in French North Africa." National Archives and Records Administration, Washington, DC.

———. D040. "Negotiations with the Representative of General Barré and the Resident of Tunis, Admiral Estéva." National Archives and Records Administration, Washington, DC.

———. D066. "Situation in OKW (Oct–Dec 1942)." National Archives and Records Administration, Washington, DC.

———. D067. "Missions of OB Sued: Battles in Tunisia--Part I (Nov–Dec 1942)." National Archives and Records Administration, Washington, DC.

———. D086. "First Phase of the Engagement in Tunisia, Up to the Assumption of the Command by the Newly Activated Fifth Panzer Army Headquarters on 9 Dec 1942." National Archives and Records Administration, Washington, DC.

———. D145. "OKW Reaction to the Allied Landing in North Africa, November 1942." National Archives and Records Administration, Washington, DC.

———. D147. "First Stage in the Battle for Tunisia." National Archives and Records Administration, Washington, DC.

———. D174. "Commitment of the 10th Panzer Division in Tunisia." National Archives and Records Administration, Washington, DC.

U.S. Department of State, Foreign Relations of the United States (FRUS). *The First Washington Conference*, 1942. University of Wisconsin Digital Collections.

———. *France, 1940.* University of Wisconsin Digital Collections.

———. *France, 1941.* University of Wisconsin Digital Collections.

———. *France, 1942.* University of Wisconsin Digital Collections.

———. *The Second Washington Conference.* University of Wisconsin Digital Collections.

U.S. Navy, Action Reports and War Diaries. Commander Amphibious Forces Atlantic (ComAmpForLant). "Operation Torch, Action Report." 3 December 1942. National Archives and Records Administration, Washington, DC.

———. Commander Amphibious Forces Atlantic (ComAmpForLant). "Operation Torch, Comments and Recommendations." 22 December 1942. National Archives and Records Administration, Washington, DC.

———. Commander Amphibious Forces Atlantic (ComAmpForLant). "War Diary, September–November 1942." National Archives and Records Administration, Washington, DC.

————. Commander Cruiser Division (ComCruDiv) 7. "War Diary," November 1942. National Archives and Records Administration, Washington, DC.

————. Commander Destroyer Division (ComDesDiv) 26. "Report of Action against Vichy French Forces off Fedhala, French Morocco." 9 December 1942. National Archives and Records Administration, Washington, DC.

————. Commander Destroyer Squadron (ComDesron) 8. "Action Report." 11 November 1942. National Archives and Records Administration, Washington, DC.

————. Commander Destroyer Squadron (ComDesron) 11. "Report of Action off Mehdia, Morocco." 16 November 1942. National Archives and Records Administration, Washington, DC.

————. Commander Destroyer Squadron (ComDesron) 13. "Report of Action against Vichy French Forces off Fedhala French Morocco on 8 November 1942." 15 December 1942. National Archives and Records Administration, Washington, DC.

————. Commander in Chief Atlantic Fleet (CinCLant). "Aircraft Operations during the Execution of Torch." 30 March 1943. National Archives and Records Administration, Washington, DC.

————. Commander Naval Forces in Europe (ComNavEu). "Action Report, Operation Torch." 25 November 1943. National Archives and Records Administration, Washington, DC.

————. Commander Naval Forces in Europe (ComNavEu). "Report on Operation Minerva." 7 December 1942. National Archives and Records Administration, Washington, DC.

————. Commander Naval Operating Bases, Oran Area (ComNOBOA). "Operations of U.S. Naval Forces, Center Task Force, Operation Torch." 30 November 1942. National Archives and Records Administration, Washington, DC.

————. Commander Task Force (ComTF) 34. "Operation Torch, Preliminary Report of." 28 November 1942. National Archives and Records Administration, Washington, DC.

————. Commander Task Group (ComTG) 34.1. "Report of Participation in Operation "Torch"; Action off Casablanca, French Morocco, November 8, 1942." 19 November 1942. National Archives and Records Administration, Washington, DC.

————. Commander Task Group (ComTG) 34.2. "War Diary." November 1942. National Archives and Records Administration, Washington, DC.

————. Commander Task Group (ComTG) 34.9. "Report on Operation Torch." 30 November 1942. National Archives and Records Administration, Washington, DC.

————. Commander Task Group (ComTG) 34.10. "Operation Torch, Assault on Safi, Fr. Morocco on 11/8/42 (Enc. A-T)." 24 November 1942. National Archives and Records Administration, Washington, DC.

————. Commander Transport Division (ComTranDiv) 3. "War Diary for Period 1–30 November 1942." 5 December 1942. National Archives and Records Administration, Washington, DC.

————. Commander Transport Division (ComTranDiv) 5. "Action Report." 15 December 1942. National Archives and Records Administration, Washington, DC.

————. Commander Transport Division (ComTranDiv) 11. 25 November 1942. National Archives and Records Administration, Washington, DC.

———. "Report on Fleet Landing Exercise No. 2." (Maj. Franklin Kibler, 1938). Combined Arms Research Library Digital Library.

———. Shepherd, Captain. "Report on Temporary Duty with Amphibious Force, U.S. Atlantic Fleet (Task Force Thirty-Four) 24 October–30 November 1942." 31 December 1942. National Archives and Records Administration, Washington, DC.

———. War Diaries/Action Reports (not otherwise included in a task group report): November 1942. USS *Algorab, Almaack, Ancon, Anne Arundel, Arcturus, Augusta, Barnegat, Bristol, Boyle, Brooklyn, Charles Carroll, Dallas, Dickman, Eberle, Edison, Edward Rutledge, Electra, Ericsson, George Clymer, Hambleton, Henry T. Allen, Hogan, Jenkins, John Penn, Joseph Hewes, Kearny, Leedstown, Leonard Wood, Ludlow, Murphy, New York, Oberon, Osprey, Parker, Palmer, Ranger, Raven, Rhind, Roe, Sangamon, Samuel Chase, Savannah, Shad, Suwannee, Swanson, Susan B. Anthony, Tasker H. Bliss, Texas, Tillman, Titania, Tuscaloosa, Wichita, Wilkes, Winooski, Woolsey.* National Archives and Records Administration, Washington, DC.

Wilson, Arthur R. "Report of Operations in North Africa," 12 December 1942. Combined Arms Research Library Digital Library.

OFFICIAL AND SEMIOFFICIAL HISTORIES

Beck, Alfred M. Abe Birtz, Charles W. Lynch, Lida Mayo, and Ralph F. Weld. *The Corps of Engineers: The War against Germany.* Washington, DC: Government Printing Office, 1985.

Boog, Horst, Werner Rahn, and Reinhard Stumpf. *Germany and the Second World War.* Vol. 6, *The Global War.* Oxford: Clarendon Press, 2001.

Caroff, R. *Les débarquements alliés en afrique du nord* (*Novembre 1942*). Paris: Marine Nationale, Service historique de la Marine, 1960.

Cline, Ray S. *Washington Command Post: The Operations Division.* Washington, DC: Center of Military History, U.S. Army, 1990.

Craven, Wesley Frank, and James Lea Cate, eds. *The Army Air Forces in World War II.* Vol. 2, *Europe: Torch to Pointblank August 1942 to December 1943.* Chicago: University of Chicago Press, 1949.

Cressman, Robert J. *The Official Chronology of the U.S. Navy in World War II.* Annapolis, Md.: Naval Institute Press, 2000.

Felmy, Hellmuth. *The German Air Force in the Mediterranean Theater of War.* U.S. Air Force Historical Study 161. Washington, DC: U.S. Air Force, 1955.

Fioravanzo, Giuseppe. *La Marina Italiana nella Seconda Guerra Mondiale.* Vol. 1, *Dati statistici.* Rome: USMM, 1972.

———. *La Marina Italiana nella Seconda Guerra Mondiale.* Vol. 8, *La difesa del traffico con L'Africa settentrionale: dal 1 Ottobre 1942 alla caduta della Tunisia.* Rome: USMM, 1964.

Garland, Albert N., and Howard McGaw Smyth. *Sicily and the Surrender of Italy.* Washington, DC: Government Printing Office, 1965.

Gwyer, J. M. A., and J. R. M. Butler. *Grand Strategy.* Vol. 3, *June 1941–August 1942.* London: HMSO, 1964.

Hinsley, F. H., E. E. Thomas, C. A. G. Simkins, and C. F. G. Ransom. *British Intelligence in the Second World War: Its Influence on Strategy and Operations.* 3 vols. New York: Cambridge University Press, 1979–84.

Howe, George F. *Northwest Africa: Seizing the Initiative in the West.* Washington, DC: Government Printing Office, 1957.

⸺. *American Signal Intelligence in Northwest Africa and Western Europe.* Washington, DC: National Security Agency, 2010.

Leighton, Richard M., and Robert W Coakley. *Global Logistics and Strategy, 1940–1943.* Washington, DC: Office of the Chief of Military History, 1955.

Matloff, Maurice. *Strategic Planning for Coalition Warfare 1941–1942.* Washington, DC: Government Printing Office, 1953.

Mayrock, Thomas J. *Air Phase of the North African Invasion.* U.S. Air Force Historical Study 105. U.S. Army: Historical Division, 1944.

McDaniel, Alva T., Francis A. Cooch III, George V. Labadie, Edwin W. Piburn Jr., and James R. Porta. *The Armored Division as an Assault Landing Force.* Ft. Knox, Ky.: Armored School, 1952.

Moran, Charles. *The Landings in North Africa: November 1942.* Washington, DC: Naval Historical Center, 1993.

Morison, Samuel Eliot. *History of United States Naval Operations in World War II.* Vol. 1, *The Battle of the Atlantic 1939–1943.* Boston: Little, Brown, 1984.

⸺. *History of United States Naval Operations in World War II.* Vol. 2, *Operations in North African Waters, October 1942–June 1943.* Boston: Little, Brown, 1984.

Page, Christopher, ed. *Naval Staff Histories. Naval Operations of the Campaign in Norway: April–June 1940.* London: Frank Cass, 2000.

Playfair, I. S. O., C. J. C. Molony, F. C. Flynn, and T. P. Gleave. *The Mediterranean and Middle East.* Vol. 4, *The Destruction of the Axis Forces in Africa.* Uckfield, UK: Naval and Military Press, 2004.

Richards, Dennis, and Hilary St. George Saunders. *The Royal Air Force 1939–1945.* Vol. 2, *The Fight Avails.* London: HMSO, 1954.

Roskill, S. W. *The War at Sea 1939–1945.* Vol. 2, *The Period of Balance.* London: HMSO, 1956.

Santoro, Giuseppe. *L'Aeronautica italiana nella Seconda Guerra Mondiale.* Rome: Danesi, 1957.

Schreiber, Gerhard, Bernd Stegemann, and Detlef Vogel. *Germany and the Second World War.* Vol. 3, *The Mediterranean, South-East Europe, and North Africa 1939–1941.* Oxford: Clarendon Press, 1995.

U.S. Coast Guard. *The Coast Guard at War. North African Landings IX.* Washington, DC: Historical Section, 1946.

Vigneras, Marcel, *Rearming the French.* Washington, DC: Center of Military History, U.S. Army, 1989.

BOOKS

Anonymous. *The Silver Phantom–H.M.S. Aurora.* London: Frederick Muller, 1945.

Antier, Jean-Jacques. *Les grandes batailles navales de la Seconde Guerre mondiale: Le drame de la Marine française.* Paris: Omnibus, 2000.

Atkinson, Rick. *An Army at Dawn: The War in North Africa, 1942–1943.* New York: Henry Holt, 2002.

Auphan, Paul, and Jacques Mordal. *The French Navy in World War II.* Westport, Conn.: Greenwood, 1976.

Bagnasco, Erminio. *In Guerra sul mare: navi e marinai italiani nel Secondo Conflitto Mondiale.* Parma, Italy: Ermanno Albertelli, 2005.

Baker, A. D. III. *Allied Landing Craft of World War Two,* edited by the U.S. Navy Department. Annapolis, Md.: Naval Institute Press, 1989.

Barnett, Correlli. *Engage the Enemy More Closely: The Royal Navy in the Second World War.* New York: W. W. Norton, 1991.

Bauer, Eddy. *The History of World War II.* New York: Galahad Books, 1979.

Bennett, G. H., and R. Bennett. *Hitler's Admirals.* Annapolis, Md.: Naval Institute Press, 2004.

Bennett, Ralph. *Ultra and Mediterranean Strategy.* New York: William Morrow, 1989.

Blair, Clay. *Hitler's U-Boat War.* Vol. 2, *The Hunted, 1942–1945.* New York: Modern Library, 2000.

Blumenson, Martin. *The Patton Papers, 1940–1945.* Cambridge, Mass.: Da Capo, 1996.

Bragadin, Marc' Antonio. *The Italian Navy in World War II.* Annapolis, Md.: Naval Institute Press, 1957.

Breuer, William B. *Operation Torch: The Allied Gamble to Invade North Africa.* New York: St. Martin's Press, 1985.

———. *Feuding Allies: The Private Wars of the High Command.* New York: John Wiley & Sons, 1995.

Bruce, Colkin John. *Invaders: British and American Experience of Seaborne Landings 1939–1945.* Annapolis, Md.: Naval Institute Press, 1999.

Bryant, Arthur. *The Turn of the Tide.* New York: Doubleday, 1957.

Butcher, Harry S. *My Three Years with Eisenhower.* New York: Simon and Schuster, 1946.

Canevari, Emilio. *La Guerra Italiana.* Vol. 2. Rome: Tosi, 1949.

Cardinell, Robert H., ed. *The 9th Infantry Division in WWII as Told by the Men.* Privately printed, 1995.

Chambrun, René de, ed. *France during the German Occupation 1940–1944.* Stanford, Calif.: Hoover Press, 1986.

Cherpak, Evelyn, ed. *The Memoirs of Admiral H. Kent Hewitt.* Newport, R.I.: Naval War College Press, 2004.

Churchill, Winston S. *The Second World War.* Vol. 2, *Their Finest Hour.* Boston: Houghton Mifflin, 1949.

———. *The Second World War.* Vol. 3, *Grand Alliance.* Boston: Houghton Mifflin, 1950.

———. *The Second World War.* Vol. 4, *The Hinge of Fate.* Boston: Houghton Mifflin, 1950.

Ciano, Galeazzo. *The Ciano Diaries 1939–1943.* Safety Harbor, Fla.: Simon, 2001.

Clark, Mark W. *Calculated Risk.* New York: Enigma Books, 2007.

Cressman, Robert J. USS *Ranger: The Navy's First Flattop from Keel to Mast 1934–1946.* Washington, DC: Potomac Books, 2003.

Cunningham, Andrew Browne. *A Sailor's Odyssey.* London: Hutchinson, 1951.

Danchev, Alex, and Daniel Todman, eds. *War Diaries 1939–1945 Field Marshal Lord Alanbrooke.* London: Weidenfeld & Nicolson, 2001.

Darby, William C. *Darby's Rangers: We Led the Way.* New York: Random House, 1980.

Darrieus, Henri, and Jean Queguiner. *Historique de la marine française 1922–1942.* St. Malo, France: L'Ancre de Marine, 1996.

Deakin, F. W. *The Brutal Friendship: Mussolini, Hitler and the Fall of Italian Fascism.* New York: Harper and Row, 1962.

Dear, I. C. B., ed. *Oxford Companion to World War II.* New York: Oxford University Press, 1995.

D'Este, Carlo. *World War II in the Mediterranean 1942–1945.* Chapel Hill, N.C.: Algonquin, 1990.

Dorrel, Thomas W. *Role of the Office of Strategic Services in Operation Torch.* Charleston, S.C.: BiblioBazaar, 2012.

Dunn, Walter Scott Jr. *Second Front Now: 1943.* Tuscaloosa: University of Alabama Press, 1980.

Dyer, George Carroll. *The Amphibians Came to Conquer: The Story of Admiral Richmond Kelly Turner.* Washington, DC: Government Printing Office, 1969.

Eisenhower, Dwight D. *Crusade in Europe.* New York: Doubleday, 1948.

Ellis, John. *World War II: A Statistical Survey.* New York: Facts on File, 1995.

Fergusson, Bernard. *The Watery Maze: The Story of Combined Operations.* New York: Holt Reinhart and Winston, 1961.

Ferrell, Robert H., ed. *The Eisenhower Diaries.* New York: W. W. Norton, 1981.

Frank, Richard B. *Guadalcanal: The Definitive Account of the Landmark Battle.* New York: Penguin, 1990.

Friedman, Norman. *U.S. Amphibious Ships and Craft: an Illustrated Design History.* Annapolis, Md.: Naval Institute Press, 2002.

Gardiner, Robert, ed. *Conway's All the World's Fighting Ships 1922–1946.* New York: Mayflower, 1980.

———. *Conway's All the World's Fighting Ships 1906–1921.* Annapolis, Md.: Naval Institute Press, 1986.

Gray, Ed. *General of the Army: George C. Marshall, Soldier and Statesman.* New York: Cooper Square Press, 2000.

Greene, Jack, and Alessandro Massignani. *Rommel's North African Campaign: September 1940–November 1942.* Cambridge, Mass.: Da Capo, 1994.

———. *The Naval War in the Mediterranean 1940–1943.* London: Chatham, 1998.

Hague, Arnold. *The Allied Convoy System 1939–1945.* Annapolis, Md.: Naval Institute Press, 2000.

Harmon, Ernest E., *Combat Commander: Autobiography of a Soldier.* Englewood Cliffs, N.J.: Prentice-Hall, 1970.

Hastings, Max. *Inferno: The World at War 1939–1945.* New York: Vintage Books, 2012.

———. *Winston's War: Churchill 1940–1945.* New York: Alfred A. Knopf, 2010.

Hawkins, Ian, ed. *Destroyer: An Anthology of First-Hand Accounts of the War at Sea 1939–1945.* London: Conways, 2003.

Heckstall-Smith, Anthony. *The Fleet that Faced Both Ways.* London: Anthony Blond, 1963.

Hezlet, Arthur. *British and Allied Submarine Operations in World War II.* Portsmouth, UK: The Royal Navy Submarine Museum. No date.

Hoisington, William A. Jr. *The Assassination of Jacques Lemaigre Dubreuil: A Frenchman between France and North Africa.* New York: Routledge Curzon, 2005.

Howard, Michael. *The Mediterranean Strategy in the Second World War.* London: Greenhill, 1993.

Howarth, Stephen, and Derek Law, eds. *The Battle of the Atlantic 1939–1945: The 50th Anniversary International Naval Conference.* London: Greenhill, 1994.

Howcroft, Ivor. *The Role of the Royal Navy in the Amphibious Assaults in the Second World War.* PhD thesis. Exeter, UK: University of Exeter, 2002.

Hughes, Terry, and John Costello. *The Battle of the Atlantic.* New York: Dial Press, 1977.

Ismay, H. L. *The Memoirs of General Lord Ismay.* New York: Viking Press, 1960.

Jackson, Julian. *France: The Dark Years 1940–1944.* Oxford: Oxford University Press, 2001.

Jordan, John, and Robert Dumas. *French Battleships 1922–1956.* Annapolis, Md.: Naval Institute Press, 2009.

Jordan, John, and Jean Moulin. *French Cruisers 1922–1956.* Annapolis, Md.: Naval Institute Press, 2013.

Jordan, Roger. *The World's Merchant Fleets 1939.* Annapolis, Md.: Naval Institute Press, 1999.

Kahn, David. *Hitler's Spies: German Military Intelligence in World War II.* New York: Macmillan, 1978.

Kammerer, Albert. *Du débarquement africain au meurtre de Darlan.* Paris: Flammarion, 1949.

Kelly, Orr. *Meeting the Fox: The Allied Invasion of Africa, from Operation Torch to Kasserine Pass to Victory in Tunisia.* New York: John Wiley & Sons, 2002.

Kennedy, John. *The Business of War.* New York: William Morrow, 1958.

Kesselring, Albert. *Kesselring: A Soldier's Record.* New York: William Morrow, 1954.

Koburger, Charles Jr. *The Cyrano Fleet: France and Its Navy, 1940–1942.* Westport, Conn.: Praeger, 1989.

Langer, William L. *Our Vichy Gamble.* New York: W. W. Norton, 1966.

Laval, Pierre. *Laval Parle.* Geneva: Constant Bourquin, 1947.

Leahy, William D. *I Was There: The Personal Story of the Chief of Staff to Presidents Roosevelt and Truman Based on His Notes and Diaries Made at the Time.* New York: Whittlesey, 1950.

Lenton, H. T. *British and Empire Warships of the Second World War.* London: Greenhill, 1998.

Levine, Alan J. *The War against Rommel's Supply Lines 1942–1943.* Westport, Conn.: Praeger, 1999.

Liddell Hart, B. H. *The German Generals Talk.* New York: Quill, 1979.

———. *The Rommel Papers.* New York: Harcourt, Brace, 1953.

Lochner, Louis P., ed. *The Goebbels Diaries 1942–1943.* Garden City, N.Y.: Doubleday, 1948.

Lorelli, John A. *To Foreign Shores: U.S. Amphibious Operations in World War II.* Annapolis, Md.: Naval Institute Press, 1995.

MacDonald, Charles B. *The Mighty Endeavor: American Armed Forces in the European Theater in World War II.* New York: Oxford University Press, 1969.

Marder, Arthur. *Operation Menace.* New York: Oxford University Press, 1976.

Mast, Charles. *Histoire d'une rébellion: 8 novembre 1942.* Paris: Librairie Plon, 1969.

Maugeri, Franco. *From the Ashes of Disgrace.* New York: Reynal and Hitchcock, 1948.

Melton, George E. *Darlan: Admiral and Statesman of France, 1881–1942.* Westport, Conn.: Praeger, 1998.

Monsabert, Goislard de, Anna Marie. *Hommage au Général de Goislard de Monsabert.* Paris: Charles-Lavauzelle, 1978.

Mordal, Jacques. *La bataille de Casablanca (8–9–10 novembre 1942).* Paris: Librairie Plon, 1952.

Moreau, Jacques. *Les derniers jours de Darlan.* Paris: Pygmalion, 1985.

Murphy, Robert. *Diplomat among Warriors.* New York: Doubleday, 1964.

Mussolini, Benito. *My Rise and Fall.* Cambridge, Mass.: Da Capo, 1948. Reprinted 1998.

Nassigh, Riccardo. *Guerra negli abissi: I sommergibili italiani nel Secondo Conflitto Mondiale.* Milan, Italy: Mursia, 2008.

Neillands, Robin. *The Dieppe Raid: The Story of the Disastrous 1942 Expedition.* Bloomington: Indiana University Press, 2005.

O'Hara, Vincent P. *In Passage Perilous: Malta and the Convoy Battles of June 1942.* Bloomington: Indiana University Press, 2012.

———. *Struggle for the Middle Sea: The Great Navies at War in the Mediterranean Theater, 1940–1945.* Annapolis, Md.: Naval Institute Press, 2009.

———. *The U.S. Navy against the Axis: Surface Combat 1941–1945.* Annapolis, Md.: Naval Institute Press, 2007.

O'Hara, Vincent P., W. David Dickson, and Richard Worth, eds. *On Seas Contested: The Seven Great Navies of the Second World War.* Annapolis, Md.: Naval Institute Press, 2010.

Padfield, Peter. *War beneath the Sea: Submarine Conflict during World War II.* New York: John Wiley & Sons, 1995.

Parrish, Thomas, ed. *The Simon and Schuster Encyclopedia of World War II.* New York: Simon and Schuster, 1978.

Passis, John A., Leo Disher, and Phil Ault. *Springboard to Berlin.* New York: Thomas Y. Crowell, 1943.

Paterson, Lawrence. *U-boats in the Mediterranean 1941–1945.* Annapolis, Md.: Naval Institute Press, 2007.

Paxton, Robert O. *Vichy France: Old Guard and New Order 1940–1944.* New York: Columbia University Press, 1972.

Payne, Stanley G. *Franco and Hitler: Spain, Germany, and World War II.* New Haven, Conn.: Yale University Press, 2008.

Pogue, Forrest C. *George C. Marshall: Ordeal and Hope 1939–1942.* New York: Viking Press, 1965.

Randle, Edwin, H. *Safi Adventure: Story of a Regimental Combat Team's First Operation,* Belleair, Fla.: Eldnar Press, 1965.

Rearden, Steven L. *Council of War: A History of the Joint Chiefs of Staff 1942–1991.* Washington, DC: NDU Press, 2012.

Reynolds, David. *In Command of History: Churchill Fighting and Writing the Second World War.* New York, Basic Books, 2005.

Roberts, Andrew. *Masters and Commanders: How Four Titans Won the War in the West, 1941–1945.* New York: HarperCollins, 2009.

Rohwer, Jürgen. *Allied Submarine Attacks of World War II.* Annapolis, Md.: Naval Institute Press, 1997.

———. *Axis Submarine Successes of World War II.* Annapolis, Md.: Naval Institute Press, 1999.

Rohwer, Jürgen, and Gerhard Hümmelchen. *Chronology of the War at Sea 1939–1945.* Annapolis, Md.: Naval Institute Press, 2006.

Rolf, David. *The Bloody Road to Tunis: Destruction of the Axis Forces in North Africa November 1942–May 1943.* London: Greenhill, 2001.

Roskill, S. W. *Churchill and the Admirals.* New York: William Morrow, 1978.

Ruge, Friedrich. *Der Seekrieg: The German Navy's Story 1939–1945.* Annapolis, Md.: Naval Institute Press, 1957.

Sadkovich, James. *Major Naval Combatants of World War II.* New York: Greenwood, 1990.

Saibène, Marc. *Les Torpilleurs de 1500 Tonnes du Type Bourrasque.* Rennes, France: Marines Editions, 2001.

———. *Les Torpilleurs de 1500 Tonnes du Type L'Adroit.* Rennes, France: Marines Editions, 2002.

Santoni, Alberto, and Francesco Mattesini. *La partecipazione tedesca alla Guerra aeronavale nel Mediterraneo.* Rome: Ateneo e Bizzarri, 1980.

Sherwood, Robert E. *Roosevelt and Hopkins: An Intimate History.* New York: Harper & Brothers, 1948.

Smith, Kevin. *Conflict over Convoys: Anglo-American Logistics Diplomacy in the Second World War.* New York: Cambridge University Press, 1996.

Stern, Robert. *The U.S. Navy and the War in Europe.* Annapolis, Md.: Naval Institute Press, 2012.

St. George Saunders, Hilary. *The Green Beret: The Story of the Commandos, 1940–1945.* London: M. Joseph, 1949.

Symonds, Craig L. *Neptune: The Allied Invasion of Europe and the D-Day Landings.* Oxford: Oxford University Press, 2014.

Thompson, Julian. *The War at Sea: The Royal Navy in the Second World War.* Osceola, Wisc.: Motorbooks International, 1996.

———. *Forgotten Voices Desert Victory.* New York: Random House, 2011.

Tomblin, Barbara Brooks. *With Utmost Spirit: Allied Naval Operations in the Mediterranean, 1942–1945.* Lexington, Ky.: University of Kentucky Press, 2004.

Tompkins, Peter. *The Murder of Admiral Darlan.* New York: Simon and Schuster, 1965.

Truscott, L. K. Jr. *Command Missions.* New York: E. P. Dutton, 1954.

Tute, Warren. *The Reluctant Enemies: The Story of the Last War between Britain and France 1940–1942.* London, Collins, 1990.

Ugaki, Matome. *Fading Victory: The Diary of Admiral Matome Ugaki, 1941–1945.* Pittsburgh, Penn.: University of Pittsburgh Press, 1991.

Vaughan, Hal. *FDR's Twelve Apostles: the Spies who Paved the Way for the Invasion of North Africa.* Guilfond, Conn.: Lyons Press, 2006.

Warner, Geoffrey. *Pierre Laval and the Eclipse of France: 1931–1945.* New York: Macmillan, 1968.

Weygand, Maxime. *Recalled to Service: The Memoirs of General Maxime Weygand.* New York: Doubleday, 1952.

Willmott, H.P. *The Last Century of Sea Power.* Vol. 2, *From Washington to Tokyo, 1922–1945.* Bloomington: Indiana University Press, 2010.

Winton, John, ed. *The War at Sea: The British Navy in World War II.* New York: William Morrow, 1968.

Wordell, M. T., and E. N. Seiler, *Wildcats over Casablanca*. Boston: Little Brown & Company, 1943.

Wynn, Kenneth. *U-Boat Operations of the Second World War.* Annapolis, Md.: Naval Institute Press: 1997.

Yeide, Harry. *Fighting Patton: George S. Patton Jr. Through the Eyes of His Enemies.* Minneapolis, Minn.: Zenith Press, 2011.

JOURNAL ARTICLES, CHAPTERS, AND PAPERS

Bailey, Leslie W. "The Operations of the 3rd Battalion, 135th Infantry (34th Infantry Division) at Algiers, North Africa." Ft. Benning, Georgia, Infantry School, 1947.

Beam, John C. "The Intelligence Background of Operation Torch." *Parameters* 13, no. 4 (December 1983): 60–69.

Ben-Moshe, Tuvia. "Winston Churchill and the 'Second Front': A Reappraisal." *Journal of Modern History* 62, no. 3 (September 1990): 503–37.

Bilgé, Kerem. "Admiral Leahy: U.S. Ambassador to Vichy." *World War II* (November 2006): 17–22.

Boyle, Harold V. "Battle on the Beach." *Chicago Tribune*, November 16, 1942.

Cafferky, Shawn. "'A Useful Lot, these Canadian Ships:' The Royal Canadian Navy and Operation Torch 1942–1943." *The Northern Mariner* no. 4 (October 1993): 1–17.

Cairns, Bogardus. "Employment of Armor in the Invasion of Oran." Ft. Leavenworth, Kan.: Command and Staff College, 1946.

Cassin, Rene. "Vichy or Free France?" *Foreign Affairs* 20, no. 1 (October 1941): 102–12.

Cernuschi, Enrico, and Vincent P. O'Hara. "Toulon: The Self-Destruction and Salvage of the French Fleet." In *Warship 2013*, edited by John Jordan, 134–48. London: Conway, 2013.

Charmley, John. "Churchill and the American Alliance." *Transactions of the Royal Historical Society,* Sixth Series (11) (2001): 353–71.

Clayton, Anthony. "A Question of Honour? Scuttling Vichy's Fleet." *History Today* (November 1992): 32–38.

Committee 25, Officers Advanced Course. "Armor in the Invasion of North Africa." Ft. Leavenworth, Kan.: Command and Staff College, 1950.

Danchev, Alex. "Dilly-Dally, or Having the Last Word: Field Marshal Sir John Dill and Prime Minister Winston Churchill." *Journal of Contemporary History* 22, no. 1 (January 1987): 21–44.

Emerson, William. "Franklin Roosevelt as Commander-in-Chief in World War II." *Military Affairs* 22, no. 4 (Winter 1958–59): 181–207.

Farrell, Brian P. "Yes, Prime Minister: Barbarossa, Whipcord, and the Basis of British Grand Strategy, Autumn 1941." *The Journal of Military History* 57, no. 4 (October 1993): 599–625.

Frank, Richard B. "The Amphibious Revolution." *Naval History* 19, no. 4 (August 2005): 20–26.

Funk, Arthur L. "Eisenhower, Giraud, and the Command of Torch." *Military Affairs* 35, no. 3 (October 1971): 103–8.

———. "Negotiating the Deal with Darlan." *Journal of Contemporary History* 8, no. 2 (April 1973): 81–117.

"G. B." "The Origins of Operation 'Torch'—Anglo-American Assault on French North Africa." *The Naval Review* 47, no. 1 (January 1959): 48–54.

Gordan, John IV. "Joint Power Projection: Operation Torch." *JFQ* (Spring 1994): 60–69.

Herman, John. "Agency Africa: Rygor's Franco-Polish Network and Operation Torch." *Journal of Contemporary History* 22, no. 4 (October 1987): 681–706.

Higgins, Trumbull. "The Anglo-American Historians' War in the Mediterranean, 1942–1945." *Military Affairs* 34, no. 3 (October 1970): 84–88.

Holmes, Julius C. "Eisenhower's African Gamble." *Colliers* (19 January 1946): 27–30.

Kirkpatrick, Charles. "Joint Planning for Operation Torch." *Parameters* (Summer 1991): 73–85.

Laiche, Weldon. "The Oran Operation." Infantry School, Ft. Benning, Ga., 1946–47.

Lyon, David. "The British Order of Battle." In *The Battle of the Atlantic 1939–1945*, edited by Stephen Howarth and Derek Law, 266–75. London: Greenhill, 1994.

Melka, Robert L. "Darlan between Britain and Germany 1940–1941." *Journal of Contemporary History* 8, no. 2 (April 1973): 57–80.

Mersky, Peter. "Naval Aviation in Operation Torch." *Naval Aviation News* (November–December 1992): 24–29.

Meyer, Leo J. "The Decision to Invade North Africa (TORCH)." In *Command Decisions*, 173–98. Washington, DC: Government Printing Office, 1960.

Millett, Allan R. "Assault from the Sea: The Development of Amphibious Warfare between the Wars: The American, British and Japanese Experiences." In *Military Innovation in the Interwar Period*, 50–95. New York: Cambridge University Press, 1996.

O'Hara, Vincent P. "America's Historian Takes Casablanca." *America in WWII* 7, no. 1 (May–June 2011): 26–35.

———. "The Battle of Casablanca: The Marine Nationale versus the U.S. Navy." In *Warship 2011*, 48–63. Annapolis, Md.: Naval Institute Press, 2011.

O'Hara, Vincent P., and Enrico Cernuschi. "The Other Ultra: Signal Intelligence and the Battle to Supply Rommel's Attack toward Suez." *Naval War College Review* 66, no. 3 (Summer 2013): 117–38

Patch, John. "Fortuitous Endeavor: Intelligence and Deception in Operation Torch." *Naval War College Review* 61, no. 4 (Autumn 2008): 73–97.

Pugh, Philip. "Military Need and Civil Necessity." In *The Battle of the Atlantic 1939–1945*, edited by Stephen Howarth and Derek Law, 30–44. London: Greenhill, 1994.

Reardon, Mark J. "Death at the Hands of Friends: The Oran Harbor Raid during Operation Torch." *Army History* 78 (Winter 2011): 6–26.

Sainsbury, Keith. "Second Front in 1942--A Strategic Controversy Revisited." *British Journal of International Studies* 4, no. 1 (April 1978): 47–58.

Sisson, J. W. "Experiences in Amphibious Landings in the MTO and ETO. T." Ft. Leavenworth, Kan.: Command and Staff College, 1946.

Smith, Edwin K. Jr. "Operation of the Anti Tank Platoon 2nd BN, 26 INF, 1st DIV, at El Ancor 8–11 November 1942." Infantry School, Ft. Benning, Ga., 1949–50.

Steele, Richard W. "Political Aspects of American Military Planning, 1941–1942." *Military Affairs* 35, no. 2 (April 1971): 68–74.

Strange, Joseph L. "The British Rejection of Operation SLEDGEHAMMER: An Alternative Motive." *Military Affairs* 46, no. 1 (February 1982): 6–14.

Thomas, Martin. "Signals Intelligence and Vichy France, 1940–44: Intelligence in Defeat." *Intelligence and National Security* 14, no. 1 (1999): 176–200.

Walker, David A. "OSS [Office of Strategic Services] and Operation Torch." *Journal of Contemporary History* 22, no. 4 (October 1987): 667–79.

Weir, Erin M. K. "German Submarine Blockade, Overseas Imports, and British Military Production in World War II." *Journal of Military and Strategic Studies* (Spring/ Summer 2003).

INTERNET

Dailey, Franklyn. "Cruiser USS *Brooklyn*: Action! Casablanca and Sicily." http://www .daileyint.com/wwii/mbgscasi.htm

Fold3. http://www.fold3com

France 1940. http://france1940.free.fr/e41index.html#North Africa

Hyperwar: A Hypertext History of World War II. http://www.ibiblio.org/hyperwar

Jackson, Richard. "His Majesty's Landing Ship Awatea: 'She Fought the Fight of a Battleship.'" *Our Naval Heritage* 10 (158), 21–23. http://www.navy.mil.nz/down loads/pdf/navy-today/nt158-web.pdf

Naval History.net. http://www.naval-history.net

Niehorster, Leo. *World War II Armed Forces.* http://www.niehorster.org/

Nye, George Thomas. *Memoirs: HMS* Martin *G44.* http://www.hmsmartin-g44.co.uk/

People's War. http://www.bbc.co.uk/ww2peopleswar

Petit, Jean. *Mémoires de Jean Louis Petit.* http://xn--pass-prsent-futur-de-stphane-ercdq .com/colonel-jean-petit.html

Trove. "Trawler's Fight: Italian Submarine Sunk." http://trove.nla.gov.au/ndp/del/article /47360609

Veterans History Project. www.loc.gov/vet

World Naval Ships Forum. "Letter: Offord, Tim." http://www.worldnavalships.com/ forums/showthread.php?t=13480&highlight=aurora+oran

Zimmerman, Dwight Jon. "Convoy SL-125: Sacrificial Lamb for Operation Torch?" http://www.defensemedianetwork.com/stories/convoy-sl-125-sacrificial-lamb-for-operation-torch/

Index

About the Author

Vincent P. O'Hara is an independent scholar who specializes in the maritime aspects of the Second World War. His recent works include *Struggle for the Middle Sea: The Great Navies at War in the Mediterranean Theater, 1940–1945* (Naval Institute Press, 2009) and *In Passage Perilous: Malta and Convoy Battles of June 1942* (Indiana University Press, 2013). O'Hara has also published with Naval Institute Press *German Fleet at War* (2004); *U.S. Navy against the Axis* (2007); and edited *On Seas Contested* (2010) and *To Crown the Waves* (2013), comparative analyses of the major navies of World Wars II and I, respectively. He has collaborated with the well-respected Italian historian Enrico Cernuschi on *Dark Navy: The Regia Marina and the Armistice of 8 September 1943* and *Black Phoenix: History and Operations of the Marina Repubblicana 1943–1945.* He has contributed to many journals and magazines, including *Naval War College Review, MHQ, World War II, Naval History,* and the annuals *Warship* and *Seaforth Naval Review.* He is a *collaboratore* for *Storia MILITARE* magazine. O'Hara is a frequent speaker for the U.S. Navy Surface Warfare Association and contributed two introductions to the U.S. Naval Institute's recent republication of S. E. Morison's *History of United States Naval Operations in World War II.* He holds a history degree from the University of California, Berkeley, and resides near San Diego, California.

The Naval Institute Press is the book-publishing arm of the U.S. Naval Institute, a private, nonprofit, membership society for sea service professionals and others who share an interest in naval and maritime affairs. Established in 1873 at the U.S. Naval Academy in Annapolis, Maryland, where its offices remain today, the Naval Institute has members worldwide.

Members of the Naval Institute support the education programs of the society and receive the influential monthly magazine *Proceedings* or the colorful bimonthly magazine *Naval History* and discounts on fine nautical prints and on ship and aircraft photos. They also have access to the transcripts of the Institute's Oral History Program and get discounted admission to any of the Institute-sponsored seminars offered around the country.

The Naval Institute's book-publishing program, begun in 1898 with basic guides to naval practices, has broadened its scope to include books of more general interest. Now the Naval Institute Press publishes about seventy titles each year, ranging from how-to books on boating and navigation to battle histories, biographies, ship and aircraft guides, and novels. Institute members receive significant discounts on the Press's more than eight hundred books in print.

Full-time students are eligible for special half-price membership rates. Life memberships are also available.

For a free catalog describing Naval Institute Press books currently available, and for further information about joining the U.S. Naval Institute, please write to:

Member Services
U.S. NAVAL INSTITUTE
291 Wood Road
Annapolis, MD 21402-5034
Telephone: (800) 233-8764
Fax: (410) 571-1703
Web address: www.usni.org